Mosques in the Metropolis

Mosques in the Metropolis

INCIVILITY, CASTE, AND CONTENTION IN EUROPE

Elisabeth Becker

The University of Chicago Press CHICAGO & LONDON

The University of Chicago Press, Chicago 60637
The University of Chicago Press, Ltd., London
© 2021 by The University of Chicago
Published 2021
Printed in the United States of America

30 29 28 27 26 25 24 23 22 21   1 2 3 4 5

ISBN-13: 978-0-226-78150-1 (cloth)
ISBN-13: 978-0-226-78164-8 (paper)
ISBN-13: 978-0-226-78178-5 (e-book)
DOI: https://doi.org/10.7208/chicago/9780226781785.001.0001

Library of Congress Cataloging-in-Publication Data

Names: Becker, Elisabeth (Sociologist), author.
Title: Mosques in the metropolis : incivility, caste, and
contention in Europe / Elisabeth Becker.
Description: Chicago ; London : The University of Chicago Press, 2021. |
Includes bibliographical references and index.
Identifiers: LCCN 2020051231 | ISBN 9780226781501 (cloth) |
ISBN 9780226781648 (paperback) | ISBN 9780226781785 (ebook)
Subjects: LCSH: East London Mosque (London, England) | Şehitlik Moschee
(Berlin, Germany) | Islam—Europe. | Cities and towns—Europe—Religious aspects—
Islam. | Muslims—Germany—Berlin. | Muslims—England—London.
Classification: LCC BP65.A1 B43 2021 | DDC 297.094—dc23
LC record available at https://lccn.loc.gov/2020051231

♾ This paper meets the requirements of ANSI/NISO Z39.48-1992
(Permanence of Paper).

For my late father, Ted E. Becker Jr., who taught me how to love cities in their fullness of life, their sparrows as much as edifices, how to tell—that is, how to hear—other people's stories, and the beauty of writing to the muddled sound of garbage trucks and waking birds, searching between the angels at dawn.

So I have erected one of his dwellings, with books as the building stones, before you.

WALTER BENJAMIN

CONTENTS

Raised in New York City, I have always experienced the shape of the metropolis as home: a place that knows little darkness, and where the lights in all of their phantasmic power obscure the stars. Beyond bright lights and twenty-four-hour bodegas, I have become intimately familiar with the metropolis as a place of myriad cultures, languages, and longings—its human density and speed uniting us strangers and, just as quickly, pulling us apart.

Snippets of the world live and lived together on our small and glowing island, bobbing between two murky rivers. For this reason, my childhood in Morningside Heights, a thin strip of upper Manhattan, was just as—if differently—idyllic as those of my friends who grew up in small towns and rural villages. In the 1980s and 1990s, everyone in my neighborhood, from the fishermen on 125th Street risking their lives to eat their catch to the dry cleaner who handed off gossip along with freshly pressed clothes, knew one another's names. The spirit of our neighborhood was embracing, reflected in its body of wide avenues hugged by two verdant parks, its churches rising from the ground to split the sky. I rode the subway from the 110th and Cathedral Parkway station and frequented its namesake, Cathedral St. John the Divine, close to my home, where saints looked on with wary eyes; there candles burned and choirs sang, pigeons perched on the gaping mouths of gargoyles at rest, closing their wings. Peacocks in the adjacent gardens splayed their majestic tails beside a peace fountain, presided over by Archangel Michael, his own wings open towards the sky. I often watched these peacocks from across the street, sat at the Hungarian Pastry Shop, a neighborhood institution owned by a Greek family, managed by Ethiopian New Yorkers, and filled with Columbia

University students fanning their faces with literature as they looked for love. Something about that space on my childhood street—its heavy, refillable coffee mugs, its refusal to install internet or outlets, its vista of cathedral and rainbow bird tails beside whizzing cars—made me know in childhood, as I still know today, that the city could speak to me from deep in its soul.

New York was never, to me, a lonely city, with its trees inhabited by fowl and its buildings by the globe. Yet it was always far more than a place of settlers and settledness, an island of comings and goings, marked by Lady Liberty in her robes of rusty green, perched on her own island in the bay. Evidence of the diverse crossings that made the city was also etched onto the face of my neighborhood—from the Lebanese grocers to the Albanian Kosovar refugees who pointed out their fatigued brothers, in both senses of the word, on the cover of the daily news. It was, and is "in so many ways, the exilic city *par excellence*," words written by the late Edward Said, long a resident of the same neighborhood.[1] New York City not only offered respite to, but was built by so many experiencing exile and estrangement, with their unbridgeable rifts and wounds unhealed. Another local resident in exile, the late Hannah Arendt, was perhaps one of the greatest thinkers on such estrangement, and appeared throughout my life, in books gifted to me by mentors and family members, prose that I imagine written where she once lived, on the bending Riverside Drive corner not far from my own.

Of the many faces of displacement in the city, I knew most intimately my Jewish neighbors whose parents and grandparents fled the Holocaust. My own Jewish family members migrated from Europe earlier, and my late grandfather, Benjamin, owned a button store in New York City's Garment District. According to our family stories, he made the first plastic button in the city. During my research, when I came across the commemorative *Stolperstein* ("stumbling stone") of Eduard Salinger, who sold fabrics in Berlin before being murdered by the Third Reich, or the park memorializing Altab Ali, a textile worker murdered by white nationalists in East London, I thought of our lives interwoven by the fates of fabrics, the colorful threads of great metropoles.

Not only Benjamin, Eduard, and Altab, but all urbanites today and yesterday are connected by the threads of the city. In fact, most on Manhattan island live within the bounds of an *eruv*, a Jewish ritual enclosure made out of thin, almost translucent wire attached to eighteen miles of utility poles. The point of the *eruv* is to mark the space of home, so that Jews do not violate the rule of carrying things in public on the Sabbath. Few of us have ever heard of it, and it's almost impossible to see with the naked eye. While there are no *eruvin* in the neighborhoods at the center of this book, East London and West Berlin, the markings of home—Jewish, Muslim, and many other forms—abound in both. And although Morningside Heights is geographically distant from metropolitan Europe, they remain intertwined through the threads of estranged and exiled lives.

From Manhattan's cathedral spires and fishing docks to Europe's diverse metropolitan mosques, I have carried a specific vantage point endowed by my own Jewishness and my own urbanity into the writing of this book, the former of which Zygmunt Bauman describes as "always on the outside even when inside, examining the familiar as if it was a foreign object of study, asking questions no one else asked, questioning the unquestionable and challenging the unchallengeable."[2] The latter, my urbanity, has been as vital as the former, my Jewishness—both forms of belonging, ways of being in the world—to this text. Or perhaps, they are really one and the same. As Leonard Barkan writes in *Berlin for Jews*, a tragically beautiful love letter to the city, "Jews are fundamentally cityfolk," relegated to this position through restrictions on owning property, limitations on livelihoods, and segregation in ethnic enclaves. In the case of Italians, he explains, "if you have a city for a surname—Ancona, Milano, Bassano—you are probably a Jew."[3]

CHAPTER 1

The European Metropolis: Where Doors and Walls Meet

Thinking the city moves towards *thinking* the world.

HENRI LEFEBVRE[1]

This is the story of flesh, bone, spirit, and stone. It is the story of two mosques, and their inhabitants called to the European metropolis by countries that wanted their bodies but never their souls. *"Man hat Arbeitskräfte gerufen, und es kommen Menschen"*—"We called for labor, but people came instead," Swiss writer Max Frisch famously wrote of the post–World War II (WWII) wave of immigration in 1965.[2] It is the story of the shells they fashioned to protect and cultivate those souls.

I begin this book on the threshold between what is, what was, and what might have been. I am standing where the Puerta de Moros once stood in Madrid, Spain, off of Cava Baja, the street where I reside. Destroyed in 1412 during the Reconquista, this door to the city and its surrounding plaza were rebuilt a century later.[3] The door is now long gone, the plaza dotted with coffeeshops, bakeries, and discount clothing stores: a center of commerce and social communion, where the city's residents sip *café con leche* and chew on brined sausage, charred pepitas, and oranges ripened by the sun. Yet each street evokes a sense of suspension in time, the past etched into the architectural face of the metropolis. As I walk through the neighborhood, I imagine the city in another time, this district once inhabited by Muslims and Jews. Although it is only by chance, by circumstance, it feels fitting for myself, a Jewish ethnographer of European mosques, to live and to pause here.

My book project is thus born, paradoxically, in the very place where my research cannot come to fruition. It is my failure as an ethnographer in Spain, itself a geographical threshold on the southern edge of Europe, where the straits of Gibraltar meet the land, that allows me to see and to feel this history, stretching from the present in a temporal backbend towards the Reconquista. This book begins to take its shape here in early 2015. It is, more precisely, early January, the week after the Charlie Hebdo massacre in Paris, when I come to recognize the deep and enduring liminality of Muslim lives. Uncertainty is alive across Europe. Muslim men and women rally at Atocha, the main train station in Madrid, holding signs above their heads: "Islam equals peace"; "I am a Muslim not a terrorist." There is a certain unsettledness not only in their words on this square, but across the city. In its streets, its stores, its mosques, a condensation of fear hovers in the air.

I have set out to comparatively study three capital city mosques across Europe, in London, Berlin, and Madrid, to understand both the constraints and the interstitial opportunities endowed by marginality on Muslim bodies and institutions. While the unraveling of my Spanish case is both sudden and unsettling, it is preceded by premonition-like moments. First, I cannot find a research site. In the largest mosques of the city, women claim that no activities take place, and security guards man entrances dually surveilled by video cameras. In a small mosque close to my home, those who have agreed to meet me never arrive. When I ask about the city's mosques, non-Muslim city dwellers shake their heads, advising me to travel south to Córdoba, once heart of the Umayyad Dynasty in Spain (756–1031).[4] Later, my interlocutors in both Berlin and London will tell me their own stories of Córdoba, the prohibition of prayer they encountered upon entering the Mosque-Cathedral. "I went to Córdoba on my honeymoon and a guard took me aside and warned me 'you cannot pray here,'" says Imani, a medical resident who I meet one afternoon at the East London Mosque (ELM). Tuba, a law student who leads tours at the Şehitlik Mosque in Berlin, similarly explains,

> I had the weirdest experience. I entered the Mezquita and literally a guard in the section came close to me and walked by me. When I left his vicinity, someone else came, then someone else came. So I was accompanied the entire duration of my stay in the Mezquita by someone in close range, and I had a feeling they were looking out to see if I was attempting to pray.

In her ethnography of Muslim encounters in Granada, Mikaela Rogozen-Soltar writes about deep historical memories of the Moors, inscribed as much into the bodies of edifices as into the collective memory of Spain's southern cities.[5] Chris Lowney calls this "a vanished world."[6] Yet in southern Spain, as in the Spanish capital, we can still see—and feel—the reverberations of this history, the blurring of boundaries between present and past. The unraveling of my research in Spain does not occur in Córdoba nor in Granada, however, but in a nearby southern city, where I am suddenly enmeshed in a day of questioning by those who appear to be covert security forces. They simply cannot make sense of my interest in Spanish Muslims. When I call the United States (US) embassy, diplomats castigate me without pause for trusting Muslim communities, and warn me not to join a terrorist organization. I am suddenly caught in the web of uncertainty and surveillance that constrains Muslims' everyday lives, the labyrinth of the minotaur-like security state—part monster, part man—guarding a blinding maze of sacrifice.

The next day, I return to Madrid. In place of ancient doors opening to the city, I now see the walls, just as old, closing it off. And I find myself at one insurmountable, immaterial wall: that of Muslims deemed uncivil. In the central neighborhood of Lavapiés, I watch West African refugees calling out the name of Allah, beating drums in rhythm with their hymns of discontent. In my own neighborhood, once inhabited by Muslims and Jews, I notice remnants of a history that castigated both: from forced conversions to expulsions and murder determined by a single drop of Muslim or Jewish blood. Standing on the Plaza Mayor, an early trade market and center of executions during the Inquisition, I now see something that I had somehow overlooked: depictions of this history carved into its lightposts, the strata of the metropolis inscribed onto its modern body in miniature form. "The city as palimpsest."[7]

My experience in Spain splits the skin of its capital open, revealing threads of continuity that weave the present to the past in its upright and crumbling body of iron welded to glass and stone. Residents speak of the Moors as if alive in the metropolis, while ignoring the architectural remnants of Islamic empire buried all around us, right beneath our feet (Madrid's Royal Palace, for example, erected at the very site where the Alcazar stood from the ninth century until 1734).[8] As I walk through Madrid one last time and night sets in, the city comes alive. I visit the Fountain of the Fallen Angel in Retiro Park, inspired by Milton's *Paradise Lost*.[9] I continue south of the park, entering the Barrio de las Letras, and glance down at the ground. My eyes together with my feet settle on a sonnet written by seventeenth-century poet and novelist Francisco de Quevedo. Inscribed onto the cobblestone streets in gold, it begins with the words "*I looked upon my native country's walls.*" Setting out in Madrid with a quest to find the ghost of a door built by the Moors, my time in Spain ends with a sonnet to the walls of the Spanish imaginary. I am acutely aware in this moment, in a city so bright that I cannot see the stars, that the door and the wall can never be pulled apart; they meet and unite at the site of the threshold, a liminal point of entry, exit, history, and new beginning.

METROPOLIS AS LABYRINTH AND AS PALIMPSEST

Stars are invoked at the conclusion of the three parts of Dante's Divine Comedy—Inferno, Purgatorio, and Paradiso—to symbolize coming into the light, into the presence of God.[10] The modern metropolis obscures the stars, just as it often obscures the lives of its many residents.[11] Much is in fact obscured by the city, with its incongruent passageways and glass that cuts into rubble. Still more can be gleaned from its daily life as a built environment made into home, where physical nearness and affective remoteness bind private and public lives.

The very word *polis*, denoting the ancient Greek city-state, references the form of the walled city, with fortifications built as a physical barrier to entry or attack. The European metropolis is both ancient and future-looking, inward- and outward-facing, today metaphorically walled off in the imaginary rather than surrounded by material walls. I primarily use the word *metropolis* to reference the urban arenas at the heart of this book, drawing on its two meanings: (1) "mother city," signifying a city of import, and (2) the colonial or imperial core.[12] The term "metropolis" is often employed in reference to cities as economic hubs during the height of the colonial era. I instead draw attention to the ways in which metropoles are today *cultural* hubs in Europe's uncertain postcolonial/postimperial age, and an evocative microcosm of global struggles over how plurality is bounded and lived. The "mosque in the metropolis" invokes both the colonial/imperial and postcolonial/postimperial connotations of the term, as at once spatial, temporal, and cultural threshold.

When I leave Madrid, I do not go home, but instead to Berlin to continue my research. As the plane lands in the German capital, I am left ruminating over the place, and limits, of the modern European metropolis. This soon draws me to the work of Walter Benjamin. Fascinated by modern cities, how they intertwine present and past, Benjamin's collected works on Berlin and Paris are often read as a manifesto on the failures of capitalism. They can alternatively be read as critical theory[13] written from a position of liminality, from exile, or as a love letter to the fragmented form of the city itself. Benjamin laments, "The pathos of this project . . . I find every city beautiful."[14] It is not only splendor, however, that Benjamin finds in urban life, but also a sense of betrayal: his childhood Berlin—"the city god itself"—in ruins, and the shattered Paris of his dreams.[15]

The modern metropolis emerged in staggered timelines across Europe from early to late modernity. Like the nation-state, it has always functioned as both idea and material reality. In *Thinking with History*, Carl Schorske traces "the idea of the city in European thought," evoking a productive tension between the city as virtue and the city as vice. For Voltaire, nineteenth-century London was particularly virtuous, allowing men to transcend social hierarchies by bringing enlightened "reason and taste" to the masses; finding "lost paradise" in the German city of the same era, philosopher Johann Gottlieb Fichte came to understand the city as an enlightened, civilizing agent of the nation.[16] In the late nineteenth and early twentieth centuries, however, intellectual social reformers like Karl Marx and Friedrich Engels, shifted from the city as virtue to the city as vice in their writings on urban poverty.[17] As a geographical condensation of imperial remnants, aftermath, and Muslim afterlives, today the metropolis rises as a lived form suspended between virtue and vice, the devastations and utopic strivings of European modernity. It rises as both palimpsest, a text to be read, with the traces of its many pasts never fully washed away, and labyrinth to carefully tread.[18]

The concurrent possibilities and shortfalls of modernity come alive in the metropolitan everyday, whether in the Parisian arcades through which Benjamin once wandered, or the mosques in London and Berlin, where I root my research. Rather than a time-centric understanding, e.g., as post-Enlightenment and temporally progressive or a distinct juncture/state, I focus on the dialectical construction of European modernity, seeking order and coherence through violently upheld hierarchies. In "Eurocentrism and Modernity," Enrique Dussel argues that modernity is "a European phenomenon, but one constituted in a dialectical relation with a non-European alterity that is its ultimate content."[19] In Dussel's understanding, modernity is created through not only contrast but imagined superiority, suggesting hierarchy, as well as its lived repercussions, including violent projects of domination that span the globe. Zygmunt Bauman argues that it is modernity's rationality—specifically, the "problem of order" in what he terms "a gardening state"—that creates both impetus and opportunity for violence.[20] "Modernity's sacrificial-mythical character," with its labyrinths and its minotaur, forges insiders and outsiders, silence, and, according to Arendt, absence of full-belonging.[21] For my interlocutors, constituents[22] of European mosques, this absence is both acute and enduring.

Within this prism of modernity, the European metropolis is not only the magnetic once-nucleus of empire, with its "knotted and complex histories" of power and marginality, but it is also a center of resistance against it as such.[23] And while it appears on the surface as the inner stratum of a set of nesting dolls, inside of the European state and the broader European imaginary, it remains a locus of community life and belonging in its own right. Like the sun, the city rises as a point of orientation for human organization and governance, while also a place of self-determination and defiance, again and again. Today, the city has risen again.

The mosque in the metropolis provides a window into how Muslims, cast as others inside of the geography while outside of the imaginary of Europe, find and root themselves in place—whether to the city itself or through the city to translocal polities. The idea of the "translocal" rather than the transnational pushes against the hegemony of a nation-state paradigm, with the nation-state largely absent from my interlocutors' reflections on geographical and emotional ties.[24] This translocality causes discomfort in the societies and states at hand, a perception of transgression notably applied to many "trans" discourses and projects—seen as unsettling coherence, while in fact exposing long-present unsettledness.[25] As Jeffrey Alexander articulates in his theory of the civil sphere, states are amoral entities that provide order, not justice; they seek domination, not solidarity.[26] The mosque in the metropolis thus offers comfort and opportunity to these at times legal, but not cultural citizens,[27] as a *phronetic* space (in the Aristotelian sense of *phronesis*, meaning moral agency consisting of practical, ethical knowledge that feeds into action) concerned with solidarity and justice.[28] As such, it becomes a locus of crossing, making (the Aristotelian term, *poiesis*), and dwelling for those perceived as strangers in Europe today.[29]

Ebrahim Moosa, a contemporary scholar of Islamic thought, sees *poiesis*—"the craft of imagination and inventive making and creating"—in and from the threshold position as imperative for critical Muslim thought. I invoke the notion of *poiesis*, as well as *sympoiesis* (making together) and *autopoiesis* (making apart) to analyze this craft—that of the stranger as maker—both in and from the sociospatial threshold position of the mosque.[30] The stranger will not be considered here in the colloquial sense of the term but instead vis-à-vis Georg Simmel's specific conceptualization:

> A stranger is not a wanderer, who may come today and leave tomorrow. He comes today—and stays. He is a potential wanderer: although he has not moved on from the society, he has not quite shed the freedom to stay or go, either. He remains within a specific place, but he has not always belonged to it, and so he carries into it qualities that do not, could not, belong there.

As Simmel asserts, "the history of the European Jews offers a classic example [of the stranger]."[31] Calling forth this Simmelian concept eighty years later, Bauman writes,

The stranger's unredeemable sin is, therefore, the incompatibility between his presence and other presences fundamental to the world order; his simultaneous assault on several crucial oppositions instrumental in the incessant effort of ordering. It is this sin which throughout modern history rebounds in the constitution of the stranger as the bearer and embodiment of incongruity . . . The stranger is, for this reason, the bane of modernity.[32]

Drawing from his own sociotemporal location in the post-Holocaust era, Bauman builds on the Jewish exemplar of the Simmelian stranger through his theory of the "conceptual Jew": the "prototypical" "ethnic-religious-cultural stranger" forged by modern European society.[33] This stranger, Bauman argues, is not only object, however, but active subject; "the stranger rebels."[34] Contemporary social theorist Richard Sennett similarly turns away from subjectivity (the stranger made by Christian/European discourse) to agency (the stranger as maker). Sennett theorizes the epitome of the stranger as the culturally displaced dweller of the modern city who embraces ambiguity as a springboard for creative self-transformation and production in her urban environment.[35] To recognize Muslims as makers in the metropolis, more than today's "conceptual" other in the European project of modernity, brings into focus how they—"included within and excluded from Europe at one and the same time in a special way"—critique and contest marginality.[36]

In the text that follows, I turn to how Muslims make sense of, and a place for themselves in the European metropolis in relation to, and also in spite of, what I term an *undercaste* status, conceptually fleshed out in the subsequent chapter. "To be rooted is perhaps the most important and the least recognized need of the human soul," writes Jewish French mystic Simone Weil.[37] But how do you root yourself on uneven ground? Sennett portrays the modern city as an opportunity not to return to clear-cut categories and boundaries, but rather to embrace plurality in individual and social body.[38] Like Sennett, my interlocutors see and grasp an opportunity for the transformation of self and community in the mosque in the metropolis, questioning superimposed hierarchies of belonging. In so doing, they reflect St. Augustine's idea that godliness can very much be experienced in the earthly city—the City of God inflected in the City of Man.[39]

MOSQUE AS THRESHOLD

Thinking about mosques as dynamic threshold spaces in the European metropolis, concrete and grounded, but not stagnant architectural articulations, shows that buildings are never complete; they are, rather, continuously made and remade over time. As Benjamin asserts, "The threshold must be carefully distinguished from the boundary. A *Schwelle* <threshold> is a zone. Transformation, passage, wave action are in the word *schwellen*, swell."[40] The mosque in the European metropolis is a threshold space in two regards: (1) as a dynamic entryway into Muslim life in Europe and (2) as an institution that is passageway or zone between the private and public spheres. Yet the mosque is also a temporal threshold, transcending modernity as an era resulting from linear time-as-progress, i.e., improvement over the past through the Reformation, the Enlightenment (including the so-called "civilizing" process), and the French Revolution.[41] It is an architectural form straddling what is and what was, built to evoke not only an orientation towards the future, in the form of paradise, but also an invocation of paradise past.

The mosque as threshold thus challenges taken-for-granted understandings about space and time, and therefore becomes relegated to the social periphery. "The occlusion of this 'periphery' . . . leads the major contemporary thinkers of the 'center' into a Eurocentric fallacy in their understanding of modernity," writes Dussel; Jürgen Habermas, for instance, conceptualizes modernity as exclusively European, ignoring Europe's development against, and through the exploitation of, its "peripheries"—many the ancestral lands of Muslim populaces in Europe today.[42] I am aware that the language of periphery and core threatens to cast this subject in light of the dominant European imaginary, and take seriously so-called geographical and/or cultural "peripheries," like mosques in the European metropolis, as moral, social, and epistemological centers in their own right. I thus herein challenge and deconstruct many Eurocentric notions, from "enlightenment" to "progress," "civility," "tolerance," "freedom," and "equality."

Betwixt and Between: Research in the Mosque

From a state of dually geographical and cultural otherness, postcolonial migrants and guest workers began the sanctioned crossing of physical boundaries to Europe in the late 1950s, "cast up on the shores of strange lands, chased into the cracks and crevices of strange economies," as Arendt wrote of Jews before them.[43] Initial migration to Europe paralleled widespread liberationist movements in the colonies. Emergent anticolonial nationalisms emphasized an explicit or implicit core Muslim identity for the nation, mobilized against the colonizing Christian "Other."[44] The majority of Muslims in the UK hail from South Asia (largely from Pakistan and Bangladesh); according to the

2011 British census, over a million ethnically Pakistani individuals and over 450,000 Bengali[45] individuals live in the UK, just over half of the latter residing in London.[46] At the same time, guest worker programs instated to address post-WWII labor shortages spanned from 1945 to the mid-1970s, reaching across the continent (e.g., to Germany, Switzerland, Luxembourg, and Sweden), with Turkey a primary sending country.[47] These individuals arrived to an uncertain future in the European metropolis. Today, the vast majority of Muslims in Germany are ethnically Turkish; according to a 2009 Pew estimate, 75 percent of the then–four million Muslims. The Muslim populace has grown to about five million since the 2015–16 refugee migration.[48]

The social evolution from provisional to permanent settlement over the past half century, from the invisibility to visibility of mosques, paralleled significant changes in citizenship laws, as legal revisions across Europe expanded access to citizenship, which coincided with an exponential increase in the number of representative, purpose-built (made to look like and be utilized as) mosques.[49] The building of these mosques emerged from Muslims' demand for dignity in the face of widely institutionalized socioeconomic disadvantage, "a space in which to affirm their worth . . . a space for expressing their own identity and competence."[50]

I chose to center my project in mosques as concrete instantiations of Muslims' collective place in modern Europe, in spite of their continued cultural marginality. I build in and out from previous research on mosques. For instance, while Saba Mahmood's formative work on the women's piety movement in Egyptian mosques takes seriously their role as centers for the co-cultivation of piety and shifting social relations, I am interested in how piety, rooted in the Islamic epistemological tradition, is fostered at two specific institutions—the Şehitlik Mosque and the East London Mosque.[51] I explore how the knowledge endowed in pious projects of the self and collective moves outwards from these mosque communities, shaping the relationships between the Muslims who constitute them and broader European civic life.[52]

My research took place over thirty months, from 2013 to 2017 at the Şehitlik Mosque in Berlin and at the East London Mosque, including the one month in Madrid with which I began this book. I chose to study these specific mosques for numerous reasons: their symbolic representation of ethnic groups (Turkish and Bengali); the size of the populations they serve; their importance for Islamic rituals and rites of passage in each metropolis; and the role that they play in society-wide conversations about Muslims/Islam in Berlin and Germany, London and the UK. In addition to the notable size of the populations they serve, and their parallel physical size (the East London Mosque accommodating seven thousand and the Şehitlik Mosque five thousand wor-shippers), they are hubs for Muslim life in each metropolis, providing religious education, preparation for religious rites such as the hajj pilgrimage and buri-als, and a space for celebrations, including high holidays and marriages. Both have also been at the center of public debates regarding Islam and Muslims in the cities and states at hand.

In Berlin, I resided largely in the Bavarian Quarter (Bayerisches Viertel), once hub of Jewish intellectual life, with the final stage of writing this book undertaken in the Barn Quarter (Scheunenviertel) of the Spandauer Vorstadt, long a Jewish area of the city. In the Bavarian Quarter, I first encountered the *Stolpersteine* (stumbling stones) of Jewish city-dwellers past—small com-memorative brass squares laid into the ground outside of what were once their homes. Stumbling stones, in contrast to stepping stones that lead somewhere in ascendance, cause a person to pause, if not trip or fall. An undeniable inser-tion in an ordinary path, they are in the most concrete of forms question marks embedded in the sidewalks that city-dwellers tread. When I began my research in Berlin in 2013, I found myself both literally and figuratively stumbling upon a Jewish past. It began with "the touch of a lone tile," a stone inscribed by the U-Bahn station at Viktoria-Luise-Platz.[53] "Here lived Selma Lehmann, born Peiser 1877," it read, "deported on July 17, 1941, Kowno Fort IX, murdered on November 25, 1941"; I paused at this particular stone when I saw "Selma," my grandmother's name. Such awareness of a Jewish past in the metropolis colored not only my neighborhoods in Berlin but also where I later resided in London's East End—first close to Bethnal Green (formerly a hub of Jewish life) and thereafter Victoria Park Village (on the edge of Lauriston Park Cem-etery, once a Jewish burial ground).

Through this suddenly intimate past, its nearness in place if not time, I made my way to the writings of Jewish thinkers, many forced into exile during the Third Reich—Hermann Cohen, Georg Simmel, Ernst Bloch, Walter Ben-jamin, Hans Jonas, Hannah Arendt, Zygmunt Bauman, Herbert Gans, and Richard Sennett —forming "time-hopping relationships with figures from the past."[54] Reading these thinkers while researching metropolitan mosque com-munities became, in a way, my very own act of *sympoiesis*—making together with the living and the dead.[55] While the fate of Muslims in Europe in no way parallels that of Jews, these two religious minorities share a history of nega-tive differentiation, partial inclusion and partial exclusion, as well as the col-lapsing of their otherness into a totalizing ethnic and racialized religio-cultural form.[56] Like their Jewish counterparts before them (and to a degree, again, beside them), Muslims in Europe assert themselves in the face of cultural subordination; they seek rootedness *as Muslims* in the cities at hand. To be clear, in my research I saw no inherent or essentialized similarities between Muslims and Jews but rather continuity in the European subject as marginalizing, unbrokenness in a chain of negative self-differentiation. And in facing the so-called "Muslim question," I heard not only the echoes of the so-called "Jewish question," but the scream of what Gil Andijar terms "the European question."[57]

In approaching this "question of Europe," Anne Norton and Anya Topolski lucidly caution that the ways in which Europe has defined itself vis-à-vis differentiation from Jews in the centuries prior to the Holocaust and how it defines itself vis-à-vis differentiation from Muslims today should not be overlooked. Mine is thus an argument about Europe's enduring struggles to create an identity, which, as in Norton's and Topolski's analyses, invoke hierarchy rather than horizontal community.[58] Benjamin writes of the glass "window mirror," "project[ing]" the interior lives of the Parisian bourgeois into the metropolis; Muslims like Jews provide a metaphorical "window mirror," seeing inside of while also reflecting the interiors of European modernity.[59]

From a critical reading to a critical writing of Europe, this book was thus born out of an act of "coproduction" between me and my interlocutors, in person and in texts, to whom I owe an unpayable debt.[60] In any critical reading or writing of Europe, one must account for the ongoing violence perpetrated by security states, a violence cast in the language of protecting the body politic and the values undergirding the Enlightenment, while directed against Muslim bodies and institutions. The stickiness of this surveillance paradigm, the depth of these murky, molasses-like waters that can so easily take hold, was the greatest challenge to my project. I have tried to write this book in a manner that both protects my interlocutors whom I met in the mosques and contends with their securitization, with what I term an "intimacy of terror" threatening their personal well-being and dignity. The explicit and extreme securitization of mosques, as all Muslim spaces and bodies in Europe, however, creates unavoidable ethical entanglements, bringing to the fore questions about the practice of ethnography, the obligation of non-maleficence in particular.[61]

Simply put, I faced questions regarding if, and how, I could participate in mosque communities without contributing to surveillance, imagined or real. To answer these questions, I turned to the communities at hand, asking on what terms I could and should engage in their daily lives, including the ongoing negotiation of my presence and participation with the gatekeepers to these unduly securitized spaces. At the Şehitlik Mosque, I discussed and planned my research with mosque director Ender Çetin and his wife Pınar Çetin, also a recognized leader in the mosque, as well as teachers and tour guides; at the East London Mosque, I discussed and planned my research with female leadership, including Maryam Centre manager Sufia Alam and teachers.[62] Reciprocal engagement not only upon entry into these mosques, but throughout my research, reduced but did not entirely eliminate discomfort with my presence and its potential for causing harm.

My interactions with and within these mosque communities were certainly colored by my own ethical entanglements: my emotional investments both different and dynamic, shifting over time as I became more familiar with each community and they more familiar with me. The Şehitlik Mosque espoused a vision of Islam that aligned to a greater extent with my own subjectivities. The East London Mosque challenged my assumptions about agency, through a self-disciplining model that I found at first not only unfamiliar but perplexing. Reflecting on her work with Christian "fundamentalists," Susan Harding introduces the idea of the "repugnant cultural other" for the ethnographer, that is not the colonized/marginalized other but an "Other" whose antiliberal tendencies disrupt disciplinary assumptions and orientations.[63] Budding from a shared bewilderment-cum-curiosity concerning the experience of "the Other" (that is, each other), the relationships that I developed with my East London Mosque interlocutors more rapidly crossed into intimate spheres, such as homes, than those with my interlocutors at the Şehitlik Mosque. As becomes clear in the chapters that follow, this difference emerged from the nexus of my positionality and community structures. Regarding the latter, my opportunities for exchange and learning were overwhelmingly collective at Şehitlik, where the cultivation of piety emerges in ongoing conversation with local civic life. My opportunities for exchange and learning at ELM were, on the other hand, overwhelmingly one-on-one or in small groups; this reflects the centrality of the individual Muslim as an ambassador of the Muslim community in the context of that mosque.

Over time, I came to see my initial disorientation as an opportunity to more fully experience the mosque in the metropolis, to learn from the intellectual dizziness imbued by new sociocultural paradigms. In his preface to Franz Hessel's *Walking in Berlin*, Benjamin discerns a difference between studying and learning. "An entire world separates these words," he writes, as studying entails the act of approaching a subject (reading, observing, etc.) while learning is the act of gaining knowledge.[64] A key drive behind my research was to *learn* how people find "the fragile magic of the 'home'" even when made dizzy in a world of great uncertainty and change: a striving for rootedness on uneven ground.[65]

Mosques are not hermeneutically sealed, and my research moved outward from the mosque into London and Berlin, the city not only rising around us but joining in, shaping the spaces, sentiments, and words shared between my interlocutors and myself. We climbed stone stairs, crossing the bridges above rivers and canals; we smelled the scent of cooking oil, and listened to the sound of walnuts, "tap-tap-tap crack," split open by hand. Of his wanderings in Berlin, Hessel asserts that "we only see what looks at us," but I would argue that we only see *who looks* with us.[66] This book was written through shared experiences of looking and learning together, under the dome of the mosque, but also the roofs of brick homes, the gaze of a gold-plated angel, and lines of laundry pulled by the wind. It is difficult, perhaps impossible, to write these senses—to put the sight of looking, the taste of learning, into words. And it is equally challenging to write the emotions imbued in these encounters, whether suffering or nostalgia, courage or joy. French philosopher Maurice Merleau-Ponty eloquently captures this unbridgeable divide between the word and the sensual world. "Like the weaver, the writer works on the wrong side of his material. He has only to do with the language, and it is thus that he suddenly finds himself surrounded by sense."[67] I still hope that in these pages readers will come to smell London's grass, wet with afternoon rain, a scent that permeates stories of displacement and home; and that they will feel the familiar ache found in voices that speak of yearning and of loss, beneath the canopy of Berlin's gray winter skies.

Sly Civility

Purpose-built mosques in Europe have come to embody not only the lives, sentiments, and histories of large postmigrant populaces, but also the assumptions and presumptions that Europe holds in relation to its growing Muslim communities. Evincing how social boundedness becomes mapped onto the physical terrain of the metropolis, they are a physical grounds for spiritual and social encounters. Disputes over, and even the destruction of, mosques has, however, increased in recent years, with conflict over their place and meaning centering on a politics of visibility.[68] Visible mosques rise as both "fraught symbol[s]" and material centers for contention over if, when, and how Islam can be part of European public life.[69] For instance, the idea of the "mega-mosque" as a symbol of Christian antagonism has stirred debate in the UK, France, and Germany.[70] Through popular vote, the Swiss outlawed minarets in 2009, seen to represent political domination rather than religious domain.[71] Effectively controlling the presence of Islam in the public sphere, visible mosques have evoked questions regarding the sacrality of space for both religious and secular political traditions in debates over *laïcité* (French constitutional secularism).[72]

In Spain, the Córdoba Mosque-Cathedral signals an enduring tension between Spanish nationalism and the echoes of Islamic history.[73]

As Muslim bodies, mosques in Europe today are most significantly constrained by the symbolic boundaries of civility rather than by law.[74] "Questions of sacred space are. . . . questions about whose feelings for a place count as civil, whose ways of seeing count as civil, and thus who is included in the cultural sphere of citizenship and civil belonging."[75] Mosques elude civility not only in their spatial structures but also in their purpose, with the social formation of the Muslim subject seen to clash with the sociopolitical formation of the citizen vis-à-vis the state. As James Holston writes, "Civility refers to the standards of behavior and common 'measure'—to the 'etiquettes, manner, and virtues'—that make public life coherent and thus possible."[76] Arguably shaped by both Islamic and European epistemologies, Muslims in Europe have come to signal ambiguity and incoherence. With its "cultural conventions, everyday performances, aesthetic codes, and foundation narratives," civility upholds social hierarchy through resulting "inegalitarian regimes of citizenship."[77] In *Citizen Outsider: Children of North African Immigrants in France*, Jean Beaman explores an inegalitarian regime of citizenship through lived experiences of the children of immigrants, revealing a deep and enduring cultural hierarchy experienced by those that she terms "citizen outsiders."[78]

Civility as a means to mark hierarchy through a discourse and system seeking coherence and order is rooted in Europe's layered colonial and imperial histories. In *Civility and Empire*, Anindyo Roy argues that civility was the very "ethos of the British colonial state," a "normative code" employed as "a means of imposing control and effecting exclusion."[79] Cultural theorist Homi Bhabha moves from this spatially oriented critique to a Benjaminian critique of "homogenous, empty time," that is a "Western nationalist discourse which normalizes its own history of expansion and exploitation by inscribing the history of the other in a fixed hierarchy of civil progress."[80] With the Enlightenment both the geographic and temporal location of the so-called civilizing process, "uncivil," "unenlightened," "backwards," and "barbaric" all rise as synonyms for "the Other" in a discourse justifying subordination and violence. This Bhabha terms "sly civility," as it offers nothing more to the colonized than what Roy terms an "impossible dream."[81]

Ignoring the very colonial and imperial histories that drove mid-twentieth-century migration to Europe, European nation-states, media, and publics have increasingly portrayed Muslims, and thereby mosques, as uncivil. In her work on Nigerian diasporas, Alice Feldman argues that self-induced societal amnesia "obscure[s] the connections" between colonial, and arguably broader imperial, histories and what is seen as the "the crises of contemporary migrations."[82] And Ann Stoler posits "colonial aphasia," signaling an incapacity to comprehend, and therefore incapacity to speak to, this history.[83] Situated in this context of collective forgetting and enduring incomprehensibility—again, *absence*—Muslims are accused of introducing transgressive difference into the possible shape of the modern European citizen, thereby threatening the social order. The real threat, of course, is not Muslim incivility, but rather the exposure of civility's own shaky ground—built upon distinction from the quite-often-Muslim "Other" in colonial/imperial projects and this postcolonial/postimperial age that still has no name.

This ground cannot hold. It gives way to an unstable albeit persistent social paradigm where civility eludes the Muslim, even when born in Europe. Algerian French sociologist Abdelmalek Sayad in fact describes the children of immigrants as "the height of both civil and political impoliteness, and the height of rudeness and violence towards *national* understanding."[84] The child of the immigrant suggests the stranger who cannot be expelled. And the mosque now rises as the architectural embodiment of strangers/strangerness, indelibly marking the European landscape.

Let us turn back now, for a moment, to the sly nature of civility, this "impossible dream."[85] Much like a dream state occupies the juncture between sleeping and waking, war occupied the juncture between colonial/imperial projects and the migration of Muslim populaces to Europe in the mid-twentieth century. While Europe recruited workers to rebuild in the post-WWII period, wars of liberation from colonial rule spanned the nineteenth and twentieth centuries. Migrating from Algeria to France in the early 1960s, the so-called Harkis—Algerian Muslims who served as soldiers in the French army—embodied the ephemerality of civility. In spite of their ultimate act of loyalty, fighting to preserve the French colony, they were initially confined to "reception estates." In 1962, Charles de Gaulle rhetorically extended myth into new geographical terrain. "The term 'repatriates' obviously does not apply to the Muslims," he asserted. "In their case, we are dealing only with refugees."[86]

The enduring perception of Muslims' and thereby mosques' deep incivility is today colored not by the context of war, but by ongoing violence, both physical and discursive, that denies full belonging, and a context, I might add, currently imbued with a rhetoric of refugee undesirables. Here and now, hypergovernmentality takes the form of the modern security state. And again, Benjamin writes, "The tradition of the oppressed teaches us that the 'state of emergency' in which we live is not the exception but the rule."[87] Building out from this thesis, Lauren Berlant discusses the "hygienic governmentality" through which particular groups, posed as dangerous to "society's common good . . . must be rigorously monitored and governed."[88] From explicit surveillance to community cohesion agendas, which implicate Muslim leaders and institutions in deradicalization initiatives, Europe's security states justify their formidable presence in mosques through a powerful paradigm of Muslim incivility.

Urban Institutions

John Bowen, an ethnographer of Islam in Europe, has long argued for institutions as sites of inquiry into Muslim life, as they produce innovative threshold spaces, straddling religious conviction, national European legal-political spheres, and localized identities.[89] In Bhabha's words, "These 'in-between' spaces provide the terrain for elaborating strategies of selfhood—singular or communal—that initiate new signs of identity, and innovative sites of collaboration, and contestation, in the act of defining the idea of society, itself."[90] Research on Islamic institutions in Europe to date has spanned mosques, schools, sharia councils, and ethnic organizations, grappling with the intersections of authority and autonomy, private/public divides, and the flexibility of space, culture, and inclusion.[91]

The mosque is, like all institutions in Europe, subject to local and national laws. In Germany, churches and synagogues are recognized under state law as public institutions (Körperschaften des öffentlichen Rechts), bestowing certain rights, responsibilities, and financial capacities. The origins of this institutional arrangement reveal an attempt to mediate deep religious conflict (from the Reformation to the late-nineteenth-century *Kulturkampf*, in which Bismarck sought to control and delimit the powers of the Catholic Church).[92] While also a secularist model, the interaction between the German state and religion diverges from the widely contested *laïcité* secularism of France, which strictly regulates religion in public life and is often misconstrued as representing European secularism writ large. Recognized religious institutions and their activities are instead made entirely public, integrated into, and managed by the German state.[93] Muslim communities have not received the status bestowed to Protestants, Catholics, and Jews, many politicians arguing that diverse interpretations of Islam thwart political representation. Instead, they are considered not-for-profit enlisted associations run by a board of directors (eingetragener Verein).[94] The United Kingdom (UK), on the other hand, where the Church of England remains intertwined with the state, designates mosques as public charities.[95]

Some mosques are also institutional centers for revivalist movements led by second- and third-generation Muslims. Numerous scholars, including

Mayanthi Fernando, Christine Jacobsen, Jeanette Jouili, Giulia Liberatore, and Olivier Roy, have analyzed this revivalism across European countries, suggesting that it is part of a transnational trend in which younger generations at once reject their parents' and grandparents' culturally imbued understandings of Islam, as well as their labeling as uncivil in "the West."[96] I argue that revivalism is an enactive, rather than reactive, form of critique; those engaged in revivalist movements critically contest the indignity and inequity imbued by partial inclusion in European nation-states through the knowledge and practice of Islam.

My interlocutors in London and Berlin often describe the mosque as "my home country," or "my home." They articulate that they can "breathe freely" within it, both literally and metaphorically "let down [their] hair," and "strengthen resolve." The metaphor of breathing freely is one employed by many in reference to the offering of anonymity in the modern metropolis. For instance, Sennett recounts the words of author Willa Cather upon arrival in New York City, where she moved with her female partner: "It's exciting, but more important at last I can breathe."[97] The city can be forgiving, as its density and plurality together create the space for difference; but the city can also be cruel. Beyond the bounds of the mosque, my interlocutors discuss when and where they can "be themselves," including how they choose to dress in different social circumstances (e.g., in wide-legged pants rather than the abaya, a typically black, loose robe-like dress/jacket worn in addition to the headscarf, in "less Muslim" areas of London). In fact, while asserting that they will not go to West London wearing a headscarf, one of my closest confidantes in London, Melia, and her university-aged daughter, Leyla, both insist that they simply will not go to West London anymore *at all*. They are, Melia explains, "just Muslims," "citizens of God," their spatial boundaries determined by the expression and protection of piety.

What does it mean to be "just Muslim" or a "citizen of God"? When my interlocutors assert that they are "just Muslims," they mean this in both senses—*only* and *ethical*. There is a namelessness imbued by ambiguity, and one countered by the embrace of Muslimness. "Who I am, who I am." "Melia." "I call myself Yusuf." "I am Mustafa." "A citizen." "A foreigner." "Not German." "A German." "Not Turkish." "Turkish." "Not British." "British." "Not Asian." "Asian." "A mother." "A brother." "A sister." "A son." "Muslim." "I am Muslim overall." There is, however, not only difference in what my interlocutors are called and what they call themselves, but also at-times contradictions within their self-understandings, between the "mosque self" and the "public self," as ethical precepts, moral practices, social relations, and spatial configurations in the European metropolis collide. In the case of the Şehitlik Mosque, women perceive clashes between the "mosque self" and the "public self" as an opportunity to politically engage, directly confronting discomfiting spaces and regulations on religious expression in the public sphere. Among my interlocutors at Şehitlik, such friction contributes to their focus on social harmonization. At the East London Mosque, my interlocutors perceive similar friction as a grounds to disengage from the mainstream and focus on redemption.

To situate the mosque in broader European debates evokes controversies about visibility, belonging, and national historical identities. The conversation about the mosque in the lives of Muslim adherents instead evokes questions of crossing, making, and ultimately dwelling, as pious Muslims, in the metropolis. Piety is, in essence, the expression of faith-based intentions (the spirit behind the deed) and faith-inspired actions ("the deed itself").[98] It is a "semiconscious, self-authoring project" based on the "search for authentic religious subjecthood."[99] The actions of the religious person—doing or making, the latter of which suggests not only the action itself but also its constructive potentiality—are stressed in the Qur'an; "Man is [deep] in loss, except for those who believe, do good deeds, urge one another to the truth, and urge one another to steadfastness" (Q 103:2–3).[100]

Carefully and purposefully enacting Islam becomes a means of authority, resisting and critiquing layered marginalities by cultivating and expressing Islamic knowledge in and beyond the mosque. As Arendt asserts, people "can resist only in terms of the identity that is under attack."[101] Islam is, at the same time, always a means of submission to God. We social scientists fear inviting God into the conversation in our commitment to that deemed objective and reasonable (which is always subjective and at times unreasonable). Yet this fear limits the possibilities of engaging with social worlds built not on the dyad of self-society, but rather the triad of self-society-God. The relational power of God cannot and should not be overlooked.[102] It is thus within this triadic paradigm that the mosque becomes an interstice, not only a concrete architectural form and institution but also a lived project in the European metropolis, where the pious subject makes and is made.

THE ABRAHAMIC STRANGER

The phenomenon of *déjà vu* has often been described. Is the term really apt? Shouldn't we rather speak of events which affect us like an echo—one awakened by a sound that seems to have issued from somewhere in the darkness of past life? . . . Just as the latter points us to a stranger who was on the premises, so there are words or pauses pointing us to that invisible stranger—the future . . .

WALTER BENJAMIN, *News of a Death* (1932–1934)[103]

A second triad emerges in this book: that of Muslims, Jews, and Europe.[104] The "Muslim question"[105] that has come to a head in twenty-first-century Europe echoes what Cohen and later Arendt termed the "Jewish question" of the nineteenth and twentieth.[106] Both are posed as contrasts or contradictions to the secular, Christian-origin body—flesh and politic alike; reflecting on Cohen's Jewish ethics, Benjamin Pollock writes, "so the stranger becomes the mediating concept" of Europe.[107] And it is within the European metropolis that Jewish and Muslim embodiments of the stranger both figuratively and literally meet. Zafer Şenocak, a celebrated writer who emigrated from Ankara to Munich in 1970 (later settling in Berlin), describes ethnic Turks in Germany as "treading in the footsteps of the erstwhile Jews" in his novel *Gefährliche Verwandtschaft* (Dangerous Relatives).[108] The title of this book does not reference, and yet captures, the insider-outsider status of Muslims and Jews as seemingly dangerous Abrahamic forms, "Others" who are also somehow, alarmingly, ours.

I am far from alone in conceptualizing the experiential overlap, in place if not time, by Muslims and Jews in Europe. Anne Norton and Anya Topolski are, for instance, key contemporary figures who illuminate this overlap.[109] Yet I innovate by turning to Jewish thought (Jews as makers) as a critically productive lens to think about both Muslim marginality as strangers and agency as makers in the contemporary European metropolis. The central thinkers undergirding my conceptualization of the status differentiation and agentive responses of Muslims in Europe—Hermann Cohen, Georg Simmel, Ernst Bloch, Walter Benjamin, Hans Jonas, Hannah Arendt, Zygmunt Bauman, Herbert Gans, and Richard Sennett—are Jewish in positionality, whether religiously, ethnically, culturally, in their persecution, and/or as part of an ambiguous ancestry. Jewishness informs their perspectives on modernity's fault lines, as part of a broader movement of Jewish intellectuals who have "reflected upon their own experiences in a wrenching reckoning with the legacies of the European Enlightenment."[110] And taken together, these perspectives forge an intellectual bridge that is at the same time an intellectual tradition, crossing three centuries from the mid-nineteenth century until today.

The earliest of these intellectuals, Hermann Cohen, was born in 1842 in Coswig, Germany, and rose as a neo-Kantian philosopher who grappled with the positionality of Jews in Europe. He abandoned rabbinical school to pursue a career as a philosopher, founding the Marburg School of neo-Kantianism. His key works include *System of Philosophy* and *Religion of Reason: Out of the Sources of Judaism*. While his life temporally mapped onto that of imperial Germany, his influence on Jewish ethics has lived on.[111] Cohen's theories on

Nebenmensch (next man) and *Mitmensch* (fellow man) as well as reconcilia-tion help me to think through the Muslim-Jewish alliance that emerges at the Şehitlik Mosque, and his interconnected ideas on prophetic Messianism and suffering, the vision of the East London Mosque.

Of the same generation, Georg Simmel was also a neo-Kantian philosopher, as well as a cultural theorist and sociologist, born in Berlin in 1858 to a Lu-theran mother (from a family that converted from Judaism) and Jewish father who converted to Catholicism.[112] Simmel is widely considered a founding father of sociology and a key thinker on cities, modernity, and the self from a psychosocial perspective. Some of his most notable works include *The Me-tropolis and Mental Life*, *The Problems of the Philosophy of History*, and *Soci-ology* (including his essay "The Stranger").[113] As noted above, I draw on his conceptualization of the stranger as a societal insider-outsider, encapsulating the particular and yet generalizable in-between position of Jews and Muslims in Europe.

Born over a quarter century later, in 1885, in Ludwigshafen, Kingdom of Bavaria (today Rheinland-Pfalz), Ernst Bloch was a German Jewish[114] Marx-ist whose writings focus on social utopia. Following his exile to the United States during the Holocaust, Bloch famously penned *The Principle of Hope* in Harvard's Widener Library, arguing that only utopic strivings, the longing and acting for a better world, can liberate humanity from systematic economic and cultural oppression. Bloch later returned to a divided Germany, first settling in East Germany, where he taught at Leipzig University, relocating to Tübingen University in West Germany in 1961.[115] I employ Bloch's theorization of hope to make sense of the hope-filled method of seeking and enacting knowledge that shapes the daily lives of my East London Mosque interlocutors.

Born in 1892 in Berlin, Walter Benjamin, known as a critical theorist, liter-ary critic, essayist, and philosopher, crossed and combined genres. Forced to flee from the Nazis, leading to his premature death, Benjamin expressed an ambivalent and dynamic stance towards his Jewishness, incorporating Jewish understandings of redemption into his fragmented writings. These include *Berlin Childhood*, *Theses on the Philosophy of History*, and *The Task of the Translator*. Benjamin not only critically examined cities, but he also actively engaged with them, embodying Baudelaire's *flâneur*—the "passionate specta-tor," as both aesthetic and critical method of exposure and excavation, born out of the desire to intimately know each city's cracks, crevices, and pasts.[116] I draw extensively on Benjamin's work, including his view of the city as the epitome of modernity, his ideas of dwelling as an active process, his recogni-tion of the ubiquity of state security, his vision of messianism—within it, hope (in relation to the messianic perspective of the East London Mosque)—and finally his theory of remembrance as a critical lens through which to view Europe's struggles with pluralism present and past.

Born over a decade later in 1903 in Mönchengladbach, Hans Jonas was a German Jewish philosopher who fled the Nazi regime in 1933, migrating to New York City where he worked as a professor at the New School for Social Research. His most significant work, *The Imperative of Responsibility: In Search of an Ethics for a Technological Age*, responded to the societal devastation he experienced firsthand; in it, he countered his contemporary, Bloch, by arguing for the centrality of responsibility rather than utopia as the animating force in the creation of a better world.[117] In this book, Jonas moved beyond the interrelationship of human beings to that of humans with nature. While, like Benjamin, deeply ambivalent towards Judaism, Jonas also incorporated Jewish theology into his writings, grappling with theodicy in the aftermath of the Holocaust.[118] Jonas's ethics of responsibility helps me to critically explore the Şehitlik Mosque in its knowledge-building practices and its relationship with the Berlin metropolis.

Hannah Arendt, born in 1906 in what is today Hannover, Germany, has been recognized as one of the seminal philosophical thinkers of the twentieth century. The power and originality of her ideas are evident in writings such as *The Origins of Totalitarianism*, *The Human Condition*, and *The Jewish Writings*. In her major philosophical work, *The Human Condition*, and in some of the essays collected in *Between Past and Future*, Arendt articulated a fairly negative conception of modernity. In a vast collection of writings, she grappled with the most crucial events of her time, including the Holocaust. She herself fled the Nazi regime, settling in the United States and teaching at numerous elite institutions of higher education, including Princeton University. While Arendt has been derided as a "self-hating Jew," she saw Jewishness at the core of her personhood.[119] I specifically engage Arendt's reflections on the absences of modernity, Jewish positionality (pariah/parvenu/"caste-like"), and the Jewish salon as a space of encounters with "the Other" in eighteenth- and nineteenth-century Berlin, as I consider similar encounters in the lives of my interlocutors from the Şehitlik Mosque community.

Of the following generation, Zygmunt Bauman, a sociologist and philosopher born in Poznán, Poland, in 1925, fled with his family to the USSR during WWII and to Israel in 1968 (in his second bout of exile, which led to the revocation of his Polish citizenship), later settling in the United Kingdom, where he taught at the University of Leeds. Hailing from a nonpracticing Jewish family, Bauman embraced socialism. His most notable contributions, *Modernity and Ambivalence* and *Modernity and the Holocaust* centered on modernity and rationality—again the "problem of order" in the "gardening state."[120] His work later turned towards postmodernity as an opportunity to transcend the dangers of modernity.[121] I specifically engage Bauman's writings on the tensions between order-seeking and ambiguity in modernity, abstracted difference in his application of Simmel's concept of the stranger to the Jewish experience (what he terms the "conceptual Jew"), and his definition of solidarity as co-constituted by the self and "the Other," the latter of which comes to life in a Jewish-Muslim alliance at the Şehitlik Mosque.

Of the same generation, Herbert Gans, a German Jew born in Cologne in 1927, migrated to the United States as a refugee in 1940, where he became one of the foremost urban sociologists at Columbia University.[122] While he never wrote of his own Jewishness, it nonetheless informed his work, much of which focused on the experience of ethnic minorities in urban contexts (for instance, *The Urban Villagers* and *The Levittowners*). Many further recognize Gans as the first public sociologist, owing to his contributions to policy and advocacy on poverty.[123] I draw on his concept of "undercaste," from early writings on inequality, in my theoretical framing of Muslim positionality today.[124]

In many ways building upon the intellectual precedent of Jewish thinkers in exile (mentored by Arendt, with Simmel, Benjamin, and Bauman explicitly woven into his writings), Richard Sennett, born in 1943 in Chicago, is a contemporary social theorist whose work increasingly centers on social life in cities. Most recently, he authored *Building and Dwelling: Ethics for the City*.[125] Although implicit rather than explicit in his work, Sennett, of mixed Russian Orthodox and Jewish descent, describes a childhood in a house filled with Jewish objects.[126] A former urban planner, he explores the relationship between the building of cities and the ways in which humans inhabit them. I draw from Sennett's reflections on the "open city" as a space for critical encounters able to foster solidarity rather than coherence, including those with strangers, and the constructive potentiality of experiences imbued with friction and pain.

Beyond—or perhaps in relation to—a Jewish positionality, implicit and explicit intellectual threads tie these thinkers together. Many of the German Jewish thinkers, like Benjamin, who were contemporaries of Cohen built their intellectual projects through distinction from his assimilatory approach to Germanness and Jewishness.[127] All of them crossed disciplinary boundaries between such areas as sociology, philosophy, political theory, theology, and literature. In terms of theoretical orientations, they all grapple with the unsettling challenges of modernity. Simmel, Benjamin, Gans, and Sennett similarly understand the modern metropolis, its many shapes and many shadows, as giving life to uniquely modern social forms; and Simmel's theory of the stranger has influenced Bauman and Sennett in their own conceptualizations of difference.

These individuals are connected not only intellectually, but also experientially—Arendt, Bauman, Benjamin, Bloch, Gans, and Jonas all fleeing from the Nazis. Their entwinement, however, both preceded and extended beyond the Holocaust. Before the rise of the Third Reich, Benjamin attended both Cohen's and Simmel's lectures in Berlin.[128] Arendt, Benjamin, Bloch, and Jonas formed deep personal bonds in their early intellectual pursuits in Germany and later in exile, bonds rooted in education and unbroken even by death.[129] Benjamin and Bloch had a tumultuous and often strained relationship until Benjamin's death in 1940.[130] Arendt and Jonas, having studied philosophy together under Martin Heidegger, forged a long-lasting friendship that traveled with them to New York City, where they both eventually resettled; "It is difficult to picture, for the remainder of my days, a world without Hannah Arendt," Jonas lamented at her eulogy on December 8, 1975.[131] Arendt mentored Sennett.[132] And Arendt and Benjamin were not only intimate friends but also, for a stint, family members; Arendt's first husband, Günther Stern, was Benjamin's cousin. Seyla Benhabib writes of the evenings the two spent playing chess in Paris in the 1930s, their lives in excruciating limbo.[133] Later, in an act of resistance and also mourning, Arendt carried Benjamin's final work, *Theses on the Philosophy of History*, with her to America after his death.[134] She proceeded to write him a poem, titled with his initials, *W.B.*

> Dusk will come again sometime.
> Night will come down from the stars.
> We will rest our outstretched arms.
> In the nearness, in the distances.[135]

It is this combination of nearness and distance that characterizes the perspective of the Jewish thinker as herself a stranger in the European metropolis. This endows a unique view of Europe; again, in the words of Bauman, European Jews were "always on the outside even when inside, examining the familiar as if it was a foreign object of study, asking questions no one else asked, questioning the unquestionable and challenging the unchallengeable."[136] As Jonas spoke of Arendt when she was laid to rest over half a century ago—"things looked different after she had looked at them."[137] This Jewish positionality has created a critical, if at times uncomfortable, perspective of European modernity, and one echoed in Islamic sources. As Moosa explains, the Prophet Muhammad himself posited that "Islam began as a stranger" and will be recovered by the stranger in exile or diaspora.[138] Moosa, in a textual conversation with formative Muslim scholar Abu Hamid al-Ghazali (1058–1111), evocatively writes of the unique knowledge thereby endowed by the stranger who inhabits the literal and/or cultural threshold space (*dihliz*); "that experience allows one to see things—to view things in a way that a domesticated or complacent gaze may fail to observe."[139]

Seeing in the Shadows, or Light Turned Inside Out

From his own abode in Morningside Heights, Edward Said cast an uncomplacent and critical gaze at Europe. In his monumental work, *Orientalism*, he writes of Muslims and Jews in Europe as unfortunate "secret-sharer[s]" on whom—in the words of Wilfried Graf—"the shadow of western civilization" is cast.[140] Yet shadows are made not of darkness, but of light turned inside out. If we shift our perspective to the shadows of the Enlightenment (including taken-for-granted understandings of "progress," "civility," "tolerance," "freedom," and "equality"), Muslims and Jews are, in their very alterity, constitutive of Europe.[141] "The idea of 'Europe' was born," Glynis Cousin and Robert Fine argue, through the persecution of Jews and Muslims.[142] And since its idea-l birth, the abstracted Jew and the abstracted Muslim have been collapsed into a similar, at times singular, "Other." During the Reformation, Jews were said to be poisoning wells through support from both the devil and Turks. In German-speaking European states, eerily similar rhetoric has been utilized to other Jews and Muslims throughout contemporary history, with global Jewish or Muslim identity posed as antinational and internal Jewish and Muslim populations antimodern. Farid Hafez points out that the slogan of today's Freedom Party in Austria, "Vienna shall not become Istanbul," echoes the words of Karl Lueger's proclamation in 1910 that "Vienna shall not become Jerusalem."[143] The recent circumcision debate and its temporary outlawing in Germany together cast Jews and Muslims as morally inferior strangers in a post-Christian, secular order, implicated in a barbaric practice against the bodies of innocents.[144] Both were and are, Graf asserts, evocative of a deep sense of "vacancy" in European modernity.[145]

While the experiences of Muslims in contemporary Europe that give form to this book are neither representative nor comprehensive, together they reveal cultural struggles at play in what appears on the surface as a "struggle over geography" but is in fact a struggle over imagined social coherence.[146] As Sennett warns, "Wholeness, oneness, coherence: these are key words in the vocabulary of power."[147] Katherine Pratt Ewing terms the stigmatization of Muslims in

Germany abjection—"the process of maintaining a sense of wholeness and identity by casting out that which is felt to be improper or dangerous to the integrity of the self."[148] Muslims in Europe, as Jews prior, are not cast out, however, but rather a caste within, inhabiting the "void between state and society."[149] In chapter 2, I thus argue that the exceptionally negative social status of Muslims in Europe can be best articulated through the analytical concept of *undercaste*, developed by Herbert Gans in his work on urban inequality.[150] I distinguish this analytical concept from the political or persecutory, as caste (very much like race) can alternatively be articulated through analytical vocabularies, political vocabularies, and vocabularies of persecution; I try to avoid the slippage that often occurs between them. Conceptualizing the status of Muslims in Europe through the analytical lens of caste sheds light on the hierarchy and high levels of social closure faced by those deemed uncivil. And it results in the abstracted understanding of diverse Muslims by the mainstream, much like Jews previously: with religion, culture, ethnicity, and race collapsed into a single form of degraded difference.[151]

While the first to conceptualize contemporary Muslim distinction in this way, I am not the first to conceptualize caste as a productive category for thinking about hegemonic identities and sociocultural hierarchy in modern Europe. In 1823, Jewish poet Michael Beer wrote and produced a show entitled *Der Paria* (The Pariah), in which a Hindu protagonist—an allegory for Jews in Europe—is denied full societal inclusion through a caste system.[152] Arendt subsequently theorized the position of Jews in premodern and modern Europe as that of a caste, caste-like, or in the "caste spirit."[153] And Isabel Wilkerson points to the caste system imposed under Hitler, its foundations visible "in the decades leading to the third Reich."[154] To think of Muslims' status similarly today—in the words of German journalist and writer Moritz Goldstein, "eternally half-other"—creates discomfort in its clash with Eurocentric understandings of progress and civility; but this discomfort is productive, as it opens new ways of seeing both the power and powerful critiques of collective subordination through associations with incivility.[155]

By no means a social theorist in the ranks of the great Jewish intellectuals who provide the theoretical backbone of this book, I aim to continue in their tradition of questioning, challenging, and ultimately unsettling taken-for-granted assumptions about European society and its (post-)Christian lens. In so doing, I draw not only from the sociological but also anthropological, philosophical, theological, and literary traditions. I am further inspired by the metropolis, and particular neighborhoods that long served as backdrops to the written works of these thinkers and now to my own, from Morningside

Heights (where Arendt and Gans sought inspiration in the Riverside Park of my youth) to the Bavarian Quarter of Berlin (where Arendt resided and Benjamin wrote on a lonely wooden desk among so many trees). This book is written in conversation with persons and texts, and—modeling an approach in both Jewish and Muslim critical thought, as between Arendt and Varnhagen, or Moosa and al-Ghazali—perhaps even friendship that transcends temporal divisions in the spaces and traditions that we call home. After all, in the words of the late Israeli author Amos Oz on the Jewish tradition, "ours is not a bloodline, but a textline."[156]

FROM MIGRATION TO INCIVILITY

The stories of my interlocutors, located within the fraught modern metropolis, begin with the crossing of the invisible lines of national borders through migration. In the UK, Caribbean and South Asian postcolonials largely migrated in the 1950s and 1960s. Yet even with their movement from the once-colonies to Europe's "core," the tiered system of colonial rule and citizenship traveled with them. Their legal status as commonwealth citizens prohibited official relegation to particular forms of labor, which rose as a major concern among British government officials, who feared their capacity to move freely within the labor market. Yet the cultural pollution of these migrants meant that labor mobility remained constricted through sanctioned discrimination, if not through law, and they found themselves overwhelmingly occupying the manufacturing and service industries.[157]

"The Post in Postcolonial": The United Kingdom

In *Mongrel Nation*, Ashley Dawson writes of postcolonial, diasporic inequalities in Britain's metropoles, with legally expanded citizenship delinked from cultural citizenship: "These ideologies of difference and innate superiority were far harder to dismantle than the political-economic system of imperial preference. Long after Britain lost its colonies, it retained its insular sense of cultural superiority."[158] S. Sayyid echoes this sentiment by interrogating the undefined nature of "the postcolonial," which "refers to a conceptual not just chronological category," a condition, a project, "the 'post' in postcolonial remind[ing] us that we have not arrived at something that can have its own name."[159] In 1978, white nationalists murdered Altab Ali, a Bengali textile worker, on Whitechapel Road, close to where the East London Mosque now stands. Protests broke out in Bengali communities across the city.[160]

This incident exposed the raw reality that entering the postcolonial city by no means resolved the cultural hierarchies of empire. In 1989, conflict over Salman Rushdie's *The Satanic Verses* reevoked felt inequalities. Incensed by the book questioning founding principles of Islam, Muslim communities responded through massive protests and book burnings across the country. Protests spread not only across the United Kingdom but the world, including the firebombing of bookstores. A year later, Ayatollah Ruhollah Khomeini, supreme leader of Iran, issued a fatwa—a nonbinding legal opinion—calling for the murder of Salman Rushdie.[161]

This event fed into Samuel Huntington's thesis that Islam and "the West" would inevitably "clash" as they drew geographically closer, whether through European consolidation or the increased border crossings that resulted from empire.[162] Contention over *The Satanic Verses* is perceived to this day as a critical juncture in contemporary British history, revealing widening cleavages between mainstream society and a growing Muslim populace. Other critical junctures include 9/11, leading to the deepened securitization of Muslim populaces, and thereafter the March 2004 Madrid train bombings and the July 2005 London train bombings. In 2003, the British government notably increased the securitization of Muslim populaces, publicly instating the Preventing Violent Extremism program (often called the "Prevent" or PVE strategy, which is part of the larger CONTEST counterterrorism strategy instated in the same year, also including "Pursue," "Protect," and "Prepare"). The Prevent strategy, which institutionalized "a politics of unease," has since been revised, entailing deepened surveillance of Muslim individuals and both Muslim institutions and institutions that serve Muslims (for instance, schools).[163] While articulated in a language of social collaboration, its exclusive focus on Muslim communities has driven a wedge between Muslims and mainstream British society. This, as Paul Thomas argues, both essentializes and stigmatizes ethnically, economically, and culturally diverse individuals collectively *as Muslims*.[164] Cloaked in claims of upholding and protecting "British values," Prevent at once securitizes and discursively externalizes Muslims from the larger social body.[165]

By the turn of the twenty-first century, the postmigrant, postcolonial British Muslim populace had become very much aware of their Muslimness as a discerning factor of difference, in spite of the diversity among Muslims. A sense of marginality deepened as such cultural difference met socioeconomic struggle; at the capital city level, the poverty of East London, Tower Hamlets in particular, where the East London Mosque is located, became bluntly juxtaposed with the shining skyscrapers of Canary Wharf. Mark, a police captain in the district, describes ethnoreligious minorities in Tower Hamlets who have "experienced levels of deprivation, Victorian in depth, something that Dickens would have written about, chuck by jowl with the ostentation and opulence of Canary Wharf." Responding to these layered, at times violent, juxtapositions, where Bengali Brits remain the most economically deprived group, Muslim identity rose as a form of alternative belonging—fixed not to fluctuating nationalities, but to an all-embracing global peoplehood. This has entailed accepting, while transforming, difference from a negative to positive status, refuting vilification through renewed and dignifying piety.[166]

Regardless of the felt distance from nation-state identities, pluralism has been, and continues to be, managed by the state. Multiculturalism emerged in the United Kingdom as the dominant political model in the latter half of the twentieth century. The term "multiculturalism" is highly ambiguous, and often used to refer in simply descriptive terms to a diverse society. Here it is employed to signal an orientation and set of policies at the interface of majority/minority relations in the UK (defined by Tariq Modood as "the recognition of group difference within the public sphere of laws, policies, democratic discourses and the terms of a shared citizenship and national identity")—policies with the potential to both create protections and reinforce divisions for certain minority groups.[167] Multiculturalism was and is a nebulous ideal and form of governance. "I think if you're looking for certainty, you won't see it," police captain Mark asserts. This brings to mind a conversation I had with Ebrahim Moosa, in which he called the postmodern an opportunity to "ask questions of unyielding certainties—certainties that are hollow."

Over the past two decades, a climate of fear, a large refugee push towards Europe, and the growing instability of the European Union (EU) have together eroded positive connotations of "multiculturalism" in British politics and publics alike. Multiculturalism has come to be regarded as a "dirty word"— its "dark underbelly" one of ethnoreligious exclusion, cultural clashes, and a decoupling of the British nation-state as such.[168] A decade ago, then–Prime Minister Tony Blair described the failures of multiculturalism.[169] The question remains, however, whether a cohesive multicultural state ever really existed, or was rather always a "paternalist" misnomer, suggesting multiplicity in name while pitting "good diversity" against "bad diversity" in the country's ethnoracial, neoliberal order.[170]

Muslims have long held a precarious place in the multicultural project and imaginary, relegated to the category of pathological diversity.[171] Some were afforded protections as ethnic or racial—but not religious—minorities during the late twentieth century, as religion does not have a similar legal status to ethnicity or race in the UK.[172] And market-driven expressions of inclusion based on consumption and consumer desire have emerged on the British landscape, such as the burkini (a full-body swimsuit for women that includes a head covering) sales by Marks & Spencer in 2015, or an annual Ramadan section at major supermarkets nationwide. Yet in spite of capitalistic strivings, the market does not comprehensively represent political or cultural norms. The public place of Islam, from mosque-building projects to the donning of headscarves in civic positions, has recently come more clearly into the national spotlight through the xenophobic Leave Campaign that successfully pushed for Brexit and a discernable shift to the political right as the UK exits from the European Union.[173]

"Foreigners Who Are Not Foreign": Germany

Germany, contrastingly, does not share a colonial history with its Muslim populace, although it does share a history of empire. As the Ottoman Empire declined, World War I (WWI) broke out in Europe, and the Ottoman-German alliance was formalized by treaty in 1914.[174] This deepened a long-lasting relationship of economic, military, and political cooperation, and Turkey therefore declared neutrality in World War II.[175] Guest workers were recruited to rebuild the fractured German state after WWII, hailing primarily from Turkey and what was then Yugoslavia, as well as Southern Europe. From mining to laying railways, street cleaning to large-scale harvesting and butchering, they were employed to do the work of reconstruction, in physically demanding occupations characterized by dirt, sweat, and blood.[176] These programs included the explicit mandate that the workers, who were not considered migrants, would only temporarily reside in Europe. The "rotation principle" throughout the initial decades of Germany's guest worker program, for instance, required that they leave the country after two years of employment, solidifying preservation of their national ties.[177] The reality of harsh economic circumstances in origin countries, as well as the relaxing of regulations in Germany, meant that while most guest workers did return to Turkey, many did not. Family reunification policies instated in the 1970s facilitated the permanent settlement of tens of thousands of guest workers.

With the "settlement of foreigners who are not foreign but remain different" in the 1970s, guest workers eventually gained recognition as migrants to Germany.[178] This shift in rhetoric bestowed few additional rights, however, with return to origin countries encouraged well into the 1980s. Settlement was recognized as extended, and residency legalized without bestowing citizenship.

Migrants faced limbo in their status, remaining entrenched in origin-country political struggles. Only in 2001 did birth-based citizenship laws replace those based on blood.[179] And only in the early 2000s, under the leadership of Chancellor Gerhard Schröder, did German politicians explicitly identify Germany as an immigration country.[180] Yet the continued, detailed discernment of what it means to be an immigration country has revealed ongoing resistance to demographic change. Ethnic Turks have been targeted in this struggle since their first wave of migration in the 1960s—today discussed via political questioning of whether Muslims and/or Islam belong to Germany.[181] One might also argue that Turkey itself occupies this liminal status in both the geographical and cultural framework of Europe, partially located on the continent, while partially set apart by the sea.

The German state finally bestowed citizenship on ethnically Turkish, German-born children at the turn of the twenty-first century, but the divisive *Leitkulturdebatte* (leading culture debate) emerged around the same time. The term *Leitkultur* was first employed in 1998 by political scientist Bassam Tibi, who argued for migrant incorporation into society vis-à-vis the recognition and embrace of so-called "European values," rooted in "democracy, secularism, the Enlightenment, human rights and civil society." He described incorporation as requiring give-and-take, calling for both the adaptation of those settling in Europe and the provision of civil rights to these new denizens by European societies.[182] Beginning in 2000, at the time of citizenship law revisions, the conservative Christian Democratic Union (Christlich Demokratische Union, CDU)/Christian Social Union (Christlich-Soziale Union, CSU) party invoked the concept of *Leitkultur* as they implored Muslims in Germany to adapt to a particular national culture rooted as much in Christianity as the Enlightenment. Backlash ensued, not least of all in response to the term's invocation of ethnoreligious hierarchy, given that such hierarchy had resulted in the extreme persecution of Jews.[183]

Rooted in a history of Catholic/Protestant church conflict, Germany contrasts with the United Kingdom in its diversity management, viewing individuals and institutions—but not communities—as autonomous. Multiculturalism is also imbued with different meanings in these national contexts. In Germany, the term "multiculturalism" was first employed by representatives of the Catholic and Protestant churches in 1980 to bring attention to labor migrants as not only economically, but also culturally beneficial to German society. The German colloquialism *multi-kulti* in essence called for the selective incorporation of traits or cultural markers seen to "enrich" German society, while excluding others—most significantly, those connected with Islam; some have thus termed

German multiculturalism the "Döner principle," drawing on the celebration of the döner kebab as a culinary source of German national pride in spite of on-going discomfort with ethnic Turks.[184] In 2010, German chancellor Angela Merkel claimed that multiculturalism, understood as living contentedly together *with* but not *among* each other, had "failed." She emphasized that minorities needed to work harder to integrate themselves into mainstream society.[185] The same Chancellor Merkel, however, opened the borders of the country to almost a million majority Muslim refugees five years later, in 2015.[186]

Germany has increasingly pursued a particular form of assimilatory poli-cies in relation to the Muslim populace, those that attempt to "domesticate Islam."[187] This entails a certain ambiguity, aiming to control the religion not by relegating it to the private sphere or explicit religious spaces as in *laïcité* France, but rather through a publicly digestible, officially recognized form.[188] The German Islam Conference (Deutsche Islamkonferenz) was founded in 2006 with this goal in mind, selecting Europe-friendly Muslim representatives to create a single Islamic interlocutor for the state.[189] Germany's Federal Min-istry for Education and Research also initiated and financed four centers of Islamic Theology at six major universities since 2010: Münster, Osnabrück, Frankfurt, Giessen, Tübingen, and Erlangen.

This move towards so-called domestication is complicated by long-standing transnational policies, as Germany has largely outsourced the man-agement of Turkish Muslim communities to the Turkish state since the late twentieth century. Thus, the role of the Turkish-Muslim Union for Religious Affairs (Diyanet İşleri Türk-Islam Birliği, DITIB) as a strong extranational force cannot be disentangled from ongoing questions over Muslim belonging. Today, DITIB administers over 900 of the approximately 2,500 mosques in Germany. It remains controlled by the Diyanet İşleri Başkanlığı (Diyanet), Tur-key's Ministry of Religious Affairs, with DITIB's secretary-general appointed by the Turkish government; this has caused recent conflicts over and within numerous mosques in Germany.[190] It is important to note here that despite diversity within both the Turkish and Muslim collectives, Turkishness and Muslimness have long been conflated in Germany.

"Imaginative Geography": Europe

The United Kingdom and Germany exemplify different state models of im-perialism, liberal democracy, and multiculturalism. At the same time, they also play unique roles in the European project, an ambiguous umbrella of economics, politics, policy, and culture. While two of Europe's largest economic powers, their positioning within this lived project has been almost oppositional—Germany at its sociopolitical and fiscal center, the UK relegated by choice to its periphery. Brexit has of course driven this wedge much further, with the UK's plan to exit the EU passed by popular referendum on June 23, 2016, and finalized on January 31, 2019.[191] This European "divorce" will have significant economic consequences for the EU and significant economic, cultural, and political consequences for the UK.[192] As divisions and uncertainty shake the Western Hemisphere, Germany—and many would argue Chancellor Merkel herself—with both trepidation and renewed vigor, has become a pivotal European leader.[193]

Beyond the city, the nation-state, and the European Union as an economic-political entity lies a less geographically tangible, but equally important, European imaginary, including what Edward Said terms an "imaginative geography" distinguishing "us" in place and personhood from "them."[194] It is this imaginary that claims secularity, but continues to be deeply affected by religious histories, trajectories, and hierarchies, "intrinsically built on the European post-Christian, post-Enlightenment and post-imperial, cultural self-understanding of majorities," where encountering Islam becomes not "encountering political or cultural difference, but . . . encountering the limits of civilization itself."[195] Such an "imaginative geography" posits an exclusive civility—the notion "civility" born in the colonial/imperial metropolis, and soon contrasted to the "otherness" encountered and emphasized in empire, echoing in and of its afterlives.[196]

The rhetoric making this marginality has shifted over time and followed a similar, if not parallel, trajectory of "onomastic moments" across nation-states.[197] "We didn't think about faith before. We were aware of the Bangladeshi and Pakistani communities, but they kept to themselves. We thought of them as shopkeepers and restaurateurs," reflects police captain Mark. In the 1980s and 1990s, the slow transformation of postcolonial and guest worker migration into permanent legal settlement, then citizenship, resulted in a rhetorical shift across Europe: the same "outsider" groups now labeled on account of their ethnicity. Rising xenophobia and discrimination were leveled against "the Turk," "the Algerian," "the Paki," and "the Asian." An exact moment in time when this ethnic labeling transformed into a dominant frame of religious labeling is difficult to pinpoint. Ferruh Yilmaz effectively traces the implications of an anti-immigrant agenda on "how the workers became Muslims" in Denmark, as in Europe more widely, showing the influence of far-right wing actors on fomenting what Werner Schiffauer terms "moral panic" over growing Muslim populaces.[198] The employment of Islamophobia in a widely

disseminated British report *Islamophobia: A Challenge for Us All* in 1997 similarly suggests that religion-based othering had gained momentum throughout
Europe in the last decades of the twentieth century, one expedited by 9/11 and
the subsequent terror attacks in Europe.[199]

Today, diverse groups are labeled first and foremost as Muslims rather
than workers, migrants, or ethnic minorities in colloquial parlance. This
has entailed an extension of pollution and dirt, with its attendant moral and
emotional dangers, to serious physical danger—an uncivil threat within the
physical boundaries, but not cultural imaginary of Europe. Osman, a social
activist and one of my interlocutors at the Şehitlik Mosque, explains the shift
that he experienced firsthand since he moved to Berlin from Turkey in the
1990s. In his office in Kreuzberg, a stark white room that contrasts with the
lush green of trees outside the windowpanes, he tips a coffee to his lips and
shakes his head.

> It's soil and blood . . . Back in the day, people were yelling, "Turks get outta
> here!" Now they are yelling, "Muslims get outta here!" So, the segregation mech-
> anisms have been altered; whereas in the past the segregation was based on
> ethnic refusal, now it's based on religious identity. So the negative connotation
> lies with the religion, more precisely, Islam. And Islam stands for a backward
> society, no human rights, no women's rights, honor killings, crime, no tolerance
> towards other religions, refusal of all other cultures, chauvinism, machoism.

Simply put, in the words of John Bowen, perceived as "incompatible with
the values of Europe and European states" and "a threat to European culture,"
"the notion of 'Muslim Citizens'" has come to appear "as an oxymoron."[200]

OVERVIEW OF CHAPTERS

In the chapters that follow, I problematize Europe and European nation-states,
invoking the metropolis as a point of reference and relationality both for the
mosque and my Muslim interlocutors. I also interweave both the critical ideas
of Jewish intellectuals, and the Jewish historical precedent in culture and
space, to help make sense of the responses of these two mosque communities
to marginalization. In the words of Benjamin, "past things have futurity," just
as present and future hold within them the past.[201] Throughout, I intersperse
short narratives of my interlocutors that personalize and enrich the larger, collective stories about Muslim space and place-making in the modern European
metropolis.

The second chapter ("Caste, or the Order of Things Defied") reawakens caste as an analytical category. The concept of caste has been analytically employed to understand the historical experience of Jews in Europe and Black Americans both in the American South during the 1930s and in the contemporary US; it can also be used to make sense of Muslim social positioning, challenges, and responsive forms of overcoming in Europe today.[202] Despite the association of caste exclusively with India, the concept is in fact native to Europe, with the linguistic term born in fifteenth-century Iberia. María Elena Martínez traces the emergence of caste as part of a broader lexicon of concepts (caste, race, lineage) meant to distinguish Christian converts from Judaism and Islam from old Christians in Europe—positing a lasting impurity through the "naturalization of a religious-cultural identity"; a system of castes was then employed in the Spanish and Portuguese colonial projects to distinguish Europeans from, and through the subordination of, colonized peoples.[203] The concept of caste is further native to the social sciences, as employed by Max Weber to describe ascriptive rather than class-based difference.[204]

I argue specifically that Muslims in Europe currently face an undercaste status based on associations with incivility; abstracted into an uncivil "stranger" like Jews before them, they experience social closure permeating all spheres of social life. Exploring this position of marginality, from its cultural underpinnings to its political, social, and economic expressions, I then turn towards the agentive responses of Muslim communities—strangers as makers in the European metropolis, the "energy in its margins."[205] Both the Şehitlik Mosque community and the East London Mosque community engage the mosque as a threshold space located between the private and public spheres, central to the making of the pious subject and pious collective. I focus on the strength found in Muslim piety as an illuminating "fragment" of modernity, with the transformation of a position of marginality into an interstitial opportunity to make (*poiesis*), and to dwell in each metropolis.[206]

The third chapter ("Kaaba in Papier-Mâché: Inside the Şehitlik Mosque") centers on the Şehitlik Mosque's trajectory from a Turkish mosque built at the turn of the twenty-first century to a self-proclaimed "Berliner Moschee" (mosque). I trace the historical and theological foundations of the mosque built on land gifted by the Prussian Empire to the Ottoman Empire for burials of their representatives abroad, close to the now-phantom border where the Berlin Wall once stood. Through a metaphor of the Kaaba in papier-mâché, I explore how this community has brought Islam into the center of their lives in the European metropolis, beginning with crossing, through migration in the 1960s and 1970s, and subsequent shaping of the mosque as a lived space by Turkish guest workers and their children. Perceived by the first generation as a place to root unsettled lives, I examine how this mosque has been shaped since 2002 by the second generation as a highly symbolic site of sociopolitical struggle over Muslim inclusion in the metropolis. I argue that their project of making together (*sympoiesis*) and dwelling as pious Berliners is rooted in what Jonas theorized as an ethics of responsibility, entailing reflections on contested belonging, a pedagogy of harmony, and a reconceptualization of pious practices, including the mosque tour.[207] Here young Muslims unite spiritual and civic orientations through an Islamic epistemological lens that interlinks obligations to God, the self, humanity, and the natural world.

The fourth chapter ("Ordinary Angels: The Şehitlik Mosque and the Metropolis") brings the Jewish salon, from Arendt's writings on Rahel Varnhagen, into conversation with today's Jewish-Muslim Salaam-Schalom Initiative in Berlin.[208] I analyze how an ethics of responsibility or obligation impels Şehitlik's youth to seek solidarity (arising, as Bauman argues, when "the 'I am responsible for the Other' and 'I am responsible for myself' come to mean the same thing") with local Jewish residents.[209] This occurs through such instantiations as the "My Head, My Choice" campaign, spurred by the rejection of a Muslim civil service candidate who wears a headscarf in the Neukölln neighborhood. Specifically, I home in how this neighborhood and the broader city of Berlin become sociospatial opportunities to develop localized identities, in acts of *sympoiesis*—drawing on the shared inhabitance of the social margins by Muslims and Jews. At the same time, I confront the different positionalities of Muslims and Jews, the latter of whom are today selectively incorporated into the state. I then turn to the role of policing, including surveillance and coerced participation in deradicalization initiatives, in the creation of the mosque as a space inextricably intertwined with the metropolis. I here reveal the constraints of an uncivil status on Muslims in the city, an enduring ambiguity evidenced by ethnically Turkish police officers who strive to escape this superimposed incivility.

In the fifth chapter ("Messianic Horizon: Inside the East London Mosque"), I focus on the East London Mosque, where constituents make themselves (*poiesis*) as Muslims through a messianic vision, articulated through a discursive halal/haram (permitted/forbidden) boundary, operationalized in gender relations inside of the mosque, Muslim-mainstream engagement, and a worldly/afterlife distinction.[210] This boundary inverts the colonial paradigm undergirding the familial histories of many of my interlocutors, which long portrayed Muslims as polluted and European colonists as pure. Through a Blochian/Benjaminian "method of hope," I explore how this community of born Muslims and converts alike confront the limits of what is possible in the postcolonial metropolis where estrangement reigns, responsively focusing on the promise of paradise both future and past.[211] As they turn away from the disappointments of everyday life and towards paradise through an Islamic epistemological tradition that prizes hope, my interlocutors at ELM come to embody anticipation and thereby move beyond the notion of time-as-progress. Here evidence of the power of redemption emerges in the form of a large, dedicated group of reverts (both converts and life-long Muslims returning to Islam).

In the sixth chapter ("Hope, Interrupted: The East London Mosque and the Metropolis"), I situate the East London Mosque in London's East End, and in the economically underprivileged borough of Tower Hamlets. I connect contemporary cultural and socioeconomic struggles to the history of the neighborhood as a place of large-scale Jewish settlement in the nineteenth century, seen as polluting the city, to explore more broadly how place today interacts with piety in a neighborhood historically home to marginalized immigrant/minority populaces. In its relation with the metropolis, this community reflects a form of *autopoiesis*, that is making itself apart from the constraints imposed by the mainstream, including notable political agnosticism among my interlocutors. The exclusive vision of this mosque can also be seen in its physical expansion, with the erection of the London Muslim Centre (seamlessly connected to the mosque, providing additional space for classrooms and events), the Maryam Centre (an entirely separate women's building), and the purchase of the Fieldgate Synagogue. In a city district where extreme deprivation abuts wealth, the economic precarity and suffering of mosque constituents becomes celebrated as evidence of salvation in another expression of its messianic vision, as found in strands of Sufism and in Cohen's writings. I again engage with policing, through the intimacy of terror that shapes the everyday lives of mosque constituents, institutionalized in the British government's Prevent strategy and complicated by the liminal positionality of Muslim youth workers employed by the government.

In the seventh and final chapter ("Unsettled Europe: On the Threshold of Remembrance"), I invoke Benjamin's concept of remembrance to complexify several inherited, taken-for-granted categories through which we look at Islam and Muslims in Europe. Through an encounter with the Paul Klee sketch, *Angelus Novus*, Benjamin's muse for his *Theses on the Philosophy of History*, I consider Europe today and its struggles with growing Muslim populaces not a moment of rupture or acute change, but rather continuity—knee deep in the "wreckage" of "what we call progress."[212] I argue that a Benjaminian turn towards remembrance, witnessed in both mosques' centeredness in the Islamic epistemological tradition, whether fostering responsibility and/or redemption, can unsettle self-affirming Eurocentric conceptualizations about modernity, including those embedded in "enlightenment," "progress," "civility," "tolerance," "equality," and "freedom." I discuss what the strivings, struggles, and hopes of these two mosque communities can teach us about marginalized histories and presents, in so doing eroding hegemonies of knowledge. Finally, I return to the idea of the mosque in the metropolis as a threshold space, both literal and metaphorical point of entry into European society, and the critical perspective of the stranger as maker, in order to shift the gaze from Muslims in/ of Europe to an unsettled and deeply unsettling European present.

CHAPTER 2

Caste, or the Order of Things Defied

Seated outside of the Şehitlik Mosque in Berlin, gazing out over a graveyard that divides the building from the street, Mustafa, a retired butcher, recalls his arrival in Germany. He wipes the sweat from his brow with the back of a callused hand, describing the guards who checked not only his Turkish passport but also his teeth at the border. Living in a barracks-like dormitory, with rows upon rows of bunk beds in what was then West Berlin, he describes his sense of disorientation in a new city and a new country, everything—from the sights to the sounds—suddenly unfamiliar: an experience not of sensory deprivation, but disorientation. Mustafa could not speak or read the German language, the signs and symbols of everyday life illegible. And he could no longer see the stars at night. But most of all, he missed the scent of wood burning in his childhood village. Trained in the *köfte* (Turkish meatball) houses set along the Turkish sea, he found work as a butcher in a supermarket chain, quickly memorizing the German words for "brisket" (*das Bruststück*) and "shank" (*der Schaft*). Even after half a century had passed, Mustafa never came to terms with the fact that he was required in his new trade to handle the meat, muscles, and blood of pigs. After a disagreement with his boss over this aspect of his job one winter, he found himself locked outside of the supermarket warehouse, where his toes literally froze to ice. "I was treated like an animal," he explains, eventually facing both physical and mental burnout, aged not by labor but by indignity into an early retirement.

Mustafa describes an enduring subordination in spite of advancing legal status in Germany—from migrant to permanent resident, his children citizens, yet still perceived as "below the Germans." As rhetorical categories of differentiation shifted from "worker" to ethnicity (reinvoking the historical no-tion of "the terrible Turk") and then religion ("the uncivil Muslim") through-out his decades in Berlin, he describes himself as a "foreigner" (*Ausländer*) in German society, a term that Cohen equates with that of the "stranger."[1] In our many encounters, Mustafa struggles to pinpoint exactly what has pre-vented his full belonging, often citing "being Muslim," "my name," "where I came from," or simply, his voice trailing off as he repeats the words, "who I am, who I am."

I invoke the concept of caste, specifically that of undercaste, to make sense of this negatively differentiated Muslim status in contemporary Europe. En-during cultural distinction that fosters social marginalization has led numer-ous social theorists to use caste as an analytical concept with salience across temporal and geographical contexts.[2] As noted earlier, caste has been em-ployed to understand the experience of Jews in Europe, as well as Black Amer-icans. Herbert Gans utilizes the term "undercaste" in his early writings on urban inequality, and it has recently reemerged in the writings of Michelle Al-exander on the prison industrial complex today.[3] "Anyone economically or socially condemned to caste status will be viewed as different in skin colour or religion," writes Gans. " 'Culture,' 'moral worth' or some other newly con-structed characteristic can also be used to exclude people and place them in an undercaste."[4] I argue that the collective labeling of Muslims in Europe with incivility—through a collapsing of religion, culture, ethnicity, and race—relegates them to an undercaste.[5]

CASTE IN CONVERSATION

Social theorists classify caste as culture-based stratification, traditionally op-posing class, which suggests economic-based stratification. Classes and their resulting power arise out of "unequal access to material resources" and there-fore differentiated standards of living.[6] Castes, on the other hand, are a mat-ter of ascription rather than achievement through education, experience, or economic attainment. They are hereditary forms of hierarchical stratification that people remain inside of no matter how much money they earn or capital they amass. And they summon social closure vis-à-vis status.[7] One may rise in economic class, but nonetheless remain inside of a particular caste. As a sociological term, Max Weber operationalized caste not in the empirical plu-ral (e.g., India has multiple castes within its caste system), but the analytical singular (a position of extreme marginality that leads to stigma); he sought to understand what happens when status is closed to an unusual extent, leading to the reproduction of this status position over time, such that people cannot get out of it no matter what class position they hold.[8]

Caste enters an established field of concepts employed to understand the cultural subordination of Muslims in spite of legal inclusion. It enters into productive, if critical, conversation with them. At the turn of the twenty-first century, the term "Islamophobia" arose as an attempt to capture this distinct positioning in a single word. In an extensively cited definition, Erik Bleich defines Islamophobia as "indiscriminate negative attitudes or emotions directed at Islam or Muslims," thereby conceptualizing a static outcome, rather than dynamic cause and effect of deep-seated aversion.[9] Yet Islamophobia erroneously naturalizes a fear of Muslims that permeates mainstream society, reducing systemic inequalities to collective anxiety. While capturing a sentiment of disdain, this concept does not explain the historical development of a collective imaginary that envisions Muslims as dangerously uncivil. By suggesting fear of Muslims as a prevalent psychosocial ill, the concept of Islamophobia cannot fully account for the origins, temporal and spatial development, ascriptive nature, and institutionalized socioeconomic implications of this negatively coded social status.

Noting the limits of Islamophobia, social scientists have come to explain the cultural subordination of Muslims through racialization and racism. But race is, as Wilkerson argues, insufficient for understanding the "infrastructure of our divisions."[10] Employing a stringent definition of racism, based on the physical expression of assumed biological difference, clearly does not fit the stratification of Muslims in Europe, as "difference is framed in terms of culture, not race."[11] For this reason, racism in its narrow definition, as phenotypically based discrimination, has become expansively redefined vis-à-vis "cultural racism" by scholars like Tariq Modood and Nasar Meer.[12] Christopher Allen claims that "while racism on the basis of markers of race obviously continues, a shift is apparent in which some of the more traditional and obvious markers have been displaced by newer and more prevalent ones of a cultural, socio-religious nature."[13] The cultural racism/racialization literature productively critiques the idea of "progress" by tracing the enduring nature of essentialized forms of difference in the modern world; it "shift[s] from a focus on product to process."[14] In so doing, it illuminates the power dynamics that create such sociopolitical divisions, fixing the analytical gaze on those doing, rather than experiencing, othering. For instance, this literature invokes the state's deep investment in the citizen's body, contributing to a process that assigns "meaning to somatic characteristics" and produces "vicariously constructed phenotypes, (including prayer caps, beards)," as "corporeal shorthand for non-Christian difference."[15]

If the intellectual project is to make sense of the how and why of this deep and enduring differentiation, then the rich literatures on race should certainly be brought into direct conversation with empirical studies on Muslim life.[16] Still, numerous challenges are posed by the blanket *framing* of Muslim cultural subordination as a racialization process or racialized form. I remain uncomfortable with the idea of a postmodern "culturalist" "racism without race," as posited by Étienne Balibar, or that "religion" can simply "be raced."[17] The idea of a neoracism, cultural(ist) racism, countering biology "as the principle [*sic*] marker of difference," "a racial logic that crosses the cultural categories of nation, religion, ethnicity, and sexuality," or a "race-religion constellation," as articulated by scholars like Balibar, Didier Fassin, Nasar Meer, Junaid Rana, and Anya Topolski, alludes to a form of differentiation that requires another analytical vocabulary.[18] That is, such adaptive conceptualizations of racism loosen their connection to the socially constructed category of race, with the "racial" transformed into an umbrella category to capture diverse forms of essentialization and xenophobia.

It is also important to keep in mind that the cultural racism and racialization literature has been almost exclusively developed (1) geographically, in the US and UK, where race is a socially constructed but also widely legible category, and (2) theoretically, through a postmodern lens, including critical race theory with its specific intellectual roots and normative bend.[19] Regarding the geographical development of this literature in the European context, in the 1970s Afro-Caribbean and South Asian minorities in the UK together embraced a movement of "political blackness," asserting a critical stance toward the colonial legacies of ethnoracial hierarchies and second-class citizenship.[20] While most South Asians in the UK reject blackness as a form of identity today, an enduring legacy of this movement is the recognition that race framing provides a protected minority status not afforded to religious minorities.[21] Emerging from this particular context, some of the UK-based literature on the racialization of Muslims shifts from theory to policy, making a stronger argument for the political salience of racial categorization than its analytical sharpness as a conceptual framework for understanding the social phenomenon at hand.[22] Exporting the unique British perspective on race to other European contexts, moreover, poses the risk of overlooking differing vocabularies, histories, and regimes of distinction, including outright discomfort with the concept of race in the post-WWII German context; here, racism links to the National Socialist imaginary, incorrectly assumed to have been overcome through a society-wide reckoning with this particular past. Racism of course exists today in Germany, as it did in Germany's imperial enterprise prior to the Third Reich, yet this anti-race discourse necessitates an analytical lens that accounts for such surface-level silencing, and the xenophobic rumblings that lie beneath.[23]

Regarding the theoretical rootedness of framing Islam through postmodernist critical race theory, Caner Dagli argues,

> The way Islam is brought into the framework of intersectionality does not add [religious bigotry] . . . to the existing matrix of oppression . . . only races, genders, classes, and sexual orientations constitute real groups. Religious bigotry sits on the lap of racism instead of having its own seat at the table of intersecting hierarchies.

That is, Islam as a religion, not only a belief system but a systematic and rational way of life, is not taken seriously. Consequently, the *meaningfulness* of Islam is lost in the framework of race, which "implies that it simply does not matter what Muslims believe or do or what kind of human beings they are."[24]

The analytical concept of undercaste offers an opportunity to more fully capture and accurately name the phenomenon at hand; it accounts for the functioning, hardening, and adaptation of divisive notions of "cultural purity," through incivility, in modernity. And it accounts for the interlinking of biological conceptions of difference (i.e., blood-based) to those based on a Christian interpretation of religion (i.e., belief) in medieval Iberia which endure to this day, forging the impure—in European modernity's language, *uncivil*—status of Muslims in Europe.[25] It thus takes religion seriously in the "matrix of oppression," by turning the lens on a (post-)Christian Europe, which has sought since its foundation to emancipate itself from Judaism and defend itself against the claims of Islam as a continuation of the monotheistic tradition. Through this concept, I argue that the justification of Muslim differentiation, like that historically of Jews, is based at once in Christian and secular narratives of historical and divine right, as European society seeks coherence and order by projecting its own liminal position onto its religious minorities. That is, Europe aims to center itself through the decentering of Muslims.

Simply put, invigorating the analytical potency of "undercaste" in the study of Muslims in Europe provides new ways of seeing the persistence, hierarchical nature, and multidimensionality of status differentiation in modernity.[26] Undercaste captures the subordinated and abstracted, not equal and individualized,[27] figure of "the Muslim," in which religion, ethnicity, race, and culture cannot be pulled apart—as previously experienced by Jews.[28] In her work on Arendt, Benhabib describes how such collapsing led to an undue focus on Jewishness. Benhabib reflects, "In answering Nathan the Wise's question 'Who are you?' with the statement, 'A Jew,' Hannah Arendt writes, 'I was only acknowledging a political fact through which my being a member of this group outweighed all other questions of personal identity or rather had decided them in favor of anonymity, of namelessness.'"[29] For Arendt, Jewishness thus becomes an "ineliminable fact" of "difference;" she aptly articulates the silencing imbued by Jewishness (as Muslimness today) so that all other identities and names become muted, erased, whited out—a making of the European self through the subordination, and silencing, of "the Other."[30] The "namelessness," the silencing of Muslims, reverberates with discomfiting echoes. Anne Norton writes, "I see the Muslim question as the Jewish question of our time: standing at the site where politics and ethics, philosophy and theology meet. This is the knot where the politics of class, sex, and sexuality, of culture, race, and ethnicity are entangled; the site where structures of hierarchy are anchored."[31] (I, as Dagli, would add religion to this entangled knot).[32]

Why, one might ask, if the analytical category of undercaste fits the phenomenon at hand, has it not already emerged in scholarly conversations about Muslim positionality in today's Europe? Caste elicits discomfort if not repugnance, as it belongs in the contemporary imaginary to the very "Other" that Europe identifies against: as a "backward," "traditional," "anti-liberal" stratification system that continues to permeate social life on the Subcontinent. It contends with the idea of European modernity as progress—exposing an unsettling darkness in the post-Enlightenment era, the clearest window into secular modernity through a reckoning with "its shadows," as posited by Asad.[33] The concept of a Muslim undercaste challenges notions of a rational, civilized Europe, as opposing the irrational, uncivilized religion of Islam and therefore also the irrational, uncivilized tendencies of the concept of caste itself.

The concept of caste, both exoticized and externalized, has thus suffered in the academy from the same Orientalist tendencies as the study of Islam. I agree with sociologist Surinder Jodhka that "such an Orientalist view of caste also denies the possibility of deploying the framework of caste for understanding caste-like ascriptive hierarchies that exist in many other (if not all) societies."[34] As Wilkerson writes of the American context (this also applies to the context of Europe): "We must open our eyes to the hidden work of a caste system that has gone unnamed but prevails among us . . . to see that we have more in common with each other and with cultures that we might otherwise dismiss and to summon the courage to consider that therein may lie the answers."[35] I do not know about the answers, but therein most certainly lies the question of Europe.

CASTE IN THE "WEST": EUROPE'S
CONCEPTUAL JEW AND JIM CROW AMERICA

Today's Muslim undercaste provokes a profound sense of déjà vu, or in Walter Benjamin's words "an echo . . . one awakened by a sound that seems to have issued from somewhere in the darkness of past life."[36] So let us turn towards that echo to yesterday's Europe, where the undercaste status of Jews became institutionalized when the third Lateran Council of the Catholic Church determined that Christians should not live together with this religious group in 1179. The council subsequently enforced yellow head ornamentation to differentiate Jews from Christians.[37] Thus, the color yellow—associated with the biblical downfall of Sodom and Gomorrah, burned by rain made out of sulfur and fire—became an external marker of Jewish impurity beginning in post-Reconquista Spain, enduring for thousands of years, and reemerging in the yellow stars sewn onto Jews' clothing during the Holocaust.[38] Another evocative symbol, the *Judensau*, appeared in thirteenth-century Germany and was soon inscribed on churches throughout Europe, including those in France, Sweden, Belgium, Switzerland, England, and Germany.[39] In 1543, Martin Luther famously commented on the *Judensau* sculpture on the Wittenberg State Church.

> Here on our church in Wittenberg a sow is sculpted in stone. Young pigs and Jews lie suckling under her. Behind the sow a rabbi is bent over the sow, lifting up her right leg, holding her tail high and looking intensely under her tail and into her Talmud, as though he were reading something acute or extraordinary, which is certainly where they get their Shemhamphoras.[40]

From the late Middle Ages until the end of the sixteenth century, Jews in Venice were relegated to the ghetto,[41] perceived as impure, imbued with "mysterious polluting powers," disease supposedly spread by touching their "alien, seductive bodies."[42] In the city's ghetto and beyond, virulent anti-Jewish sentiment transformed into anti-Semitism (which I here understand as a "knot" of prejudice against Jews as a religious, cultural, and ethnic group, and through their racialization, based on the supposition of biological difference), which endured far past the Middle Ages.[43] For centuries, Jews continued to experience second-class citizenship (I would argue that this was in fact an *undercaste* citizenship)[44] across Europe, restricted in occupation, segregation that led to further ghettoization, regulation against intermarriage, and ultimately demonization, from the French Dreyfus affair that began at the end of the nineteenth century to the rise of Hitler and his policies of extermination.[45]

In her writings from exile, Arendt argues that in spite of economic integration, Jews remained distinct in status as "a society outside of a society, a caste," "retain[ing] characteristics of a caste," and/or constrained by a "caste spirit" in modern Europe.[46] She theorizes this particular differentiating "spirit" through the idea of the "Jew as Pariah"—*pariah* defined as "social outcast" or "members of a low caste," the word entering English by way of Tamil in the seventeenth century.[47] Arendt was not the first to employ the word *pariah* to make sense of the Jewish experience in Europe. In an arguably derogatory text, Weber terms the Jewish experience "a pariah existence" ("separated formally or de facto from their social surroundings"), a term earlier used to describe Jewish social positionality by nineteenth-century Jewish French journalist and literary critic Bernard Lazare.[48] Here it is also relevant to note that Weber described Jews not only as pariahs, but also *Gastvolk* (guest people), invoking a discursive parallel with the subsequent status of Muslim *Gastarbeiter* (guest workers), that suggests both foreignness and impermanence.[49]

Across the Atlantic, in the postslavery period prior to the Civil Rights Movement, Black Americans also experienced exclusion along caste lines, through institutionalized "racial mores" and a "one-drop rule" eerily similar to that of the Spanish colonists.[50] Here "incongruity" was shaped in terms of race. From the back of the bus to the poverty-stricken edges of urban centers, laws prohibiting everything from mixed-race bathrooms to mixed-race marriages, "blackness" transformed into a pretext for concurrent ordering and exclusion in the United States.[51] The semantics of this category suggested white purity in contrast to black pollution. In the American South, Jim Crow laws institutionalized the subordinate status of Black Americans, denying civil rights in everyday life.[52] In the worst cases, this led to the lynching of Black Americans by organized criminal groups sanctioned by authorities, most notoriously the Ku Klux Klan.[53] In his seminal 1937 work, *Caste and Class in a Southern Town*, John Dollard names this systematized exclusion based on indignity and blood impurity a caste.[54] Allison Davis, Burleigh Gardner, and Mary Gardner echo this conceptualization in *Deep South: A Social Anthropological Study of Caste and Class*, based in Natchez, Mississippi, a community decisively ruled by Jim Crow.[55] And historian Amy Louise Wood argues that violence against Black men permeating the American South in this period was not only racially motivated, but justified as a religiously sanctioned act, "laden with Christian symbolism and significance . . . ordained and consecrated by God."[56] Reflecting on these "religious rituals," journalist Jamelle Bouie concludes that "the God of the white South demanded purity."[57] Today, Michelle Alexander argues, the prison industrial complex has forged a "New Jim Crow" set on purifying society through the mass incarceration of Black men, and therefore "the rebirth of caste" in contemporary America.[58] She terms the resulting undercaste "a group defined wholly or largely by race that is permanently locked out of mainstream, white society by law, custom, and practice."[59]

The Terror Specter

Such systems of extreme cultural differentiation have remained a troubling dimension of modernity, entwined with the inherent fallacy of "progress as a 'fact.'"[60] The persistence of social closure based on impurity, hierarchy, and exclusionary ideologies has thus characterized modernity in diverse geographic locales. As Zygmunt Bauman argues, insider-outsiders have continuously been forced to contend with the belligerent rationality of modernity that upended prior socioeconomic orders.[61] In what Bauman terms "the conceptual Jew," "the individuality of the [Simmelian] stranger is dissolved" into a feared collective; as society moved from premodernity to modernity, Jews were no longer set apart, but seen as dangerously ambiguous in an increasingly ordered world.[62] This effectively created a scapegoat for the uncertainty that undergirded European modernity. Bauman writes, "Whoever felt thrown out of balance, threatened or displaced, could easily—and rationally—make sense of his own anxiety through articulating the experienced turbulence as an imprint of Jewish subversive incongruity."[63] As with "the conceptual Jew" in early modern Europe, the Conceptual Muslim has today risen as a "vivid, obtrusive reminder of the erosion of old certainties," "perceived as standing close to the centre of the destructive process."[64] The culturally and geographically liminal position of Muslims, perpetually caught between crossing (borders, languages) and dwelling on uneven ground, reinforces this perception. Such liminality is not innocuous; "we experience ambivalence as discomfort and a threat."[65] In what Bauman describes as modernity's quests for order ("impossible tasks"),[66] Muslims are thus seen to jeopardize society.

Perhaps nowhere is an association with a destructive core more potent than the terror specter that dominates mainstream discussions of Muslims in contemporary Europe. The particular cultural impurity of the Muslim has evolved through the transformation of social taboo from "symbolically" to "literally injurious," relying on associations not only with dirt or pollution (first as "street-sweepers" and today as uncivil denizens), but with direct threat to European survival (as potential terrorists).[67] This widely held association of Islam with terrorism evokes fears of unpredictability, irrationality, and willingness to risk life and limb. And no one is exempt from this association at the heart of a narrative of looming demise, in which Muslims threaten to destroy Europe from the inside.

From the halls of schools to the homes of converts, the pages of a book, schoolchildren, and a woman lounging on the beach, potential terrorists are feared to hide among us. In fact, the usual innocents—refugees, children—have become the nucleus of antiterrorism efforts in all of their nebulous forms. Journalist Emily Badger reports, "After the Paris attacks, you hear politicians equating Syrian refugees with terrorists. Of course, many of those refugees are *fleeing* the same terrorists Europeans fear. 'But it's a fact that they are Muslim,' says [Maarten] van Ham [editor of a book on segregation in Europe]."[68] In a recent Pew report, those with anti-Muslim views were significantly more likely to associate refugees with terror and threat.[69] Pew also found that majorities in Hungary, Poland, the Netherlands, Germany, Italy, Sweden, Greece, and the UK (eight of the ten countries surveyed) believe the 2015 influx of refugees increased the likelihood of terror attacks.[70] And across Europe, teachers in schools and universities are given the responsibility of identifying students at risk for radicalization. They must look for signs—a Qur'an, a headscarf—that a child increasingly identifies with Islam.[71] "Few things seem to scare the French as much as the sight of Muslim schoolgirls wearing head scarves," writes journalist Eduardo Cue.[72]

A MUSLIM UNDERCASTE

For Muslims in Europe, an undercaste status came into being over time as a system of concurrent ordering and exclusion. During the Spanish Reconquista, a formative moment in the making of Europe, Christian leaders instated a social order based on blood purity (*limpieza de sangre*) to distinguish "Old Christians" from those tarnished by a single drop of Muslim or Jewish blood. Muslims who converted to Christianity were termed "Marranos," meaning both "faithless convert" and "filthy pig."[73] The Spanish extended this notion through colonial rule of the American continent, establishing a classification system (*sistema de castas*, system of castes) to rank mixed races, with the purer in blood (lighter, European-origin) superior to the more polluted in blood (darker-skinned Native Americans). Government officials in the colonies had to provide a "certificate of purity of blood," proving the complete absence of Muslim or Jewish ancestry.[74] "So if 1492," writes Dussel, "is the moment of the 'birth' of modernity as a concept, the moment of origin of a very particular myth of sacrificial violence [by the security state, that familiar minotaur], it also marks the origin of a process of concealment or misrecognition of the non-European."[75] The cultural legacies of this misrecognition, itself a form of sacrificial violence, persist to this day. Contemporary Spanish history textbooks, for example, continue to highlight Muslim-Christian conflict and "the negation of the *moro*" in the construction of national identity, with Muslims in Spain referenced as "Moros" or "Moriscos" (Moors). This includes depictions of Islam as incompatible with modernity, fixated on conquering the world, and threatening to peace.[76]

Spain, however, was not and is not alone in negatively differentiating Muslims. A cursory look into the imperial projects of Western Europe at the end of the nineteenth and first half of the twentieth century reveals deep-seated discrimination against geographies with large Muslim populaces, even those seen as direct extensions of a European state, such as "French Algeria" or "British India." In the French colonial apparatus, the unveiling of Muslim women[77] was a highly symbolic act of an imperial power "bent on unveiling Algeria."[78] Through individual unveilings, it mandated the neutralization of religion in the public sphere, and also a visual boundary between civility and incivility (mirroring that between "citizen" and "subject")—one paradoxically accomplished through force.[79] Similarly, suspicion and conspiracy characterized government dealings with Indian Muslims during British colonial rule, as seen in the early texts of Alfred Lyall and W. W. Hunter—colonial scholars fixated on the degree to which Muslims were inherently similar to, or incompatible with, Christians.[80]

Cultural stereotyping developed in Western European countries through hierarchical relations not only in colonized territories, but also in relation to the Ottoman Empire. In her seminal work, *Purity and Danger*, Mary Douglas argues that pollution leads to perceptions of danger, long coloring characterizations of the Ottomans.[81] Orientalist views of the "barbarian other," the "Terrible Turk," penetrated European society far prior to actual migrations from Turkey to Europe.[82] Since the height of the Ottoman Empire, popular discourse has revolved around the "Turkish threat," whether in terms of violence or seduction—a trope that remains in contemporary Europe vis-à-vis perceptions of the Muslim man as both violent and sexually potent, and paralleled in other projects of gendered ethnicization/racialization, such as that of the Black man.[83] After Napoleon invaded Egypt in 1798, the Ottoman Empire slowly but steadily shifted its alliance to Germany, serving as its ally in World War I. Despite cooperation, the Ottoman Empire crumbled as Germany rose to regional power; Imperial German Navy admiral Wilhelm Souchon took charge of the Ottoman Navy in 1914.[84]

Recruited as guest workers into undesirable occupations in the post-WWII period, or "permitted" to migrate from colonial states as subordinated citizens, this undercaste status elucidates the enduring afterlife of European empire. It is rooted in hierarchical global relationships dominated by the European metropolis through the mid twentieth century, eventually producing large flows of migration from Muslim-majority countries—reformulating spatial, but not necessarily cultural, inclusions. Perceptions of Muslim danger based on associations with incivility are thus not new to Europe, although they come to life in modern forms.[85]

Media accounts throughout Europe over the past decade and a half portray the wide-reaching implications of associating Muslims with threat, with migration narratives increasingly couched in security terms; borders not only shut, but surrounded by barbed wire fences, manned by armed national guards.[86] The inflammatory words of French presidential candidate Marine Le Pen summarize this growing sentiment: "If it's about occupation, then we could also talk about it (Muslim prayers in the streets), because that is occupation of territory."[87] The late left-wing Jewish writer Ralph Giordano similarly called mosque building "a declaration of war," responding to the controversial erection of Germany's largest mosque in Cologne.[88] In this now-prevalent narrative, the foundational sources and figures of Islam come into question. Danish newspaper *Jyllands-Posten* famously portrayed the Prophet Muhammad as a radical with explosives in hand.[89] Far-right Dutch politician Geert Wilders termed the Prophet Muhammad a "terrorist worse than Bin Laden," and the Qur'an a "license to kill."[90] This demonization has been extended to mosques, described by Wilders as "hate palaces."[91] In the words of Josep Anglada, president of Fuerza Nueva, a Spanish far-right party, "We are against mosques because they are not only places of worship. They are places where social and political rules are imposed. The Muslim world does not distinguish between social, religious and political aspects of life, so that mosques become a nest of Islamism and radicalism."[92]

While arguably its loudest proponents, not only the far right espouses essentialist visions of Muslims and Islam that perpetuate associations with incivility. The claim that both Islam and Muslims are uncivil and thereby eroding Europe's sociopolitical fabric has been justified across the political spectrum through historic means (protecting hard-fought-for secular political systems, by the left), as well as contemporary renditions of divine will (protecting the [Judeo-]Christian history of Europe, by the right).[93] Left and centrist politicians, jurists, and intellectuals have painted the dangers of Islam in space and time, with Muslims portrayed as barbaric remnants, threatening to pull Europe backwards into a dark, irrational past. For instance, the centrist Cologne regional appellate court temporarily outlawed circumcision in Germany when it came under attack in 2012 as "violent" following complications from the procedure on a young Muslim boy.[94] And leftist movements in France, Germany, and Switzerland fixate on complete relegation of religion to the private sphere, with the aim of producing an idealized, albeit impossible, "neutral public sphere," by regulating public expressions of religion, most notably the headscarf.[95] From Salman Rushdie's publication of *The Satanic Verses* to French Communist parliamentary leader André Gerin sparking the debate that ultimately led to France's ban on the niqab, such cultural moments reveal that a fear of Islam, and a resulting need to control it, cannot be deemed a right-wing phenomenon.[96]

On the level of popular sentiment, a 2016 Pew Research Study shows anti-Muslim sentiment rising across Europe.[97] And in a German-, French-, and UK-based Gallup survey, Muslims are perceived as among the least desirable neighbors when compared to other groups, ranked above only drug addicts.[98] A powerful weaponization of this subordinated cultural status has recently gained momentum in Germany, where resident Muslims are blamed for rising levels of anti-Semitism and Holocaust denial—arguably the worst of cultural crimes.[99] This perception of civic incompatibility also contributed to the decision of many to vote for Brexit in 2016, with the Leave Campaign espousing xenophobic rhetoric pointedly targeting Islam. In the aftermath of this vote, Muslims across the United Kingdom were cornered and confronted at an unprecedented rate, told to "get out, we voted leave!"; halal butcher shops burned to the ground; headscarf-wearing women spat on; and mosques threatened.[100]

Support of groups with xenophobic agendas has, in parallel, exploded over the past five years. Once marginal if not marginalized, such political "alternatives" now permeate mainstream politics. The frontrunner in Austria's 2016 presidential election, Norbert Hofer, was one such case (although eventually defeated by Independent candidate Alexander Van der Bellen).[101] Far right-wing candidate Marine Le Pen similarly came in second in the French 2017 run-off for presidency.[102] Le Pen gained popularity following her design of policy initiatives targeting Islam, including the "eat pork or go hungry campaign," which pressures schools to stop offering alternative meals to their Muslim students.[103] Even former national "exceptions" to this institutionalization of the right are home to largescale anti-Islam parties. For instance, the far-right party Alternative for Germany (Alternative für Deutschland, AfD) garnered 15 percent support in political opinion polls across Germany following its adoption of an anti-Muslim manifesto.[104] While tens of thousands of individuals attended the infamous march of Patriotic Europeans Against the Islamicization of the West (Patriotische Europäer gegen die Islamisierung des Abendlandes, PEGIDA) in Dresden in January 2015, it is perhaps more telling that an opinion poll showed that one in three Germans express support for this movement.[105]

The Institutionalization of Incivility

Muslims in Europe today cannot access a narrow and elusive civil space, its exclusions and inclusions determined by "the West," exclusive "broker of the civilized."[106] To the contrary, the deep and lasting association of Islam with incivility has become institutionalized across Europe in determinate spheres of social inclusion. This association has many consequences, not least of all heightened surveillance and imprisonment, as Muslims make up disproportionate and surging percentages of European penitentiary systems, but also ongoing exclusion across the economic, educational, and residential spheres.[107] The following discussions of these marginalities are far from comprehensive. Instead, they serve to provide a sketch of trends in marginalization and exclusion, from occupational subjugation to educational penalization and residential segregation.

Occupational subjugation began with the guest worker programs and migration of colonial subjects, recruited to fill labor shortages, working in mines, construction, and service. They became relegated to the bottom not only of the economic but also social hierarchy, dehumanized, differentiation of "us" versus "them" embedded with notions of savagery: "the internal partition between humans and nonhumans . . . through which the [so-called] moderns have set themselves apart from the [so-called] premoderns."[108] Treated like animals, former guest workers like my interlocutor, Mustafa, recounted their teeth being checked at the border, experiencing what Arendt terms only an "illusion of liberty and unchallenged humanity."[109] Upon settlement in Germany, they were called *Kanake*, a derogatory term, which often means "wild man" in its origin language (Polynesian).[110] A British documentary on postcolonial South Asian migration to the Midlands features a discontented white British interviewee echoing this sentiment: "They are content with Kitekat (cat food) and dog food instead of ordinary meat."[111] Samia Fekih, a digital project manager in Paris, told the *New York Times*: "I was curious to see if, in the cities where they forbade women in burkinis, dogs could swim. The answer was yes for some of them . . . dogs can have more rights than a scarfed woman."[112] Idealized "Euro-Islam," reforming and moderating religiosity, has tellingly been designated "domestication" in colloquial parlance across Europe.[113]

Employment opportunities have been affected by perceptions of immutable difference. Statistical data starkly evidences that Muslims—irrespective of ethnic group or national status—not only have far lower labor market participation, but also experience significantly higher job refusal across Europe than non-Muslims (including those identifying with other religious groups). Matthias Koenig, Mieke Maliepaard, and Ayse Güveli find employment gaps between Muslim and Christian immigrants to Western Europe.[114] Claire Adida, David Laitin, and Marie-Anne Valfort have shown that a Muslim candidate is significantly less likely to be called back for a job interview than an African-origin Christian in France; their research reveals that for every one hundred positive responses to a job application under an African-origin Christian name, an equivalent job application under a Muslim name receives only thirty-eight positive responses.[115] In 2015, Valfort conducted the largest experimental study to date measuring the effects of religion on hiring in France. In her study, practicing Muslims receive callbacks only half as often as practicing Catholics with the same ethnic background.[116] In Germany, a study on internship applications shows that those with Turkish-sounding names receive 14 percent fewer callbacks than those with German names.[117] And Moroccan and Turkish Belgians experience an unemployment rate (38 percent) five times the national unemployment rate (7 percent).[118] While this is more notable in some cases than others, Muslims throughout Europe remain not only significantly underemployed, but underrepresented in managerial and other well-paid positions. Pointedly overrepresented in the service industries, obstructions to labor mobility continue to determine a subordinate position in the occupational hierarchy.[119] Labor market disadvantages persist even with high educational achievement and professional training.[120]

Labor market discrimination against Muslims has been documented by human and civil rights organizations as well as through limited academic study. In Belgium, Amnesty International found that "in 2010, Muslims filed 84 percent of the cases of religious discrimination collected by the Centre for Equal Opportunities," most often regarding women's dress or a failure to accommodate religious needs in the workplace.[121] Explicit prohibition of religious symbols in public has been accompanied by relegation to back-office positions in the private sector.[122] A recent parliamentary report in the UK describes Muslim women as the single most disadvantaged group in the labor market, encountering a "triple penalty" on account of being Muslim, (usually) ethnic minorities, and female.[123] And, according to the Equalities Review Commission in the UK, "more than two in three Bangladeshis and more than half of all Pakistanis live in the bottom decile for deprivation."[124] The 2011 British census maps this economic deprivation, finding that "46% (1.22 million) of the Muslim population resides in the 10% most deprived, and only 1.7% (46,000) in the 10% least deprived local authority districts in England, based on the Index of Multiple Deprivation measure."[125]

The *educational penalization* of Muslims, in particular when wearing religious symbols, is also widespread. Those with migrant backgrounds in Germany are seriously overrepresented in vocational training schools and underrepresented in the high schools that feed into the university (*Gymnasium*), and thus underrepresented in universities.[126] A recent study conducted by researchers at the University of Mannheim found that teachers grade students with migrant backgrounds worse than those without, in spite of equal performance levels.[127] Much of the regulation in schools relates to female dress. In Spain, 37 percent of the populace believes girls wearing headscarves should be expelled from school, although no clear-cut regulation exists, with individual school boards determining the guidelines on worn religious symbols. In one case, a sixteen-year-old girl attending a public high school, Instituto Camilo José Cela de Pozuelo de Alarcòn in Madrid, was banned from classes and forced to sit in the visitors' room when she refused to remove her headscarf in 2010.[128] In France, the 1994 ban on religious garb in state schools singularly targeted the headscarf and not "discreet" symbols such as the Jewish kippah or the Christian cross; the so-called "headscarf debates" in France culminated in the outlawing of all conspicuous religious symbols in 2004, with Muslim girls inordinately targeted thereafter. For instance, the *New York Times* published a piece on Sarah, a young girl from Charleville-Mézières, France, who was suspended twice for wearing not a headscarf but a long black skirt—"an ostentatious sign" of her religious belief in 2015.[129]

Interconnected with labor market discrimination and educational penalization, *residential segregation* has been an implicit reality for Muslims living in European cities since the first waves of postcolonial/guestworker migration over half a century ago. As Thomas Gieryn asserts, "place sustains difference and hierarchy."[130] In the 1950s–70s, guest workers lived only among each other in segregated housing units, reflecting expectations of temporary residence.[131] Today across Europe, many cannot access central housing on account of their "Muslim" names, relegated to the French *banlieue* or other doubly—socially and physically—marginalized areas across Europe; "the picture painted of Rosengard [Sweden] could just as well be that of any other stigmatized borough, suburb, or big city neighborhood such as Clichy-sous-Bois in Paris, Molenbeek in Brussels, or Tower Hamlets in London; these are the famous 'no go zones' for the average non-white citizen," writes Per-Erik Nilsson.[132] Muslims in the Netherlands overwhelmingly reside in neighborhoods with similarly weak infrastructure and high rates of crime.[133] In the UK, 28 percent of Muslims live in low-income social housing, and Tower Hamlets, the London borough with the highest percentage of Muslims, ranks among the most deprived local authority districts in all of England.[134]

Together, these data suggest that Muslims in Europe experience a state of multiple deprivation and social distance: an enduring institutionalization of hierarchy based on their abstracted status as a collective, uncivil other, rather than as distinct, individual citizens. The extent of social and economic deprivation of course differs both within and across country cases. However, the cultural marking of Muslims with incivility; notable economic and education inequalities; and the persistence of high levels of residential segregation beyond the second generation together point to significant social closure. Here, I disagree with Rogers Brubaker's claim that "Muslims in Europe are indeed deeply and multiply disadvantaged; but they are not disadvantaged, in the first instance, as *Muslims*."[135] While there is no singular Muslim group in Europe, Muslims in Europe are very much disadvantaged *as Muslims*: not through their self-identification as such, but rather the externally imposed classification of "Muslim" in its abstract form by the societies in which they live.

STRANGER AS MAKER: CASTE, INTERRUPTED

"The idea of society is a powerful image," writes Mary Douglas in *Purity and Danger*. "It is potent in its own right to control or stir men to action. This image has form; it has external boundaries, margins, internal structure . . . There is energy in its margins."[136] Such energy in the margins can be witnessed in communities like Şehitlik and the East London Mosque, interrupting mainstream discourse that casts Muslims as uncivil through *poiesis*, the making of alternative visions of the self and the collective. That is, these mosque communities not only critically reflect upon, but critically *act* upon the marginality endowed by their undercaste status, elucidating how moral agency functions under constraints of discursive and material power—and in so doing, "transform[ing] difference from being a source of weakness and marginality into one of strength and defiance."[137]

The enactment of moral agency in the European mosque entails the capacity to exert power in and from the margins: power to cultivate Islamic virtues rooted in Islamic epistemology while under the constraints of the liberal state; and power to refute, or flat out refuse, disempowering discourses, policies, and sociopolitical positioning. Both mosques in this book are, in Benjaminian terms, "fragments" of the modern metropolis, pieces of a broken whole; and as Greil Marcus writes of Walter Benjamin's written and social project, "the fragment exerts its own gravity."[138] These mosque communities exert their own gravity by acting on what Benjamin terms a "conviction, or instinct, that the totality ha[s] to be resisted, even chipped away, even defeated by the fragment: the street, the sign, the name, the face, the aphorism, the evanescent, the ephemeral."[139] Benjamin found Ariadne, goddess of dawn, using a ball of thread to lead Theseus out of the Minotaur's labyrinth in Berlin's largest park, the Tiergarten. My interlocutors in Berlin and London find God in the metropolis, led by piety out of a labyrinth of superimposed incivility, guarded by the minotaur of the security state.[140]

Since the time of the Prophet Muhammad, stigma has been met with resistance time and again through turning towards Islam as source of ethical knowledge and moral agency in the remaking of bodies. Cultivating piety entails, as Rudolph Ware writes of Islamic education in Senegal during the height of colonialism, an "effort to remake supposedly 'impure' bodies as bodies of knowledge."[141] Reflecting on her mother's decision to wear the headscarf after taking the hajj pilgrimage to Mecca and Medina, Mina, a law student in Berlin, makes sense of her mother's turn towards piety. "I think many people come back from Mecca more conservatively dressed because they have had the experience of feeling similar to others, being in a group with the same values, feeling comfortable in Mecca," she explains, pausing for a moment. "*They want to feel that their religion is not strange, they are not strangers*" (emphasis added).

Turning towards Islam is a religious response based in deep theological sources to marginality, but it is also a social response to—and through—superimposed "strangerness." In the stories that follow, turning towards Islam recasts the stranger as made by society to the *stranger as maker*. Islamic practice provides a means to "self-author," critically countering assumptions about incivility through an active search for selfhood and collective belonging both in and beyond the mosque.[142] In its spatial form, the mosque is at once literal and figurative edifice (from the Latin words *facere*, make, and *aedis*, dwelling), a building where a complex system of knowledge, beliefs, and practices, shaping both selfhood and belonging, comes to life. While many twentieth-century philosophers, from Martin Heidegger to Theodor Adorno, have asserted the impossibility of dwelling in modernity, Benjamin relegates dwelling to a nineteenth-century obsession with "the shell" encompassing the (imprint of the) person, albeit exposing a kind of naturalized longing as an "age-old" "motif of primal history": that humans yearn, and therefore strive, to dwell. Benjamin writes, " 'To dwell' as a transitive verb—as in the notion of 'indwelt spaces'; herewith an indication of the frenetic topicality concealed in habitual behavior. It has to do with fashioning a shell for ourselves."[143] I witness this dynamic "fashioning" of dwelling among my interlocutors at both mosques.

Here not only geographical but also spiritual stirrings, a striving for virtue, shape the visions and actions that contribute to the fashioning of each mosque, as in the Aristotelian sense, "virtue is a habitual mode of dwelling in the world."[144] Personhood, community, and place are rooted in a virtue-rich discourse that emerges from Islamic thought, in which the theological concept of virtue (*taqwa*) can mean piety, God-consciousness, or fear of God. Virtue, according to al-Ghazali, is *achieved* by linking knowledge to "good habit," i.e., the *phronetic* perfection of the individual through ongoing acts towards God.[145] Yet virtues are also shared goods that link individual behavior to broader norms, "not determined by isolated individuals but . . . generated in reference to a field of social relations."[146] More specifically, as Islamic philosopher Abu Nasr al-Farabi (872–950) argues, the striving of the modern individual towards virtue is inherently interconnected with urbanity: the well-being of the person both constitutive of, and dependent upon, the well-being of the city.[147]

The site of the metropolis is important as it provides a topographical opportunity for the "activist dimension of group solidarity," beginning with the Prophet Muhammad and reinvigorated in Muslim collectivities across the world throughout time.[148] Through the metropoles at hand, both urban mosque communities rise as protective and enactive spaces that decenter narrative monopolies, where piety not only defines sanctioned religious practices and engagement with the mainstream, but also defies the status quo in an "anticipatory consciousness" of what could be, either soon in the city or ultimately in the afterlife.[149] And both move beyond the nation-state as a dominant interlocutor that too often determines the direction of the conversation towards conflict and threat, elucidating the stark limits of citizenship through the discursive and material constraints of civility.

The Şehitlik Mosque and the East London Mosque further contend with a widespread misconception that Muslim collectivities in Europe are either embracing of or adversarial to so-called European values—as Nadia Fadil critiques, an "unequal ethical importance attributed to conducts in a liberal-secular regime" that overlooks alternative forms of agency.[150] Such values are, to put it mildly, ambiguous. Positing individual freedom as a European value, for instance, while taking seriously the potency of the security state evokes a question posed by one of my interlocutors, Kasia, in London, and one that I will return to later in this book: "Freedom for who?" In her formative work on the women's piety movement in Egypt, Saba Mahmood pushes back against agency as inherently countering or questioning norms, arguing that to choose to inhabit norms is a no less agentive act.[151] Jeanette Jouili shows through her scholarship on pious women's circles in Germany and France that dignity and self-delineation are not necessarily rooted in liberal discourses of autonomy and empowerment, but also in the Islamic discursive tradition.[152] And Mayanthi Fernando illuminates how the cultivation of Islamic piety both reinforces and challenges the autonomy of the female French subject.[153] While indebted to the vital contributions of the moral anthropological school, where the relationship between norms and agency, as well as the limitations of liberal discourses of autonomy and empowerment, has been fruitfully explored, I focus on how the specific spatial and social form of the mosque reveals the dialogical relationship (a third triad) between Muslim communities, the metropolis, and God.

From declaring faith to participating in the pilgrimage, fasting, almsgiving, and praying, Islam is lived through five pillars of individual practice that are part of a comprehensive daily comportment. Yet living Islam concurrently transcends the experience of the individual in a larger vision of group identity and belonging, an ethically driven social practice not only of personhood but the making, and rooting, of a people. Reflecting on the diasporic memories of early-twentieth-century Yiddish migrants in East London, Ben Gidley writes,

> Although diaspora theorising has importantly helped us think in terms of routes as well as roots, we still need a richer understanding of journeying, one that avoids the postmodern image of endlessly deferred free-floating motion, that enables us to conceptualise not just diaspora's routes, but also its ever renewed *rootings*.[154]

I thus see mosque constituents' acts of *poiesis* as enacting both identity and integrity through renewed piety and "renewed rootings," in the Islamic tradition as much as the metropolis, in relation to God and society alike. These parameters are learned and practiced within, while extending piety as a sociopolitical act far beyond the mosque. As Ebrahim Moosa points out, *poiesis* does not entail mere action without meaning, but is rather "an art of doing and reflecting"; this intercourse between action and reflection emerges among my interlocutors in both mosques, with religious resources employed to make sense of social positionality in the metropolis, while also cognizant of the nexus between worldly and otherworldly life.[155] My interlocutors are, in other words, with eyes towards other-worlds, constrained but not contained by their social contexts, reflecting and acting beyond the here and now.

This beyond is both future-facing and rooted in the past; thus, in looking forward, I, in this book, also look back. Peter Demetz writes of late nineteenth- and early twentieth-century German Jewish thinkers such as Benjamin, born into assimilated bourgeois families, whose intellectual projects—"building their counterworlds in spiritual protest"—set them apart from their forebears.[156] Some who came of age in that era, like sociologist Leo Löwenthal (1900–1993), did not even know they were Jewish until a politics of anti-Semitism took hold; forced to reflect on their Jewish heritage, many rooted themselves deeper in Judaism as an epistemological tradition. The refusal to partake in the assimilationist project, their perception of its violent erasures of collective identities and silencing of histories, compelled them to enact Jewish knowledge in the social world, to construct another way.[157]

Echoes of this experience can be heard in the Şehitlik and ELM mosque communities. The children of economic migrants relegated to the dehumanized position of worker, ambivalent position of migrant, externalized position of Turk or Bengali/Asian and now subordinate position of Muslim, today seek—through Islam—another way. Explanations of the revivalist movements that have gained momentum in the second and subsequent generations of Muslims in Europe describe their aim as shedding ethnicity- or culture-centric visions of Islam for pure or universalistic visions in reaction to mainstream exclusions. Revivalist movements, however, are not reactionary but critical; they do not merely respond, but critique through Islamic epistemological projects. Like the thought projects of modern Jewish thinkers, the projects of these two mosques communities are similarly at once (anti)political and personal, at once theological and sociological: dialectical ways of not only thinking but making through renewed rootings in Islamic knowledge.

The twenty-first-century mosque in the metropolis is thus an "entry point" into understanding the layered, critical ideas and actions of Muslims in Europe's metropoles. It is at the same time a point of refraction, a fragment able to pierce through the false coherence of Europe, present and past.[158] Of agency in the urban context, Henri Lefebvre writes:

To think about the city is to hold and maintain its conflictual aspects: constraints and possibilities, peacefulness and violence, meetings and solitude, gatherings and separation, the trivial and the poetic, brutal functionalism and surprising improvisation. The dialectic of the urban cannot be limited to the opposition centre-periphery, although it implies and contains it.[159]

The stories that follow "cannot be limited to the opposition of centre-periphery," nor the hierarchy and subordination inherent to an undercaste status. They are hope-filled stories of strangers as makers, and the energy that moves across the symbolic boundaries of the modern metropolis into, and out from, the threshold space of the mosque. As Moosa eloquently stated in a conversation we had on his work, "The stranger and strangerness create the opportunity for hope." Here the opportunity for hope emerges where the dialectic of Islam intersects with what Lefebvre terms the "dialectic of the urban," its "constraints and possibilities, peacefulness and violence, meetings and solitude, gatherings and separation, the trivial and the poetic"; *poiesis* is, after all, at the root of poetics, which entails critique through narrative.[160] Paul Ricoeur argues that "a poetic work . . . re-describes the world," and I argue herein that my interlocutors redescribe the European metropolis—both imagined and real—it all of its poetic possibility.[161]

CHAPTER 3

Kaaba in Papier-Mâché:
Inside the Şehitlik Mosque

My project begins in earnest in the West Berlin district of Schöneberg, where a beautiful fountain opens high into the sky and barefoot, laughing children dip their toes into the dirty water with glee. There are no angels atop this fountain; but in the winter, children throw themselves to the earth beside it, forming snow angels as the water ceases to rise. They splay their arms and legs, new ephemeral bodies beside memorials to the city's murdered Jews.

"Everywhere a dead and resurrected world of play is framed in the perspective of exile," writes Howard Eiland in his translator's foreword to Walter Benjamin's *Berlin Childhood Around 1900*.[1] This fountain at Viktoria-Luise-Platz, at once a place of death, of flight into exile, and a "resurrected world of play" marks the end of my street, as well as the beginning of the Bavarian Quarter, where both Hannah Arendt and Benjamin resided. I almost overlook the signs, taut on metal posts as tall as the trees, signaling the "places of remembrances." "Jewish doctors could no longer practice medicine." "Jewish children could no longer attend public schools." The increasing restrictions on Jews remain inscribed in urban memorials, whether signposted above our heads or on the thousands of brass plates (*Stolpersteine*) bearing the names of Jewish families who once lived here laid into the ground beneath our feet. This past is similarly inscribed into the texts of German Jews who fled Nazism, as they grappled with the Holocaust in exile, inspiring such writings as Arendt's *Origins of Totalitarianism* and Jonas's "The Concept of God after Auschwitz."[2]

It is odd and uncomfortable, the presence of this particular past in Berlin's city streets. And yet such inscriptions both to and into the metropolis, these etchings of home, come to bridge our stories in place and over time. It is 2013, the year that I lose my home in the city of my childhood, New York, and find a new home in the lost city of Benjamin's. And it is also here that I begin my own courtship with the figure of the *flâneur*—"to be away from home and yet to feel oneself everywhere at home"—wandering the city's streets without a map, a form of "walking remembrance."[3] Each morning, I am reminded of this past by the glinting brass beneath my toes and the signposts in the sky, of those who were at home here and then found themselves nowhere at home—in the "double absence" of exile if not death (drawing on the name of Abdelmalek Sayad's book, *La double absence: Des illusions de l'émigré aux souffrances de l'immigré*).[4] In Benjamin's words, "The street became an Elysium for me—a realm inhabited by shades of immortal yet departed."[5]

Each morning, I depart from this corner of the city, traveling to another "realm inhabited by shades of immortal yet departed," the Şehitlik Camii (mosque) in Neukölln. The Şehitlik Mosque was erected on a symbolically potent border at the turn of the twenty-first century, not long after German reunification in 1989. In certain respects, Germany became a new country after this iconic event of overcoming, reinvigorating an old geography while unable to shed its twice-fractured history—first, by World War II, followed by a communist-capitalist divide.[6] With reunification, Berlin became the new state capital on October 3, 1989; this was also an act of return, with Berlin the capital of Prussia and the German Empire until 1945. In this new (old) capital of a new Germany, Neukölln is today one of the most diverse neighborhoods. Of its 326,000 residents, over 40 percent have a migration background and 76,517 do not have German citizenship. In North Neukölln, the most populous part of the district, 80 percent of those under the age of eighteen live in immigrant households.[7]

Both Neukölln and the adjacent district of Kreuzberg transformed into ethnically Turkish neighborhoods in the late twentieth century, and are now increasingly settled not only by new immigrants, but also students, expats, and ethnically German Soviet Jews. With rapid gentrification following the closure of the Tempelhof Airport on the plot of land directly next to which Şehitlik stands, *Time Out* calls Neukölln "the latest Berlin borough to be hailed as the centre of all things hip."[8] The gentrification of Neukölln breathes life into experimental cafes, coworking spaces, bars, and boutiques. In this way, it resembles Tower Hamlets, where the East London Mosque is situated, long a post–migrant Bengali London district increasingly settled by students and artists. Urban studies scholars similarly describe and even compare the plurality and rapid gentrification of these two neighborhoods, citing in both "the allure of diversity, creativity and space."[9] Like East London, Neukölln's perceived gritty cool results at once in the push-out effects of gentrification and a struggle by urban minorities to retain cultural ownership of a space. And a rising wave of contention over the plurality of Berlin, in Muslim and Jewish populaces in particular, emerges in public conversations about this neighborhood.[10]

FORMING THE MOSQUE

As a microcosm of the metropolis, the topography of the Şehitlik Mosque tells multiple stories: the metropolis in constant contact—and at times conflict—with the national and transnational, the present with the past. The comings and goings on Columbiadamm, one of Neukölln's largest avenues, have increasingly centered on the mosque since the Tempelhof Airport closed in 2008. Reaching towards the sky, the traditional Ottoman structure of a grand white dome and twin minarets today marks the avenue, and therefore the cityscape. The mosque marks the landscape of a country that long denied its migration status. Its location is symbolic not only because it stands so close to where the Berlin Wall once stood, but also as a site of friendship forged between the Ottoman and Prussian Empires. In the eighteenth century, the two empires exchanged ambassadors, with then–Ottoman ambassador Giritli Ali Aziz Efendi moving to Prussia to strengthen political and cultural ties. Along with two of his consular officials, Efendi died soon after his arrival. As distance thwarted the return of their bodies, the Prussian king gifted land for their burials in what is today Berlin to Ottoman Sultan Selim III. On November 1, 1798, the three were buried in Berlin at a cemetery on Uhlandstrasse; their bodies were moved in 1866–67 to the Şehitlik Mosque, which was named after the cemetery ("Şehitlik" means "of the martyrs graveyard").

Diyanet and Diaspora

A mosque was first erected at this site on Columbiadamm in the 1980s. At the turn of the twenty-first century, that mosque was deconstructed and the new, far more ornate Şehitlik Mosque was built there. The care, detail, and grandeur of this new mosque, under the management of DITIB, reflected the reality of permanent settlement for many of those who had migrated as guest workers.

Designed by architect Muharrem Hilmi Şenalp from Turkey, the mosque was built under the supervision of Berlin architect Tarkan Akarsu from 1999 to 2004. The architecture reflects the sixteenth- and seventeenth-century Ottoman design of mosques. Numerous Turkish influences mark the Şehitlik Mosque, including both the external form of its edifice and its ornate internal

FIGURE 1. Exterior of the Şehitlik Mosque, Columbiadamm Avenue. Photo by author.

FIGURE 2. Burial ground outside of the Şehitlik Mosque. Photo by author.

décor, overseen by the famous calligraphy artist, Hamid Aytaç. Specialized workers from Turkey temporarily resided in Berlin to participate both in the initial design and in the building of the mosque, funded primarily through community donations from within the Turkish diaspora in Germany.[11]

As a DITIB mosque, Şehitlik's theological profile is influenced by the Diyanet in Turkey. The Diyanet, established in 1924 after the emergence of the Turkish Republic, is a state institution that effectively succeeded the Institute of the Shaykh al-Islam, office of the highest religious authority during the Ottoman Empire.[12] The Diyanet is not only supervised but also allocated funding by the state, which in turn facilitates state control over the largest organized religious entity in the country, and to a degree also in diaspora settings. For decades, the Diyanet managed to walk a fine line between political dependence and theological independence, and until recently was considered a semiautonomous body. Due to a series of legislative reforms under President Recep Tayyip Erdoğan, however, it is now directly attached to the Turkish executive branch, leaving it more vulnerable to political manipulation than before.[13]

Theologically, the Diyanet has been influenced by the Hanafi school of Sunni Islam, as well as strands of Sufism. The multicultural constitution of the Ottoman Empire effectively created a theological center that integrated diverse strands of Islam, encouraging consensus. In many ways, the Diyanet continues this methodological approach, focusing on ameliorating the contention that arose from the political and societal changes in the aftermath of World War I, as Kemal Atatürk's revolutionary reforms radically altered the status of religion in the new Turkish Republic. At the time, the Diyanet demanded unequivocal inclusion in the changing political scene. This, in turn, created immense tension among state elites, eager to implement *laiklik* (secularist) policies, and a large pious populace that showed opposition to the far-reaching depth of reform. In the long history of Turkey's struggle to define and redefine its identity, the Diyanet was called upon time and again to present solutions to the conflicts that arose from this very specific mix of official secularism and popular piety.[14]

The Şehitlik Mosque was explicitly designed at the turn of the twenty-first century to emulate the Diyanet's stance in diaspora. As in Turkey (and throughout the Muslim world) neither the (rationalist) Mu'tazila school nor the (scripturalist) Ash'ari school of Islamic thought are prominent in the teachings of Şehitlik, but more so the Maturidi school of thought, which initially tried to overcome the conflict between them. Abu Mansur al-Maturidi (853–944 CE, born in Samarkand) sought to bring an end to the sectarian schools of thought that created a dynamic of exclusivism that he perceived at times as dangerously close to radicalism.[15] Maturidi is therefore consistently upheld as an example of how controversial positions can be brought into a convincing compromise, preaching *wasatiyya* (moderation) or the "middle path."[16] Since its erection, Şehitlik has implicitly followed the Maturidian model, overcoming political divides in the diaspora populace in order to unite Sunni Muslims under the roof of a single, representative mosque.[17]

Since the founding of DITIB, the Diyanet has provided imams for all affiliated German mosques, with the mosque administratively run by a combination of Turkish state and civilian employees. In 2003, Ender Çetin, a second-generation Turkish Berliner, was elected as mosque director; Şehitlik has since transcended its status as an ethnically Turkish mosque. Under his leadership, this mosque became a locally and nationally celebrated space for civic engagement and city-level solidarity. It remains rooted in the Hanafi school of law, the Sunni strand dominant in Turkey and the Middle East, but with a particular adaptability and openness that many attribute to early theological developments (Maturidi), historical facets of the Ottoman Empire (accommodating diversity), and a deep Sufi tradition largely born in what is today's Turkey.[18] Under the leadership of its second generation, Şehitlik comes to privilege a harmonizing vision, fostering responsibility for local society through Islamic tradition and practice.[19] Tradition is here, and throughout this book, understood in the Asadian sense as

> discourses that seek to instruct practitioners regarding the correct form and purpose of a given practice that, precisely because it is established, has a history. These discourses relate conceptually to a *past* (when the practice was instituted, and from which the knowledge of its point and proper performance has been transmitted) and *a future* (how the point of that practice can best be secured in the short or long term, or why it should be modified or abandoned), through *a present* (how it is linked to other practices, institutions, and social conditions).[20]

Today, young Muslims at Şehitlik make sense of their complex present, including multiple connections spanning from the local to the global level, in an assertion of leadership in the body of the mosque. Located in this at-times-fraught middling space, second-generation leadership straddle many lines—privileging Islamic sources, tradition, interpretation, and community engagement—and in so doing many sociocultural communities, present and past. Such broad inclusivity becomes enacted by stressing social horizontality rather than hierarchy, and commonality that cuts across groups assumed to be in conflict with one another, with Berliner identities described as founded upon the same principles as Muslim identities, and German values as reflecting Muslim virtues. Şehitlik's youth leadership enacts Muslimness inflected with, while influencing, the specific urban context, transforming the mosque into a space where piety emerges as part of local life. While Wilkerson writes of caste as "the architecture of human hierarchy," the mosque here becomes an architectural opportunity for equality and harmony.[21]

This specific vision of piety as harmonized with the metropolis has brought Şehitlik political praise at both the local and national levels, including attendance of the former interior minister, Thomas de Maizière, at a 2015 iftar (the meal that breaks the fast after sundown during Ramadan) and numerous visits from Germany's former president, Joachim Gauck. It has resulted in bountiful media coverage, characterizing Şehitlik as a place of "openness."[22] This is a double-edged sword, as such recognition of one community—contrasted with others—fortifies the good Muslim/bad Muslim binary based on a widespread perception of the average or nonexceptional Muslim as uncivil.[23] State governance is, after all, accomplished through regulated, selective, and often temporary inclusions of Muslim bodies and institutions. We see in the rise and the subsequent fall (the latter of which I explore in the book's afterword) of Şehitlik as what police officers term a "model mosque," both the empowering agency of a mosque community to make itself as part of the metropolis and the powerful limits of perceived Muslim incivility that keep it apart.

A word of caution here. Şehitlik's project is often misread from the outside as assimilatory. It is anything but, refuting Europe's monopoly on knowledge—both ideas and ideals—and the linearity inherent to notions of "progress" in its teachings on the intertwined responsibilities/obligations of Muslims to God, themselves, society, and the natural world; in its tours that bring the city into the mosque; and in the solidarity built with the local Jewish community. In *Religion of Reason: Out of the Sources of Judaism*, Hermann Cohen argues that Enlightenment ideas, such as individual autonomy and freedom, are far from novel; they emerged from the Jewish foundational religious sources, including the Old Testament.[24] Şehitlik similarly shows that conceptions of justice, human equality, and appreciation of pluralism do not elucidate the adaptation of Muslims to European society, but are rather intrinsic to Islam, present in the Qur'an and the Sunna (the ways, both sayings and doings, of the Prophet Muhammad). Şehitlik, like Cohen, thus inverts the Foucauldian perspective, which counters the universality of the Enlightenment.[25] Instead, the community critiques and contests the *particularity* of the Enlightenment and resulting liberal democratic values.

Unsettled Lives: On Migration and Pilgrimage

The story of this mosque does not begin with the children of immigrants, but rather in the journeys of their parents to, and later within, Berlin. My first visit to the mosque takes place on Kandil, the anniversary of the birth of the Prophet Muhammad, which is a holiday celebrated in Turkey. I arrive to the mosque overflowing, cars parked along Columbiadamm Avenue, men and women carrying dishes to share, and a service of almost continuous prayer. The co-transmission of knowledge and etiquette commences here, as first-generation women school me on how to dress for, sit within, and engage with the mosque as both built environment and lived community. What I initially perceive as micro-aggressions ("you cannot expose your ankles," "you cannot sit with your legs crossed") are in fact a crash course in the cultural subjectivities of the mosque, with knowledge accrual a project of body and mind—at the same time revealing my own subjectivities and the assumptions embedded within them. Muslims are, after all, called to follow not only the word of God (i.e., the Qur'an), but along with it the words and actions of the Prophet Muhammad. In his melodic text on Islam in West Africa, *The Walking Qur'an*, Ware lays bare the centrality of embodiment in Islamic knowledge formation and transmittance, as "knowledge in Islam does not abide in texts; it lives in people."[26]

Of varying generations and backgrounds, my interlocutors share an active practice of Islam, many counting their duties, the five pillars of Islam, on the five fingers of a single hand—the *shahada* (declaration of faith), salat (prayer), *sawm* (fasting), zakat (giving alms), and the hajj (pilgrimage). They emphasize the role of the hajj pilgrimage to Mecca and Medina as a specific embodied experience and a requirement for all physically and financially capable Muslims. Discourse on the pilgrimage is particularly potent among the first generation of Turkish migrants, dislocated from their birthplaces in Turkey, placed by economic possibilities and/or marriage in Berlin. Unlike their children, they were not born in Germany, and while many have no formal Islamic schooling, they often describe Islam as the singular entity grounding them in border-crossing lives. The dislocation felt by the first generation is both acute and enduring, with a female elder at the mosque describing the city of Berlin as a "stop" on her "journey." There is a certain sense among those who migrated that they are still living unsettled lives.

During the hajj, pilgrims perform numerous embodied rituals, including the circumambulation of the Kaaba (the holiest site in Islam, a building at the core of Al-Masjid al-Haram in Mecca built by Abraham and his son Ismael), running between the hills of Safa and Marwa, a vigil for the Prophet Muhammad at Arafat, the symbolic stoning of Satan, and Eid al-Adha, a celebratory feast that concludes the pilgrimage with an animal sacrifice. These rituals are based in Islam's foundational stories. For instance, Hagar, wife of Abraham, ran between the hills of Safa and Marwa to find food and water for her dying infant son, Ismael. Her patience and dedication to God was rewarded with the Zamzam well, opened from the ground by the Angel Gabriel, saving them both from death by thirst.[27] Women I meet at Şehitlik's Kandil celebration have just returned from the pilgrimage, dates in hand, along with holy water from the Zamzam well to share. Here, I drink that water for the first time.

Pilgrimage means journeying, often to a sacred place, an intimate action imbued with great intent. As a pillar of Islam, the hajj pilgrimage is a once-in-a-lifetime experience for many who make it to Mecca and Medina. The economic cost means that most do not make it at all. Hope for this pilgrimage dots the life histories of Muslims across continents and across time. Here in Europe, in Germany, in Berlin, at Şehitlik like many other mosques, those who cannot join may partake in reenactments. In fact, papier-mâché Kaabas are used in preparation for the hajj, practice to complete the correct bodily movements during the ritual. And they are also employed for demonstrations upon the pilgrims' return. With a simple mixture of paper, water, glue, and flour, artists create lifelike figures of humans, animals, and other forms. While static in structure, a papier-mâché Kaaba is a communicative tool about the hajj, representing practices of crossing and making across planes of belonging: to a mosque in metropolitan Europe, while also to a broader Muslim peoplehood. As material representations of the center of divinity and orientation in Muslim life, these papier-mâché forms at once evoke tradition and hope.

Beginning with the Kandil celebration, Esra, a middle-aged mother of five, immediately takes me under her wing. Over butter-fried bread and kebabs in the heart of Kreuzberg, Esra's family, celebrating the Qur'anic recitation award won by their young son at Şehitlik, tells me of their daughter, Fatima, who saved for the pilgrimage with the hope to win back her lost love. They laugh deep belly laughs and roll their eyes. But just like love, dreams don't make sense or follow rules. She didn't win him back, they explain, spoon-feeding meat and yogurt along with their tales. When I later speak to Fatima, she assures me that she found something else on hajj: acceptance of a different path. She "found peace in the pilgrimage"—and "what more is there to wish for, really, than peace?" Peace is, after all, in Cohen's words, "the fundamental power of the human soul."[28]

Peace, as power, remains remote, relegated to the past for many who feel that they were forced by economic circumstance to leave their homes in Turkey, long dwelling in a liminal legal state as migrants but not residents, and still dwelling in a liminal emotional state whether as German residents or citizens. My first-generation interlocutors see themselves on the margins of German society and yearn for lives once lived in Turkey, recounting stories of their mothers beating fresh milk to butter, while notably silent on the economic precarity that motivated moves abroad. Their yearning remains an endlessly giving well of conversation and conundrum, with children born in Germany, leaving them perpetually torn between two worlds. None "feel German," even with German citizenship. "I am Turkish. The passport I have is another thing." "My children are Turkish, even if they have German passports, their parents are Turkish," they say.[29]

As law does not guarantee belonging—"the passport I have is another thing"—the embodied act of pilgrimage links the first generation to a sense of self-recovery from migration, as "not only a physical state of removal from one's ancestral land, place of birth, kinship, or nationality . . . [but] also a psychological condition that produces a certain estrangement."[30] It is simply impossible to articulate what it means to take the pilgrimage for those who feel an enduring sense of estrangement and absence, knowing that they can never really go home. The pilgrimage, as a future-facing form of border-crossing rooted in tradition—evoking nostalgia but no real promise of return—is described as "full," "shared," "ours," opposing the vacancy experienced in the Berlin metropolis. Many do not have photographs. "I wanted to remember it *here*," my interlocutors say, pointing to their hearts. "Beautiful," they whisper, voices trailing off as their minds wander abroad. Others have no words at all. As Mehmet, a man who migrated half a century ago as a teenager from Anatolia, tells me upon returning from the hajj, "*There are no words.*"

Language has its limits in its capacity to capture the full range of life's colors and many shades of gray. The experiences of first-generation Turkish migrants, from being called to build a new Germany to the hajj, can only be translated and therefore approximated. No language can capture how it feels to stand in ripped shoes in old West Berlin hauling pig carcasses into a van, like Mustafa, once a young Muslim "guest worker," now retiree in the first generation who sought opportunity in this new life, but certainly "not this." I can imagine and yet not feel what it was like for Mustafa to learn those cuts of pork, how to handle something so linked to his sacred as impure; and how it is for millions of pilgrims like him to stand where their ultimate prophet, Muhammad, once stood, to walk their way through oceans of bodies that share a history and a practice leading them to the same hills and the same well, quenching thirst for dignity.

Esra, the woman who invited me to this post-hajj gathering in Berlin, returned from the hajj in the late 1990s donning a perfectly taut headscarf
and flowing black coat. Born in an agrarian village outside of Istanbul, she had
previously worn a triangle-scarf that covered most of her hair, ankle-length
skirts, and fitted button-down shirts tucked into the waist. She found strength
in spirituality during the pilgrimage and "wanted to scream it" to her critics in
Germany. She found relief there, a place to rest her feet on what many in the
first-generation feel is a life of endless, dizzying movement. There was "nothing wrong" with her, she tells me. In fact, the pilgrimage helped to set things
straight. This is not surprising, she explains, as the hajj (the dress, the norms,
the shared experience) emphasizes human equality. "Equality of all." Many
women in the first generation describe hajj as the experience through which
they recognize their own equality to others, no matter how much they have
been put down—whether in Mecca or Berlin, in Istanbul or the villages of Anatolia that still "smell like home." The hajj presents not just a space but a time of
transformation that can transcend geographical boundaries: the opportunity
to reorient oneself towards God. It allows for change (as for Esra), as much as
acceptance that things may not change at all (as for her daughter, Fatima). Both
play important roles in the life of Muslims in contemporary Germany, and in
Europe at large.

Two middle-aged women drag a papier-mâché Kaaba into the center of the
room, to reenact—with all of its indescribable emotionality—their journey to
Mecca and Medina for those who cannot afford to make the trip. Sitting in a
straight line, each reflects on the pilgrimage, with a glance, weeping, very few
words. When they speak, it is of the unifying experience connecting all corners
of the earth, a moment of belonging fully there, while being present here in
Berlin. This act, the construction and reenactment with papier-mâché, is one
that I see in two of Berlin's mosques: it is an act of *sympoiesis*, making together,
a practice that transcends the boundaries of both space and time, as replicas
connect the pilgrimage to, thus creating the pilgrim in, a European metropolis. Today the tears fall fast, some women weeping so hard that they are unable
to speak more than a *mashallah* (literally translated as "what God has willed,"
used to express appreciation or thankfulness) or *al-hamdulillah* ("all praise is
due to God alone"). I may not see what they see, but I still see clearly that these
women who belong neither here, exactly, nor fully in their birthplace anymore
together make something in and of this city. One elderly woman walks around
the room carrying a plate of dates, tucked like a child into the nook of her waist,
her knit sweater swinging to the rhythm of her hips, and another, small plastic
cups holding sips of water from the Zamzam well.

Maps of Desire

This early experience with my first-generation interlocutors from the Şehitlik Mosque illuminates a longing shared by those who migrated from Turkey
to dwell in spite of what Michael Heller calls the "scattered scatterings" of
diaspora and the importance of space for embodying this longing; they seek
respite from a sense of un-belonging, settling within both community and self,
emplacement amidst the shifting winds that blow their lives in different directions.[31] They are, like Mary Poppins, pulled to the sky by these winds—
reaching through the mosque both for the future, with and through God, and
for the past. In the words of Arjun Appadurai and Carol Breckenridge, "diasporas always leave a trail of collective memory about another place and time
and create new maps of desire and of attachment."[32]

Sevgi, a DITIB leader born near Cologne, describes the affective power of
the physical transformation from makeshift to permanent mosques for the first
generation, new loci of "desire and attachment" on maps that cut across the
world. "They remember the times, twenty years in the old backyard mosque,
twenty years hidden away, maybe the first five years without any network. Having just this one place. It's so important for the emotions of the first generation."

The Ottoman "architectural mimicry" of this mosque —at once familiar
and new—also helps the first generation to recollect their Turkish origins, to
"rebuild the glory of the past in today's conditions," here linking a Turkish-
Islamic ancestry to a present and a future in Berlin.[33] This results in a deep
sense of both material and emotional ownership. In the words of law student Yusuf, reflecting on his parents' rooting in the city of Berlin, "Muslims
here answered life's questions through architecture."

As she slowly ascends the steps to the main prayer sanctuary, Ayşe, an elderly instructor of Qur'an recitation, explains how Şehitlik, first a graveyard,
later a sanctuary for the living, encapsulates her forebears, her children, and
her grandchildren all at once. In so doing, she describes her own embodied
experience of migration and settlement.

> I came to Germany in 1970. I remember the date even, October 5. I came be-
> cause I was married to someone who had come earlier, three years after him,
> and began working three years later cleaning schools in Berlin . . . Every day
> since the mosque opened I have come here. This is my second home. Ever
> since I retired, I have been asked to teach Qur'an . . . If I stay home, I feel I will
> get sick. My body is telling me that I have to leave, my bed telling me to get out.
> I'm escaping loneliness at home, being in a community, doing volunteer work.

When I see this place, it reminds me of Turkey. On Fridays, when a specific supplication is performed, I am transferred to Turkey. When I enter this place, I am transported to Turkey . . . I was about to leave to return to Turkey but this mosque made me stay.

For many, like Ayşe, who emigrated from Turkey, Şehitlik creates a space for smaller everyday pilgrimages, a both literal and metaphorical circumambulation of the Kaaba in papier-mâché.[34] While physically representative spiritual institutions like Şehitlik certainly bestow dignity, they also offer a space that transcends the geographical and temporal divisions that shape life trajectories of migration and settlement.

Esra at one point uses the untranslatable Turkish word *hüzün* to describe life in Berlin before the mosque was built. This word suggests more than melancholy, spiritual anguish because one feels distanced both from God and from the past. This sense of exilic homesickness, at once backward- and forward-looking longing, lies at the heart of Benjamin's writings on his early life in Berlin; his description of a baked apple pregnant with "fugitive knowledge" rouses the question of whether he alludes to his own Eden in the city of his childhood (that is, again, the "city god itself"), not innocent but alluring—and from which he was ultimately cast out.[35] This sense is similarly invoked in the words of my interlocutors who yearn for their lives once lived in Anatolia, imperfect but alluring in the now. In the words of Turkish novelist Orhan Pamuk, "for the poet, *hüzün* is the smoky window between him and the world."[36] The Şehitlik Mosque provides the space, the pedagogy, and the inspiration for a great feat, fostering a closeness to God that eases and mends, lifting the fog from the glass not for poets, but for persons entranced in the haze of *hüzün*.

In spite of such poetic possibility in the mosque, it must be acknowledged that the transformation of Şehitlik from an ethnically Turkish mosque to a Berlin mosque focused on civic harmonization, comes with a certain cost borne by the first generation. They largely adjust to the opening of the mosque to everyday mainstream engagement, where schoolchildren shriek at the site of ostrich eggs hanging from the ceiling to ward off spiders, and visitors walk in front of prostrating men, violating their prayer. Still, as I discuss later, their discomfort and at times sheer discontent with such disruptive moments rises to the surface in reflection and in recollection, having built Şehitlik from the ground to the sky—in cement and stone, wood and papier-mâché, trees transformed into edifice to hold unsettled lives.

Sadiye: "There is loss"

When she visited Istanbul as a young adult, Sadiye felt a certain pull. In the center of the city, she stood outside of a mosque alight, men praying in rows within its open form. "Sometimes I feel disconnected from who I am," Sadiye explains, eyes filling with tears. Her parents moved to Berlin at the end of the 1960s, and she was born over a decade later, in the early 1980s. Sadiye worked beside her father in the city's supermarkets to help support her family during adolescence. She found it exhausting to defend herself against the men who berated her for wearing a headscarf during those years, ongoing commentary about how she did not, could not, would not belong to Germany, despite being born and raised in its capital. Sadiye met the same bigotry in school and later at university. Still, she refused to give up either her Turkishness or her Germanness, insisting that she was made of both. Eventually, she felt that the stereotypes about women who wear headscarves would limit her capacity to thrive, grow, and economically succeed in her burgeoning craft as an artist. She considered leaving Germany. Instead, she removed her headscarf. "Modesty, it's not only about your body, it's how you conduct yourself," Sadiye explains, securing her headscarf for prayer, the *adhan* (call to prayer) sounding on the loudspeakers inside of the Şehitlik Mosque. She steps forward in line with other women and lifts her hands, palms open to the sky.

After she prays, Sadiye sits beside me on the floor and continues her story. She slowly rescinded her decision to don the headscarf in her late twenties, while working as a graphic artist in Berlin. First, she tied the scarf on top of her head, during a summer that she lived abroad in the United States. Soon after, she wore a bandana, and one day nothing on her hair at all, which quickly unraveled her closest childhood friendship. "No matter which way you look, there is loss," she says. In Sadiye's process of unveiling, the tension between the lived experience of the individual in practice and conflicting Muslim-mainstream discourses on the meaning of the headscarf emerge. Her decision, like that of so many others, illuminates a nexus of social pressure and individual agency—an unrelenting liminality—transforming her conceptualization of how best to harmonize internal and external expressions of Islam, as she navigates piety and socioeconomic life.

Today a successful graphic designer in Berlin, Sadiye invokes her time in Istanbul with nostalgia, not as a place where she yearns to live, but rather one where she imagines that such choices would not constrain her opportunities. There is something easier about a city that moves to another rhythm, with the signs and symbols of Islam mundane rather than profane. Still, Berlin remains her one and only home: her family, her business, her childhood memories are here. I ask whether she feels more accepted by society now, with her economic success, or continues to feel torn. Instead of speaking, she opens her bag, removing a sheet of paper carefully preserved inside of a book. It is a picture drawn by a young artist, a sketch of a young woman's face, scarf partially covering her hair, pulled in all directions by the wind. There are flowers falling everywhere.

CONTESTED BELONGING

The second generation is differently unsettled than the first, as they face associations with incivility beginning in their childhoods. Born in Berlin, they experience negative differentiation that is often rooted in school and continues into adulthood. Here I turn towards experiences of being "downgraded" and surveilled, leading to the fragmentation of the Muslim body and a monopoly over language that also does violence.

On an exceptionally bright autumn afternoon in 2014 following a tour of the mosque, I meet Yusuf by the gates to the street. Women on roller skates fly down Columbiadamm Avenue, absorbing the last warmth of day. A law student with an always-jovial demeanor and neatly pressed jeans, Yusuf is running late for dinner. He apologizes and then asks with a smile if we should return together on the bus to Schöneberg, the Berlin district in which we both reside. While many of my interlocutors at the Şehitlik Mosque work in the service and labor industries, a sizable minority of the second generation—most notably the mosque's youth leaders—are employed in white-collar professions such as law, education, and engineering. Largely thriving in their educations and careers, youth leaders like Yusuf describe social challenges as doors to a better future rather than walls, some utilizing their knowledge of Islam to carve out professional niches in social work, pedagogy, and governance.[37]

As we wait for the bus, Yusuf recounts his experiences as an exchange student in the United States with a certain nostalgia. Between anecdotes relaying the curiosities of everyday life in a new country, he injects larger lessons from his time away. Here Yusuf draws a distinct line between American and German understandings of belonging.

> One of the greatest experiences I had was in Louisville, when I met an African American Muslim. He was the first I met there and I thought he would be from West Africa, so an immigrant who came there to work. He was really

traditionally dressed like West African people. And I went to him and said, *"Salam 'alaykum."* He said, *"'Alaykum salam."* And I asked, "By the way, where are you from?" "I'm from Louisville." "And where are your parents from?" "From Louisville, as well." "Their parents?" He said, "Man, from Louisville." "And their parents?" "Actually, they are from Alabama, but why are you asking me questions like this?"

Drawing on his own experiences in Germany, Yusuf had equated Muslimness with foreignness, a sentiment and self-perception that this American Muslim did not share. Yusuf pauses and looks at me intently, gesturing a lightbulb going off in his head. "And so, I was like, oh, *it's possible*, it's possible to have this connection and to still be American and be Muslim as well. Germany is different. It hasn't gotten to that place where being Muslim and being German can uncontestably belong together." Although born and raised in Berlin, Yusuf remains noticeably uncertain about how he belongs to Germany. He feels that there is something inherently unsettling about his Muslim identity to others, who maintain that he is "guest" or a "foreigner" (*Ausländer*) in the ways that they look at, speak to, and struggle to characterize him—despite being a German national.

Who I am, who I am. It's a question I am trying to cope with. When I was born, I had Turkish citizenship, but later on when I was sixteen, I got the German one, so I had two citizenships. And when I was eighteen, I was forced to decide. It was really hard for me, but I am someone who likes to travel and I looked at the one I could travel the best with, the German one . . . For me, it doesn't mean anything to have a piece of paper in my hands. I had so many different experiences. I had times in my life when people came to me and told me that I should "be quiet" because I am "only a guest" in this country and I have nothing to say . . . So, society expects a lot from you since according to them you are not from the society and it reflects in every aspect of your life . . . Sometimes, I tell my mom, "I don't even have a name."

Yusuf is not the first, nor the last, of my interlocutors to equate German citizenship with a passport (recall the words of my first-generation interlocutors)—an object representing to them not rootedness but the capacity to cross borders, move through the world. This sense of dislocation echoes in his statement that "I don't even have a name," laying bare the space between full legal and cultural inclusion, even for individuals born in Berlin. Names matter; they represent a history, ancestry, offerings of offspring. They suggest the possibility of continuance, a mortal nod at the never-ending story. And they at once represent unity, in family and community, as well as separation (of the latter, Benjamin writes, "he communicates himself by naming *them*" [emphasis added]).[38] When Sadiye accompanied her father, complaining of sharp chest pain, to the hospital in winter 2015, the doctors and nurses belittled him. "If his name were Hans, they wouldn't be acting like this," she laments. Seated in his office, Osman also considers the importance of names. "Our colleague has a Syrian father but a German mother and when she was looking for an apartment she always used her mother's name instead of her father's, because when your last name is Muslim you have no chance." Not only names, but any markers of Muslimness, can lead to discrimination—in securing residences and health care, schools and employment.

When invited to talk about her profession in her daughter's kindergarten class in spring 2015, Ecrin, a young mother of three, asks to discuss her work in the mosque. "We don't educate children in religion. Religion has no place here," the teacher remarks. And when Selim, a history teacher in a Berlin public school, requests Fridays off to attend the Friday prayer each week the same spring, the principal not only refuses but draws a line between him and Judeo-Christian civility. "This is not a religious school and you cannot indoctrinate students. You don't see Jewish and Christian people asking for this," she remarks.

The discursive vision of the Şehitlik Mosque begins with the recognition of this culturally subordinate position in public life, one often juxtaposed to the secular and/or (Judeo-)Christian norm, upheld through fragmented representations of the Muslim body and an accompanying vicious discourse. Here I bracket "Judeo," as Jewish inclusion remains tentative, which I later explore vis-à-vis the 2012 circumcision ban.[39] Almost all of the youth at Şehitlik recount being discriminated against by their schoolteachers—"never being called on," "chosen last," "told I would never accomplish anything." Yusuf explains that "in school when a German student just put up his hand three times, me as a Turkish student had to do it six times to prove that I am on the same level. So, it meant for me to do more, always to do more, to do more to show that I am on the same level." Timur, a university student, describes a similar experience of having to perform at a higher level than non-Muslims.

> Personally speaking, I find it very hard to be a Muslim in Germany. We are still being discriminated against. Others are being favored, even when we [Muslims] are better [at something]. We are being constantly downgraded. We are being always neglected, we are never the first choice. We really have to make a huge effort to be recognized. We have to perform not at 100 percent but rather

200 percent to actually achieve anything here in Germany. Without any ambition, we'd just go straight downhill.

Turning towards the marginalizing force of gendered stereotypes, Yakup, a law student in Berlin, laments that his sisters were not recommended for the *Gymnasium* (the highest academic level of high school) based on "the expectation that they would marry young rather than pursue an education." And Meral, another law student, reflects on her own experience with gender-based assumptions growing up:

> I feel like we are still struggling with stereotypes, especially gender relations, what people think women are not allowed to do in Islam. I have an anecdote to tell. I had a German friend, we were close in fourth grade, then our school was closed. We got separated. I ran into her . . . she was shocked when I told her I was going to law school. "What are you going to law school for? You are not supposed to be going to law school, a Turkish woman. . . ." That was her facial expression.

While anti-Muslim discrimination is rooted in early periods of socialization, my interlocutors born and raised in Berlin face ongoing unequal treatment in universities and workplaces, as one has to "do more" than others, is "downgraded," "neglected," "not on the same level," and "never the first choice." Osman describes the underlying social atmosphere normalizing such experiences, which range from neglect to outright violence in the public sphere. "People don't scream, 'Poles get outta here!' They yell, 'Turks get outta here!' You're constantly reminded that your presence in Germany is not appreciated, sometimes even violently reminded." The resulting sociocultural hierarchy is one based in, and justified by, fear. "I was always tested, twenty-four hours a day," Yusuf explains, paralleling Bauman's description of the stranger as "permanently on trial, a person vigilantly watched and constantly under pressure to be someone else than he is."[40] "I think Germany is somewhat afraid of us," Timur echoes. "They don't want to boost us up. They want to keep us down. They don't want us to hold high positions. I feel like they are looking down on us . . . they only want Germans to be in high positions so that they can tell us what to do."

The Body in Pieces

This fear, and its repercussions on belonging, has come to center on a particular embodied and gendered aspect of Muslim life: the headscarf. Both veiling, and its counterpart, unveiling, emerge again and again in my conversations with Şehitlik Mosque constituents, as they discursively navigate the limitations on inclusion to both mainstream and Muslim collectivities. The headscarf has become the most regulated religious symbol in Europe, a point of obsession in the struggle over what and who can fully belong to contemporary European nation-states. This obsession with the headscarf entails both totalizing abstraction and disintegratory fragmentation, with the Muslim body pulled not only in many directions, but pulled apart. Rather than conceptualizing the Muslim body as part of a physical and spiritual whole, its fragmentation casts it as broken and incomplete: their bodies in pieces, a metaphor of violence usually reserved for the ravages of war. It is only through the literal and discursive reconstruction of the shattered Muslim body in new, assimilated form (as with Arendt's parvenu) that Muslims can potentially, albeit conditionally, cross into the civil realm.[41]

Here I turn to the French case, since it set off the discursive fixation on and regulation of veiling across Europe, both quickly echoed in German discourse and policy. In his description of the unveiling of Muslim women in French Algeria in *A Dying Colonialism*, Frantz Fanon analyzes the veil as a universalized symbol of Islam, with its forced, public removal paradoxically justified as a civilizing act: a secular baptism into the civil order. Yet as in the French colonies, even the ritual purification of removing the headscarf, still rife with violence, can never truly overcome the cultural branding of Muslim bodies with incivility.[42] Moving from the colonial/postcolonial nexus to the present, the promise of potential inclusion is again betrayed. Joan Scott describes the politics of the veil today as continuing this "civilizing process"—the unenlightened Muslim juxtaposed to the enlightened European/French—with which Muslims have to contend.[43] Even with the removal of the headscarf in compliance with the bans in French schools, however, the referent of incivility simply shifts to a different embodied fragment; recall, for instance, the long skirt of schoolgirl Sarah in Charleville-Mézières, France, read as an "ostentatious" Muslim signifier, leading to her suspension.[44] And few contemporary moments invoke the continued fixation on unveiling the Muslim body like the burkini bans in southern France, which lay bare the brute incivility of "civilizing" by force. I am still haunted by the image of a woman with a headscarf on the beach of Nice, encircled by three police officers, removing her shirt under their collective gaze.[45]

While the headscarf debates that ensued in Germany differed from those in France, regulating teachers rather than students in public schools, and justified through constitutional laws on state neutrality rather than *laïcité*, they similarly centered on delimiting the Muslim body.[46] In Germany, the bounds of such regulations have been determined by the Federal Constitutional Court (Bundesverfassungsgericht, FCC), specifically through in its 2003 and 2015 rulings, but enacted at the federal state level. In 2003, half of Germany's sixteen federal states instated such bans, with most soon amended as broader bans on all religious symbols, given that singling out the headscarf violates the constitutional principle of nondiscrimination. Notably, in many cases, these expanded regulations excluded Christian symbols, deemed historical and cultural, rather than religious.[47] Berlin, however, upheld a ban of all religious symbols, including the cross.[48] In 2015, the language of threat again came to characterize the Muslim body, with the FCC decision that such blanket bans violated the constitution; they could only be upheld in cases where a teacher's donning of a religious symbol proved a "tangible danger" to state neutrality or school peace.[49] This ruling appeared, on the surface, to contend with discriminatory practices, but in fact reinforced both the interpretative ambiguity of headscarf bans and the broader bifurcating discourse of Muslim "danger" and mainstream "peace" in official state language describing the Muslim body.

The headscarf, its presence and its absence, remains deeply fused to the imaginary of the Muslim body. Şehitlik Mosque leader and tour guide Tuba laughs as she describes students' curiosity about how she can shower with a headscarf on, yet reveals in this anecdote the disturbing depths of such fusion: merged with the image of the Muslim as vestibule of subversion, subordination, and strangerness. A Berlin journalist describes an interview she held with an engineer who wears a headscarf. "Whenever she goes to see one of her clients, a lot of people assume she is a cleaning lady." Gülay, a university student often found reading in the mosque, recounts similar experiences regarding the symbolic power of the headscarf in public life.

> I constantly encounter people who believe that I can't think, that I can't speak German because I am wearing a headscarf. I was once in the subway on my way back home from the university, an elderly lady was sitting next to me and she goes, "Can I sit here?" And I replied, "Most certainly." And she goes, "Oh I thought you couldn't speak German."

As we board the bus to Schöneberg, Yusuf paints the picture of a woman on the street, hand wrapped around a dripping ice cream cone—or rather two women, one his mother and one me. In his powerful description of a potential encounter, Yusuf posits the different reactions that this scene would evoke depending on the simple presence or absence of a headscarf. "It's like, for example, when you would walk on the street and eat ice cream and drip on the ground—people wouldn't say anything. But if my mom would do that with her headscarf, people would say, '*Don't you see what Muslims do?*'"

My interlocutors recount not only the fraught representation of the headscarf, but also overt and covert pressures to remove it. With the veil removed, whether by physical or psychological force, society seeks exposure of the true, possibly dangerous person, who can only be saved by Europe. Yet even with the potentiality of individual inclusion, the pollution assigned to Muslim qualities remains.[50] And here the person underneath the controversial cloth, still Muslim without it, remains degraded. That is, exposure, nakedness, nothing forgives the Muslim her Muslimness; for even underneath the veil, she is Muslim and therefore incongruent with civility.

Muslim bodies are not only systematically marked with incivility, but also disciplined in public life, beginning with early education and continuing throughout adulthood in widespread surveillance. On a warm spring day, I meet Nora, an engineering student, for cake in the Schöneberg neighborhood, where she speaks of her elementary school experience. "I decided to wear a headscarf, but my mom didn't want me to. She had had so many bad experiences, and she took hers off. What happened was, I failed gym because I wouldn't take off the headscarf in class." Even though she participated in all requisite activities, when she refused to take off the headscarf, her gym teacher failed her, claiming that it "endangered" her well-being, illuminating the unbound power of a securitized discourse, officially upheld by the FCC. This very personal experience reflects a larger debate over religion-based exemptions from school activities, a subject of numerous lawsuits by Muslim families, and deep social contention, through mainstream associations with female oppression in Germany. In 2016, the FCC ruled that all girls must participate in swimming alongside boys at school.[51] Here the civic disciplining of the child's body through sports, including a culture where undressing is equated with purity and freedom (signaling civility), contends with Islamic norms of modesty, privacy, and purity.[52]

Within this conflicted social realm, the individual decision to veil or not to veil responds to fragmentation through the assertion of wholeness. This is an act of *phronesis*, where one negotiates the self vis-à-vis multiple, at times contending, collectivities and traditions and their normative aims. The process of unveiling, as Sadiye explains, is fraught, as the lived experience of the veiled woman in a context of social marginality—leading to implicit and explicit sanctioning—and the idea behind the veil as an expression of piety diverge. Sadiye discusses both as informing her "old" life in Berlin and the eventual decision to embody her religion in a new way. However, she also echoes what

Nadia Fadil finds in her study of unveiling among Belgian women of Maghrebi descent that it is not simply an assimilatory practice nor conformity to a secular norm, but rather an agentive choice regarding which norms to inhabit and when.[53] It is a process as much of internal as external negotiation, learning how to move between realms of social and moral life. While noting the influence of discrimination that led her to first consider unveiling, Sadiye felt a strong pull from within her Turkish community to continue to veil. A feeling of distance from both the Turkish community and mainstream German/Berlin society, and the opportunity of physical distance through her time abroad, spurred this eventual shift in her bodily practice, as did her sense that she would be "no less of a Muslim"—maintaining her moral agency, her wholeness in body and spirit alike, when she removed the scarf.

It is clearly not the scarf itself, but rather the female Muslim body that is here "at issue—the body and its forces, their utility and their docility."[54] The male Muslim body is also "at issue," in similar (fragmented by focusing on such markers as "the beard") and different (perceived as threatening both to mainstream society and to Muslim women) ways. Katherine Pratt Ewing traces the stigmatization of Muslim men in Berlin through imaginations, "social fantasies," that include embodied forms seen to signal danger.[55] This dualistic discourse of danger does more than stigmatize the male Muslim body, however, also falsely externalizing hierarchical social relations, attempting to turn Islam on itself by painting the headscarf as a symbol of male domination over women; in so doing, it solidifies a broader social hierarchy in European states and metropoles, the undercaste status of Muslims sustained through the contortion and breaking apart of bodies. *Their bodies in pieces.*

Vicious Discourse

On a Saturday afternoon in summer 2015, I meet Meral in the main sanctuary of the Şehitlik Mosque. Leaning against a pillar, she recounts her upbringing in the adjacent Kreuzberg neighborhood, from a tight-knit family to struggles in school. When Meral speaks of her secondary school experiences, she reveals the power of discourse in shaping the possibilities of belonging, excluding herself from the category of "German," as she was once excluded from the category of "German speaker."

> My school was a very German school in Kreuzberg. Over 90 percent of the students were German and I feel like specifically the teachers had some stereotypes about us. I mean, I can give you one example. I started attending this

school and our German teacher barely knew us. She knew us for two weeks. And she immediately sent every student with a migration background into the course "German as a second language." . . . So, we started attending a German-as-a-second-language course, and then they abolished the class after the month because they realized, OK, these kids actually speak [German]. We were forced to go, we had to go because we were afraid for our grades; if you didn't go, they would penalize you.

Such a monopoly on language—seen in relegating Muslims to "German as a second language" courses or encounters like Gülay's on the subway, where the ability to speak German elicits surprise—feeds into a broader experience of subordination, which disciplines both bodies and minds. In the words of Toni Morrison, "Oppressive language does more than represent violence; it is violence; does more than represent the limits of knowledge; it limits knowledge."[56] Edward Said has long articulated that Orientalism is not a concept but an enduring form of vicious discourse, and Stuart Hall has argued that the discourse of "the West and the Rest" continues to morally exclude racial and ethnic others to this day.[57]

These moral exclusions not only forge boundaries, but become internalized by those othered. By at times inhabiting such discursive norms, my interlocutors move from describing their externally imposed labeling as "foreigners," "outsiders," "migrants," and "guests" by "Germans"—here referencing ethnic Germans, rather than German citizens since the 2000 citizenship law pulled these two categories apart—to calling themselves "Muslims in Germany" instead of German Muslims. Many in fact speak of themselves and their religio-ethnic communities as *Ausländer*, "foreigners," in spite of German citizenship, most born in Berlin. "At my school, we had about 99 percent foreigners and only 1 percent German kids," explains Murad, who had just begun university, assigning himself to the former category through a speech act. It is this very form of internalized difference that Simmel evokes in his conceptualization of the stranger, "suggest[ing] that foreignness is a psycho-cultural as well as a geographical matter."[58]

Within the prism of language, the powerful trope of the "successful" or "exceptional" Muslim also emerges at the Şehitlik Mosque, not least of all when police officers nominalize the mosque itself as their "best-case scenario." Some might argue that this exceptionalism negates my claim of an undercaste status. In the powerful words of a female Shaykh whom I met in Oxford, however, "There are two ways to dehumanize someone: to idealize or demonize him." Even Hitler conceptualized the *Edeljude* (noble Jew) to describe his doctor,

Eduard Bloch, an exception that he contrasted to millions of other Jews.[59] Additionally, as Zygmunt Bauman argues, acculturation is an individual process, accomplished by the fragment broken away from the whole, whereas " 'cultural strangeness' is always aimed at a collective."[60] Such exceptionalism, in its juxtaposition to the collective, helps to maintain the system of subordination. Michelle Alexander makes this very argument regarding the prison industrial complex in the contemporary United States that relegates Black Americans to an undercaste status. "Highly visible examples of black success are critical to the maintenance of a racial caste system in the era of colorblindness. Black success stories lend credence to the notion that anyone, no matter how poor or how black you may be, can make it to the top, if only you try hard enough."[61]

Turning back towards Europe, just as "good Muslims" have become contrasted with "bad Muslims," "good Jews" have long been contrasted with "bad Jews." Anya Topolski traces the practice of *shtadlanut* (having an intercessor), a term that emerges in Hannah Arendt's critical writings, as a means to reinforce a good Jew/bad Jew division; in this case, European states selected *shtadlans* as privileged Jewish representatives and state interlocutors—not only solidifying a hierarchy in which Jews were subordinated by the mainstream, but also producing a sociopolitical hierarchy among Jews. In twentieth-century Germany, Topolski argues, this hierarchy became transferred to the *Judenräte*, the Jewish councils used and abused by the Nazis to control the German Jewish population.[62] The moral of this story reflects Arendt's conclusion that the Jew—whether pariah or parvenu—is never fully belonging and therefore never really safe, but rather that the pariah and the parvenu remain together "in the same boat, rowing desperately in the same angry sea."[63]

Muslims, whether labeled precarious or exceptional, remain confined to the same boat of an undercaste status in Europe's unsettled and unsettling seas. Situated in this sphere of contested belonging, where violence in language conditions violence against bodies, young Şehitlik Mosque constituents row not desperately, but determinedly against the currents of sociopolitical life. They localize their pious expressions and broader societal connections, making social and political claims on the metropolis through acts of moral agency, acts of making rather than making do. The mosque provides an institutional and spatial opportunity to contest their acknowledged cultural subordination, fostering an ethics of responsibility that stresses horizontality, acting upon Islamic obligations to the surrounding social world through an Arendtian vision of "*harmony* as the morally relevant experience."[64] This begins with countering the violence of oppressive language and the fragmentation of bodies through individual and collective rooting in bodies of Islamic knowledge.

Tuba: "The point of no return"

Tuba carefully paints henna onto the hands of a woman visiting the mosque on the annual Open Day, her fingers steady as they create swirls and flowers, vines and lines on the woman's skin. She is silent in this moment, biting her lower lip as she concentrates. I often see Tuba at Şehitlik, where she gives tours, attends Wednesday evening lessons on Islam in German, and drinks tea outside in the sun. The mosque is central to her life in the metropolis; she describes it as increasingly "a reference point of Islam" for Muslims born in Berlin, as it "pushes the envelope on outreach" into the mainstream.

Internally, Tuba perceives generational conflict in the community over such outreach. "The elder generation view this as a sacred place that cannot be violated, where you need to be quiet and not talk and just observe the service, whereas we want this to be a lively place where we laugh, get together, unite, and discuss." The vision of the mosque's youth "fits the historical experience" of Islam, Tuba argues, as "the mosque was always a communal place, a place of gathering, of exchange, where you celebrate, where you cry." These divergent perspectives are, of course, dependent on the focus of making and of dwelling alike. The first generation, in their lives of ongoing crossings, many of whom expected to eventually return to Turkey, long maintained a closed ethnic community. For the second generation and beyond born in Berlin, "these tendencies to segregate oneself and operate within your own borders have changed entirely." They individually experience, and collectively embody, a "point of no return."

Tuba began her work as a tour guide three years ago, when the mosque director was traveling and needed someone to cover his tours, and she sees her role in the community today as primarily pedagogical, guiding students and their teachers through the mosque. She tries to overcome assumptions about various topics in German public life during these tours, including the headscarf and gender relations. Still, she finds visitors often steer the conversation into unproductive and unrelated directions, such as the political situation in Saudi Arabia.

Tuba is concerned with fostering knowledge, whether on tours or in Berlin's city schools, where she has recently devoted herself to a project on Europe's Islamic heritage.

We are confronted with the notion that we do not belong here, you didn't go through the Enlightenment phase, you guys didn't contribute to our culture at all, we have a Christian culture, one might say Jewish-Christian leading culture and Islam doesn't have anything to do with this. This is wrong, I mean look at our language, many words we use like "coffee," "algebra." There are so many words people aren't aware of and we said, "We are going to look into this." Not what came to Germany with the guest workers but way before that in history, all the way back to the Middle Ages. So we organized and designed workshops as we collected data on these issues. Now we are instructing people to go into school classes and offer these workshops to kids.

Stereotypes can be overcome, Tuba believes, only through knowledge of Islam's deep and lasting influences on European society. Tuba sees herself as a trailblazer in this respect, as "unapologetically" Muslim, Turkish, German, a Berliner at the forefront of the Şehitlik Mosque as more than building or place of respite—as an "opportunity to learn."

"MY NAME IS *INSAN*:" THE PEDAGOGY OF HARMONY

"The first mosque was the place of knowledge, learning, science," Deniz, the evening's teacher, asserts, seated at the front of a room filled with Muslim youth. Deniz not only teaches about Islam at the mosque, but also in Berlin's city schools, helping both students and teachers to navigate their plural classrooms. Nearly every day, however, Deniz can be found at Şehitlik, whether providing lessons to Muslim youth or leading visitors on tours. "I should see the mosque as a training ground. I forget things. I am reminded when I return to the mosque. I should develop myself and my knowledge." His toddler son, crawling back and forth across the floor, laughs in delight as he stops to pull himself up on his father's knee to stand. The child claps his hands, suddenly unbalanced, crashing with an "oomph" to the ground. A visual lesson in the curve of learning, Deniz continues to speak as he pulls the fallen child into his lap.

On Wednesday evenings like tonight, Muslim youth from across Berlin unite for lessons on Islam in German, led by both mosque director Ender Çetin and an eclectic mix of second-generation Turkish Berliners and converts who attend. Demand for German-language teaching and sermons on Islam arises not from the growing membership of non-ethnically-Turkish Muslims, but instead overwhelmingly from Turkish German youth in the mosque seeking to overcome externally imposed divisions between their Muslim and Berliner identities. Tuba explains, "We . . . have a language we share, *German*, and interestingly I would say a sermon held in Turkish is not necessarily speaking to us anymore." These lessons center on the interlinked harmonization of the self and society, speaking at once to spiritual and civic life, bringing together that which is so often pulled apart by political and media portrayals of Islam.

Wednesday evening lessons at Şehitlik invoke a German concept for which there is no direct English translation, *Bildung*, the cultivation of moral character through education. Like the interior ring of a set of concentric circles, moral character is cultivated through an ethics of responsibility for the self, the community, society, and the natural world—enlivened through an Islamic pedagogical approach highlighting the interdependent obligations (*taklif*) of the Muslim.[65] Hans Jonas developed the idea of an ethics of responsibility from exile in 1974, looking for respite, understanding, and protection against extreme human suffering in the post-Holocaust era. Responsibility emerged not only as a rallying cry, echoing of lives lost and the threatening technological advances of modernity, but also a critique of utopia, a concept at the center of both Karl Marx's and Ernst Bloch's work; Jonas writes, "It is the rule, stated primitively, that *the prophecy of doom is to be given greater heed than the prophecy of bliss*."[66] While first and foremost centered on human beings' responsibility to one another, Jonas extended his ethics of responsibility to human responsibility for the earth. Within Islam, obligations, the *taklif*, similarly undergird both an individual's world-centric acts, through law, and those aimed at the hereafter, through moral cultivation; thus, the *mukallaf*—the one subject to the obligation—is called to concurrently act upon intertwined responsibilities towards humanity, the earth, and God.[67]

Founded a decade ago as a weekly educational endeavor for non-Muslims interested in learning about Islam, this informal Wednesday evening group quickly morphed into a space for religious pedagogy by and for young Muslims, bringing to life an "open" vision of the mosque as a place to at once ground oneself in Islamic knowledge and engage in mainstream society. Obligations are taught to extend far beyond the embodiment of religious duty to enactments of civic duty, themselves understood as pious acts. This pedagogical approach draws extensively from Islamic sources to show how virtue is in fact attained through a particular form of *phronesis*: knowing and acting upon an obligation—as explicitly laid out in the revelation—to agentively harmonize the self and the Muslim community with the social and natural world. It further stresses the vitality of "affective knowledge," knowledge of the spirit, a concept developed by Jeanette Jouili in her research on women's revivalist learning circles in Germany and France.[68] In the words of Şehitlik Mosque teacher Arman, "Knowing God is knowledge of the heart." The epistemological project of this mosque thus emerges as an affective project of harmony and responsibility/obligation that moves from the heart of the moral subject outwards.

The Wednesday evening teachers, all young adults, many of them converts, describe the draw of Islam in emotional terms, inspired to embrace the religion by feelings of acceptance, connection, even love. Their knowledge-seeking projects, and later knowledge-sharing roles in the mosque, at once emerge from and remain rooted in affect. Maryam, born in Eastern Europe, recounts the acceptance she felt among Muslim students in her small Berlin school. Through them, she gained exposure to Islam, deciding to convert in her late teens. Huseyn, born to a German mother and an Arab father in Berlin, grew up in a "semi-Christian," "German-German" household, akin to most in his generation. Although his father did not play an active role in his life, Huseyn increasingly identified with Islam while attending high school with Maryam; he felt deeply drawn to Islam and at the same time to Maryam, whom he later married. The other teachers, a second-generation Turkish German man (Deniz) and a Jewish man who converted to Islam (Nasar), have long been part of the same group of friends.

bookmark Before the 2015 attempted coup in Turkey, three of these teachers (Arman, Huseyn, and Nasar) read from a book with the word "al-Nur," meaning "the light," inscribed on its cover during their lessons. The Light Movement, founded by Ottoman Kurdish scholar Said Nursi (1877–1960), reflects Şehitlik's vision in that it stresses Western modernity's easy marriage to Islam. Throughout his lifetime, Nursi commented extensively on the Qur'an and pushed for mass religious and science education; his compilation of writings, known holistically as *Risale-i Nur*, provided the foundations of a major revivalist movement that remained strong even during the secularist regime of Mustafa Kemal Atatürk, the war hero turned statesman who founded the Turkish Republic.[69] The *Risale-i Nur* also inspired the work and movement of Fethullah Gülen, former friend and now foe of Turkish president Erdoğan.[70] While these teachers describe learning about and through the Light Movement, they also assert that they do not remain part of it; and yet this connection is important for later sociopolitical developments at the Şehitlik Mosque. Even twice removed, it does not bode well for the community in the aftermath of the attempted coup, as the Turkish state accuses them of ties to Gülen (an accusation that I will return to in the afterword).

One immediately encounters the live, harmonizing vision of piety as reflective of, and reflecting on, the surrounding metropolis in the visual of this weekly meeting: pastel-blue Qur'ans open in the laps of attendants mouthing supplications in sync with babies crawling across the floor; fingers filled with prayer beads and tapping on iPhones. Most women wear headscarves, a few the abaya, others neither. Men wear jeans or khakis, a few prayer caps. Underneath this visual harmony, however, lie common experiences of disharmony—spurred by contestations over Muslim bodies, symbols, practices, and institutions in the public sphere. One Wednesday evening in early 2014, Nora explains that her negative experiences wearing a headscarf have continued to implicitly shape her educational experiences as she cannot find a place at her university to pray. She is afraid to ask university administrators, she says, as this would mark her as "more different." Such experiences lay bare how and why the mosque remains a protective space beyond the first generation, with the sense of being strange or stranger replaced by the opportunity to positively locate the self in shared affective knowledge.

A Change Inside

The self here emerges as a relational form (recall the triad of self-society-God), rooted in pedagogy that supports the individual in aligning her inner and outer selves, thereby transforming *Erlebnis* (individual lived experience) into *Erfahrung* (collective experience that can be communicated to others). In Arendtian terms, this entails a movement from *poiesis* (making) into *praxis* (habituated being/acting); in Aristotelian terms, it entails the integration of *poiesis* into *praxis* through *phronesis*, acts of moral agency constituted by practical, ethical knowledge.

Aristotle, and later Pierre Bourdieu, theorized habituated being/acting as *habitus*, the former giving greater credence to agency and the latter to social structure. In her influential work on women in the Islamic piety movement in Egypt, Saba Mahmood invokes Aristotle's original conceptualization of habitus, ingrained with self-reflexivity and choice, as she explores the cultivation of Muslim moral selves,

> Aristotelian in origin and adopted by the three monotheistic traditions, *habitus* in this older meaning refers to a specific pedagogical process by which moral virtues are acquired through a coordination of outward behavior (e.g. bodily acts, social demeanor) with inward dispositions (e.g. emotional states, thoughts, intentions).[71]

Bourdieu builds on the Aristotelian concept, reconceptualizing habitus as structures of norms that shape thinking and doing, discourse and action,

> Systems of durable, transposable dispositions, *structured structures* predisposed to function as *structuring structures*, that is, as principles which generate

and organize practices and representations that can be objectively adapted to their outcomes without presupposing a conscious aiming at ends or an express mastery of the operations necessary in order to attain them.[72] [emphasis added]

Daniel Winchester fuses the Bourdieusian and Aristotelian traditions in his US-based work on the "making of a Muslim moral habitus" among converts in Missouri. He argues that an interplay of cultural structure and agency, embodied in the repeated pious acts of adult converts to Islam, results in a Muslim moral habitus.[73] At Şehitlik, ideal and idealized embodiments of piety are often referenced vis-à-vis the Sunna, itself a prophetic habitus rooted in responsibility for the self, humanity, and the natural world; as Ware writes of the Islamic epistemological tradition, explicitly linking pedagogy to embodiment, "human 'bodies of knowledge' are made, not born."[74] This relates, he argues, not only to the vitality of human exemplars in Islam (a long line of prophets), but also to the very incarnation of each person, crafted by the hands of God.

Both Moosa and Jouili echo the centrality of the body in learning through the Islamic concept of *adab*, which Moosa defines as "a disposition toward knowledge."[75] This disposition, the infusion of knowledge into the project of the self, is not inherent; it requires work. One Wednesday evening in early 2014, Arman translates social experiences into theological terms, explaining that disharmony within a divided self and divided society calls for the active habituation of virtue in a turn towards God (invoking, again, the relational triad). As Jouili points out, virtue work in Islam diverges from Aristotle's idea of the stable, virtuous person; the virtuous Muslim is never complete, with virtue a constant effort, emerging only through ongoing struggle against one's *nafs* (here connoting the desiring soul).[76] As Armando Salvatore writes, "*Islam* as the keyword denoting surrender to Allah/God does not signify an accomplishment, but a new, continual beginning."[77]

In Spring 2014, Arman stresses that moral habitus first and foremost requires harmony within the self, fostered through the regular, embodied practice of Islam. Prayer, in particular, is fundamental to building knowledge of and sustaining internal harmony, as it binds the person through regular introspection and interaction with God.[78]

The aim of life, first it is *shahada* (declaration of faith), then we say salat (ritual prayer). This comes from our prophet, that it's second most important. First *iman* (faith)[79] and then directly after it comes prayer. Prayer is a form of supplication, *'ibada* (worship). Prayer is a support for *iman* . . . Prophet Muhammad *salla Allahu 'alayhi wa-salam* (God bless him and grant him peace) says it is a one-to-one dialogue between God and a person, a very meaningful interaction between God and human, nothing less. Prayer is the most important way that the Prophet created a binding with God—"So did I create a connection with him and you can also have this." Our prophet says that prayer is the aim of our life, religion, duty. He says, "One who destroys his ritual prayer destroys his religion."

Arman continues by discussing the reward of investing oneself in the five daily prayers, a moment of centering and connection that can transcend even the "double absence" entailed by familial histories of migration, colored by belonging fully neither to Germany nor to Turkey.[80] This act, this presence, being with God, is not linked to a particular geographical location—prayer can be carried out nearly anywhere on earth—instead evoking the casting off of an inherited estrangement. "Why is prayer important? How can you motivate yourself to pray even when it seems like a difficult task?" Arman provides an analogy to the German transportation system, how one can decide whether or not to buy a ticket. Here he signals what Jouili finds among her interlocutors in the revivalist movements in Germany and France—that every "process of self-transformation," laden with "doubts, ambiguities and tensions," is not naturalized but instead continuously achieved through effort and discipline.[81]

> If you buy a ticket, you can relax, whereas if you don't, you are more stressed and worried you will get caught. The end payment if you get caught is much higher (40 Euros) than the ticket (2.60 Euros) and thus it is better to just pay the ticket. Prayer is a kind of payment for eternal life, access to paradise. God has given us time and expects us to spend just one out of twenty-four hours praying, giving back to God, for which he will give eternity in heaven. So it's like someone saying, "I will give you 1,000 Euros and if you give me 100 back, then I will give you a million in return." It may be difficult to motivate yourself to pray, because you need to work, to make money, etc., and so that seems immediately important, but you are in essence paying your way into paradise and this is important. Also, who feels bad after prayer? Who says, "Now I feel shitty"? You always feel better after prayer. Now what about when someone says, "I can't do it anymore, five times a day, for a life of sixty years." How can he be motivated?

A teenage girl seated in front of me replies, "We eat to survive and it is a part of our daily routine and we could do the same thing with prayer." Arman nods his head, affirming, "Yes, it would be good if we could feel the same way about prayer as we do about eating. We pray in that we want to survive." The notion that repetitively undertaking the same act, through discipline, will cultivate its integration into the self as a means of daily subsistence, not praying *for* survival, but rather praying *to* survive, demonstrates how practice is seen to foster, sustain, and advance faith. As Arman says, "*iman* dies without practice." According to this lesson, depending on prayer will result in the deepening of knowledge, a "knowing of God" necessary for salvation, whereas a failure to pray will result in the "destruction of faith" through distance from God. "The greatest wisdom of prayer, what is the greatest wisdom? What happens? What should happen? Our purity changes. We change inside."

While Pierre Bourdieu maintains that habitus is socially determined in early life (through primary and secondary socialization in family and school, respectively), his related concept, "habitus *clivé*" ("cleaved," split, or divided habitus), produces an opportunity for its transformation—for what Arman terms "change inside." This concept suggests that habitus responds to new social realities, as "attitudes and dispositions are nurtured" through dynamic "cultural environments"; Bourdieu argues that significantly changed "conditions of existence," such as his own upward mobility, can forge a habitus *clivé*.[82] The Islamic tradition, however, contends with the idea that ways of being, rooted in both affective and practical ways of knowing, are never complete—with the human being endlessly malleable through learning and acting on knowledge, modeling the self through encounters with the prophetic tradition and the surrounding social world. At Şehitlik, it is thus not a shift in external "conditions of existence," but rather the internal cultivation of piety that continuously transforms a Muslim moral habitus, allowing for the reshaping of the self and with it one's relationship to the world.[83]

A Place in the World

Religious commitment turns the body of the Muslim not only inwards towards God, but also outwards towards society, in another layer of "corporeal remolding," a civic commitment that emerges from religious commitment.[84] Şehitlik's epistemological form, built on an ethics of responsibility—again in Islamic terms, an ethics of obligation—entwines the inward-facing cultivating of the soul and the outward-facing sustaining of the world which Arendt perceived as in conflict with one another.[85] As Deniz emphasizes, "People have a place in the world, each that exists has worth and responsibility. There is a reason people exist. They have a place in the mosque and in the world." This interweaving of place in the mosque and place in the world allows young Muslims in Berlin to develop identities tied to local social life in spite of their deep marginality.

To explicitly challenge social divisions both in and beyond the Muslim community, teachers invoke human unity. "Are you Sunni or are you Shiite? Are you Arab or Turk? Are you metal or rock?" asks Arman. "I am first and foremost a person, half-Arab, half-German, but very Muslim. What I mean by Muslim is that I understand that I am a guest of God's world, we are all kids of Adam. My name is *insan* [human]. Then I am Muslim." He pauses. "*Similarities*, give people a chance, get to know them, take the opportunity to get to know them." This is taken one step further afield, from society to the earth, in plans for the 2013 Open Mosque Day, held on October 3, the symbolically potent anniversary of German reunification. Its theme is "Environmental Protection: Mosques Are Engaged." Here collapsing place in the mosque to place in the world, Deniz calls on his students to recognize their obligation to care for the earth, as "the whole earth is a mosque." As he draws out in this lesson, not only can prayer take place nearly everywhere on earth, but the earth (water, and sand when there is no water) is also used for purification before prayer, again suggesting the interdependence of piety and the natural world. Deniz continues, "The entire earth is a mosque, which is why tomorrow we are talking about environmentalism. One interpretation is that the mosque must be clean and the whole world is a mosque so this means that all people should be responsible for the whole world."

Such harmonization of the self with society and the earth that holds us is not a modest project; it is a strenuous act of fulfilling religious obligations in spite of significant sociopolitical constraints. It bears weight, the heavy lifting in its constancy, to continuously invoke belonging while meeting exclusions, facing resistance with determination in daily life. By refuting top-down hierarchies superimposed onto their very beings in discourse and action—"so many times, I have been told to go back home, to my country"—these self-identified Muslim Berliners transcend taken-for-granted oppositions between piety and civility. For instance, they encourage one another to "dress Islamically" for the outward-facing Open Mosque Day as they discuss the Islamic roots of environmentalism. When they recount their struggles, daily brushes with discrimination—being yelled at, spit at, belittled—teachers respond not with the salve of comfort or affirmation, but rather questions meant to spur critical reflection: "What do you do in this case? Give up or go further? The way is the goal? Or is the goal the way?"

In this series of questions, Arman signals Cohen's idea that consistency, through ongoing striving and practice, is the path to fulfillment both in this

FIGURE 3. Interior of the main sanctuary of the Şehitlik Mosque. Photo by author.

FIGURE 4. Chandelier, adorned with ostrich eggs, in the main sanctuary of the Şehitlik Mosque. Photo by author.

world and the next.[86] Islam does not provide these Muslim youth with answers, but instead the moral agency to question the status quo in body and in
soul through the acquisition of affective knowledge reflected in both, to "overcome evil with good," seeking "satisfaction through God" as they confront the
inequities of German society. They reject a prism of "either/or" (either Muslim or German, Muslim or citizen, Muslim or civil) replacing it with a vision of
"and, and, and" (Muslim and Berliner and human being and, ultimately, "guest
in this world"), in the cultivation of pious harmony through the interwoven
layers of self, society, and nature. This is an act of reconciliation, rather than
hyphenation. Cohen writes of the layered act of reconciliation, with the self
nested within society under the reign of God.[87] "Without the peace, which I
establish with my fellow man, I cannot have any hope of reconciliation with
God, and as little can I hope for inner peace in myself."[88] Cohen understands
peace as the ultimate form of harmony, as "the Bible calls this harmonization
of the whole of morality peace."[89] At Şehitlik, reconciliation of the self with
society and the larger natural world is similarly sought by the *mukallaf*, the responsible, the obliged, through moral and social harmonization. This vision
of harmony infuses not only the words of mosque teachers, nor only the bodies of their students who act upon the knowledge herein endowed, but also
this building that holds them, where sparrows' wings touch ostrich eggs, opening beneath arches that emulate trees; and where a golden chandelier throws
shadows like the sun that rises and falls for everyone.

Yusuf: "What is kosher?"

"In Germany you don't have this borderline. There is no difference between
Turkish and Muslim. There is no difference between, I don't know, Arab and
Muslim. There is no difference between turban and Muslim. There is no difference between headscarf and Muslim. So it's really, they just look at you as
different. They just look at you, that's the point. They just look at you." Seated
on the carpet in the main sanctuary of the Şehitlik Mosque, Yusuf leans against
the wall and sighs. He comes to the mosque often to give tours to schoolchildren, police officers, government employees, retirees, and parolees, among
others.

Yusuf grew up and lives in Schöneberg, a nearby West Berlin district. And
he realized when he entered university, also in West Berlin, how little he
knew about Islam; he wanted to learn and thus began exploring mosques
throughout the city. He settled on this mosque four years ago because of the
feelings it evoked in him, its affective power as a visual reminder of his child-

hood visits to Turkey. Soon, it gave him the opportunity not only to learn, but to teach.

Last year, Yusuf's curiosity led him farther afield, to an exchange program in Kentucky, where he spent a semester abroad. His perceptions of German society were shifted by this experience.

> I told them I was from Turkey and they told me, "But I heard you and your friend speaking German, so why are you speaking German if you're from Turkey?" And I said, "Yeah, I live in Germany. I didn't move there. I was born there." "OK, doesn't that make you German?" So that was a new perspective for me. I met people who were born in Ethiopia and still defined themselves as American . . . They asked me, "Why is it so hard for you to identify with the country you live in?" And I said, "When the country you live in accepts you the way you are is different from when it forces you to adapt certain ideas that are not even necessary to live in a harmonic community."

"Harmony." It's a word Yusuf regularly speaks, and it colors his motivations to give tours of the mosque. He strives to show the inherent harmony between Islam and mainstream society on his tours, from the dome of the mosque and the dome of the church reaching towards the same heavens, to the origins of the university in Muslim societies. He doesn't always find time for prayer, he explains, but sees the tours themselves as a pious practice. "I can't participate in everything. I just put my priority on doing tours, working with young people and I think that's what I can do right now. Right now, that's enough for me, sometimes even too much."

When I ask him what he has learned by leading these tours, he first says "patience" with difficult and provocative questions. Most of all, he later reflects, he has learned the vitality of knowledge in the intertwined shaping of himself as a better person and the shaping of a better world. "Everybody has to learn from each other and it's one of the most important intentions of Islam, that the Prophet Muhammad, peace be upon him, he said 'if the knowledge is in China, go there, go to China.' So this connection between different cultures is so important. That's why we are here." Today, Yusuf is especially interested in interreligious work—"our bigger family are people of the book"—and has participated in events like Weihnukkah (combining the word *Weihnacht*, meaning Christmas, and Hanukkah), a theater show for the Jewish community in the mosque. With laughing eyes, Yusuf recounts the first time that he recognized the affinity between Muslims and Jews, stood in front of a vending machine with kosher Haribo, a German gummy candy that in its nonkosher form is made with gelatin. "I asked, 'What is kosher?' And so, for the first time, I put coins inside and bought some Haribo."

TOURS AS PIOUS PRACTICES

Judging by the skies, today is the first day of spring, clouds opening to a blue that hibernates for Berlin's long winter of short, gray days. In the early afternoon, children sit at the threshold of the Şehitlik Mosque, carefully unlacing their shoes, subsequently placed in rows by the door. They push it open in unison, heavy against their small frames, moving their feet—whether sock-clad or bare—across the literal threshold of the mosque. "To step across the threshold was to take leave of the upper world," writes Benjamin, describing his immersion in the waters of a swimming pool near Krummestrasse in Berlin.[90] A century later in same city, Benjamin's words echo in my mind as I watch a class of children step into the mosque, an architectural form long coded as opaque and dangerous, if not as a lower world. Juxtaposed with these stereotypes, the beautifully ornate dome, split open by stained glass, rises towards the sky; below it, children sink their feet into carpets the color of the sea.

From the softness of the carpets to the firmness of prayer beads pressed between forefinger and thumb, mosque tour guides—Wednesday evening students transformed into teachers—engage visitors through deeply sensual experiences paired with riveting storytelling. Stories from the Qur'an and the life of the Prophet Muhammad intersect with seeing and touching in the mosque to build affective knowledge in the guide and visitors alike, with "knowing . . . produced as much by the limbs as by the mind."[91] This layering of experience gives texture to the Islamic tradition and to a Muslim space in the metropolis, while the stories told translate religious texts and lives to unfamiliar audiences. Here the guide contends with marginality vis-à-vis the interweaving of embodied and discursive Islamic forms that stress social horizontality in place of hierarchy.

Twice each day, second-generation tour guides break down assumptions about Islam and Muslims by leading diverse groups of visitors through a crash course in the religion's theology, history, and architecture. Not only schoolchildren, but also university students, government employees, police officers (for a period, all officers in the city), and the formerly incarcerated attend tours at the Şehitlik Mosque, many required to undertake such visits as part of a larger diversity curriculum or training. While serving outsiders of the community, the tour also serves to cultivate the body and mind of the guide; this repeated daily act is part of a larger process of self-cultivation achieved through hard work and discipline. Guides describe tours as jihad (defined by my interlocutors as "a spiritual struggle in the name of God"), in the tradition of the Sunna, and even "more important than prayer." They term leading tours a "calling" that crosses spiritual and civic realms: contending with their undercaste status, as they move from positions of subordination in mainstream public life to positions of authority on their own literal and epistemological grounds.

While unique among Muslim communities, affect for Jews in Germany has long been invoked via requisite site visits to former concentration camps and Jewish memorials. Tours of former concentration camps center specifically on Denkmal-Arbeit, memorialization work, in which visitors, most often students, become imbued with a deep sense of responsibility for Germany's historical wrongdoings. They are linked to Germanness through physical encounters with a shared, dark past.[92] The Şehitlik Mosque tour, on the other hand, focuses on overcoming contemporary marginalities by deconstructing stereotypes about the Islamic tradition. In both cases, the tour is an embodied means to build affective knowledge and responsibility across groups, aiming to transcend "moral exclusion" present and past.[93]

During these tours, schoolchildren hold turquoise prayer beads in their hands, with police officers invited to run their fingers along the large ostrich eggs inscribed into the mosque interior. Through multiple sensory experiences, they call on those guided to "feel the feel of carpets underneath your feet," "walk under its archways," "touch prayer beads," listen to the "sound of birds flying through the room" or the "call to prayer with intent." "Hold this in your hands," "the mosque is a space open to everybody." This multidimensional experience of body and mind purposefully contends with the view that Muslims are strangers, if not dangerously deviant, by fostering affect, sentiments of familiarity and unity in particular. These linked moments of physical and emotional contact undermine the untouchability fostered by associations with incivility, at the same time countering colonial or imperial aphasia.[94] In the words of Yusuf,

> When we started tours here, our motto was not to discuss with people, or not to justify anything or not to debate. Our intention is to build bridges, that's the important thing for us. Because you can discuss everything. You can sit here and discuss the Super Bowl and it will take one month and we still wouldn't come under one roof, we would still discuss. So, building bridges is the most important thing, to have a connection, a healthy connection and to live in peace. Islam means peace. And that's why this is our intention.

Here Yusuf invokes Cohen's dualistic understanding of peace: as both power and goal. Cohen scholar Peter Schmid argues that "this double definition forms the basis for the idea of harmony of the individual and humanity."[95] This double harmony, at once within the individual and within humanity, lies at the heart of the mosque tour as it does the Wednesday evening lessons— with the harmony cultivated in the embodiment of the tour as a pious practice inextricably linked to the cultivation of collective harmony. As students seat themselves on the floor in a circle at the center of the room, Yusuf quotes the Qur'an. "One day, We shall make the mountains move, and you will see the earth as an open plain. We shall gather all people together, leaving no one: sura [chapter] 18, verse 47." He continues in a soft voice, just loud enough for the group to hear. "People, We created you all from a single man and a single woman, and made you into races and tribes so that you should recognize one another: sura 49, verse 13."

A Mosque Without Pillars, a World Without Trees

While the Kaaba in papier-mâché is meant to symbolize the place of Islam in the world, equalizing access to a divine place and act through its symbolic diffusion across other social contexts, the mosque is invoked in the tour to symbolize the larger world within Islam. Of the tours, mosque teacher Aida reflects, "We always want to show this to the outside. To say 'we are like you, so to speak. We can live together with one another.' That is what we show in these activities . . . I am everything, I have a piece in me from all." Highlighting the civic ideals of broader German/Berlin society in their tours, guides at no point break with a rootedness in the religious tradition. Rather, they employ verified Islamic sources that evidence latent commonalities between mainstream civic ideals and Islamic ethics. This includes emphasizing the role of female leaders and a democratically elected mosque board, and discussing environmental concerns (Germany long referenced as "the Greenest Nation") in Islamic terms.[96] Tour guides describe the mosque as a smaller replica of the globe that must be cared for and preserved, while engaging mosque visitors in this exercise, asking them to locate representations of the natural environment in its physical form. As Yusuf says to a tour group:

> Your task: look around. Do you see anything that makes you think of the world outside? . . . Now use your imagination . . . the carpets are seas, the blue and white decor the heaven and clouds. The gold chandelier in the middle of the room, the sun . . . What would happen to this mosque if I were to cut down all

the trees [the pillars] here? It would collapse. What would happen if we cut all of the trees in the world? It would fall apart. You take off your shoes, sit, are respectful, but this is a copy—there are no real rivers, no real trees, and when I treat this well, then I also have to treat the true trees, the true lakes, the true world with respect.

Tour guides also move beyond finding common ground with secular German ideals, as they explicitly draw parallels with Christianity—a key historical and many argue present-day normative cultural structure in Germany as Europe— and also Judaism. Bringing attention to overlapping traditions and symbols that constitute a larger Abrahamic whole, they highlight the Christian origins of the dome structure, as suggesting connections to a higher place and higher being. They describe prayer beads held in their hands, passed around the circle of visitors, as similar to a rosary. They note the importance of Jesus to Muslims; and the long line of prophets, such as Moses, Abraham, and Joseph, shared with Christianity and Judaism. Deniz explains to neighborhood residents that the word "Allah" is used by Christians in Muslim-majority societies when they speak of God, e.g., in Egypt, where Coptic Christians too call on Allah in their prayers. In his tours, Yusuf focuses on connections to Judaism, as he describes the physical layout and material symbols in the mosque.

> You won't find any traditional mosques without the Star of David—even in Russia directly above the mihrab [a niche within the mosque wall, to which congregants orient themselves during prayer]. In the village of my mother [in Turkey], there is the first verse of the Qur'an and under it the Star of David. Two hundred, or 150 years ago, if you had a Star of David around your neck, they thought you were Muslim, not Jewish. You will find them in every traditional mosque.[97]

On multiple occasions, those touring the mosque join the discussion by drawing their own parallels between the familiar religious tradition, Christianity, and Islam. On a neighborhood tour in autumn 2014, one woman cites the Crusades "as proof that not only Muslims, but also Christians have misused and employed violence for political means." A young man, at the mention of Jesus, claims he was the "second most important prophet for Islam . . . not the same, but still majorly important." Years later, this moment replays in my mind at a dinner in Charlottesville, Virginia. "Who's the Jesus figure in Islam?" the man seated next to me asks. "Jesus," I respond, transported in spirit if not body to that evening in the mosque, and the fluttering of lace curtains like eyes about to open, as they let in the day's last light.

Such discussions in the mosque are not always tinged with optimism or centered on finding common ground. During the same autumn tour, an elderly man from the neighborhood insists on discussing suicide bombers. This evokes a friction-filled exchange. "What religion allows you to strap bombs to your body and [blow] other people up?" he asks. Deniz, the evening's guide answers "no religion," and many voices in the room respond in unison, "great answer!" A woman beside Deniz interrupts, explaining that other religions, including Christianity, have "also used violence" and that "danger lies in all forms of radicalism." A man seated on the other side of Deniz defensively interjects, attempting to draw an at-once temporal and symbolic boundary between Christian civility and Muslim incivility: "That was a different time. Christians don't do that anymore!"

At no point, however, do such moments of friction produce critiques of the colonial and imperial projects that violently unsettled whole societies, leading to the mass migration of Muslims to Europe in the mid-twentieth century. At no point is violence *against the Muslim body* by, and in, European state projects interrogated. The tours thus do not create the space for overarching political critique of the deep marginality and parallel surveillance experienced by Muslims; they instead offer a view into an apolitical and often dehistoricized Islam, in a project that seeks to foster and maintain harmony at a potentially very high cost. With the bracketing out of the political, friction may disrupt stereotypes about Muslims, but it does not shake the foundations, the founding myths of the system that produces them.

This particular silence and the question it evokes brings to mind another project of the children of immigrants, that of the Harkis' daughters in France. Beginning in the early 2000s, Hadjila Kemoum, Zahia Rahmani, Dalila Kerchouche, and Fatima Besnaci-Lancou wrote texts situating the individual memories of their fathers within France's collective memory. Nested within a larger political movement to incorporate colonial histories into official national history, these emerged after then-President Jacques Chirac declared that "the Harkis are entirely French. They enjoy the respect and the recognition of the national community," soon after followed by the first official Harki Remembrance Day on September 25, 2001.[98] Before then, knowledge of the Harkis had remained largely relegated to family histories, a private, intergenerational reckoning with the dual rejection of the Harkis, as traitors by Algeria and as so-called "refugees" and Muslims by France. Through these written acts of unsilencing personal histories, their daughters exposed the discrimination and scapegoating at the heart of the Harkis' experiences, and the memories of these "Others" came to infuse collective French memory. Controversial, political, and also deeply historicized, what was long an identity imbued with shame became contextualized in the French colonial project by writers "from below."[99] This aside serves as the provocation for further questioning about the mosque tour as a critical project among the children of immigrants in Berlin: Would exposing and interrogating the violent histories that have led to present marginality offer an agentive opportunity to crack open collective memory "from below"? Or is there a reason for this silence, this absence?

The First Universities

Over time I come to see the mosque tour not as shaking, but rather building foundations: that its greatest offering lies in the moral agency it cultivates in Muslims who learn and teach from the Islamic epistemological tradition. The mosque tour is a natural extension or enactment of the Wednesday evening lessons, further cultivating *adab*, a disposition towards knowledge in both the guide and the guided. Stressing the vitality of fostering knowledge within the self and imparting knowledge to others, guides consistently note that mosques were, in fact, always places of learning: "the first universities." On Yusuf's school tour, he calls on the visiting children as they exit the mosque to continue to build on their knowledge about Islam. Again employing the hadith literature, he smiles widely and says: "The Prophet Muhammad, may peace be upon him, said that 'seeking knowledge is an obligation for everybody, from the cradle to the grave.'" Yusuf later describes his duty as a Muslim to not only seek, but share the knowledge he has gained. Similarly, Tuba asserts, "In Islam you learn that once you know the Qur'an, once you really know it, it is *your obligation* to teach it the best that you can."

Piety thus not only motivates the assumption of the role of tour guide, but the tour becomes itself a way to express piety through knowledge sharing by the student-cum-teacher. This capacity to move from student to teacher is described through notions of human equality, as religious leadership does not stand "above" but rather "on the same level as the community;" Yusuf points this out during a tour in which he explains that the imam must bend down to enter the mihrab, an act of humility (a virtue often assigned to the Prophet Muhammad), signaling submission to God. On her social media platform, another guide, Betül, similarly describes humility, as well as the prophetic example, in the mosque tour.

There are people who have never been in a mosque, and they don't know how Muslims pray, they don't know what they wear and what should be worn and they are uncertain, sometimes afraid. When such a person comes to visit the mosque then I have great respect for his openness, interest, and courage. It's not always easy to open yourself up, to get to know something foreign. I believe that we as Muslims in our community must have a lot of openness and thankfulness for this courage, for those who stand uncertain in front of the door . . . In our training, we learn from mosque leaders: community work is relationship work. What will be recalled from the mosque visit is not the definition of zakat [almsgiving], but the emotions that you feel when you visit. And that alone is a community in our hands . . . Let us shine, especially in our mosques, where we act as believers and represent our faith—it's Sunna!

In enacting the Sunna (virtues and habits modeled by the Prophet Muhammad), guides not only draw from the religious tradition during the tour but cast the tour within it—an invocation of the habitus that they strive to foster within themselves. Seen as a link in a chain of tradition, the tour is a way for Islam to be learned, taught, and *lived* in the Berlin metropolis. As young German residents and citizens, Berliners, and ethnic minorities, these guides consistently note how this position of the guide also guides them in becoming "good" or "better" Muslims.

While they avoid uncomfortable reckonings with an uncomfortable past, the tours remain an agentive means of both making the self and making a dwelling for the Muslim community in Berlin: "to stand for something in Germany" (as Ali puts it) as the second generation and beyond come to straddle multiple social worlds, while remaining or becoming rooted in their piety. The children of immigrants—the ultimate strangers, in that they have migrated from nowhere, yet occupy an ambiguous position in the German nation-state—are different from their parents and grandparents in how they straddle Islam, Europe, Germany, Turkey, and Berlin. They innovate as they strive to articulate and harmonize their identities perhaps not first and foremost for mosque visitors, but for themselves, in the necessary negotiations entailed by "doing religion" in a context of marginality.[100] The position of the guide thus uniquely endows young Muslims with the capacity to transform social hierarchy into horizontality through the Islamic tradition and to powerfully communicate this tradition to mosque visitors.

While guiding is a pious practice among the second generation, generational tensions relating to the meaning of the mosque as space and opportunity for exchange emerge here. For the first generation, the mosque as a place of emotional ownership and protection has proved the antidote to experiences of inequity and indignity in public life. Ayşe, for instance, contrasts her work

F I G U R E 5 . Cultural center next to the Şehitlik Mosque. Photo by author.

cleaning Berlin's public schools with her position as an Islamic school teacher in the mosque. Contextualized by the echo of her personal past, she, like many others, takes issue with the disturbance of religious practice, such as "tours that interrupt prayer," "women who enter without headscarves," and "events that disturb" the quiet recitation of the Qur'an. This tension is deepened with the erection of a cultural center next to the mosque in winter 2015, which hosts art exhibitions and academic conversations; tellingly, it has a separate entrance from the street.

This tension is not unique to Şehitlik, however, but instead reflects a broader schism in revivalist movements across Europe, where the first genera- tion are castigated for being too "ethnic" rather than embracing "true Islam" by subsequent generations—enlivening a critical Islamic lens that comes to bear not only on mainstream society, but on their Muslim communities.[101] Elif, a young public school teacher, recounts an iftar at the mosque in which her mother refused to eat with a South Asian Muslim family, expressing nothing short of disgust—thereby alluding to internal ethnoracial hierarchies in the mosque community. "I told her that Islamically that is wrong," Elif says, shak- ing her head. Yet the second generation and beyond do not simply dissolve such ethnocultural hierarchies, as their own celebration of both society-wide and inner-Muslim diversity exists alongside of the valorization of Turkish

Islam as the exemplar par excellence of a religion of harmony. Even a vision of harmony, it appears, is not free from hierarchy, contradiction, and dissonance.

Esra: "Tap-tap-tap-crack"

In her kitchen, as the everyday sounds of the city—children playing soccer on the street, cars skidding to a stop at lights—mingle with the sounds of home, Esra's husband opens walnuts at the table with a "tap-tap-tap-crack." Each shell burst open makes her laugh and shake her head. "Stubborn," Esra says, nodding at the large bag of walnuts sat beside him, a "deal" that absorbs hours of his day. Having grown up on a hazelnut orchard outside of Istanbul, she is familiar, she is intimate, with the sound of nutshells opened and the soft skin inside.

Today, Esra's phone is ringing off the hook. Friends and acquaintances from the mosque are calling. "There are women's breasts in a painting at Şehitlik," she says, shaking her head. She is referring to a cultural center erected beside the mosque building, hosting art exhibitions and academic workshops. The first installation displayed in the cultural center covers the history of the Tatars. One of the posters depicts a line of women in a sketch, two with the tops of their bosoms exposed. At the opening event, first-generation Turkish Muslim women including Esra express dismay at this brazen portrayal of cleavage, regardless of its historical veracity, a conversation that continues beyond the mosque. "Who knows who did this," she continues, intermittently picking up her phone to converse about the controversy. The walnuts are opened—"tap-tap-tap-crack"—as the children below shriek in revelry. Esra's daughter interjects from another room. "It's a historical fact!" she says of the depiction, "and anyway, it's art, you can't fight it." She joins us in the living room. "Don't be shattered," she advises her mother.

Esra is a closed book with an open mind. A private extrovert. Curious and determined. Soft-hearted but hardened by life. She looks for opportunity, and protection, in the mosque and other corners of the city—leafy green gardens and homes—where she meets her friends. She taught herself to read the Qur'an as an antidote to her retired husband's sudden presence each day at home, soon after they returned from the hajj over two decades go. These days, she attends a recitation class at Şehitlik, led by the imam's wife, meeting her friends before and after in the women's room above the teahouse. Sometimes she invites me to meet her at a neighborhood mosque or to her garden in the city to socialize with the same friends. Sometimes, when we walk home, to the garden, or to the mosque, men in cars shake their heads, sharing their disapproval of her form in a city they believe to be theirs alone. Here she also laughs—a laugh ringing with anger rather than amusement—and also shakes her head. Sometimes, she curses them or yells. Every time, for a second, so quick to pass, she winces, her face moved by the pain that she cannot mask.

Men in cars. Bosoms in the mosque. They have more in common than one might suspect. When I think of Esra now, what Mayanthi Fernando terms "the right to indifference" again comes to mind.[102] And I recall Yusuf describing the power of a differentiating gaze ("they just look at you as different. They just look at you")—normalcy and, with it, freedom to move through the city's streets, appears as a taken-for-granted luxury.

When we arrive, whether at Şehitlik, the garden, or her home, Esra always removes her shoes, slides on slippers and makes her way to the bathroom to cleanse herself of the city's soot. In these mundane moments, she brings not only water but relief to her face. "Don't be shattered," her daughter says. She is far from shattered; yet she is wounded again and again and again by those faces, their mouths turned upside down. She has struggled to make a life in this metropolis, to dwell by "fashioning a shell."[103] "Tap-tap-tap-crack," the walnuts sound, their splitting shells her symphony.

CHAPTER 4

Ordinary Angels: The Şehitlik Mosque and the Metropolis

In an office outfitted in neo-Ottoman style, perched on an intricately embroidered sofa atop hand-tied Turkish carpets, Deniz plans the Open Mosque Day with a group of community volunteers. Tea glass filled to its brim, balanced between forefinger and thumb, he explains to the room of young community volunteers that "no one is going to put this mosque on his shoulders and take it back to Turkey. This is a Berlin Mosque. It should represent and be embraced by Berliners." Deniz speaks of the mosque as not only in but *of* the metropolis, demonstrative of what Richard Sennett terms the "open city" in its architectural and social form. An "open city" depends on the creation of dynamic spaces for encounters; yet an "open city" is not only a material project, made malleable with "ambiguous," "porous wall[s]," but also an ethical project made of plural encounters intent on forging cohesion.[1] Similarly, the Şehitlik Mosque community is not made, nor made into a dwelling, in isolation from the metropolis in which it stands; it is also an ethical project that carves out spaces for plural encounters both within and beyond its architectural form. This mosque community invokes a process of *sympoiesis*—that is making together with and in the city, on a richly symbolic piece of Turkish land in Berlin. And this making together takes many forms, including bringing the city into the mosque through tours, or, as in the story that follows, bringing the mosque into the city through the Jewish-Muslim Salaam-Schalom Initiative.

The Salaam-Schalom Initiative, which both holds meetings at the mosque and encourages mosque constituents to participate in other urban spaces, draws on a shared sense of dislocation from the nation-state, fostering instead a rootedness in the metropolis. During a symbolically potent Salaam-Schalom art installation held in Jewish and Muslim homes throughout the Neukölln neighborhood in winter 2015, I find myself at the threshold of an unidentifiable apartment—a Jewish mezuzah protecting the entryway, beside it Qur'anic verse inscribed onto the wall. "There is a desperate need for a third way, one that neither strives to divide nor wants to be divided, but seeks to bring people together around something closer and more tangible: the cities we live in and share as our homes," writes journalist William Glucroft in his subsequent coverage of this initiative.[2] "It is ours," says a young Salaam-Schalom member, bumming a cigarette on the apartment's balcony, when I ask who the home belongs to. "It is ours," I repeat, as my toddler, born to a Jewish mother and Muslim father, traces Arabic letters with his tiny forefinger on the wall.

This home, in its ambiguity, powerfully disorients by stopping our categorizations of each other, of "the Other" in their tracks, reflecting the larger vision of Salaam-Schalom. In so doing, it fosters the power to tell the story of the city in terms that challenge the civil/uncivil divide. "The power to narrate," writes Edward Said, "or to block other narratives from forming and emerging, is very important to culture and imperialism, and constitutes one of the main connections between them."[3] One of the most powerful and enduring cultural narratives, integral to Berlin and the German nation-state alike, is that of lost Jewish life. Here, the act *sympoiesis*, fashioning a dwelling in the metropolis that is "ours," both at and extending outwards from the Şehitlik Mosque, meets the Jewish populace in Berlin's lived present rather than its potent, vanished past. Here, in the mosque as in the apartment with its twin inscriptions of Old Testament and Qur'anic verse, spoken and embodied narratives challenge the supposed Jewish-Muslim divide. At the same time, the complex social arena of Jewish-Muslim relations reveals the limits of agency, delimited by the perceived Muslim threat that disrupts the everyday life of the mosque and its bonds with the metropolis.

Yakup: "Raised by Berlin and a village"

Yakup grew up in the heart of West Berlin in a one-bedroom apartment with his parents and two sisters, their windowsill a haven for the city's sparrows. He played soccer with the neighborhood's children on the flat concrete beneath their home, called up each evening by the siren song of his mother's cooking— cornbread charred at the edges and yogurt fermented in the kitchen. Having spent his childhood summers in Turkey, he still sees himself as part of the

"1.5 generation," straddling two places in body and spirit alike (not so much either nation, but the city of Berlin and an Anatolian village that he does not name). "I was raised by Berlin and a village outside of Istanbul," he once told me. As he entered adolescence, Yakup read novels in Turkish in his living room and novels in German in bookstores until they closed their doors at night, releasing him into the quiet of the city center's streets. He biked home past the Siegessäule, a "victory column" built to commemorate Prussian victory in the 1870–71 war with France; moved to its current site by the Nazis in 1938, it is today located at the "Great Star," an urban axis connecting east and west.

Yakup loved history and stories, the remnants of what was and the dreams of what could be. He loved the concrete jungle of his youth, the Brothers Grimm buried side-by-side in a graveyard where he wandered aimlessly, throwing stones into the willing mouth of grass. He didn't love the teachers who failed to call on him, or later, the university professors who questioned his capacity to complete a graduate degree.

Yakup's negative experiences motivated him to seek respite in the city, his city. On the weekends, he attended Islamic school at a local Turkish mosque. A model recitation student, he won competition after competition and the fatherly heart of his Islamic school teacher. As he explored the city, he began to work with the Jewish community in Berlin. And always, from childhood until adulthood, he read and he read, devouring texts in his two mother tongues. Yakup describes the wandering spirit that led him as a young adult out of Berlin, to France, where between the sloping mountains and the never-ending sea, he embraced an anonymity gained by speaking a foreign language.

Even when he looks back with nostalgia today, to the overgrown stones celebrating masters of the German fairy tale, there are wounds: the wounds of his mother who migrated as a teenager, too young to leave home, and the wounds of his father, a worker who was anything but guest—worked to the bone. And there are his wounds alone, of being told in no uncertain terms that he "could not do everything a German could do," "being downgraded time and again," beginning in primary school with a spelling bee.

Still, almost two decades later, what others see as his weakness, his piety, Yakup knows as his greatest strength. It connects him to his ancestors, to his family, to his first strivings and successes in Islamic school, and to the knowledge that he would thrive, in spite of everything. It helps him to hold the past, the present, and the future in his heart and his mind at one and the same time. It allows him to cross into other communities in the city where he resides and far beyond. It grounds him, again and again, in Berlin as in Anatolia.

WINGS OF DESIRE: MUSLIM-JEWISH AFFINITIES

To dwell in Berlin—heavy with history and hard-edged soul, reborn through acts of severing and reunification—requires a reconciling with its layered histories and the stories that they carry forward. It is a new (old) capital scattered with old angels, ephemeral and material, made of cement and gold, the epitome of the latter erected in the Siegessäule, subject of Walter Benjamin's *Berlin Childhood* epigraph: "O brown-baked column of victory, With winter sugar of childhood days."[4] Before the Berlin Wall fell—or was rather ascended en masse by East Germans, bringing the Communist project to an end—German filmmaker Wim Wenders wrote and produced the film *Himmel über Berlin* ("The Sky over Berlin," called *The Wings of Desire* in its English-language rendition). In it, he captures the spirit of a city brought to its knees, with the victory column, the place in the film where angels meet, rising as an emblem of both triumph and defeat. In the melancholy, often-desolate images of Berlin in its post-WWII era of partition, an angel searches for an ordinary sense of dwelling, a place to close his wings and ground his feet. The angel speaks: "Instead of forever hovering above I'd like to feel a weight grow in me to end the infinity and to tie me to earth. I'd like, at each step, each gust of wind, to be able to say 'Now. Now and now.'"[5]

"Now. Now and now" Muslims seek to dwell, to ground themselves, their families, and communities in Berlin. And the narrative of Şehitlik as site of not only crossing and making, but also dwelling, harks to an unexpected space and time: modern Jewish Berlin. While the markings of the Holocaust, from the *Stolpersteine* to the stone labyrinth of the Memorial for the Murdered Jews of Europe, imprint the cityscape, so too do other, lesser-known Jewish histories, which belong—even if so often silenced—to the conversation about pluralism in the metropolis.

Although Jews were present in what are today German territories, including Berlin, since the Middle Ages, the social and economic thriving of Jewish communities followed the eighteenth-century emancipation of Jews. In Berlin's east, Jewish life centered around the Scheunenviertel, a neighborhood still marked by the once-central synagogue (the Neue Sinagogue, or New Synagogue, built 1859–66), and a Jewish graveyard, burial place of Moses Mendelssohn, father of the Haskalah (the Jewish Enlightenment).[6] In its west, the Bavarian Quarter once had a large Jewish populace (an estimated 7–8 percent of its population was Jewish in the early twentieth century, in comparison to an estimated 4 percent of the city's overall population) and flourishing intellectual life. The markings of this past remain only in memorials, such as the plaque where the Münchenerstrasse synagogue stood until it was burned to the ground during Kristallnacht, and of course the signposts, the stumbling stones.[7]

By bringing Şehitlik into conversation with the echoes of this Jewish past, a productive parallel can be made with the Jewish salons at the turn of the nineteenth century, subject of Hannah Arendt's writings. Throughout this city the salon thrived as an "idyllic mixed society that was the object of so many dreams," uniting Jews and Christians in a rich discursive environment, at once subculture and rebellion against ethnoreligious and gendered social restrictions.[8] More than utopia, salons promised egalitarian innovation and intimacy—attempting to break boundaries through the leadership of enterprising Jewish women (like Rahel Varnhagen, whose biography Arendt wrote), delivering if for a moment the hope for "an alternative form of public sphere."[9] While the institution was the home, and the host intelligentsia, the spirit of the Jewish salon is echoed by the Şehitlik Mosque today, in the fostering of *Bildung* through knowledge-building practices in gatherings with "the Other," and the infusion of this knowledge into new narratives that are both spoken and lived. An openness of "the Other's" intimate space, whether living rooms or spiritual sanctuary, and the narratives inspired—in the form of art, literature, and music in the salon or a harmonizing of religious and civic life in the mosque—transcend taken-for-granted divisions in chosen encounters, colored by the promise of a moment, the wrenching beauty of a passing song.[10]

"Narrativity is constitutive of identity," writes political theorist Seyla Benhabib.[11] And the narrative constituting the identity of Berlin is one laden with Jewish legacies, from the intermezzo promise of the salon to the haunting of the Holocaust.[12] Today, nothing, nowhere, and no one in the city is exempt from reckoning with the many strata of, in a collective striving for, reconciliation with the past. Monuments have been built from the ground to the sky, school pedagogy imbues children with a responsibility for history, and a strict criminalization of the incitement of hatred (*Volksverhetzung*) marks the young federal constitution.[13] Nested within this larger historical narrative about Jewish life is the contemporary narrative of Jewish-Muslim relations in Germany and its capital. Over the past decade, Muslims and Jews in Berlin have faced overlapping conflicts with the mainstream vis-à-vis the governance of religious expression, while also facing conflict with one another over Israel-Palestine.[14] The recent resurgence of anti-Semitism in Europe, often blamed on Muslims albeit coinciding with growing anti-Muslim sentiment, has merely added to the complexity of Jewish-Muslim relations in this metropolis, laying metaphorical stumbling stones on a topography with abundant Muslim and Jewish life.[15]

The potentiality of the city, its histories, arteries, softly beating heart, emerges in the specific form of the Salaam-Schalom Initiative, as contemporary form of intermezzo, where the self is cultivated through encounters between Muslims and Jews in the mosque and in Berlin. By inhabiting this complex and at times uncomfortable reality, Jews and Muslims show the ways in which difference is perceived, maintained, and/or overcome, fostering harmony with one another and with the metropolis itself. "This city is ours," says Muna, a Şehitlik Mosque community member and member of the Salaam-Schalom Initiative, evoking my earlier experience in that ambiguous Neukölln home, with its mezuzah and its Qur'anic verse. Muna's eyes widen as she speaks of all that Berlin has to offer, a city broken open in her encounters in the mosque, Neukölln, and the larger metropolis—embraced by the shadows of old elms, under the gaze of a golden angel and ghosts memorialized in stone.

Familiar Strangers: Making Together in the Metropolis

Literary scholars have argued that Benjamin appears in *Wings of Desire* implicitly in its evocation of recollection and rebuilding, as explicitly in the narrator's voice: "Walter Benjamin bought Paul Klee's watercolor, *Angelus Novus*, in 1921. Until his flight from Paris in June 1940, it hung in his various workrooms. In his last writing, *Theses on the Philosophy of History* (1940), he interpreted the picture as an allegory of a look back over history."[16]

Amidst the rubble of post-WWII Berlin, the fallen angels in *Wings of Desire* speak to this shared, plural history: "We are greater than just the two of us. We embody many. We occupy the square of the people and the whole square is full with persons who wish what we wish."[17] Such shared embodiment of history in the city, in its still-unfulfilled yearning for repair, reverberates in Muslim-Jewish affinities, like those developed through the Salaam-Schalom Initiative. Some have asserted that Muslims share not only experiences of cultural discrimination with the Jewish community today but also with the Jewish community of the past, as the "new Jews" or "Jews of tomorrow."[18] Here again the notion of "progress" is broken open in comparisons with the period that followed the thriving salons —including the prominence of xenophobic cartoons and the incitement of widespread fear of Jews among the mainstream populace in early twentieth-century Germany. Yasmin, a young Muslim poet I meet through my interlocutors at Şehitlik explains, "Germans don't want to hear that—but in my opinion, you can really compare it to the pre–Second World War situation with the Jews. Some happenings in recent times are definitely comparable in terms of how people are marginalized." Mara, a German-born

Salaam-Schalom Initiative leader who has recently moved back from a period living in Israel, identifying as "half-Jewish," echoes this sentiment,

> I especially felt very uncomfortable with Germany and how Germany is act-ing towards Muslims, given the German past, the sub-sub-sub-sub-subtext you know is always like with Muslims, "They're bad, they're bad guys, bad religion, bad everything, bad culture." I remember two years ago when friends, as Muslims, were treated as how I imagine Jews were treated in the twenties of the last century, that was my motivation to take part in [the Salaam-Shalom Initiative]. It is like, "OK, Muslim, that explains everything." I don't want to say that there is a Holocaust or signs that it is going this direction but I think the atmosphere in the streets is maybe what happened here a hundred years ago towards Jews. Such a black-and-white thing. You know, there are liberal Muslims, well-integrated Muslims? But it's like it's either German or Muslim and there is no possibility that you can be a German Muslim. It's strange and I think it's worth saying in public.

Both Yasmin and Mara invoke the undercaste status shared by Muslims today and Jews in the twentieth century: "comparable in terms of how people are marginalized"; "Muslim, that explains everything"; "they're bad, they're bad guys, bad religion, bad everything, bad culture." They portray continuity in the othering gaze of mainstream German society. In their evocative descrip-tions of the historical portrayals of Jews echoed in the mainstream portrayal of Muslims today, potential "chaos and devastation" resides within the bodies of strangers in the same city, divided by the schism of time, somehow shattered, and yet somehow made anew.[19]

In August 2012, Rabbi Daniel Alter was walking with his then six-year-old daughter in Berlin's Friedenau district when four Arab Germans jumped and beat him, fracturing his cheekbone.[20] The following year, Ármin Langer, a German-born Jewish Berliner raised in Hungary, founded the Salaam-Schalom Initiative in response to Rabbi Alter's unfounded claim that the southeastern Neukölln district, among others, had developed "no-go areas" for Jews, made dangerous by a large Muslim populace. "I was surprised when I first heard this statement [about 'no-go areas']" says Ármin, at the time a rabbi-in-training in Berlin, "since I have a lot of Jewish friends here and we all feel at home here in Neukölln. I think this statement is counterproductive, only strengthens stereo-types and doesn't bring us closer to the peaceful coexistence we all yearn for." By founding the Salaam-Schalom Initiative, Langer wanted to outwardly dem-onstrate, both to enliven and to *live* the connection between Jews and Muslims in Berlin through what he terms "multicultural cohesion"—an alliance that not only respects but protects and upholds plurality.

The Salaam-Schalom Initiative, a seemingly unlikely alliance between Neukölln's Muslims and Jews, emerged in 2013 amidst a social atmosphere of rising anti-Semitism and anti-Muslim sentiment, contributing to the ambivalent relationships both groups have with the German nation-state. Tracing the discourses, pedagogies, and actions of Salaam-Schalom Initiative members shows how they not only practice but habituate, embody, and teach responsibility for one another in the metropolis. In the face of national exclusions and othering, the metropolis provides an opportunity to renegotiate both selfhood and collective belonging. "The modern city can turn people outward, not inward," argues Sennett. "The power of the city to reorient people in this way lies in its diversity; in the presence of difference people have at least the possibility to step outside themselves."[21] Through solidarity with the Jewish populace in Neukölln, Şehitlik Mosque constituents both step outside of, and root more deeply within, themselves; the city—"full with persons who wish what we wish," in the words of the fallen angels in *Wings of Desire*—turns both inwards and outwards, in the co-constitution of the self and the collective.

From a starting point of commitment to their cause, the leadership and members of this organization forge solidarity, emerging when, as Zygmunt Bauman writes, "my link with the stranger is revealed as responsibility, not just indifferent neutrality or even cognitive acceptance of the similarity of condition." This again relates to the internalization and embodiment of an ethics of responsibility. That is, "the 'I am responsible for the Other' and 'I am responsible for myself' come to mean the same thing."[22] Here we witness transformation through responsibility for the other "Other," from what Cohen terms *Nebenmensch* (next man) to what he terms *Mitmensch* (fellow man).[23] Similarly, Bauman argues that solidarity is forged in a double awakening—"awakening to being for the Other is the awakening of the self."[24] When one accepts responsibility for the *Mitmensch*, the self and "the Other" can no longer be pulled apart.[25]

Social realities, old and new, serve as the grounds on which members of this initiative collectively confront twofold struggles against boundaries to belonging. This is very much an act of making together, *sympoiesis*, as they strive to dwell in the Benjaminian sense, to "fashion" a place in which both can belong to the metropolis.[26] More than *convivencia*, a state of living together, making together (*sympoiesis*) entails dynamic knowledge-based acts of moral agency (*phronesis*) in the creation of new imaginaries that entwine Muslims and Jews in the metropolis. Throughout my research, Muslim members of

Salaam-Schalom consistently respond to questions about their core identities with ambivalence to nationality—as Yusuf says, "It's complicated. When I speak to Turkish people, I say I am German and when I speak to German people, I say I am Turkish"—and yet self-affirmation in relation to the city—in the words of many, "I am a Muslim Berliner" or "this is a Berliner mosque." New conceptualizations of selfhood and belonging thus emerge from the interaction between the Islamic tradition, a relationship with Berlin, and a responsibility for the other urban "Other," strangers made familiar in the city.

Salaam-Schalom activities move from the mosque, where for instance, seated in a circle on the heated winter carpets, members discuss the role of art in undermining bigotry in 2014, outwards into justice-oriented activities in the metropolis. In 2015, Salaam-Schalom leads the "My Head, My Choice" campaign at Neukölln's city hall, in response to the banning of religious symbols in civil service positions. This campaign emerges when Betül (the mosque tour guide mentioned earlier), a second-generation Şehitlik leader and member of Salaam-Schalom, is denied a position in local government on account of her headscarf. Betül refuses to stand down in the face of this slight, instead uniting young Muslim and Jewish women to stand up together in protest. On July 14, 2015, children carry signs with the words spoken in unison by their mothers— "My head, my choice," "It matters what is *in* a woman's head, not what is on it," or "I am a Berliner"—printed beside sketches of women donning headscarves. This campaign employs the language of liberal values, articulating the headscarf as a matter of individual autonomy and freedom in the German city and state.

In 2016, in another evocative moment, Salaam-Schalom members participate in a tandem bike ride organized by a related initiative, Meet2respect, which creates "encounters" between groups in order to foster respect and mutual understanding in Berlin; led by imams and rabbis sharing bicycles, this entails a dynamic display of solidarity through conavigation of the city's streets.[27] Still, while they may navigate the city, Salaam-Schalom members are not able to navigate all sociopolitical challenges together. In their meetings, Muna explains, "Israel-Palestine politics must be left at the door":

> What Salaam-Schalom does really well is when these groups come together (Jewish, Muslim) they start talking about the Middle East conflict and we don't have anything to do with the Middle East conflict in Berlin. We may be affected emotionally, but nothing that should come between me and a Jew for our work in Berlin. Many people have difficulties to put that aside, but it works really well with Salaam-Schalom because we emphasize issues that are theologically

important, which center on the human condition, and always have a sort of relation towards the practical world we are affected by, here. Now. Day-to-day business. Questions like, "Can a Jew go to a mosque?" It's simple, you start discussing it and then you go have a cup of coffee together. So, *it's not political* and if there are any political questions raised, those are political questions that relate to Berlin.

Here, by chance, and yet not to be overlooked, Muna employs the same terminology as Arendt's most famous work, *The Human Condition*. In this seminal text, Arendt argues that the layeredness of plurality—the concurrent sameness (as humans) and distinction (as individuals)—is what makes action possible: "because we are all the same, that is, human, in such a way that nobody is ever the same as anyone else who ever lived, lives, or will live."[28]

The centrality of shared humanity echoes the Wednesday evening lessons and tours at the Şehitlik Mosque, where both sameness (as human) and distinction (as Muslims) enlivens a harmonizing project, rooted in an Islamic epistemology that emphasizes responsibilities/obligations towards the self, others, the earth, and God. Over coffee, Menon, a Muslim Salaam-Schalom member and lawyer, explains,

> We tell stories about how people changed. For example, a story about two Nigerian rivals who are out there to kill each other and once they met in person they changed—they toured the world and tell people how wrong they are. One lost his arm. One lost his son. They were enemies and are now friends.

In Bauman's words, "There are friends and enemies. And there are *strangers*."[29] Menon continues by discussing how direct contact between these two groups of "strangers," in both senses of the term, shifts perceptions to the point that they are not only friends and not only imbued with empathy, but experience a loss of distinction between the self and "the Other"; as Ármin asserts, "they see each other as one and the same." In an interview with *Mozaika*, Ármin explicitly links the shared experiences of contemporary Muslims and Jews in Berlin to the particular history of Germany and its capital city. "We have to support each other as minorities, because if there is something that history has taught us, it's that today it might be somebody else who is being oppressed, discriminated against, victimized, but tomorrow it could be you."[30] Ármin was, in fact, expelled from his own rabbinical studies in Germany after writing a newspaper opinion piece in which he claimed that "Muslims are the new Jews" in 2014.[31] The capacity to build solidarity therefore emerges from experiences of both a general "common humanity" and a particular "shared othering," spanning present to past—making Berlin into what Ármin aptly terms "a home in exile," another rendition of Said's "exilic city."[32]

Regardless of the solidaristic success within the discrete sociocultural space of Salaam-Schalom, the surrounding local and national political context has become increasingly tense for Muslims and Jews. Support for Palestine is now explicitly equated with anti-Semitism in the mainstream German political arena; in May 2019, the German Parliament officially labeled the BDS (Boycott, Divest, Sanction) movement anti-Semitic. The move was implicitly connected to a debate over the dismantling of the Jewish Museum Berlin's leadership following the invitation of BDS supporters to a public event on Islamophobia and anti-Semitism (explored in further detail below).[33] As in the mosque tour, the complete bracketing of difficult, albeit pertinent conversations here raises the question of what is at stake when political questions that are at the same time ethical questions cannot be asked. Is this a choice—whether silence or absence—borne out of fear? Or is it an act of refusal to quash any chance at unity under the weight of one of the world's most divisive conflicts? Ármin alludes to the latter: "We are not soldiers standing against each other on the front. We are average people living in the same city."[34] In his view, Salaam-Schalom fosters solidarity through its focus on ordinary, local life, rather than global political strife.[35] It is concerned first and foremost with pluralism in this city, this neighborhood, this home that is "ours."

My interlocutors who participate in Salaam-Schalom are far from naïve; they recognize the inherent grayness of a plural society and their own perceived grayness, which endows them with a unique critical perspective and a call to act. In the summer of 2017, I meet Ármin at a Neukölln café. Here he asserts the responsibility he feels as a contemporary Jewish Berliner,

> I think that I as a Jew have certain responsibilities. And I don't see any other option. I won't sit at home and watch the country going down . . . I don't believe we can change everyone. I'm naïve, but not that naïve. But there is a gray zone which we *can* change.

This "gray zone" is again transformed through encounters—"the realm of doing"—motivated by an ethics of responsibility, holding the promise of Sennett's "open city" as both a material and an ethical project rife with ambiguities, overlaps, and ongoing possibilities: made with porous walls.[36] Valuing plurality, at once unfixed and unfamiliar in all of its shades of gray, gives way to the discarding of social narratives built on assumed incompatibility; instead, the othered self is altered through its encounters with the other "Other," becoming together at ease in the threshold spaces (the salon, the mosque) of the modern metropolis.

Salaam-Schalom thus operates at the level of the city, but also within the realm of unrealized dreams. When Arendt writes of Rahel Varnhagen, she also writes of herself, bridging biography and autobiography as she transcends time through the dreams of two women living in society's margins, a hundred years apart.[37] Today in Germany, two religioethnic groups living in society's margins do the same, blurring the lines between the narrative of the self and the other by fusing responsibility for both at the level of the metropolis. In so doing, they contend with a secular state, imbued with power as order-maker and arbitrator, struggling with the tensions between religious freedom and religion-lite publics; they respond to failed national belonging, creating an urban mecca in which to reach for their dreams, albeit constrained by a political reality that does not appreciate their shades of gray. Even under such constraints, however, Salaam-Schalom carries the German past into its present in order to both contextualize and rebel against exclusions—aware of, and attending to, the city's own unrealized dream, that of reconciliation with its Jewish past. In striving for solidarity in the metropolis, Salaam-Schalom members reconcile the unique symbolism of urban spaces where history speaks with the present, spaces of loss, unification, and rebirth, through creative forms of conversation and local activism; rather than coherence, they foster cohesion—speaking to yesterday's Jewish living rooms, now marked by *Stolpersteine*, through a neo-Ottoman mosque named for its burial ground.

JEWS AND MUSLIMS IN-SECURITY

At a celebratory iftar in July 2015, a policewoman from the neighborhood stands on the outdoor steps of the Şehitlik Mosque that lead up to the main sanctuary, a wire trailing from her pocket to her ear. She surveils the premises, dozens of men circumventing her as they ascend the same steps for prayer. The policewoman appears like a statue, unmoving, left foot positioned squarely below her right, the shadow of her body growing as the sun dims beneath the clouds.

Muslim bodies, individual and collective, experience inordinate levels of surveillance across Europe, as state-level policies over the past two decades have increasingly associated Islam with violence and threat.[38] This has bred "reciprocal skepticism" between Muslim communities and the police, tasked with managing difference and intergroup relations as well as protecting state interests through widespread security presence.[39] Strategies of surveillance include both overt and covert police presence at mosques, as well as coerced "cooperation" between mosque leadership and police on city-level projects, specifically those aimed at preventing extremism. The habitual police presence at the Şehitlik Mosque straddles all these of realms—at times overt and others covert. Justified by the supposed incivility of Muslims, it wears the mask of civility. Mosque leaders describe police presence as a manifestation of discrimination against Muslims, with so-called cooperation cloaked in a language of "opportunity." Like it or not, these leaders often become de facto makers in the state security project, delimiting their own agency in the modern metropolis.

It is worth noting here that the history of policing in Germany is one characterized by deep ambivalence. During Prussian rule, police rose as a formidable entity representing state interests.[40] Recognizing their established authority, Hitler created his own police force for fear that dissent from state police could undermine his rapid consolidation of power.[41] In the post-WWII era, German society bifurcated into a police state in the East and a state where citizens felt suspect of the police in the West. In the first instance, the Stasi infiltrated the daily lives of East Germans, while in the second, the West German police force provoked revolt, culminating in the 1968 student protests.[42] Incensed by high levels of police violence in response to their protests against the Vietnam War, students criticized the continued entrenchment of fascism in German society, allowed to fester through decades of silence. They argued that the state apparatus, including the police force, had not been fully purged of Nazi influences, an old suppressor emerging in new uniforms under the discursive guise of democratic order. In the face of this perpetuation, they lamented that neither closure nor repair had occurred in the post-WWII era.[43] While attenuated in the postreunification period, a suspicion of the police has remained since, resurfacing most recently with a series of corruption scandals and exposed linkages between state police and the far-right AfD party.[44]

Circumcision: Modern Stigmata

In summer 2013, I meet Şehitlik community member Harun at the Jüdisches Museum Berlin café. We sit in a glass courtyard, described as a "sukkah made of glass and steel," that throws shadows in the shape of Jewish stars. While it is peaceful under this covering of metal and sky, the museum and, institutionally nested within it, the Akademie of the Jüdisches Museum Berlin (hosting public-facing events in a building across the street, its architectural concept one of "in-between spaces") is in the midst of a conflict.[45] This conflict centers on how to balance representation of Jewish life in Germany present and past within the broader context of contemporary social plurality. Like Şehitlik, the Jüdisches Museum is an urban institution struggling with its space, and place, in contemporary Berlin.

This struggle is not entirely new, as the museum has increasingly turned towards Jewish-Muslim dialogue in its exhibitions and events over the past fifteen years. In 2005, it instated a tour comparing the religious practices and rites of Judaism and Islam. From 2013 through 2019, many of the academy's events centered on bringing discrimination against Jews and Muslims into conversation, through the Muslim-Jewish Forum and/or the program in Migration and Diversity. In 2013, in response to the temporary ban on circumcision in Germany, the museum hosted an exhibition, *Snip It: Stances on Ritual Circumcision*, including perspectives from across the Abrahamic traditions. In 2017, it installed another exhibition, *Cherchez la femme*, which brought the voices of Jewish and Muslim women to bear on head coverings, including a series of visuals, such as photographs and a sculpture made out of hair.[46] In 2018–19, the museum's exhibition, *Welcome to Jerusalem*, portrayed Jewish, Muslim, and Christian claims on the city. Both the Israeli government and Berlin's largest Jewish body—the Central Council of Jews in Germany—expressed outrage at this portrayal, arguing that it exhibited anti-Israel sentiment in content and form (citing, for example, a model of the city where the Kaaba appears larger than other religious sites), thereby privileging the claims made by Muslims on the holy city.[47] Later in 2019, an academy event on anti-Semitism and Islamophobia included known BDS supporters, which appeared to be the straw that broke the camel's back; both museum president Peter Schäfer and academy director Yasemin Shooman stepped down.[48]

This flash summary of key events linking Jewish and Muslim life in the Jüdisches Museum serves as a backdrop to the tension at the heart of the institution's recent unraveling, a tension that reverberates throughout the German capital and beyond. An aptly titled *New York Times* article published on July 9, 2019, captures the conflict with a single question: "What and Whom Are Jewish Museums For?"[49] This gives way to other questions, including: Is the museum a place to emphasize the particularity of the Jewish experience in Germany and Berlin? Or is it a place to explore the particular and yet universal experience of strangerhood in and beyond any geographical locale? These questions emerge in a context where, unbeknownst to many, numerous guides in the museum are ethnically Turkish Muslims motivated by a sense of empathy emerging from their own position of alterity. Harun is one of them. The question that colors my conversation with Harun is not explicitly about the museum, however, but rather implicit in the museum's unsettledness—what and whom is Berlin, is Germany for?

Harun, wearing a red scarf adorned with the outline of the museum building, sits across from me in the modern sukkah and quickly turns to a recent crisis faced by Muslims and Jews together in Germany: the circumcision ban. On May 7, 2012, the Cologne Appellate Court ruled that circumcision constitutes bodily harm (*Körperverletzung*), following a Muslim boy's complications from the procedure in Cologne.[50] Articulated in a language of liberal rights rather than religious obligation, the court ruled that circumcision violated an individual's autonomy over his body, leaving Jewish and Muslim populaces across Germany reeling. Facing stark critique from across the globe, the German parliament passed legislation agreeing to accommodate circumcision, requiring a doctor's presence if the procedure occurs after six months of age. Still, in the months of discord that followed the initial court decision, a language of incivility prevailed, with circumcisions described as irrevocably damaging the bodies of children: modern stigmata, marking each as a Muslim or a Jew.[51] Here again, Muslim and Jewish bodies are reduced to pieces, with circumcision described as disfigurement of the individual's body rather than part of a larger configuration of shared religious traditions, incomplete human projects that have not arrived in modernity. As Harun puts it:

> What was very significant is that this practice was portrayed as a barbaric practice and "OK, now we teach you what to do, we Christian society, we German society, we have overcome certain barbaric traditions, we have modernized with the Enlightenment and everything. We have left things behind, you know, we have overcome this. So now it's time for you guys to, you know, arrive here."

Nested within the concept of "the barbaric" and its juxtaposition with modernity are associations not only with brutality, but also the twin characteristics of the uncivil: primitiveness and foreignness. As modernity turns away from rites of passage, "we have grown very poor in threshold experiences," writes Benjamin.[52] Yet modernity is characterized not only by scarcity in, but also discomfort with, threshold experiences—whether circumcision, or the everyday happenings in the metropolitan mosque. Reflecting the ambiguity of strangers and their strange practices as antimodern, Benjamin asserts that "in modern life, these transitions are becoming ever more unrecognizable."[53] They are cast as belonging to another place and another time. And thus, in the circumcision ban, Muslims and Jews, often portrayed as at odds with one another over

Israel-Palestine, are collapsed into a single stranger. Harun explains, "The anti-Semites, they were kinda happy actually, and also the anti-Muslims, you know, they were like 'these are the two strangers in our society and now we have one case where we have the two strangers in our society together.' For them, it was the perfect chance."

Schirin Amir-Moazami argues that not only the legal ruling, but also the surrounding secular discursive framework centered on individual freedom and integrity, reveals the incomprehensibility of a common Islamic and Jewish moral framing of circumcision.[54] At first, the dominant language and affect of the secular body prevails—focusing on medicalization (for instance, treating rather than experiencing pain) and liberal rights, thereby further marginalizing embodied religious traditions that do not shy away from pain. In the words of Holston, here "civility's idioms of inclusion and consensus create habits of the public which entrench citizenship's inequalities."[55] This grappling for a coherent body of the citizen—rather than a cohesive body of citizens—reveals the incongruities of the European nation-state and its hierarchies of belonging. To critique this debate through an Islamic or Jewish lens, where circumcision is not primarily about pain and yet also recognizes the presence of pain, is to call forth the vitality of obligation rather than "rights" in shaping the pious body.

In *Flesh and Stone*, Sennett opens a new possibility for solidarity through the recognition of pain—in the self and in the other—that can create cohesion beyond any single community, identifying value in transcendence of the status quo.

> Arousing sympathy for those who are Other . . . can only occur, I believe, by understanding why bodily pain requires a place in which it can be acknowledged, and in which its transcendent origins become visible. Such pain has a trajectory in human experience. It disorients and makes incomplete the self, defeats the desire for coherence; the body accepting pain is ready to become a civic body, sensible to the pain of another person, pains present together on the street.[56]

Perhaps most importantly, this sensibility to pain "defeats the desire for coherence," arising from a dangerous modern myth that creates and yet casts thresholds—including the strangers that inhabit them—as threats to the order of modernity. In its creation of a civic body, this sensibility to pain suggests an alternative to coherence, with solidarity or cohesion forged through empathy, recognition of human sameness and human difference at one and the same time. In so doing, it echoes Arendt's theory of action, emerging from this nexus of resemblance and distinction, as well as Bauman's notion of double-awakening to the self together with "the Other."[57]

Anti-Semitism's New (Old) Face

Harun laments the lost chance for a shared awakening among Muslims and Jews, who could have used their shared pain during the circumcision ban, not of the body through the ritual itself but the mental anguish of public sanctioning, to act together. Yet not only a lost chance for collective action, but also differences between Muslim and Jewish experiences in today's Germany arise throughout our conversation. For the Jewish community, re-rooted in Germany after the Holocaust, the circumcision ban constituted a "shock moment"—a frightening reinvocation of the Jewish body as stigmatized form. Muslims, on the other hand, expect no less than continuous intervention in their religious institutions and practices, with the circumcision ban one among many instances of mainstream hegemony. Harun explains,

> I have a lot of [Jewish] friends who said, "This is something we never expected, never in Germany with this past," and this was a disappointment for them and *unfathomable*. On the Muslim side, it was somewhat different. Muslims have had many such experiences in the last years, prohibitions by the state, the majority society, mosque building, halal, everything is a problem . . . the shock moment was not so big.

Harun describes these divergent responses as elucidating "the secondary placement" of Muslims in Germany. For instance, he notes that while Muslim institutions, like mosques, experience ongoing surveillance, Jewish institutions, like synagogues, receive police protection. Still, the somehow primary placement of Jews as a religioethnic group in Germany alludes to the strange, liminal position that they continue to occupy as European Jews more broadly. In one widespread narrative, Jews are seen to represent the body of Germany/ Europe and its vulnerability to Islam, as one-of-us in the post-WWII era; Jews have become institutionally recognized in the same manner as Christians in Germany and culturally recognized in the European discourse of a (Judeo-) Christian imaginary. In this narrative, anti-Semitism is thus perceived as a threat against the nation-state. Anya Topolski, however, traces the notion of the "Judeo-Christian," demonstrating that it emerged not as an inclusive but rather a supersessionist concept—suggesting Judaism as temporarily preceding and replaced by the supposedly morally superior religious form of Christianity.[58]

The differentiation between Jews and Muslims similarly takes a supersessionist turn, in social if not in theological terms, with Muslims now the primary "Other," occupying the most subordinate position in a hierarchical social order, as undercaste. Harun notes the role of the educated elite in solidifying this distinction between Muslims and Jews. These include Social Democratic politician Thilo Sarrazin, philosopher Rüdiger Safranski, and historian Jörg Baberowski, colloquially described as displaying *Altersradikalität*, radicalization that comes with age. Sarrazin's first book, the 2010 *Deutschland schafft sich ab* ("Germany Is Undoing Itself"), quickly caused a national controversy; in this text, Sarrazin argues that genetic inferiorities among minorities have detrimental effects on German society, effectively "undoing" it.[59] Large segments of German society responded with the assertion that Sarrazin showed not bigotry but bravery; he had the guts to say what many believe, but struggle to express given Germany's history.

And yet this book also reflected the tension between collapsing Muslims and Jews into a shared position of otherness and divergent treatment of these two religious groups in Germany's public life. Even Sarrazin discerns between those tolerably othered (Muslims) and the clear cultural boundary to demeaning Jews. The history of the Holocaust—constructed both as "a moral universal" and as particular to Jews—means that any expression of anti-Semitic sentiment garners widespread dissent in Germany.[60] The same does not hold true for anti-Muslim sentiment. Harun laments:

> When he mentioned genes and Jews, then he got so much critique—I mean he was mentioning all the time Arabs and Turks and about their genes—talking about how strange and weird they are and how wrong they are. Then in an interview, he talked about Jews and their genes and all of a sudden, he got so much critique from the public and he said, "Oh I'm sorry, that was wrong, I didn't use the right terms, I'm sorry." But he never did that for Turks and Arabs, for Muslims.

In 2018, Thilo Sarrazin published his second text, which quickly became a bestseller on Amazon, this time with a title more clearly targeting Islam: *Feindliche Übernahme: Wie der Islam den Fortschritt behindert und die Gesellschaft bedroht* ("Hostile Takeover: How Islam Prevents Progress and Threatens Society").[61]

In spite of the red line regarding anti-Semitism in the German public sphere, Berlin and Germany as a whole have witnessed a rise in anti-Semitic attacks, reflecting a broader pattern of violence targeting Jews across Europe over the past few years.[62] Muslims are tellingly blamed for heightened anti-Semitic activity in Germany, although facts and figures prove otherwise. Even a 2014 op-ed in the *New York Times*—written by German journalist Jochen Bittner and titled "What's Behind Germany's New Anti-Semitism?"—exemplifies this sentiment.[63] This opinion piece equates acts of violence perpetrated by a small minority of ethnically Arab youth to a "Muslim" problem (much like Rabbi Alter's claim of no-go zones in Berlin), evidencing the universalizing tendency to label incivility and threat as "Muslim." The idea of a "new anti-Semitism" connects to anti-Zionism among the parents of young Muslims in Europe today (those from the Middle East, in particular); it alludes to a transformation on and by an emergent Islamic left rather than the ethnonationalist European right who espoused—and still espouse—so-called "classical anti-Semitism."[64] The Central Council of Jews in Germany recently echoed a concern over this "new" form as emerging from within the Muslim populace, asserting that "the whole of society needs to take the problem of Muslim anti-Semitism very seriously."[65] While a Bundestag report released in spring 2017 explained that ring-wing extremists pose the most significant threat to Jews, it also highlighted the "increasing threat" of Muslims in Germany without statistics to match.[66]

This false projection of new anti-Semitism that is anything but new solely onto Muslims is not inane; it is a politically motivated portrayal of incivility. Jews come to represent the perceived vulnerability of Europe juxtaposed against, rather than those marginalized in Europe alongside of, Muslims. While Pew polling in fact uncovers the linkages between anti-Jewish and anti-Muslim attitudes across Europe, the mere *popular sentiment*—powerfully supported by media discourse—that Muslims are to blame for this reinvigoration of anti-Semitism has deepened the rift between two groups often othered in the very same way.[67] Let me be clear: anti-Semitic sentiment persists among many first-generation Muslims whom I meet in Berlin, with anti-American and anti-Semitic tropes together invoked to explain social and economic struggles in Turkey; Jews and Israel, through the support of the US, are on multiple occasions described as controlling the global financial system. Yet anti-Semitism is neither exclusively nor even primarily a "Muslim problem."

Here it appears politically savvy to externalize the issue, rather than grapple with anti-Semitism's twin survival and revival in a country that has shaped pedagogy and public space in order to contend with this particular form of xenophobia: a country and a capital city with their own impossible dreams of reconciliation with their Jews. "Sometimes, as with the Pegida marchers," writes Sennett, "images of the stranger define exactly how a people does not want to see itself, as in the portrait in Oscar Wilde's *The Picture of Dorian Gray*."[68] The image of the Muslim as anti-Semitism's new face in post-war Europe is akin to that portrait—a false cover for a metaphorical window mirror (of the Muslim, of the stranger) reflecting the untenable face of an exclusive European modernity: shadowed by the Enlightenment, weathered by progress, and wounded by civility.[69]

POLICING INCIVILITY

The Muslim as stranger and the Muslim as window mirror appears again in my research at another urban institution in Berlin, the police precinct responsible for Neukölln; here behind the luster of an intercultural "new way," the incivility of a civility discourse and its accompanying security agenda shines through.[70] When I arrive at the precinct in late spring 2015, I check in with an officer at the front desk. He directs me to sit in the waiting room on a metal chair in a line of metal chairs, all bolted to the ground. I am accompanied only by the loud, lonely hum of a mostly empty vending machine and church bells that echo in the air. After about ten minutes, a young, dark-haired officer enters the room and asks my name, explaining that he will drive me across the compound to meet Torsten, the officer in charge of intercultural work.

The police working with Şehitlik have won numerous awards for their intercultural focus, at the forefront of this "new way" of engaging diverse communities through building relationships and open exchange. When I meet Torsten at the bottom of a staircase in one of the compound's many identical buildings, he shakes my hand with friendly vigor, inviting me into a conference room with his partner, Katja—the same woman who appears earlier in this book, standing on the steps of the Şehitlik Mosque as she oversees a public Ramadan event. A spread of soft drinks and snacks between us, Torsten and Katja discuss not only the unique approach of their team, supporting diversity in the Berlin metropolis, but also the increasing urban diversity within the police force itself as evidencing their socially progressive agenda. "For example, that guy who just drove you, he was Turkish, right?" Torsten half-asks, half-asserts.

At the same precinct a few weeks later, I meet two other police officers, Berat and Ateş, both ethnically Turkish and in their mid-thirties. Berat was born to a Muslim family in Neukölln but no longer practices Islam. He describes his upbringing as "very modern." As our interview takes place during Ramadan, I ask if he is fasting. Berat quickly retorts that he stopped fasting because it is "almost only cultural." He describes the exhaustion of attending evening prayers at the mosque during Ramadan, while stating that everyone must choose his or her own path. Religion is not only questioned, but cast aside through its nominalization as "culture," which continues throughout our conversation, and connects to a broader trend in Europe of labeling Muslim practices as "cultural" in order to devalue them; for instance, the avoidance of pork and alcohol are similarly delimited to the "only cultural" realm.[71] His colleague, Ateş, belongs to the Alevi community, a heterodox Muslim religious group long persecuted in Turkey; its ties with the Sunni majority both in Turkey and in diaspora remain strained.[72] Ateş consistently remarks that Berat lives an ideal, "modern" form of Islam—that is, explicitly not practicing. These officers, I soon realize, embody Arendt's conceptualization of the parvenu, striving to assimilate while never able to fully shed an undercaste status.

The radicalization of youth lies at the forefront of concern for police officers as they engage with Muslim communities in Berlin and beyond. By 2015, 760 German residents or citizens had joined ISIS (Islamic State of Iraq and Syria), according to former interior minister Thomas de Maizière.[73] Yet far before the emergence of ISIS, arguably since the 1980s, Muslim communities have been under watch for their supposed linkages to violence.[74] And after 9/11, Germany introduced two packages of security legislation. The first, enacted on September 19, 2001, essentially reformed existing law in order to more easily prosecute suspected terrorist groups and the individuals embedded within them; it expanded the capacity to ban extremist organizations and to take legal action against those rooted in Germany. The second, enacted in 2002, increased the capacities of the German intelligence service, counterintelligence, and the federal border guard.[75] Although undergirded by such federal powers, much surveillance takes place at the city and state levels, often shifting between hard and soft power. An example of the latter, the Islam Forum Berlin established in 2005, unites police, leaders of Muslim, Jewish, and Christian communities, and other civil society actors to address radicalization in the city.[76]

Although reflective of this two-sided city-level paradigm, the officers at this precinct perceive themselves as spearheading a uniquely cooperative approach to security. According to Berat, "our goal is prevention. For some [others] it's repression . . . this is the future, to work this way." Berat and Ateş explain that to accomplish prevention, they collect information on individuals and groups through regular visits to different communities, including mosques. Most of their information on individuals is, however, honed from teachers and administrators in local schools, as not only Muslim institutions, but institutions serving Muslims, have become implicated in the security agenda. The local Hermann-Sander-Grundschule, an elementary school in Şehitlik's Neukölln neighborhood, was the first to produce an actual handbook—"Promoting Integration, Recognizing Radicalization"—for its teachers tasked with this surveilling role in 2017.[77] The handbook rules that teachers can ask children to fast for shorter periods during Ramadan, must penalize missing school for the Friday prayer, can request that mothers uncover their faces if covered, and should require all children to participate in all sports. It further emphasizes that no "religion rebate" should be given, mandating that students must first and foremost comply with the community culture of the school. Here we see again the mask of civility, the metaphorical portrait of Dorian Gray, a false cover in the explicit targeting of Muslims.

In Germany as across Europe, teachers are now involved in identifying Muslim children and adolescents at risk for radicalization, keeping track of visible shifts in religiosity, innocuous save their connection to Islam.[78] Teachers vetting both the religious practice and "the direction" of students poses numerous challenges, including lack of Islamic education/knowledge and undermining the already-weak trust of teachers among students with immigrant and/or Muslim backgrounds in state schools, as described by almost all of my interlocutors. Ateş reveals the lack of knowledge about Islam by those called to surveil their students and the resulting penalty of being discernably Muslim in school.

> When a teacher doesn't have a lot to do with the religion, and sees a school child holding a Qur'an in his hand, reading it, it's like when a Christian holds the Bible and reads it. Well, it's seen differently, with the current politics in the world, it's put in another box. When there is a Muslim who now holds the Qur'an, or changes her clothing . . . one who dressed in a modern way puts on the headscarf for the first time, or the next level would be to go to the burqa [a loose, full-body covering and face covering with a mesh screen over the eyes], then you can't see anything. These are already indications for us that we need to see in which direction things go.

Remaining illegible by default in a secular liberal discourse, the opaque Muslim student—"then you can't see anything"—is "put in another box," illuminating the hierarchy inherent in her undercaste status. The Qur'an, the headscarf and the burqa together become material symbols not of Islam but of an uncivil unsettling of modernity by the Muslim child. This has not only emotional but also discernable material impacts, discrimination that feeds into grading biases and decreased educational opportunities.[79] Moving from student to teacher, despite public claims that efforts are being made to increase the presence of Turkish and Muslim teachers in German public schools, they remain a small minority even in the most pluralistic cities and federal states.[80] Recently, a Muslim woman in Berlin-Brandenburg was outright—and therefore unlawfully—rejected from a teaching position on account of her headscarf,

suggesting the continued hurdles faced by visibly Muslim educators in securing positions.[81] This school-level decision was first struck down by the Berlin-
Brandenburg labor court, and subsequently by the Federal Labor Court, who
ruled that it was unconstitutional on August 27, 2020.[82]

Although Germany's Federal Constitutional Court deemed such general-
ized bans on the headscarf unconstitutional in 2015, controversies regarding
the public signaling of Islam in schools continue to span the country, including
a 2017 ban on "provocative prayer" in a West German high school. A local district counselor describes this decision in terms of protecting the peace of the
school, espousing the language of the 2015 FCC decision; "the ban on praying
in a 'provocative way' in the school is intended to promote peaceful coexistence and ensure the school peace."[83] The ambiguity of laws regarding religious
symbols and public practices not only endows state and city authorities such
as teachers and police with great power, but also allows perceived danger to
justify the targeted regulation of Muslims.

Berat recounts the discomfort of a teacher whose Muslim student changed
his appearance—donning a prayer cap and carrying the Qur'an—and his own
intervention to convince the student not to wear a prayer cap in school.

> For example, there was a sixteen-year-old schoolchild who dressed very tradi-
> tionally for three to four months . . . head covering, and wants his Qur'an with
> him . . . The parents don't know. The parents said in the beginning, "Oh great,
> he prays. He is no longer on the street. He has become believing." But they
> don't see in what direction he has developed. And one needs to trick him, when
> one speaks with this boy. When we speak with him, he has Qur'an experiences
> already, we also have Qur'an experience but we aren't believers. He might say,
> "You aren't believers, you play with [Islam] . . . Where is it in the school rules
> that I have to take off my hat? There is no school rule that I have to take off my
> hat." We say, "OK, that's true, you are right, but there is a school order . . . one
> takes off the hat out of respect." And then we ask, "Where is it in the Qur'an [to
> wear the hat]? When one goes to the mosque one takes off shoes. This is also
> not in the Qur'an but you do that also, because of respect and not to make it
> dirty." That was a good idea of ours and he accepted it.

That Berat takes pride in "tricking" a student by making spurious connections
between an outwardly Muslim appearance and threat to the school environment, citing Islamic traditions (here not wearing shoes in the mosque in order
to keep it clean) again speaks to a taken-for-granted social hierarchy: the comfort of the teacher explicitly privileged above the student's expression of piety.

Here Berat exposes the power of discourses where danger or fear prevail in the regulation of the Muslim body, while also alluding to a prayer cap making the school "dirty," effectively polluting civic space.

The Muslim Parvenu

Dirt and danger reside in the discourse of "darkness." And throughout our interactions, darkness also emerges as a discourse attached to Muslim life. I am assured by these police officers that Şehitlik is a "best-case scenario," diverging from the utter "darkness" of "basement" or "backyard" mosques. They offer to show me these closely monitored spaces and thereby illuminate Şehitlik as an exceptional mosque that stands out from the ordinary, an architectural embodiment of Arendt's parvenu.[84] This is a warning disguised as an offering, an invocation of the good Muslim/bad Muslim and good mosque/bad mosque divide, a nod towards the impossibility of Muslim civility towards which they themselves strive.[85] As Berat puts it,

> Şehitlik is a model mosque. With our politics, they were often in the press and TV. And more and more mosque tours are happening, the people come and go, the buses drive in front and maybe you have been on one of the tours? Şehitlik has to be considered differently than other mosques without tours. In those one has to be covered but in Şehitlik one can go with a t-shirt, normally dressed.

Ateş adds,

> To me personally, Şehitlik is the model mosque, but for me personally it could be more open, even more open. I was not brought up so religiously, I know Muslims as much as I know Christians. My vision of the future for Muslims is exactly how he [Berat] and his family are: open, tolerant, not closed, still believing but not so believing as in AD 536 when Muhammad came out, stuck in these old traditions. But in reality, we are in year 2015. They must develop into that.

The same tropes of the abstracted Muslim as embodied incivility, from opacity to the persistence of "old traditions" rather than enlightened progress, emerge in these police descriptions of Şehitlik's exceptionality. And yet these officers not only describe a civilizing process in the twenty-first-century metropolis, but *partake in it* themselves. In this process, the individual Muslim (like Berat) or individual institution (like Şehitlik) reaches for a promise to escape incivility, explicitly undergirded by the expectation that he/it distance himself/itself (disregarding religious rituals, revising the Qur'an, stressing "modernness") from Islam. Here again "sly civility" rears its ugly head, in a system of surveillance that supposedly offers inclusion—again "an impossible dream."[86] These heterodox/former Muslim police officers, as explicit state intercessors (recall Topolski's analysis of the Jewish *shtadlanut*) embody this striving, as they explicitly grapple for Muslim forms that, paradoxically distanced or distinct from Islam, can belong to contemporary Germany.[87] At once surveillant and surveilled, they expose just as they impose the violence of a civilizing discourse, with fraught liminality hidden under words of progress, "a new way" as old as Europe itself.

The coding of Muslims as uncivil through a dichotomy between tradition and modernity occurs not only in conversations with police officers but also with other state representatives, as during a 2015 community discussion at Şehitlik with a psychologist who works for family services in Berlin. The psychologist speaks of the hurdles in families with migration backgrounds—home structures that create barriers to higher education, the failure of parents to play with their children, and a lack of ability to develop individual selves. She shows a slide with the graphic of an upside-down triangle, detailing how kids from "traditional families" emphasize the collective, whereas "the modern" emphasizes autonomy. She then criticizes fathers in these communities who "never kiss their kids." Mosque leader Pinar interjects, responding to this abstraction of the Muslim father—the imagined, traditional Muslim man as "oppressor" rather than caretaker—with a concrete example from the prophetic tradition.[88] In so doing, Pinar agentively shifts the narrative, articulated in a language of German values (including broad misconceptions about Muslim families) to one articulated in a language of Islamic virtues—replacing a discourse of hierarchy with one of horizontality. She draws on the Sunna, in which the Prophet Muhammad is said to have walked through the streets, engaging with children. "When he spoke to them, he knelt so as to be on the same level," she explains.

The harmonization project of Şehitlik does not crumble but meets its limits here, in the stories told and stories enlivened by civil servants, most notably the police officers who term it a best-case scenario that is simply not good enough, still positioned in the social imaginary far below the mainstream. The incivility of Islam so potent in the mainstream reverberates in the constructed images of cold-faced fathers, or little boys clutching their Qur'ans. And it hovers, always, in the backdrop of conversations with city authorities about Islam. "They should do more," the police officers contend, be "more open," "go to the streets" to demonstrate against terror attacks, "show that [they] are distanced from these things." Ateş asserts,

> You have to say that you [Şehitlik] are absolutely against this: go to the streets, have events, demonstrations, involve non-Muslim society, Germans, and those not involved in Islam, show them that you are distanced from these things . . . They are also victims of the attacks, they are seen as the image of an enemy. Şehitlik organized a large event to show "We are against Islamism. We are against terror. We are against killing."

Whether exceptional or not, mosque communities like Şehitlik, as all mosque communities, are guilty until proven innocent. They are tasked with demonstrating their loyalty to the city and to the state, again and again and again. That is, the parvenu remains dangerously close to the pariah, "in the same boat, rowing desperately in the same angry sea."[89]

Recognizing the security lens under which they are scrutinized, Muslim leaders aim to prevent police contact with their communities, creating a space between them; in so doing, however, they come to straddle both spheres, inhabiting a positionality of great social dis-ease. At Şehitlik, for instance, the Bahira Project, a partnership between the mosque and the Violence Prevention Network (VPN), an NGO that receives funding from city and state governments, tackles both prevention and intervention when individual radicalization is suspected. Headed by Pinar Çetin (Şehitlik), Thomas Mücke (VPN), and Levent Yükçü (VPN), it works with schools, youth, parents, mosque communities, broader Muslim collectivities, and other religious organizations. From its inception in 2015, the Bahira Project intervenes in families concerned that a child/brother/sister might radicalize, aiming for deescalation before police involvement becomes necessary. My interlocutors express ambivalence towards the police, some emphasizing the respect they are due as authority figures who maintain social order—at times turning to the police, for instance, when mosques receive threats. Yet when Muslim leaders become themselves implicated in state surveillance, coercion cloaked in discursive terms of partnership, cooperation, or community work, they may also lose legitimacy within the Muslim community. This is inarguably violence by another name, an impossible choice amidst impossible dreams.

We are thus reminded here too in Benjaminian terms that "the 'state of emergency' in which we live is not the exception but the rule."[90] Police, the eyes of the security state, reveal an inherent and enduring discomfort with, and sanctioning of, Islam *as Islam* and Muslims *as Muslims*. From physical markers to pious practices and even familial structures, officers reiterate discourses of danger and threat. The dominance of gendered and embodied distinction also comes to the fore in these conversations; while the covering of a girl's body, or a boy's head, becomes a perceptible sign of threat, allowing "normal dress" such as t-shirts in the mosque is held up as a symbol of civility. Like mosques, Muslim bodies in all of their forms, including those of Muslim security personnel themselves, remain ceaselessly insecure objects of security.

To write of latent discrimination in security forces in Europe, along with the pariah and parvenu, evokes one of the greatest scandals in French history, the Dreyfus Affair. In 1894, Alfred Dreyfus, a captain artillery officer, was falsely accused of high treason and sentenced to life in prison. Although major Ferdinand Esterhazy was in fact guilty of the crimes attributed to Dreyfus, French army officials not only attempted to hide this information when it came to light but even created fake documents to continue Dreyfus's imprisonment. The ongoing condemnation of Dreyfus was spearheaded by Éduard Drumont, author of the deeply anti-Semitic book *Jewish France* and editor of the newspaper *La Libre Parole*, in which he described Dreyfus in a headline as "the Jewish traitor."[91] While Dreyfus was eventually pardoned after a series of trials in 1906, the Dreyfus Affair exposed deep-seated anti-Semitism across the military, politics, and society writ large. I am reminded of a personal story that I encountered in my readings on the Dreyfus Affair, not about Alfred Dreyfus himself but rather about Bernard Lezare, a nineteenth-century French literary critic and journalist (mentioned earlier in reference to his writings on the Jew as pariah), who was one of Dreyfus's greatest supporters. Lazare, who grew up apathetic about his Jewish roots and enamored with France, was jolted awake by the Dreyfus Affair from his own impossible dream of civility. Nelly Jussem-Wilson describes Lazare's self-transformation in the aftermath of this face-off with anti-Semitism in France in poignant, painful, and still-relevant terms. "The Jew-philosopher once had a dream: he was a son of France without allegiances outside his native land. Then somebody called him 'stranger' and he woke up a Jew, without knowing what it meant to be a Jew."[92] In the years that followed, Lezare came to embrace his Jewish identity, and summoned Jews writ large to demand respect and dignity *as Jews* in the nation-states that refused to fully include them.[93]

It was not only in France but also in Germany that such suspicion in the military came to characterize all Jews as a threat to the civic order in the early twentieth century. In 1916, not long after the Dreyfus Affair, the Imperial German War Ministry, specifically War Minister Adolf Wild von Hohenborn, called for the "Jewish count" or "Jewish census" (*Judenzählung*), on the grounds of conspiratorial accusations that Jews were shirking their responsibility to participate as soldiers on the front lines. As with the Dreyfus Affair, the *Judenzählung* set off fierce debates across the sociopolitical spectrum, revealing the depth and breadth of anti-Semitism. Stereotypes of Jews as weak, conniving, disloyal—and ultimately responsible for Germany's defeat in World War I—quickly took hold, devastating the hopes of German Jews that they could be truly emancipated in and by the state. The experiences of many German Jews mirrored that of Lezare, being marked as a stranger and waking up a Jew, resulting in increased support for Zionism. The findings of this count, which showed German Jews as serving in the military in great numbers, the vast majority on the front lines, were not made public during the war. Instead, military leaders like General Erich Ludendorff ("the man who made Hitler possible") used the idea of the *Judenzählung* to foment divisions, feeding into the widespread scapegoating of Jews that undergirded the rise of National Socialism.[94]

I end here by returning from the past to the Ramadan celebration at Şehitlik with which I began, an evocative visual still imprinted on my mind. As the sun sets beneath the horizon, Katja remains on the mosque steps like a statue, a physical obstruction in the path of men who ascend the steps, hands clasping the hands of their children, as they move towards prayer. Katja's presence reveals only the tip of the iceberg—one among innumerable uncomfortable moments in which the deep security state, and the dangerous stories it tells about the civil/uncivil divide, rises to the surface of everyday life. The constituents of the Şehitlik Mosque believe in God and believe in the city, often holding both in the same breath as they describe a sense of belonging under the "undivided sky over Berlin."[95] They are, however, never "free" from this "straightjacket" constraining "the [un]fixed and the [un]familiar"—in a threshold held hostage, and a dream that fails to fully include them.[96]

CHAPTER 5

Messianic Horizon:
Inside the East London Mosque

Pushing a skinned cow carcass in a mangled shopping cart with fierce speed, a butcher catches my eye. His lips part in a whistle, hands so thick with callouses they barely close. He passes me in a bloodied white jacket made unremarkable by the opal and cerise saris on discount outside of shops, sent high to the skies by the wind. Upon exiting the Whitechapel tube station in Tower Hamlets, East London, I am greeted by street market workers and shoppers; swaths of gem-colored silks cut into wearable shapes in front of my eyes; baskets of mangos sold in bulk for a pound. The market bustles with men in traditional Bengali *kurta* pajamas, women in black donning a diversity of headscarves and niqabs.

London has always been a city of villages, centered in and around each neighborhood. And these streets of the east are the beating heart of a plural metropolis, once its center of Huguenot and Jewish life, and today home to a large Bengali, as well as growing Somali, populace. What a local police officer calls the "beating spiritual heart" of the Bengali community, the East London Mosque stands high above the other buildings on Whitechapel Road. It is a typical brown-brick edifice in London's East End, largely integrating into the urban landscape, albeit with a small dome and two small minarets suggesting something more. Being not only central but integral to this slice of Tower Hamlets, it melds fluidly into the city's surroundings. While only three decades old, the East London Mosque, a meeting place for local Muslims and also many who come from outside of the Tower Hamlets borough, appears on this broad avenue as if it has always been here. Each day, its *adhan* can be heard in nearby streets.

FIGURE 6. Exterior of the East London Mosque, Whitechapel Avenue. Photo by Vikram Kushwah.

Whitechapel Road is home to numerous discernably Muslim establishments beyond the mosque, from Kalam Solicitors to Bismillah Hotel, Al-
Furqan Bookshop, and Alhambra Clothing. Qur'an reading schools stand
side-by-side with Islamic banks, halal butchers, Bengali restaurants and clothing merchants, and an all-purpose Islamic store. It is also home to establishments like Aldgate Coffee House and Whitechapel Gallery. Tower Hamlets,
like East London more broadly, is in the throes of two levels of gentrification:
with the middle class moving into the area—the proportion of professionals
and managers in Tower Hamlets having risen 72 percent in the 1990s—and
commercial gentrification, like that in the docklands.[1]

TOPOGRAPHY OF DIFFERENCE

The topography of the East End is one long marked with cultural difference
and hierarchy. Jews first arrived in London in the eleventh century and were
forced to leave during the Jewish expulsion in 1290.[2] Marrano families (Jews
and Muslims who converted to Christianity) from Spain and Portugal then resettled in the British capital during the Reconquista.[3] Fleeing pogroms and expulsion from Russia and Prussia in the seventeenth century onward, the Jewish
population eventually came to center in East London, reaching approximately
150,000 by the mid-1880s.[4] Drawing on common stereotypes, Jews in the East
End were portrayed as dangerous, conniving tricksters set to outsmart others
in the market and beyond, and associated with "dirt and disorder"—"Jewish"
employed as a descriptor for the abject character of the area's garbage-filled
streets. As David Englander reflects, "immigrant Jews, it seemed, lived within
English society but were not part of it," a positionality experienced by Muslims, similarly associated with dirt, disorder, and danger following their mass
migration to the London metropolis in the mid-twentieth century.[5]

These topographical overlaps can be seen in the architectural face of today's East End, including the Brick Lane Mosque, converted from a Huguenot Protestant chapel into a synagogue in 1898 and from a synagogue into a
mosque in 1976.[6] Until recently, as it closed in 2015 due to dwindling membership, the Fieldgate Synagogue not only stood beside the East London
Mosque, but was also hugged from behind by the London Muslim Centre
(erected in 2004). In fact, the architects who expanded the ELM complex cut
windows into the adjoining walls to shine light on the Star of David above
the *bima*, an elevated platform for services or oration in the synagogue. For
years, this window allowed sight from the mosque into the synagogue and
from the synagogue, through the same window, into the mosque. In 2013, with

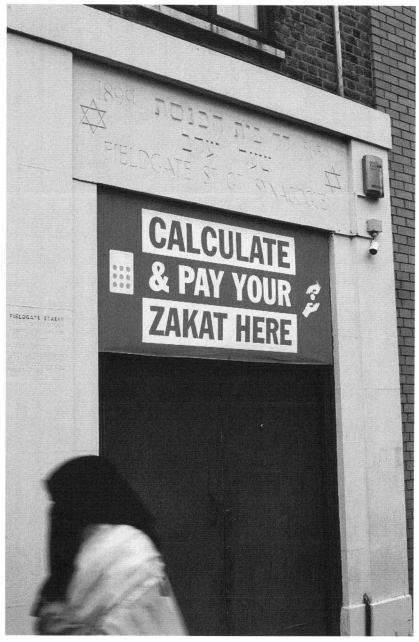

FIGURE 7. Exterior of the building that was previously the Fieldgate Synagogue. Photo by Vikram Kushwah.

FIGURE 8. Exterior of the Maryam Centre after Friday prayer. Photo by Vikram Kushwah.

the construction of the Maryam Centre, three sides of the synagogue abutted the mosque. Shortly after the synagogue halted services, ELM purchased the building in 2017. Today, below Hebrew lettering and Jewish stars etched into its edifice, a red and white sign reads "calculate & pay your zakat here."

The story of the neighborhood is not only one of topographical overlaps, windows cut open to let in the light of plurality present and past, but also conflict. Just one block south of the East London Mosque on Whitechapel Road, across from the Aldgate East Tube Station, Altab Ali Park commemorates a recent instance of ethnoreligious contention. The park was named following the murder of Altab Ali, a twenty-five-year-old Bengali man, by a group of teenagers in 1998.[7] A line from a poem by Rabindranath Tagore cuts through the green: "The shade of my tree is offered to those who come and go fleetingly." Today, broader societal tensions penetrate the borders, both geographical and imagined, of the borough. Whether myth or reality, some have come to perceive Tower Hamlets as a beacon of plurality to take down.[8] The right-wing Christian patrols drive in armored cars suggestive of violence, seeking to provoke by drinking beer in front of the East London Mosque. The Muslim patrols stand behind "non-gay zone" stickers pasted on street lamps and the burqas spray-painted on H&M bikini ads at a bus stop in ELM's neighborhood. Mark assures me that both groups have infiltrated the diverse mecca of Tower Hamlets, external forces continually forcing their way in. They choose this district as their stage, he asserts, its mixture of residents at odds with the divergent, imagined homogeneous societies championed by both.

At Home and Away

Established in 1910, the London Mosque Fund provided spaces of worship for the local Muslim populace in the East End. In 1926, it became a registered charity, a "floating mosque" of sorts renting prayer rooms on Fridays and holidays.[9] In 1941, the East London Mosque and Islamic Cultural Centre opened its doors to congregants at its first site on Commercial Road. In the post-WWII era, the East London Mosque became a center of spiritual life for local Bengalis, who make up one-third of Tower Hamlet's residents, the borough long home to the largest Bengali population in the UK.[10] In 1982, the London Council, a government administrative body, appropriated the mosque buildings, and the community moved into a temporary space, with a new building— that which stands today—planned for Whitechapel Road. This came to serve not only the local Bengali populace but also a growing Somali population since the 1980s.[11] While the main building on Whitechapel has been in use since 1985, additions of the London Muslim Centre, the Maryam Centre, and the Fieldgate Synagogue building have expanded the mosque complex both upwards and outwards.

Although a small Bengali populace already resided in London, the first large wave of immigration took place in the 1950s and 1960s, with most migrants hailing from Sylhet, a northeastern region of what is now Bangladesh.[12] Undergirded by a history of empire, as part of Britain's expansive colonial holdings, theirs was a labor migration explicitly encouraged by the British government, which needed industrial workers.[13] This need declined in parallel with the industrial sector in the UK towards the end of the twentieth century; however, the same migrants soon came to dominate service sectors in London, including laundries and restaurants. In Katy Gardner's oral histories with first-generation Bengalis in London's East End, the dominance of work in their daily lives resonates. "I used to sleep, eat, work, and sleep. Get up in the morning and work and work. I would just work and work," said one of her interlocutors, a narrative very much akin to those of my interlocutors who migrated from Turkey to Berlin.[14] With their husbands employed in the London economy, many first-generation Bengali women in East London lived their lives almost exclusively in the private sphere, providing comprehensive care to their immediate and extended families. Some provided further fiscal support to their families through domestic jobs, like housecleaning.

In the discourse of her interlocutors, Gardner finds that the first generation tends to classify Sylhet as "home" (*desh*) and Britain as "away" (*bidesh*).[15] Like the feelings their Şehitlik counterparts express towards Turkey, many who hail from Sylhet feel that they still belong in and to the towns and villages from which they emigrated. Located in the liminal space between "home" and "away," the East London Mosque affords a sense of grounding in a diaspora setting. Although it primarily serves the Bengali and Somali communities, it has also increasingly catered to a large group of reverts (people converting or returning to Islam). As it has expanded both inward and outward, the mosque's myriad spaces, incarnations in form—from the main building to the Muslim Centre, the Maryam Centre to a beehive on the rooftop—have bolstered a sense of shelter in what can be a vicious city, where cultural distance and economic struggle collide. "So we may dwell by being both home and away," write Timothy Oakes and Patricia Price on the expansiveness of cultural geographies.[16]

Anthropologist Pnina Werbner has reductively argued that two contrasting hegemonic public spheres emerge among ethnically Pakistani and Bengali communities in the UK: one hybrid (a reflexive British South Asian culture) and the other espousing a purist vision of Islam.[17] The simplicity of such division in fact gives way to complex moral-social-material universes. The ELM community, for instance, grappling with a sense of partial inclusion in British society, seeks protection, certainty, and rootedness in other forms, demarcating all aspects of life through a halal (permissible)/haram (forbidden) boundary. On the surface, this halal/haram boundary preached in sermons and taught in mosque learning circles appears to replicate the mainstream/Muslim divide. Yet it in fact powerfully inverts group positioning, with the Muslim community representing the halal, encompassing not only the permitted but the pure, and the mainstream site of the haram, operationalized as the forbidden and polluted. This inversion is based in a messianic vision of salvation—an idea, shared by Muslims and Jews, that the messiah will arrive and lead the pious back to God. And it helps the community to make sense of, as well as contend with, their positioning in earthly life: a history of colonialism and a present concurrently characterized by low socioeconomic status and stigma attached to Muslim identities in the mainstream. By providing for most social needs at the mosque (gym, school, speakers, cultural events, etc.) and opting out of main-stream media, establishments, and institutions, the ELM community is able to create both emotional and physical distance from the forces of marginality.

The theological underpinnings of the ELM community, spanning both time and space, are impossible to condense into any single tradition, draw-ing from (1) the Jamaat-e-Islami, (2) the Deoband movement, (3) Wahhabism, (4) Salafism, and (5) Sufism (through and beyond the aforementioned Deo-band movement). Mosque leadership historically belonged to either the Jamaat-e-Islami, founded by Syed Abul A'la Maududi (1903–79), or the Deo-band movement, merging Sufism with the Hanafi legal school. Yet the mosque has also increasingly become linked to Wahhabism through deepening Saudi Arabian influences, including the training of imams, financial support for the mosque building, and celebrated visitors, as well as Salafism through contem-porary teachings of scholars like Yusuf al-Qaradawi.[18] Finally, leaders at ELM are influenced by Sufism not only through the Deoband movement but also through writings like those of Sufi Imam Mawlud in his Matharat al-Qulub (1844–1905), translated and commented on by Hamza Yusuf. This kind of theological diversity combines schools of thought (some assumed to be incom-patible, like Wahhabism and Sufism), revealing a modern project of fusion and translocality.[19]

Rather than state connections, my ELM interlocutors describe connections that transcend the nation-state—from Mecca and Medina, vital to the birth and flourishing of Islam, to their mosque and neighborhood in London, vital to their flourishing as Muslims. In Gardner's oral histories with first-generation migrants, emotional connections to cities, towns, and villages in Bangladesh, and neighborhoods in London, rather than the state, similarly emerge; here it is important to recall that Bangladesh was founded in 1971, after many individ-uals and families had already migrated to the UK.[20] Translocality also appears on a symbolic rather than geographical level, as the teachings at ELM move beyond taken-for-granted boundaries inside of Islam in order to solidify new boundaries that demarcate it as a sociocultural space separate from both ethno-national cultures and the mainstream. In addition to theological influences, past social influences—colonialism in particular—and present economic precarity pair with sociocultural marginality to shape a particular expression of Islam.

The East London Mosque has long been influenced by Jamaat-e-Islami, as London's hub for the movement beginning in the 1960s.[21] In 1962, Jamaat-e-Islami followers founded the UK Islamic Mission (UKIM), and in 1984, the Young Muslims UK (YMUK) for UKIM youth. In 1978, the Dawat al-Islam organization was also established at ELM by UKIM—specifically aiming to appeal to the large and growing Bengali population in the East End. The youth wing of the Dawat al-Islam, the Young Muslim Organisation (YMO), was created soon after, and the Islamic Forum of Europe (IFE) established to serve the Bengali intellectual elite in 1988. When Dawat al-Islam broke away from the mosque, the IFE became linked to the YMO.[22] The IFE and the YMO, both rooted in Maududian thought, have since been the subject of great controversy due to their Islamist political agendas.[23]

While divorced for many, but certainly not all, of its increasingly diverse community—including a growing constituency of Bengali Brits born in London—from South Asian politics, Maududi's ideas consistently emerge in community discourses. This includes the dominance of Islam in all aspects of life and the mark of absolute obedience discerning a "true" Muslim from a "cultural" Muslim. Such discernment between pure Islam and the "non-Islam" lived by most self-identified Muslims is a marked aspect of Maududi's theological treatise.[24] ELM also reflects Maududi's stance that Western society, while not modernity in its entirety, clashes with Muslim piety, although its main imam, Shaykh Abdul Qayum, has suggested the acceptability of some sociocultural adaptability in a society without viable Islamic institutions.[25]

One must keep in mind that reformist movements like Maududi's Jamaat-e-Islami emerged in the context of colonial rule, undergirded by a drive towards liberation. In response to the colonial and postcolonial experience, Maududi's teachings have become interwoven with myriad other reformist doctrines, such as those undergirding the Deoband movement, Wahhabism, and Salafism. Colonialism fomented widespread belief that Muslims had done something wrong, bringing upon themselves political conquest, disease, and suffering through immorality—as predicted in the Qur'an. The idea that only moral purification, a righting of past wrongs, can redeem a people, has thus been a common response to the unfathomable abuse, as well as political and social destruction, that characterized colonialism.[26] Pakistan, of which Bangladesh was formerly a part, was founded on the idea that a Muslim state could provide a place for the pious to thrive; and in recent years, Bangladesh has increasingly tied itself to purist religious leadership.[27] The trope of immorality or sin as cause of extreme human suffering continues to be preached in many Muslim communities, including ELM, today.[28] As Imam K. of ELM puts it:

> Due to all this immorality spread in society . . . Allah will enable their enemies to overpower them and take some of what is in their hands, which is taking place in many parts of the Muslim world . . . Allah will cause them to fight

among one another. Civil war will be in many places, which is happening in many places. Allah *Subhanahu wa-ta'ala* praise those people who don't commit these kind of sin, the major sin, they are the people of Janna [heaven]!

Many of the most revered contemporary religious figures at ELM hail from, or are trained in, Saudi Arabia, where Wahhabi doctrine, entailing purist and literalist interpretation of Islamic sources, dominates. As Khaled Abou El Fadl explains, "According to the Wahhabis, it was imperative to return to a presumed, pristine, simple, and straightforward Islam, which was believed to be entirely reclaimable by a literal implementation of the commands and precedents of the Prophet, and by a strict adherence to correct ritual practice"; this ideology emerged from a centuries-old political alliance between the Saudi ruling family and the followers of Muhammad ibn Abd al Wahhab, an eighteenth-century theologian.[29] If not initially theologically linked, ELM has had a close association with Saudi Arabia since its foundation. The booklet distributed at the opening ceremony of the mosque on Friday, July 12, 1985, begins with a message from King Fahd Bin Abdulaziz of Saudi Arabia, presented by Hafiz Wahba, the Saudi ambassador. Wahba in fact led the first prayer at the original ELM mosque. According to this archival document, "Since 1949 their excellencies, the Ambassadors for Saudi Arabia, Pakistan, Egypt and their successors have been ex-officio permanent Trustees." The Saudi Arabian government donated more than half of the funds used to build today's purpose-built mosque.[30]

Marginality and Flight

Rooted at once in the city and the *umma*, the mosque itself has become a place of home in "away," a temporary respite in lives displaced, as lives are oriented towards paradise. For the first generation, it rises as an opportunity to bolster dignity and authority in a space of emotional ownership. For the subsequent generations and for converts, the two groups with whom I spend most of my time, it becomes a center for learning and enacting an unadulterated, "culture-free" Islam while critiquing surrounding society. As at Şehitlik, this relates to a sense of marginality and yet here also to the idea of flight. Conversations about marginality are, however, significantly more limited than at Şehitlik, arguably owing to less engagement with civic life. The disappointments of everyday life in the city do, however, emerge in the discourses of my interlocutors, and contribute to their messianic vision, rooted in a method of hope, which I explore in the following chapter.

In *London Youth, Religion, and Politics*, Daniel DeHanas characterizes Muslims in Tower Hamlets as highly civically engaged, whereas my interlocutors describe, display, and celebrate both emotional and physical detachment from local and national civic life beyond the Muslim community. At least some of these differences arise from our chosen methodological lenses and their gendered components; while DeHanas interviewed those engaged in myriad institutions throughout the borough, including numerous men, I spend my days with women whose locus of public life is the mosque.[31] Yet our differing lenses, when brought into conversation, raise similar questions about the boundaries of civic activism, including: How and where are civic actions oriented? Who participates in these actions and who is left out? What are the gender dimensions of such engagement? And where does the mosque fit into the larger stories of the neighborhood and the metropolis?

The motivations behind mosque leadership holding positions on local interfaith or civic boards remain unclear, elucidating their investment in the neighborhood and/or a way in which to agentively respond to surveillance while buffering the community from external influences. Social and even political participation appears motivated by an aim of protecting separate but equal Islamic space—according to DeHanas, being a "Muslim first," and for many of my interlocutors, "just Muslim."[32] This exclusive identity results not from a lack of knowledge about the state, politics, or civic life among my interlocutors, but instead feelings of detachment fostered by inequality, undergirded by assumptions of incivility.[33] In spite of our differing lenses, DeHanas and I both witness a process of gaining faith while "losing faith in the state," with the city, and the imagined global *umma*, central to the articulation of belonging—complicating notions about the locus of home, which appears both dynamic and plural.[34]

On my first day at the mosque, I sit inside of the main prayer room at the Maryam Centre, where Amaya teaches Qur'anic recitation to a teenage girl and her mother in a mixture of English, Bengali, and Arabic. As I exit the room, another woman extends her hand and asks who I am. She introduces herself as Melia, a retired teacher and mother of two. Lithe, beautiful, and yet sickly looking, Melia exudes an air of loneliness. She assures me that I too "will soon learn" through Amaya's instruction, learning circles, and workshops. Soon I am learning from Amaya, in a weekend learning circle for "New Muslims" that caters both to converts and Bengali Londoners seeking to deepen their practice of Islam, and through a variety of other workshops, spanning topics from purification to preparation for the hajj.

Weeks later, as we cross Weaver's Field, an expansive green dividing the Bethnal Green neighborhood from Whitechapel Road, Melia takes my arm. "Tower Hamlets is different," she says, gesturing around us to the sweeping verdant fields. "British society is not so open and accepting." She pauses, shifting her eyes to the sun crossing the horizon. As a not-so-gentle reminder of the larger, wealthier cityscape, the skyscrapers of Canary Wharf peek out from behind the clouds. "Non-Muslims want to get out of here, move to East Ham [a district in the London borough of Newham] and other areas where they can hate us from afar." This comment evokes Richard Sennett's critique of flight from the city as response to discomfort with cultural difference—"Jew then, Muslim now"—poignantly embodied by Martin Heidegger during the rise of National Socialism.[35] Heidegger fled to the German Black Forest as he embraced anti-Semitism, in spite of his longstanding mentorship of Jewish students, including Hannah Arendt and Hans Jonas.[36]

Melia describes uncomfortable moments where cultural differences collide, the reign of civility measured through what Holston calls "cultural conventions, everyday performances, aesthetic codes"—"qualities of inclusion" that notably exclude visible symbols of Islam, like dress.[37] She recently moved to a new house near Bethnal Green, where neighbors were friendly to her husband and son before they met her daughter and herself; afterwards, they became distant and assumed "that we don't know anything. They offered to fill out our bureaucratic forms . . . 'You know, she is a teacher trained in special education,' my husband told them." Hasan, a local youth worker, describes the blows of stereotypes that not only color mainstream perceptions of Muslims as ignorant and uncivil, but can lead to violence. "For instance, at the Whitechapel Market my mother has started wearing a burqa, full covering, niqab. She was called a 'ninja' and spit at." And yet he hopes to shift perceptions in mundane encounters, exposing what Mayanthi Fernando describes as "the desire to be ordinary" among those marked as negatively extraordinary in the public sphere.[38]

> I feel now I need to try to prove [myself], to help a woman with her carriage across the street and hope that she thinks, "No, Muslims aren't like that." If she sees something on the news, or if she is with friends saying, "Muslims are like this and that," she can say, "No, a Muslim man helped me to carry the carriage, or my bags."

Flight from such an environment pregnant with tensions over plurality occurs not only outwards in the literal sense (as from the city), but also inwards

FIGURE 9. View of the London cityscape from the Maryam Centre. Photo by Vikram Kushwah.

in the spiritual sense (both within the city and within the self). At ELM, the inward-focused opportunity found within Islam for the individual is often spoken as "truth" and for the community as "equality." It appears as both affective opportunity and shelter from the steel faces—human, economic, architectural—of the metropolis. Having returned to root himself in the East London Mosque community and its surrounding neighborhood after studying Arabic abroad, my Qur'an class teacher, Jamal, contrasts his disillusionment with Hinduism, experienced during a visit with relatives in India, to his experience with Islam:

> I went to eat a street snack in Mumbai and the shop was closing. I asked the old man working to sit with me and eat, but he said he couldn't, he was one of the untouchables. He couldn't really talk to me, he couldn't sit with me. Because he learned that if he stayed within his caste and did what he was supposed to do—served, cleaned the streets—he would be reincarnated into a high caste. With us, in Islam, it is different. Everyone is equal. We stand shoulder to shoulder as equals.

At the East London Mosque, everyone is equal and yet they are not: equal in spiritual potentiality within Islam, but neither in cultural nor socioeconomic status as Muslims in the London metropolis. Many of my interlocutors live in the stifling social housing flats where I too resided during my research, a constant flow of marijuana spiking the air, urine-filled stairways beside broken elevators, metal doorways etched with keys. Many experience discrimination on a daily basis, bellowed through the back of a bus, shoved, or spit on: proof of the broken promise of pluralism, yet again that "impossible dream" of "sly civility."[39] Like "civility," "equality" must be deconstructed in the liberal democratic context as it is pregnant with both power and contradiction.[40] "The root meaning of equality is negative," writes Michael Walzer. "Egalitarianism in its origins is an abolitionist politics. It aims at eliminating not all differences, but a particular set of differences, and a different set in different times and places."[41] That is, equality is not bestowed upon, but rather forged in its juxtaposition to, certain forms of difference, such as Muslim difference and its many signifiers.

Situated in this complex arena of economic and cultural marginality, my interlocutors at ELM are motivated by sight beyond the colonial afterlife of the London metropolis, not only in space but in time, reassured that in doing what they are supposed to do for God *and more*, the fruits of paradise will fall onto their tongues after death. The difficulties and disappointments of this life "as only a drop in the ocean" of all life become easier to endure. It is not so different from the Hindu man in Mumbai described by Jamal after all, who stepped away and held his tongue for hope that his life in the here and now would be just a drop in the ocean of all lives to come. Both remain constrained by systemic marginalization, differentiated by the only religiously righteous way out: one through the caste system itself, the other through a transcendent system designed by God that will release him from "the world [that] is of course a prison . . . indeed it is forever, that is what you are waiting for," in the words of Hawa, a speaker at a women's event. Here a sense of detachment from the dystopic reality of the metropolis—teeming with impossible dreams—comes to contend with the unrealized but redemptive *topos*: the place, and time, in which the pious will be reunited with God.[42]

Amaya: "You can never trust the weather in Britain"

Amaya's father opens the door to her rowhouse, peeking outside to greet us. He kisses Amaya on both cheeks and then waves us in. "He's just here watching TV," she comments, removing her abaya and headscarf as soon as she shuts the door. "I need to get out of this right away." She hangs both items of clothing on the knob of the staircase banister, entering the kitchen and turning the kettle on. "First, let's have some tea," she says with a smile, as we have arrived damp from the midday rain.

"Amaya." Her father says her name with affection, as he speaks to his daughter, a woman in her mid-thirties, and with pride in the education she has pursued to become a teacher. She not only teaches *tajwid* (recitation) to women from the mosque in her spare time but also children in Sunday school. A *tafsir* (exegesis) course drew her back towards the religion, from a life of clubbing, which now feels a world away. Beside us in the kitchen, her youngest child, a girl on the brink of adolescence, balances stuffed animals on the counter: a fox beside a zebra beside a lion. Amaya smiles as she removes them, ushering her family members out of the room towards the staircase so that we can begin our lessons, filling their arms with these inanimate characters, looking on with wide plastic eyes.

"It's important to be educated, educated properly," she asserts, as she pours tea into two ceramic cups, their mouths lined with silver. "But then I have a lot of friends whose children are given a proper education in a *madrasa* and reject the religion, go to university and give up on it." She talks about her husband, whose gambling and drinking problems threatened their union. While he has relinquished both and turned towards Islam, now reciting the Qur'an in an off-key voice that she cannot stand, Amaya says he was at first envious of her return to Islam. He was in fact initially even afraid of her invigorated religious devotion. Then, he started learning himself. "I'm way ahead," she assures. Yet when she began Arabic lessons, she wept each evening because the other women were far ahead of her. As she grasped the language, learning not only to read but to "think it," she found herself yearning to change her life. Her three children all nearly grown, her dream of moving to Saudi Arabia and teaching now seems within grasp.

Amaya grew up in London with her brothers and her parents, who migrated from Bangladesh in the 1960s. She feels safe here, even though "you can never trust the weather in Britain." Her mother passed away and her father lives nearby in Stepney; "not a religious man," but more "culturally Muslim," he visits her for company or to share meals. Over the past few years, she has "come back to the religion," as she was looking for something else in her life. She knew in her heart that she was Muslim because her parents were Muslim, but didn't know what this meant. She changed the way she dressed, from jeans and t-shirts to modest clothing. Within the local Muslim community, she got "much more respect" since she "started covering."

In her kitchen, we begin the recitation lessons slowly, pronouncing the Arabic letters with care, focusing on how I shape my lips and tongue with each sound. Amaya retrieves a *tafsir* book from the top shelf of a tall cabinet, which at first she does not want to touch, as she is menstruating. She reconsiders; "I won't touch the Arabic," she says, opening it at the corner of the page so that I can see inside. We turn to the letters, her finger carefully hovering above the text. "Before, like you, I knew nothing," she says.

IN THE SENSE OF A POSSIBILITY: THE PEDAGOGY OF REDEMPTION

Like many in her Tower Hamlets neighborhood, Amaya is barely getting by. Positioned within a nexus of cultural and fiscal marginalization in one of the UK's most disadvantaged neighborhoods, the East London Mosque largely serves an economically insecure community. While not a site of emotional identification, citizenship is both a recognized and esteemed legal status among my interlocutors, who make fiscal claims on the state. At the same time, they describe their mosque and the global *umma* as interconnected loci of emotional belonging, both vital to their strivings to be "just Muslim." On a concrete level, the prospect of paradise fosters devotion to the mosque itself as a protective and emancipatory space in the city, neither home nor away but a liminal bridge between them. And focusing outwards on the *umma* allows the individual to locate herself within a larger collectivity, in spite of dislocations in lived sociopolitical circumstances, emotionally rooted in this greater imagined sphere. Here salvation is achieved through a messianic vision transcending the notion of time-as-progress so central to Euro/Christian historicity. Socioeconomic struggles and cultural marginality are transcended through what Giulia Liberatore terms new "forms of aspiration" in anticipation of the future to come—"not *yet*, in the sense of a possibility"—through self-cultivation and social cohesion that draws on an Islamic past.[43]

Messianic Time

This anticipatory focus of the East London Mosque can be fruitfully explored through the messianic strands of Hermann Cohen's and Walter Benjamin's writings. In these interstitial fragments of urban life—one architectural (the mosque), the other textual (the writings of these Jewish thinkers)—what Benjamin terms "the present, as 'the time of the now' . . . is shot through with chips of Messianic time."[44] Cohen and Benjamin both expose the tension between historical and messianic perspectives, specifically their incongruity in scales of time. Cohen in particular sees the Jewish perspective as endowed with the capacity to critique time-as-progress through a focus on the future rather than a Euro/Christian-centric historicity.[45] And the inherent tension between historical materialist critique and messianism lies at the heart of Benjamin's writings; over time, he delinks himself from the former, arguably deficient of religious experience, as he turns towards the latter. Like Cohen, recognizing and rejecting the dominance of a uni-historical lens, Benjamin instead looks to the ideal future, built upon a new, more complete blueprint of the past, one revealed to the critical eye through the cracks of modernity.[46] As Benjamin scholar Peter Demetz writes, here "we are left with hope."[47]

East London Mosque constituents *begin* their projects of *poiesis* with hope. As at Şehitlik, the limits imposed by oppressive language are contested through a deepening of Islamic knowledge in both body and mind.[48] ELM, at once as institution, as community, and as vision becomes an opportunity: a place of worldly, if temporary, respite from which to critically counter superimposed cultural and socioeconomic hierarchies through the Islamic epistemological tradition. Here hope rises in, and as, an anticipatory interstice cutting through the soon-to-be rubble of the distracting and devastating present. And it is projected not only to the future, but through the past. At no point do my interlocutors seek emancipation within the material world through, for instance, socialist paradigms; instead, they seek emancipation *from* the material world by anticipating the messianic promise. Aiming to revive a purer past in future form through the cultivation of Islamic knowledge and practices, ELM thereby forges an alternative to the Eurocentric conceptualization of progress.

Enlivening their messianic vision, striving for truth and justice in the future through the past, is a deeply *phronetic* act rooted in a pedagogy of redemption. This pedagogy teaches pragmatic ways of both knowing and doing, drawing a discursive line between the halal, described not only as "permitted" but "pure" Islamic practice, and the haram, the "forbidden" and "impure." As one woman in our learning circle asserts, explaining that there is no gray in a life piously lived, "Black is black, white is white." The halal/haram boundary is constantly invoked within the knowledge-building activities of the mosque (learning circles, sermons, workshops) in three interrelated ways that delineate worldly acts as either oriented towards, or opposed to, the divine. Inside the mosque, it is operationalized as a gendered boundary; in the city, as a boundary between the Muslim community and the mainstream; and on a universal scale, as a boundary between this life and the afterlife. These layered delineations are reiterated in materials used by mosque leadership, including *Purification of the Heart*, based on the writings of Imam al-Mawlud, sold at a women's weekend workshop by the same name.[49] From the mihrab to inspirational graphics shared on social media, the mosque stairways to the nearby streets of Tower Hamlets, a halal/haram pedagogy positing pure "Muslimness" as key to redemption dominates. On the surface, this binary discourse suggests a simplification of the Islamic tradition in the life of the mosque community, but it in fact results in a nuanced system of learning and reflecting to determine on what side of the line each intention or action falls.

In his Friday sermons, Imam K. consistently articulates the need for gender separation as an expression of the larger halal/haram boundary that distinguishes true Muslims from non-Muslims, including both "cultural Muslims" and the mainstream. In one particularly evocative speech, he differentiates between halal marital relations and haram romantic encounters, encapsulated in the celebration of Valentine's Day.

> How to make our life pure, not touched by impurity . . . When you are not guided by Allah, there is no restriction, there is no halal and haram boundary. We are not alone with our desires, our *nafs*, but there is somebody else always trying to confuse us, he has many means and that is Shaitan [Satan] . . . He had the weapon of Jahannam [hell], of not having the proper dress code. He had the weapon of music, dance . . . many other things, to spread immoral love, illegal love. Legal love between husband and wife is beautiful. First thing, it is

coming from eyesight, big tool of Shaitan . . . The sight, the eye, looking at somebody who is haram to look at, is a poisonous arrow of Shaitan . . . That's why Allah commanded . . . "Tell believers they need to lower their gaze"[50] . . . and that women should not have interactions with someone who is haram.

He continues:

Valentine's Day: some people, many of them are doing some kind of function, some kind of party, seeing each other, sending cards, roses, many other things. What is this? The heart, the colors red and pink, roses, images, and statues of cupids and cupid's bows and arrows symbolize the feelings of love. Cupid in their understanding is an angel, a good helper to create love between one person and another. An angel is created to do this evil job, immorality.

With not only a separate space but an entirely separate building for women, encounters between the genders at the East London Mosque remain few and far between. Relations with men outside of one's family are strictly regulated both within and beyond the mosque. "When we have these barriers, or screening, it's just to delay the inevitable that could happen. It doesn't mean it happens all the time. It *could* happen," explains Rua, a women's leader at the Maryam Centre. Again, this pedagogy is rooted in possibility—anticipation of what could be. Women cover when venturing outside, often increasingly over time, first donning the headscarf, later head-to-toe niqabs. When they do on rare occasion walk through the men's section of the building to attend a talk, my female interlocutors, dressed with only hands and faces exposed, shield all but their eyes; each time, the words of a women's learning circle teacher, Samiya, echo in my mind: "If a man sees you and lusts after you, then it's your sin, isn't it?" We view most talks not in divided rooms but rather on large white screens that descend from the ceiling of the Maryam Centre's main prayer space. Visiting male speakers are obscured in tall, blue felt-covered boxes when inside of the same room as women, and thus women also obscured to them.

Love of the *Dunya*

In this paradigm of learning and doing, not only are halal/haram boundaries between the genders (as the mainstream and the world/afterlife) carefully maintained, but every moment is lived as the last; "for every second of time was the strait gate through which the Messiah might enter," writes Benjamin

FIGURE 10. Interior of the main prayer room in the Maryam Centre. Photo by author.

in his final thesis on history.[51] Spanning physical places and moments within London's East End, moving from the mosque itself to homes, walks through ever-green parks to restaurants, my time with women from ELM both inside and beyond the mosque bounds focuses on building, and constantly invoking, Islamic knowledge—providing both a metaphorical and a metaphysical door to redemption. Here Islam comes to occupy all spatial and temporal areas of life through a saturation with Islamic knowledge seeking, discourses, and practices. In the mosque and within my interlocutors' homes, we memorize Arabic letters, flick through texts on the Prophet Muhammad, and practice reciting Qur'anic verse. "What do you want to learn?" Kasia, a young friend of Melia whom I often see at ELM with her daughters, asks me, when we meet at her home. The first time she poses this question, I request a lesson on angels; she searches YouTube, and settles on a Merciful Servant channel video in which an angel saves a man lost in the desert after he prays to God. She pauses it throughout to encourage her husband to leave the house so that we can use the kitchen, always cognizant of maintaining separation between unrelated women and men.

During a Friday sermon, Imam K. iterates the totality of Islam. "Islam would like to see every individual is having a pure life, life of honesty, dignity, life of, *subhanallah*, beautification. It's not only *'ibada* [worship] it is everything in our life. All behavior, conducts, everything." From the declaration of faith to the five daily prayers, fasting, almsgiving, and the pilgrimage, life in this community is largely shaped by learning about, and adhering to, the five pillars of Islam. And yet it reaches far beyond them, enacted in all layers of daily comportment, with piety invoked in thoughts, emotions, speech, dress, and relations to persons and objects in the mosque and the metropolis alike—in "all behavior, conducts, everything." Social events take place in the mosque and/or revolve around Islamic principles, for those both chosen and choosing to express their freedom to act by actively relinquishing all freedom to God.

Along with my interlocutors, I attend a series of gender-segregated talks held at the mosque, dealing with the pilgrimage, finances, family, and the afterlife. As the main form of entertainment, we save seats and gossip throughout, snacking on chips and halal gummy candies in tandem with the sometimes-solemn sound of Qur'anic verse. Men accompanied by smartphones snap selfies with eminent visitors, their very own celebrities, often hailing from Mecca. Cell phones do not ring, but spout the call to prayer. Love is studied not simply as love, but "love for the *muslima* [female Muslim]." Women tell each other not "I love you," but "I love you *for the sake of Allah*." And teachers assure that "the shortest distance between a problem and its solution is the distance between your knees and the floor." "Spell *need* backwards?" requests a woman in my study group [*din*, often spelled phonetically as deen, means religion in Arabic]. "Yep! That's all we need. That's all we need."

Not only social discourse, but language itself becomes saturated with Islam. Events include a "halal drumroll please" spoken in the voice of a presenter, speech studded with countless "*inshallahs*" and "*mashallahs*." "We will begin in a few moments, *inshallah*. We are waiting on a few sisters, *inshallah* and once they arrive *inshallah* we can begin, *inshallah*," says Ranya, a community member. "It's heavy on the tongue but light on the scale. If you say *alhamdulillah, alhamdulillah* from your heart then it goes into your bank, if you know why you are saying that and what you are saying," Melia explains.

Filling all spaces and aspects of life with Islam further includes nuanced behavioral regulations: no nail polish ("sister, did you know your prayers will be invalidated?"), no exposed hair ("please cover—this scarf is a gift for you"), no alcohol-serving establishments ("we don't go there"), and no music or dance ("halal drumroll"). After hearing this spoken drumroll—"duh-duh-duh-DUH" at the mother-daughter fundraiser, I ask Shaykh P., a male mosque teacher, about the place of music in Islam. He responds from inside of the tall blue box, erected to avoid sight between him and the women in the room.

Many scholars say music is haram, music with instruments, especially bad lyrics. Many say it's haram to listen to music. A minority say musical instruments are OK if used for good purposes, *nashid*s [chants that often have an Islamic focus]. There is a difference of opinion. Definitely if you listen to mainstream music, then definitely this is love of the *dunya*, this is love of the world.

Love of the *dunya*, or love of the world, draws on the Islamic theological concept of *wasatiyya*, a "middle path," urging Muslims not to focus exclusively on the here and now, but instead remain cognizant of the hereafter.[52] Leadership at the East London Mosque encourage not a middle path, however, but rather an exclusive focus on the hereafter in order to "earn" paradise.[53] This directly relates to—both reflecting and solidifying—the omnipotence of the halal/haram binary, rooted in a messianic vision, providing the potential to transcend a present rife with socioeconomic struggle. Along with gender segregation, community separation, and saturation with Islam, the living of a halal life entails explicit prioritization of the afterlife, with emotional attachment to this world (*dunya*) understood to be an "illness of the heart," as Shaykh P. puts it. The final stanzas of a poem in a book (*Purification of the Heart*) disseminated at a workshop read: "As for the one whose heart is encrusted with the love of this world, his only cure is having certainty [of his mortality]. Thus, if he keeps death constantly before his eyes, this acts as a cleanser for the soiled matter encrusting his heart."[54] Moral boundaries divide not only the spaces of the mosque and the broader city, but also the world and the afterlife. And yet they also bring the world, as a means to earn paradise, closer together with the afterlife.

At the beginning of a workshop on *Purification of the Heart*, a young girl of perhaps eleven years old recites a chapter of the Qur'an and provides an emotional reflection on death to the women in the room. She holds a microphone to her lips, bending her small head forward, while rhythmically bellowing:

If anyone is dealing with a disease and the doctor says you have only one month to live, he repents, changes life, repents! But it has no effect when Allah says in the Qur'an that you will die! Allah doesn't care what place you are from, worship him—verse 26! Everyone on this earth will perish, only Allah will remain! Angel Jibreel asks the Prophet Muhammad for permission to die! Jibreel said, "Allah cannot wait to meet you!" Prophet Muhammad said, "Do what you have to do, take out my soul!" Did death let him out? "Prepare yourself before you come to me! Prepare yourself before you come to me!" Out of dust you are created and to dust you will be returned!

Obviously moved, an older woman seated beside the young girl shakes her head in disbelief. "I am at a loss for words. *Dunya* is nothing. *Dunya* is nothing," she repeats.

From inside of the blue box, Shaykh P. further discerns between the temporary nature of this world and the everlasting hereafter. "The world is a bridge, so pass over it to the next world but do not try to build on it." He invokes the halal/haram boundary and its consequences, noting: "There are two types of people in this world at the end—the happy and those miserable and sad. There's no third type of person. As soon as you die, you will see your place in hellfire or your place in Janna." Three "signs of people who will be sad/ wretched": "having a hard heart," "lack of modesty or shame," and "wanting the *dunya*, coveting the world," with "time and energy spent on the *dunya*, not the hereafter, because of lack of certainty, lack of faith."

On Eid al-Adha in 2016, the feast of sacrifice, a guest speaker reinvigorates this topic, implicitly alluding to the connection between the halal/haram boundary and love of the *dunya*.

> Worldly life is both extremely short-lived and insignificant in value. Important to note that *hayat al-dunya* (worldly life) is only referring to those actions/pursuits that are void of any benefits in the next world, so not everything is blameworthy, because our life here is also a means to earn paradise.

For Melia, this perception of worldly life as a means to earn paradise motivates a refusal to eat at many local restaurants, as she moves from relinquishing any form of alcohol (in cooking, perfume, etc.) touching her body to avoiding all establishments that sell liquor. This messianic temporal perspective also helps to make sense of why Qur'anic verse is played in the background as a sensory-rich reminder, even when we speak of family issues, and why giving beyond one's financial means is described as proof of piety, providing "rewards" in the next world. As undergirds a great deal of Sufi thought (including that embedded in the Deoband movement), the true path to paradise entails the rejection of materiality inherent to earthly life.[55] At ELM, a pedagogy of redemption moves the individual to embrace an ascetic form of Islam and even suffering in this life in order to access paradise. This relates to the haram that may arise from misspent wealth and ephemerality of *dunya*—in Benjaminian terms, the lived experience site of the myth, with remembrance site of the truth. "We will wake up in our graves and know that this life was a dream," warns Shaykh P.

That "*dunya* is nothing," "insignificant," speaks through a pedagogy of redemption to the future and past, but also to the often-silent sufferings of the present. It is a powerful phrase, pregnant with both hope and disappointment, emerging not only in sermons, but also casual conversation among my inter-locutors. "*Dunya* is nothing" remarks Melia when she describes losing her job in an early childhood education center, able to make sense of a significant fi-nancial and emotional hit—as she "watched kids take their first steps . . . raised them"—through a focus on other times. The prospect of paradise thus soothes as both spiritual and social salve. As Sennett writes of the Jews in the Venetian ghetto, "Separation also turn[s] the oppressed inward in new ways."[56]

Turning inwards at the East London Mosque—internal flight in a city and nation-state that so often flee from Muslims as they once did from Jews—entails a pedagogy of redemption, calling the adherent to fill all spaces with Islam. Through hope that forms and directs their knowledge, my interlocutors bear the sharp edges of metal and glass, stigma and caste encountered in the London metropolis. They thereby shape and are shaped by ELM as a place where the pious can agentively grapple with the many strata of marginality through Islam, gazes fixed not on the material horizon—with its skyscrapers piercing the sky (a visual echo of that "impossible dream")—but instead on the messianic horizon, a dream deferred.[57]

A Method of Hope

On the island of England, surrounded by the Atlantic seas, this community dreams and acts in anticipation of the messianic horizon above and beyond earth. The horizon moves closer through hope-based practices of devotion en-acted in the here and now; domination and marginalization can, after all, only be contested in the time of the now (what Benjamin terms the *Jetztzeit*).[58] In his work exploring knowledge practices among Fijians, anthropologist Hirokazu Miyazaki invokes the work of Bloch and Benjamin as he explores hope as nei-ther feeling nor subject, but rather an epistemological method, emerging from disappointment that looks at once to the future and the past.[59] "Hope's meth-odology," writes Bloch, "dwells in the region of the not-yet (with its pendant, memory)."[60] Many of my interlocutors at ELM similarly dwell in the region of the not-yet, while tying themselves, through the acquisition of knowledge, to a glorified Islamic past—Amaya learning and teaching Qur'anic reading and recitation to support a move to Muhammad's "heartland" in Saudi Arabia; Melia expanding her repertoire of memorized Qur'anic verse to promote heal-ing, in body and soul, through recitation; and Kasia perceiving complete root-edness in the Islamic tradition, knowing its history inside out, as the only way out of a bad marriage.

Orienting the present towards the possible redemptive future while ground-ing oneself in an Islamic past suggests a responsiveness to the disappointments of an undercaste status—from economic strain to the powerful sentiment shared by my interlocutors that they do not, and cannot, fully belong to British society. Yet "hope's methodology" also forges an opportunity for "the radical tempo-ral reorientation of knowledge," as suggested by both Bloch's and Benjamin's writings; it is thus a method of critique and transformation in the making of the self and the community in spite of, that is apart from, present structural inequalities.[61] Hope without prophets may foster submission (as for Spinoza, with hope linked to fear), but here interrupting hope shines through the cracks of an imperfect world, replacing the narrative of the unrelenting incivility of the Muslim with a narrative of dignity and potential itself made possible through Islam.[62] Henry Giroux terms such interruptive hope "subversive hope," as it "gives substance to the recognition that every present is incomplete."[63]

"Subversive hope," is, I would argue, also "educated hope," rooted in the opportunity to forge a sense of belonging to another time, to somewhere or something else.[64] At ELM, hope thus emerges as an epistemological method employed to cultivate the always-incomplete Muslim. Again, a Muslim moral habitus is an ongoing project of the self: here a project of self-recovery through the acquisition of knowledge, rather than reconciliation with civic life—of hope adorned by memory.[65] Hope as a method of coming to know the world as, and thereby becoming, a "better Muslim" is rooted in the Proustian notion of "intertwined time" so integral to Benjamin's writings—stressing a return to that which was or should have been, and the future, that which will or could be.[66] Here Sayad's "double absence" of the present is countered by the double presence of an Islamic future and an Islamic past.[67]

This process of dislocation from time-as-progress begins with recovery of the self within the Islamic past; it begins with what Paul Ricoeur describes as "re-appropriation of our effort to exist," first by recognizing, "I am lost, 'led astray' among objects and separated from the center of my existence."[68] Yet a finding, uniting, and centering of the self through self-recovery requires more than an unreflexive turn towards any or all hope as a source of knowledge and betterment. It requires the discernment of "false hopes" from a "good type of hope." Shaykh P. explains,

It's quick-acting poison, extended false hope, assuring self-death is a long way off leads to inroads to the prohibited. Ignorance to the fact that entire affair of this life is God's, Allah's—quick-acting poison out of all diseases of the heart. Certain types of snake, if they bite you, five to ten minutes to live. What is false hope? When we think that we have a long, long life ahead of us. Death is not near us, we are young . . . *Inshallah*, I will become better when I'm older, will go to hajj at fifty, start praying at thirty or when I get married. Relying on the fact that we will be here for a long time, change in the future . . . just an excuse. This generates hard-heartedness and indolence regarding obligations, prayers, fasting, zakat, hajj. You won't feel anything if you don't do it, it's insignificant to you, heart is hardened with extended false hopes.

Acting against false hopes and thus in line with God is described as an act of *poiesis*, making oneself Muslim and thereby redeeming oneself in daily life. This entails not only sanctioned religious acts such as prayer, but also what I would argue becomes the sanctified treatment of all mundane acts as *'ibada*, and therefore connected with the divine. This habitual practice is at the same time a centripetal practice, revolving around the Qur'an and the Sunna, moving the individual out of the diaspora of the self and towards key Islamic sources of knowledge, forging solidarity with the past.

Reflecting on Benjamin's *Theses on the Philosophy of History*, Stuart Jeffries writes of how those disaffected with the present "reach back in time to express solidarity with previous role models"—in the case of my ELM interlocutors, as of many Muslims, first and foremost the Prophet Muhammad.[69] In contrast to Şehitlik, at ELM such solidarity does not emerge in tandem with broader metropolitan society, but rather fills a felt, affective absence in the larger metropolis. Here again knowledge calls for embodiment, the past spoken not only through lips, but limbs; as Ware notes, Islam's "classical texts typically insist on the inseparability of *'ilm* (knowledge) and *'amal* (deeds)."[70] In one of our weekly learning circles, the teacher, Biva, turns towards the embodied integration of the Qur'an and the Sunna. These are deeply interconnected, the prophetic habitus imbued with Qur'anic knowledge and affect. The prophet and the revelation cannot be pulled apart.

"Good Muslims," Biva explains, both "carry the Qur'an in the heart" and become, like the Prophet Muhammad, a "walking Qur'an" or "a walking *aya* [Qur'anic verse], Qur'an that is walking the streets . . . Not only did he have the Qur'an in his memory, it was live beating in his heart. It was his heart." As Saba Mahmood emphasizes, "These mimetic ways of realizing the Prophet's behavior are lived not as commandments but as virtues, where one wants to ingest, as it were, the Prophet's persona."[71] This ingestion occurs through meticulous embodiment in a processual "positing [of] the self" through regular acts of piety that become second nature.[72] "If we hold ourselves accountable," Biva assures, "whatever we start, it becomes a habit. If you fixate on your

Qur'an, it becomes a part of that routine." As Cohen argues, a habitus that incorporates the future, the "not yet," and the traditions of the past, allows the individual to not only strive for, but move ever closer to, God.[73] As at Şehitlik, a Muslim moral habitus thus emerges as eternally incomplete, with *phronesis* and *poiesis* both directed towards a *telos* "that is . . . by definition, never really achieved"—at least not in this life.[74]

Painted onto the wall of the stairwell in the Maryam Centre, a telling quote stands out in an otherwise naked space, with English letters following Arabic script: "The most beloved of actions to Allah are the most regular, no matter how small." Such consistent moral practice reflects an anticipatory consciousness, rooted in hope-filled knowledge. "You've had a homework. What was the homework? It starts with *alhamdulillah*," says Munira, a teacher sitting on the carpet at the front of a Maryam Centre classroom. She leads the room of women awaiting the workshop on purification of the heart through unified recitation of Qur'anic verse, speaking each syllable with utmost care, encouraging perfected pronunciation as an integral, integrated part of everyday life. "It starts with *alhamdulillah*" and it also ends "with *alhamdulillah*." "All praise to God alone." In the words of Hamza Yusuf, quoted at the same women's workshop:

> It's like silverware: one may polish it with a few hard strokes and then put it down; or one may gently polish it regularly so that its shimmer is maintained. Left unattended, the heart becomes encrusted. Unwholesome deeds accumulate and take away its purity. But with consistent work on self-purification, the heart becomes cleansed and is kept that way.[75]

"Everything I do, I do for Allah. It's strict but sometimes I make mistakes. It's strict. It's clear, but sometimes I mess up and I try to do better," Rua tells me. One attempts to do better every day through training the body and mind, thereby shifting the disposition over time. This process of self-cultivation entails the interaction of an embodiment that supports, but may precede, belief (eating foods that the Prophet Muhammad once ate, dressing modestly, thanking God in speech), undergirded by the power of intention to continuously remake the self in the image of the Prophet Muhammad. The first time that I visit her home, Amaya explains that this process is "about effort," not ability. Everyone is able. She notes, for example, the difference in Arabic letters. "If you use the wrong one while saying the first sura of the Qur'an, Al-Fatiha, you are talking to God about fornication." She giggles. "One letter makes a big difference." As we practice individual lines of this verse, Amaya explains that as long as I "say each letter the right way," I will "say the whole thing correctly. It's about knowing where to place your tongue. It's about putting in the effort and not being lazy." This serves as a fitting metaphor for the meticulousness I observe among my interlocutors, motivated by hope, as they seek to achieve virtue in their smallest of daily intentions, actions, and interactions. Together such sentiments, practices, and knowledge become a means to condition a wholly pious subject—putting in the effort, saying each letter correctly in order to say the whole thing correctly.

This condensation of affect, knowledge, and action not only sets the pious subject, or even the larger Muslim community, apart from a mainstream that deems them uncivil and unworthy of full belonging; through a transcendental view, moving from dyad (Muslim-society) to triad (Muslim-society-God), it expands, thereby collapsing the dominant European view of space and time.[76] This method of hope thus decenters from the margins, endowing the pious subject with the *phronetic* capacity to expose and see through the cracks in notions of "progress," "civility," and "enlightenment," and their accompaniment, linear time. This critical perspective, Amaya emphasizes, is rooted in the revelation itself, the Qur'an not chronological, but transcending time, enlivened by an unbroken chain of recitation. And it is deepened through internalization and expression of the Sunna. "This," she emphasizes, pointing at her body— her heart?—"this is where the Prophet's light shines through."

Melia: "I used to sing"

When she moved to London in the 1990s, Melia liked to walk in the park by her house. She studied childhood education by day, and wandered the park with friends from her university as day turned to night. Her now-husband played pick-up soccer in the same park, and sometimes she would pass by him and smile. "She likes you!" her friends would cry out, as they slowed their stride beside the pitch. One day, he stopped playing and approached her. "And that," Melia says matter-of-factly, "was that." While her family is largely Hindu (her mother recently converted to Islam), Melia long felt dislocated from any religious tradition. After she got married, two young children and a full-time job as an early childhood teacher kept her busy for many years; yet as her children entered adolescence, she felt a familiar loneliness creep back in, and began to move closer to Islam. She started praying regularly and visiting local mosques. Only the East London Mosque "felt right" to her, without the ornate distraction of others, like a nearby mosque built in neo-Ottoman style that we visit together on a particularly rainy day.

A year before we met, struck by a debilitating illness, Melia found herself confined to bed. With a strange sense of satisfaction, she watched her husband and children fend for themselves. Doctor after doctor, perplexed by her mysterious illness, prescribed rest. She slept for nearly a year, eating just enough to survive, emerging from bed a month before we met like a heroine from a fairytale, suddenly roused from a spell. It was "a blessing," she assures me, to have slept for so long: the opportunity to begin again. For months, the remnants of the illness gave her sea legs, her body shaky and uncertain. Yet the illness also fostered a determination to deepen her practice, as she reoriented herself to God. "Allah wanted me to become ill, so that I could change the way that my life was going . . . I have to do things for myself," she says, explaining that she no longer "run[s] after" her family; how if you do everything for a man, he will expect you to do more and more and more. "As long as I fulfill my basic duties, I run away from home," she asserts. Melia spends time at the East London Mosque almost every day, whether practicing recitation, reading the Qur'an, or conversing with friends. And she becomes the backbone of women meeting together outside of the mosque to practice Qur'anic recitation, enlisting Amaya to teach us inside of her home.

Melia meets me in Kasia's home on a blistery winter afternoon and Kasia asks if she can sing. "When I have the sisters here, they don't like it. They say it's not Islamic." Melia responds, "I used to sing. I don't mind, though I don't sing anymore." In this moment, as many others, she signals her own progression to a higher level of piety, which she describes as "climbing up a ladder of Muslimness." She wants to "do things perfectly." Soon after, at a mother-daughter fundraiser, Melia will be the only woman in the room who does not take off her headscarf. "It's become a part of me," she will say, visibly embarrassed by her daughter Leyla, who will beg her to remove it. Today, Melia no longer listens to music, watches mainstream television, or reads mainstream newspapers. Still, she sympathizes with Kasia's worldly attachment as a "good sister," who remains caught inside of the same web of economic and marital strife that she herself must face each day.

PIETY IN RETURN:
REVERTS IN LONDON'S EAST END

On the same afternoon, Kasia quickly turns the discussion from song to singer, recounting the conversion of Cat Stevens, now Yusuf Islam, with awe. "Yusuf Islam was stuck in the ocean on a boat, with waves coming at him," she explains, "He asked God to save him and said he would worship God. That happened and then he opened the Qur'an and it said, 'Didn't I save you from the waves?'" She looks from me to Melia, her wide eyes filled with conviction. "Didn't I save you from the waves?"

Seeking refuge from "the waves," a symbol of personal and social tumult, reverts—the term rooted in the notion that all humans are born Muslim and thus return to Islam through conversion—also "dwell in the region of the not-yet" so fundamental to messianic thinking.[77] Whether newly converted or returnees (life-long Muslims who have reinvigorated their practice), they describe a desire to "go back to the natural state of things," pushing back against the ascriptive and abstracted form of the Muslim as stranger through concrete acts—the Muslim as maker—that foster piety. Arendt writes, "The miracle that saves the world, the realm of human affairs, from its normal, 'natural' ruin is ultimately the fact of natality, in which the faculty of action is ontologically rooted. It is, in other words, the birth of new men and the new beginning."[78] Rebirth, or beginning again—often, like Yusuf Islam, with new names—is an act of *poiesis*, making a dwelling in the unforgiving metropolis, where socio-economic marginalities and opportunities to cultivate the self collide.

Each week at the East London Mosque, a life-long Muslim or "long-term Muslim" gives a lecture in the New Muslim Women's Circle, followed by group discussions and one-on-ones to address individual challenges and needs. From teenagers to grandmothers, hailing from Europe, the United States, the Middle East, Africa, and Asia, these women have at least one thing in common: their turn or return to Islam. The reasons for reversion are varied and multiple, but cluster into particular trends. About half of the women in our learning circle converted through marriage to Muslim men, the other half having returned or newly turned to Islam on their own. The latter group describe Islam as their answer to a search for peace or purpose in life. About a third in this group are life-long Muslims who feel that their familial upbringings did not teach them true Islam, a third middle-aged converts (racially diverse, but mostly from the neighborhood around ELM and exposed to Islam while growing up), and a third young British women considering conversion. This last group of women explore the possibility of conversion through regular engagement with the learning circle, as well as dabbling in religious practices, including communal prayer, at the mosque. For new Muslims familiar with economic struggle and/or discrimination based on their race, particularly Black British converts, Islam emerges as an alternative and attractive alterity; rejecting the individualistic and capitalist mainstream, they find an opportunity to belong to a community. Here again, being Muslim entails both spiritual and social experience—a dynamic identity and an agentive response to disempowerment.

For reverts, new and life-long Muslims alike, belief acts as the bridge, with habituated practices embedding the individual into her new habitus and new religious community through acts of *phronesis*.

Across all of these groups, many speak of the day that they "changed." From this day forward, dress, mannerisms, speech, and friendships all experienced revision. An older convert in our circle likens this shift to a chameleonic "shedding [of] one's old, peeling skin for new, pristine skin." In this process, one not only modifies her exterior, but transforms her interior being. Rather than reinvention, however, regardless of being born into a Muslim household or not, the women in our ELM learning circle perceive this experience as waking, or bringing the self back to life, beginning at the beginning again (with paradise punctuating both beginning and end)—as Benjamin writes, "a worldly restitution . . . the rhythm of messianic nature."[79] As they breathe life into new old selves in the metropolis, moving to a new rhythm in their daily lives, my interlocutors distinguish between being idly Muslim or culturally Muslim (again, Muslim as a noun) and actively "Muslim-Muslim" (Muslim as a verb), seeking and embodying Islamic knowledge. "I was born Muslim, but I only returned to my practice a few months ago," explains Nabila, a Bengali British woman who grew up in the Tower Hamlets neighborhood.

Amaya splits her own life into two distinct stages, the before and after of her transformation four years before our meeting. "Before" was marked by economic prosperity, the ability to "have everything" she wanted, but "something was missing in my soul. I was missing my Lord. I was missing peace." Clubbing and alcohol, her husband's gambling habit, and miniskirts all marked "before." She describes her process of returning to Islam, beginning with reading the Bible that her son was assigned in his high school religion class and culminating with reading the Qur'an. Before, she continues, "I knew in my heart that I was Muslim but I didn't know what this meant." Amaya has found peace since she "changed," although plummeted into far poorer economic circumstances, including dependence on state welfare.

All of those from Muslim families returning to Islam are young women born in London, between eighteen and their mid-thirties. Amaya pinpoints the role of generation in her own refocus on Islam, a discursive thread shared among the life-long Muslims in our learning circle.

> There is a new generation, in which I am a part, coming up, who wants to learn things right, learn things perfectly—we are coming back to our religion and want to do things right, not partially. My parents, for example and many of their

friends, they didn't learn what you should say before beginning a sura. *They were only partial in their knowledge.*

This admonishment of the first generation is based on a striving to erase cultural particularities and replace them with a universal Islam rooted not in a specific ancestry or language, but rather a holistic epistemological system.[80] There is a sense among the ethnically Bengali women leading this learning circle, and preached as a central tenet of the larger ELM community, that cultural misinterpretations resulting from a lack of knowledge disfigure Islamic virtues. Henna, a young volunteer in the circle, explains:

> I put my religious belief before my culture. There are some cultural things that clash with the religion. For example, I cover quite a lot. In the culture, this is seen as quite a lot, over the top. The way you cover and the way you socialize as over the top, such as not wanting to mix with men outside of the family. [It is] increasing that young women are covering because they have more understanding of Islam. More people are practicing now than when my parents came. It depends how much they practice . . . if they cover.

This "problematization of culture" characterizes diverse second- and third-generation revivalist circles in London—this is, for instance, also prevalent among the Somali women studied by Giulia Liberatore—while emerging across Europe and Muslim-majority countries more broadly.[81] And it is invoked both within religious communities and from the outside, by mainstream society (e.g., the police officers I interview in Berlin) in order to distinguish "authentic" from "inauthentic" Islam, in a striving to delineate static group boundaries in spite of overlaps and change.

Whereas Mikaela Rogozen-Soltar finds converts in Granada grounding themselves through Islam's local history and Esra Özyürek notes the ways in which German converts "giv[e] Islam a German face" (locating Islam in the Enlightenment, for instance), reverts at the East London Mosque embrace the universal potentiality of Islam as a hope-filled method of acquiring knowledge, dislocated from any particular place, ethnicity, or race.[82] The power of reversion releases the individual from the constraints of the liberal, globalizing nation-state by casting the self in a new paradigm that does not focus outwards on socioeconomic opportunities or disappointments, but instead inwards, backwards, and forwards on redemptive possibilities. This is not only a form of resistance, but emancipation, by transcending the civil/uncivil divide and thereby reframing the self and the collective in the dynamic threshold space of the metropolitan mosque.

Good Endings

In our learning circle, returning to Islam is seen as the single most explicit act of purification; as Samiya puts it, "Once you accept Islam, anything prior, sins are forgiven. You enter Islam with a clean slate." With clean slates, reverts have a unique advantage in learning "true" Islam without muddying cultural norms.[83] Their status is particularly honorable, as "all around Muhammad were reverts—the Qur'an was not revealed to people born into this religion. The first generation of Muslims were reverts," explains Biva, another of our learning circle teachers. And the care for reverts, as new bodies filled with enduring traditions, is thus also seen to bring great spiritual rewards.

In the words of medieval Sunni Muslim scholar Ibn Taymiyyah, a quote shared by a young convert in our learning circle, "what really counts are good endings, not flawed beginnings." This striving for "good endings" among "flawed beginnings" again points towards overlapping spiritual and social realms, reinvoking messianism while relating to a sentiment of being left out and/or left behind by socioeconomic insecurity. I learn from my revert interlocutors that a combination of economic precarity, cultural dislocation, and deep loneliness—the desire to be part of a whole, to be known and no longer alone—motivates their search for new ways of being in, if not of, the metropolis. "Many marvelous things have emerged from the lonely city: things forged in loneliness but also things that function to redeem it," writes British author Olivia Laing.[84] Distance, disappointment, disenfranchisement; all are ameliorated by a community promising redemption, providing new ways of knowing, and new ways of being, through Islam.

Mary-now-Maryam, who grew up in the ELM neighborhood, recounts her first day wearing a headscarf, evoking Zygmunt Bauman's idea that one can overcome estrangement through solidarity.[85] "I was crossing the street and a car stopped to let me pass and I could see in their eyes. They were Muslim, they looked at me and smiled, like I was one of them. It wasn't like that before." As she tells her story of conversion, she links eyes with another woman in the circle. "Olivia! Is that you?" She asks, her eyes widening with a smile. The face of the woman she references, known to us as Khadija, registers a combination of discomfort and surprise. Khadija has tried to burn the bridges to her former life, not least of all the nearby social housing unit where she lived an unhappy childhood—having sought fusion with a redemptive community. And yet here before her sits Mary-now-Maryam, the upstairs neighbor from her childhood estate, a headscarf loosely wrapped around her face, which breaks into a smile as she recounts memories of their shared abode across Whitechapel Road. Carrie, a middle-aged woman from the London suburbs, joins the conversation on fractured pasts that led to this present, here in this very room at the East London Mosque, describing her own recent conversion right before Ramadan in summer 2016. She speaks of the estrangement underlying her search for solidarity, "how important it is to have some sense of belonging, to feel that you belong to a community."

Over toast and tea in the London suburb where she resides, Carrie later describes her former "life without," feeling distanced from both society and God. "There is no way to describe it," this sense and sentiment of Sayad's "double absence" that runs like a river through my interlocutors' stories in London as in Berlin. It is a sense of being both outside of and within two places at the very same time (in spirit and ongoing migrations of the body alike).[86] I cannot help but think, in this village café, with tables adorned in floral, plastic coverings, of the word used by my Turkish interlocutors: *hüzün*. This word, again meaning a collective spiritual, bittersweet melancholy—of feeling distanced from God and the weight of history's ruins—is where loss meets yearning.[87] *Hüzün* is "an ache that finally saves our souls," writes Nobel Prize–winning Turkish author Orhan Pamuk, who uses the word to describe the power of Istanbul's urban form.[88] While she never speaks this word, Carrie invokes its sentiment in another great metropolis by describing a "life without," grappling through Islam with her fractured past; her parents, Jewish Russian ballet dancers, fled to Britain and never danced again, what with their broken toes and ankle bones, broken homes, and broken hearts. So too is Mary-now-Maryam's earlier description of recognition as she crossed the street imbued with *hüzün*: no longer disempowered by her estrangement from the city, but instead empowered as a maker in her new urban Muslim community.

For the new Muslim, like Carrie or Maryam, solidarity with the stranger—in both the colloquial and Simmelian senses of the word—is chosen over estrangement within the mainstream. And it emerges from the opportunity presented by *hüzün*, a "critical ache" that endows "poetic license" to "read life and the history of the city in reverse"—locating the self in Islamic tradition, and in a marginalized group identity.[89] As for all of my interlocutors, moral worth and dignity emerges from the Muslim identity. Yet this flipping of the lens that dramatically decenters a liberal gaze (a gaze that sees Muslims as undercaste) through critical knowledge is perhaps nowhere more potent than in the conversion of new Muslims. Converting not only purifies, but empowers the new

Muslim to make a dwelling for herself, becoming the ultimate *phronetic* and poetic act in the London metropolis. The agency imbued herein illuminates the power of Islam, beyond the bodies of born-Muslims, in its offerings to the searching inhabitants of this lonely city, choosing against estrangement and vacancy at once. In looking for another way, converts are at once animated by, and embodiments of, hope—finding in Islam the capacity to transcend the exclusive and excluding cultural-spatial-temporal constraints they encounter in the East End.

The Plural Faces of Pure Islam

Each week, we sit in a room filled with a dozen languages, a deep northern melody of speech responding to a Texan drawl. Arabella's Italian accent breaks through the cover of a black abaya when she speaks about her new blog on being Muslim, Italian, and living abroad. Even with this collective quest for redemption vis-à-vis pure Islam, familial, cultural, and historical heritage does not vanish into thin air.

The inescapable diversity within and among reverts, the impossibility of its condensation into a singular Muslim form, comes most fully to life in our few meetings outside of the mosque. In summer 2016, we unite for a post-Eid celebration picnic in Shandy Park. Whether through birth or seeking in adulthood, it is clear that these women have come to Islam from different walks of life. Our teacher Samiya sits beside Ayla, a French Tunisian woman. Across from them, Saba, a single mother of a ten-year-old boy, dressed in rainbow cotton pants and a t-shirt, ring in her nose, explains that she does not fast. She laments that her mother is ready for her to get married. To each of her sides sit Carrie and Zainab, a young East Asian woman who has changed not only her religion but also recently her name. Some talk of Brexit, the only time it is casually mentioned during my research. "I can't believe this, in London, I've heard of lots of incidents. I always thought that London was protected," says Samiya, reflecting on violent verbal and physical attacks against visible Muslims in the city. Ayla interjects that she drinks her tea black. "You're a European?" asks Samiya, as she pours tea from a thermos into small paper cups, "don't you know that the UK left the EU now?" Ayla responds with a smile. "If you want us to get out we will get out, but us Arabs don't add milk."

Remaining keenly aware of, and connected to, their "flawed beginnings," new Muslims reside in a threshold space within and beyond ELM—socially and culturally located between the mosque and British society. They are particularly ambiguous, as supremely suspect by the mainstream. They remain under suspicion for their transformation, perceived as lost, desperate, easy to influence, unstable, and erratic; as such, they become equated in the Western imaginary with extremism.[90] The "choice" of Islam, adopting an identity coded as uncivil, deeply stigmatizes the act of conversion.[91] It does not—cannot—make sense within the framework of mainstream discourses on Islam and Muslims. The "non-normative whiteness" of white British converts makes them particularly suspect, as they choose out of a privileged position in society's ethnoracial hierarchy and into a position of social marginality.[92] And yet they are uniquely able to cross the metaphorical moat between the mosque and the mainstream in the metropolis; for instance, converts regularly man Open Mosque Days. On the Open Mosque Day in July 2016, a male convert spritzes the air with alcohol-free perfumes, while female converts arrange dates and pomegranates on a table, tying different styles of headscarves around the heads of hairless mannequins. They describe their experiences incorporating the pillars of Islam into their lives to visitors, from daily prayer to the once-in-a-lifetime pilgrimage to Mecca and Medina.

The layered, liminal position of the convert is not only a result of mainstream-Muslim relations; many also face race-based discrimination inside of the mosque. "Muslims are equal in the eyes of God, but not in the eyes of mothers-in-law," says Nala, half laughing. She explains that she hopes to get married but has not been able to find a husband in the Bengali community because she is a Black British woman.

> I want to get married. There I see the divisions. They won't marry me because of who I am, my background . . . one man even said that he would have a secret marriage with me, he doesn't mind, but his parents wouldn't accept it. I said, "No, that wouldn't be fair to the child that I have nor to children if we had any together." There I saw the divisions in our *umma*.

Race and ethnicity emerge as decisive dividing lines inside of a community that remains overwhelmingly Bengali. Despite the growing number of Somalis in the community, the two groups still largely occupy separate spaces within the mosque. As one young woman, Hanan, explains to me of her own failed engagement to a Pakistani British man who was rejected by her family, even marriages within the larger Muslim South Asian community are discouraged because of perceived ethnic differences. Since her family prevented her marriage, her mother has approached her with the CVs and pictures of numerous Bengali men, to which she says, "No, no, no."

While undergirded by a discourse and pedagogical model stressing the

purity of true Islam, the plurality of reverts—converts and returnees alike—
and the layered marginalities of their particular incarnation of the Simmelian
stranger come to life in their everyday social interactions inside of the mosque.
Their very presence in the mosque community evokes questions of inner-
Muslim divisions, as they embody multiple identities, presents, and histories,
made known in the casual utterances of social life: "I am global," "us Arabs."
"I've realized how French I am, how straightforward," comments Aliya one afternoon over *jilapi*, a fried South Asian sweet, with her two young sons. While
seeking refuge, community, and redemption by learning and participating in
the ELM community, their diversity breaks through the surface of everyday
life, shining light on inner-Muslim alterity even in shared acts of making, that
is *remaking*, dwellings among the echoes of so very many pasts.

As the midday sun rises above Shandy Park, in our learning circle completed by dozens of bodies—somehow so different, somehow much the
same—Arendt's words take human form: "because we are all the same, that
is, human, in such a way that nobody is ever the same as anyone else who
ever lived, lives, or will live."[93] Here we share prayers along with laughter; and
for those who drink it, fresh milk for tea. Of course, this does not erase the
violence of the discourse that led to the outcome of the Brexit vote, which is
casually mentioned, then cast aside. Yet in this moment—accompanied by the
sounds of children's revelry, as they dig for worms in uneven ground—a new
beginning ("the miracle that saves the world"), a new name, and a better ending appear within reach.[94]

CHAPTER 6

Hope, Interrupted:
The East London Mosque
and the Metropolis

From Asian supermarket to halal butcher, Biryani house to money-transfer shop, Whitechapel Road is a sociocultural artery of Tower Hamlets, infusing Bengali culture into London's cityscape. Near the Whitechapel tube station, middle-aged men curl dough the flaming color of the sun in a deep fryer that spits dangerously into the air, pulling fresh *jilapi* from the bubbling oil with silver tongs. It is June 2016 and summer Ramadan fasts lead to a languished stroll among many who walk beside me, shopping bags swaying loosely as extensions of arms. During Ramadan, life is slow here. Bursts of life happen around prayer times and after sunset, an alternative rhythm of time in a city known for its prowess on the global market.

For the East London Mosque community, the metropolis is site not of reconciliation, but of reckoning. Rather than the *sympoiesis*, or making together, seen in the Şehitlik Mosque's relationship with Berlin, my interlocutors at ELM exhibit a form of *autopoiesis*, making themselves and their community apart from the broader city. It is not only the delineation of place and space through a halal/haram boundary that separates this community from the larger cityscape, but also a time-space continuum based in religious obligations rather than economic strivings. "You pray." "You put on your hijab [headscarf or other modest apparel] before the postman comes." "You pray." "You read the Qur'an." "You practice recitation." "You read about the life of the Prophet." "You pray." "You try not to speak badly of others." "You may fast." "You give something, whether food or money or kind words." "You pray." "You work and/or study and/or take care of your children." "Maybe you go to the mosque." "You pray." "You begin again." Such a time-space continuum does not undermine the fraught socioeconomic reality of my interlocutors but instead reframes it through a messianic vision, leading to both a celebration of poverty and notable political agnosticism. Dwelling as Muslims in Tower Hamlets requires the capacity to at once make sense of, and somehow transcend, socioeconomic inequality, increasingly deepened by the retreatist state and sociopolitical inequality, magnified and maintained through aggressive state securitization.

The disintegration of the British welfare state with the turn to neoliberalism in the 1980s coincided with the permanent settlement of postcolonial populaces.[1] The resulting economic retreat of the state has disproportionally affected ethnoreligious minorities, and the Bengali population of Tower Hamlets in particular. Again, Tower Hamlets registers among the poorest districts in all of the UK. Today, the most deprived borough in all of London (10th of 326 local authority areas in England), it also ranks first in three out of five measures of city-level deprivation, most notably income, and has some of the highest rates of both childhood and pensioner poverty in the nation.[2] Reflecting the precarious economic state of the borough, most of my interlocutors, along with their spouses, are un- or underemployed. Many live in social housing between the districts of Whitechapel and Mile End, in mazes of government blocks, their fiscal struggles dramatically contrasting with the rapid gentrification of the neighborhood.

Not only transferred to, but transformed within the modern metropolis, the disillusionment among postcolonial migrant and postmigrant groups in London transcends Muslim communities, cutting across the social, economic, and political spheres, inspiring and appearing in the texts of diverse writers like V. S. Naipaul, Zadie Smith, Hanif Kureishi, and Monica Ali.[3] These writers, like my interlocutors, give voice to a metropolis of cultural strata far deeper, and far more contested, than its glamorized portrayals of cosmopolitan charm. The specific apolitical stance expressed by my interlocutors can also be witnessed in diverse postcolonial populaces in London including Afro-Caribbeans, who have little confidence in the political apparatus.[4] As Christian Ball writes, "The old Empire (the 'new Commonwealth') is compressed into London." And yet it is under the continuous cloud of lived inequality, in metropolis as once in empire, that the detachment and resulting *autopoiesis* of the East London Mosque community takes root, is nourished, and grows.[5]

Kasia: "There is good in it somewhere"

On a windy London afternoon with skies promising rain, laundry hangs with little hope to dry, and Kasia awaits me in her East London home. "I had to get past the dirt to see the gold," she remarks over Nescafé in her warm living room, the pull-out bed shared with her husband closed by day. By dirt, she means Bengali culture, by gold, pure Islam. An active constituent of the East London Mosque community, her identity revolves around being Muslim, whether performing the five daily prayers or quietly proselytizing in our increasingly intimate encounters. "I say I am Muslim. And that is all. Just Muslim!" she exclaims, each time I ask her about Bengali or British belonging. Kasia hands me a small book on the life of the Prophet Muhammad wrapped in the folds of a dress I once admired, a gift inside of a gift—an offering of exchange. "*Mashallah*," a term of appreciation and thankfulness, she whispers upon embrace, as my pregnant belly grazes her niqab.

Whether by chance, choice, or the nexus between them, Kasia's home becomes a place of communion for women at ELM as the damp 2014 winter turns to a wet spring. Here mundane acts of *poiesis* come to life in the kitchen, linked to sacred acts of *poiesis* through the cultivation of piety. Although we are soon in her kitchen grinding spices to dust, I have not been invited to Kasia's home only to cook and to learn about Islam. Kasia also wants me to help make sense of the bureaucratic hurdles that stand between her and an impending spousal separation. She met her husband as a teenager and joined an unnamed "radical group" to which she belonged for twelve years, a fact that emerges twice in our conversations inside of her home, spoken in a hushed tone that reveals her desire to forget. Getting out was a challenge, fraught with fear. She pioneered the process, followed by her husband, her brothers, and others she had recruited into the organization. Kasia explains that she is still finding her way back to "true Islam." And "true Islam" is "sullied by the sexism of Asian men . . . men shouldn't try to control women, because they were made from Adam's rib. You can bend them, but if you break them, they are destroyed," she says. Her deepening dependence on God and independence from her husband is rooted in a time of increasing ad hoc women's organization at the mosque, friendships that span daily prayers and weekly home cooking lessons. "The wonders of the world are of God," Kasia remarks, dipping her finger into a bowl of crushed onion and garlic, as we stand side-by-side in her kitchen. "Humans have the idea that they are above all else in the universe." She pauses, smiling widely, placing her hand on mine and then pointing to a fly. "But can you make a fly's wing? Can *you* make a fly's wing?"

Soon after I arrive at her home, Kasia retrieves a pile of letters from the British state, envelopes torn open with care. She wants to be certain that divorce will not affect the welfare payments that she and her two young daughters receive from the state. Kasia struggles with what it means to be a Muslim woman of Bengali descent born and raised in the social housing of Tower Hamlets, London, where in spite of rapid gentrification, economic opportunities remain scarce. "We must keep turning to God," she asserts, "and that which comes, if it is good then good and if it is bad then there is good in it somewhere."

MY POVERTY IS MY PRIDE

I pass a church on my first day in Victoria Park Village, a bohemian neighborhood skirting the borough of Hackney and abutting Tower Hamlets where I reside during summer 2016. Bold white letters in front of the church spell out the sentiment expressed in the weekend women's learning circles at ELM. "For what shall it profit if he should gain the whole world and lose his own soul?" Many of my interlocutors at ELM live by this adage, echoing the words of the Prophet Muhammad—"my poverty is my pride"—in a habitus imbued with the prophetic past. They prize their economic position in this world as a reflection of their chosenness in the hereafter, as place (Tower Hamlets) interacts with piety (including ascetic Deobandi influences) to forge a celebration of poverty. In so doing, they reflect their embeddedness in messianic time, both contending with notions of "progress" and rising above capitalist strivings.

While all strands of Sunni Islam call for a life without excess, Sunni thought largely espouses the belief that poverty undermines the capacity to live as a pious person and fully functioning member of society. Instead, drawing on Qur'anic verse, a "balanced path" or "path of moderation" is stressed: "Seek the life to come by means of what God has granted you, but do not neglect your rightful share in this world" (Q 28:77). The living of a balanced life that does not overemphasize material wealth diverges from the embrace of poverty in asceticism. The earliest Muslim ascetics, *zuhhad*, emerged in the eighth century, including such figures as Hasan al-Basri and Ibrahim ibn Adham; asceticism since then has been an aspect of Sufi theology and practice.[6] The East London Mosque appears "at home both in the idiom of ascesis" and traditional Sunni orthodoxy.[7] In terms of direct influences on the ELM community, the Deoband movement calls for asceticism in its specific combination of the Hanafi legal school and Sufi *tariqa* (path to the ultimate truth), encouraging worldly detachment.[8] ELM constituents respond to their life situation of low socioeconomic status through an Islamic lens that perceives poverty as a religious virtue rather than a social stigma, a metaphorical stumbling stone on their path to the ultimate truth, emancipating them from economic woes by detaching them from earthly concerns. That is, they come to dwell in the metropolis by focusing their sights and deeds on salvation.

Throughout history, Islamic theology has largely discussed socioeconomic status with reference not to social *class* but to social *justice*.[9] Omid Safi notes that "justice lies at the heart of Islamic social ethics" as moral and social concerns in both the Qur'an and Sunna, just as body and soul, cannot be torn apart.[10] The Qur'anic metaphor of weighing scales can be read as calling for the economic-distributive component of justice.[11] In addition, justice is represented as a prophetic mandate in the Sunna, with Muhammad's prophetic work characterized by an ongoing struggle against injustice.[12] A focus on social justice has thus arisen rather seamlessly in Islam, in which the individual is imbued with deep social responsibilities, and in which local circumstances and sharia continuously inform one another.[13] Sharia is understood not simply as law, as it is often mistranslated, but rather pathways of legal interpretations and living traditions that emerge from the Qur'an and the Sunna.[14] Justice has also historically undergirded emancipatory projects in Muslim communities worldwide, from the time of the Prophet Muhammad to the present, e.g., in the struggle against apartheid in South Africa and the Arab spring.[15] From giving large sums of money to celebrating personal sufferings, detachment from earthly life can also be understood as a means to engender justice.[16]

While economic status, as much as opportunity, defines the bounds—both material and immaterial—of the life one lives, my interlocutors stress that they also define the bounty of the heavens in direct inverse to earthly consumption. This reflects Cohen's philosophy of religion, specifically the centrality of poverty in his messianic vision; he writes, "The poor have become the pious. And the pious are the forerunners of the Messiah . . . This identity is the high point of ethical monotheism."[17] Similarly, on the first day that I visit her home, Amaya explains that "people who suffer in this life, poor people are rewarded more in heaven than rich people." She perceives poverty as a test of God. She knows this for certain, as she recently faced the test herself. In finding her way back to God, she simultaneously lost her wealth. She simply did not need material goods to fulfill herself or her calling. In fact, Amaya found that material wealth had stifled her soul.

Mosque leaders also posit the preferred positioning of the poor. During his Friday sermons, Imam K. draws in his diverse audience, many employed in the service industry, others unemployed and thus dependent on state welfare, by discussing the dangers of wealth:

Now, the problem is the wealth, 90 percent of the instances it is related to the wealth . . . maturity of other desires, wealth leads to it. If you have the money, yes, I can do that, I can do this. I can get that desire. I can get that haram. If

I don't have it, even if Shaitan comes with that source of deception and whispers to you . . . but you don't have so you can't get it. Then you might think how to get wealthy, because I won't get this haram unless I have this money, so I want to go and get the money from haram. So, I go and get the money from haram, then I go to spend it on haram. This is the way of Shaitan.

If Satan can lure the person into haram acts through material wealth, ascetic acts can counter this temptation, allowing her to remain in the halal realm. Ascetic acts can also alleviate false hopes and thereby a false sense of security in the constructed, at times alluring, material world—as embodied in the skyscrapers cutting through the city's clouds. Shaykh P. perceives denying oneself or giving away worldly objects as a means to soften the heart, as both foster distance from emotional attachments, including those to material wealth, rooted in *dunya*. Giving either that which one treasures or is beyond one's means, acting on the belief that "God is all you need," is a form of self-recovery and protection from worldly concerns that not only lead to disappointment but erode piety.

Forc[e] self to do difficult things, eating less, and spending money on charity. We want to keep all of our money, all our possessions. Abu Bakr was promised paradise but in one battle gave the Prophet Muhammad all of his wealth. He asked: "What have you left for your family?" "I have left Allah *Subhanahu wa-ta'ala.*"

Enacting this lesson, Rua responded to a near accident by donating her gold, reminded by the incident that she should detach from worldly objects and wealth and focus on her connection to God.

The other day in Ramadan, I was driving, very tired listening to the radio and then I suddenly just saw a BMW. She swerved, I swerved, I saw my life flash in front of my eyes. I said, "I have to give *sadaqa* [voluntary charity]" to my brother. Someone recently asked me, "Where is your gold chain?," and I said, "I gave it away."

Intertwining asceticism and giving as a means to influence spiritual and social lives demonstrates agency in a context of external constraints, facilitating detachment not only from objects, but also from overarching social and economic inequality, upheld by securitization, as I will later explore—in other words, an undercaste status in the London metropolis.

The Professionalization of Giving

The conceptualization of an inverse relationship between piety and wealth leads to high levels of charitable giving in spite of the precarious socioeconomic status of my ELM interlocutors. Mosque constituents not only place their scarce spending money into the collection buckets during the weekly Friday prayer without pause, but they agree to raise thousands of pounds at fundraisers. Zakat, or almsgiving, is one of the five pillars of Islam. While understood as an individual duty to God, mosques often spearhead philanthropy at the community level—from funding sources for the actual mosque project to raising and distributing alms. Throughout my research, ELM is extremely successful at fundraising for numerous causes: from the mosque building itself to Syrian refugees and Palestinian farmers.

The philanthropic vision of ELM is undergirded by a professionalization of giving, with mosque volunteers in official uniform who approach individuals following prayers and motivational speakers who fundraise before well-attended events. The first event where I witness collective fundraising occurs prior to a talk on "the Qur'anic generation" as well as a visiting muezzin (one who calls Muslims to prayer) from Mecca in March 2014. Here men and women sit in the same room, but remain physically divided by a screen. A master of ceremonies of sorts takes to the stage. He dons a shirt with a yellow collar, along with a red and white scarf. *"Al-salamu 'alaykum,"* he greets the crowd. The audience replies in sync, " *'alaykum salam."* He begins with Qur'anic recitation, pausing before he continues,

As said in the hadith, believers are like a building, they support one another. Like Muhammad *salla Allahu 'alayhi wa-'alihi wa-sallam*, we are part of one body, if one part hurts, all hurts. From the sura, Allah is the one who created death and life—will see who is doing last deeds to get to Janna. [We live to] age sixty, seventy, that's why life is very short and why we must work extremely hard before time runs out, for the benefit of our *dunya*. The one who is planting a seed should continue planting. The concept of *dunya*, you should work for the earth like you will die tomorrow. We are in severe need of others to take care of our *umma*. You must come more to these gatherings, to increase our *iman*. An *iman* is to believe, that you believe in the message of Allah. You believe in angels . . . We need to learn. We are people of knowing. Muhammad *salla Allahu 'alayhi wa-'alihi wa-sallam* said "read." So that we must read. And I repeat that I am very happy to be amongst you today. Thank God for coming today. It is a sign that there is goodness in your heart. There are three parts of the program, but first comes Salman from [a relief charity].

In contrast to the sermons and discourses of teachers in the mosque, positing the *dunya* as fleeting, "nothing," this speaker focuses on a responsibility towards the world, the need to treat it as a dwelling; "you should work for the earth like you will die tomorrow." As he emphasizes, *dunya* is not inherently or strictly haram, but it becomes haram when it "impedes [one's] *din*." In other words, if worldly life, in particular possessions/wealth, is utilized as a means to strengthen one's *iman*, it remains halal.

Next, Salman approaches the stage with a warm, smiling face,

> I am here to speak about a big problem taking place in Syria . . . I will copy some words of brothers and sisters in Syria, a particular sentence we always hear from them, a scream, a shout. "Ya Allah, we are the Muslims. Ya Allah, we are the Muslims. Ya Allah, where is our help, our brothers and sisters in Islam?" These are the cries in the last three years. Every day, 2,500 people have to leave home, half of Syria needs human aid, and three million had to leave in 2013. Seventy-five percent are women and children. This is the reality, the reality that I have seen three weeks ago when I went there. We went to one camp. They said, "Yesterday we had 500 people, today we have 2,500." Next to the camp, we built a village . . . *Wallahi* [I swear to God], it was so cold, it was even colder than London on a winter night. *Wallahi*, they have nothing other than that.

Salman raises his hands in the air, his voice a desperate cry as he repeats a single Arabic word. "*Wallahi, wallahi!*" He continues,

> When the Prophet said in the hadith that the believers are just like one body, if part of the body would ache the rest of the body would feel it. May Allah *Subhanallah* bless you. May Allah *Subhanallah* bless those who donate. I come from that with a big responsibility, with the promise that I gave to a grandmother ninety-three years old, to orphans, where there were no men at all. They will tell you how their fathers were killed, how their husbands were killed. We're funding tonight for flour, to provide some food, some bread, 10,000 pounds, 4,000 for a month, five trucks sent. And we are also fundraising to build another village, to provide safety for children, widows, and the disabled. Will anyone pledge 10,000 pounds? To donate or to fundraise. There is the hadith that mentioned an evil woman, she was very thirsty and went to the well to get some water. She saw a dog and decided to give the dog some water—only

from that were all her sins forgiven. People will assist you, they will help you. Anyone to start us? Anyone to take responsibility for 10,000 pounds? 5,000?

Two men volunteer for 5,000 pounds, reticently raising their hands. "Even if you can't raise all the money, at least you will get the reward." The arms of two women bolt into the air.

Remember, once you put your hand up, the reward is written . . . 2,500? Anyone from the sisters? Brothers? Allah will help you. I will never forget this. One brother went to Syria and saw a girl suffering. "How's life?," he asked. She said, "You know we don't cry anymore. We've been crying for two years now." They have lost faith in others. It's worse, 60 percent of hospitals damaged or destroyed. How many have seen the video of kids frozen? Put your hands up. A pound a day, you could have donated and that could've saved a life. A pound a day today and you *can* save a life. Stand in front of Allah—"At least I have tried. I have tried to raise 2,500 pounds. I raised 1,000 or 10,000. At least I have tried." One more person and we move down . . . now 1,000 pounds to be donated or raised.

Men and women throughout the room begin to raise their hands.

We have two, can we have a third, a fourth, a fifth person? We have five. Can we get five more? 1,000 pounds within one year, remember the hadith . . . We have six, one last person, make it seven and finally we are done. I ask for 500 pounds. We have two, two sisters in the back.

Salman steps down from the podium with the promise of 20,000 pounds.

Soon after this talk, I attend a mother-daughter event with Melia and her daughter. The evening commences with a video showing footage from the conflict in the Central African Republic. The real-life protagonists speak of the massacre of Muslims, forced to flee from their homes, some seeking refuge in churches and mosques soon burned to the ground. Following the video, two young women approach the stage. The first gives a brief overview of the nonprofit organization for which they are raising money. The second describes the conflict in vivid detail. Tears begin streaming down her face, slowly at first, then faster. She does not pause her speech to cry. Instead, she asks for a pledge of 5,000 pounds "to donate or raise together" as she swallows back sobs, wiping her eyes with the back of her hand. She repeats her request multiple times, but no one volunteers. She raises her voice, describing a YouTube video she saw in which a Muslim man was killed in this conflict, his flesh then eaten inside of a baguette. She weeps, the sobs now pulling her shoulders forward. "No child should have to witness this, should have to know that such things are going on in this world." Head bent, she exits the stage.

A third woman, in her mid-thirties, dressed in professional attire, walks to the front of the room. She appears to be another organization representative. She assures she "will not ask for a 5,000-pound donation"; she "will not ask for any particular donation." She calmly asserts, "This is not about money, I am not asking for money, but who wants to help?" Hands across the room shoot up in unison. "You should all have your hands raised," she declares. She then asks, "Who has spent thirty pounds this week, which is the amount for a family food pack which would last a family one month?" Most of the women in the room raise their hands. She asks, "Who has thirty pounds?" The same women in the room raise their hands a second time. She pauses and then asks again if they would like to donate money to the cause. Volunteers hand out paper forms for either one-time donations or standing orders from a bank account. Glancing around, I see most of the women sitting at my table offer thirty pounds, the number that she discussed. Melia starts to collect the papers, and announces that someone has offered a 1,000-pound donation. Then, with a shriek of glee, Melia declares that someone has pledged to raise 5,000 pounds. The girls and women throughout the room clap their hands and chant in unison "Allahu Akbar."

William Barylo describes European Muslim charities as opportunities to unite ethics and modern, neoliberal forms of organization; what he finds—communities utilizing foundational Islamic sources to support "a 'Muslim prosperity theology' in which material success is deemed as a sign of divine approval"—contrasts with the East London Mosque, employing the same religious sources to draw out fiscal giving from individuals in situations of great economic insecurity.[18] The lived realities of ELM constituents who see proof of piety, and therefore find pride, in poverty demonstrate both how and why some of London's urban poor contribute at high rates to fundraising campaigns, offering money they have not yet secured. At fundraising events, the emotion of the speakers draws in the audience, guttural cries, streams of tears, personal experiences, and horrors described in detail: a performance of anguish for the brute suffering of fellow Muslims. This tactic of fundraising invokes empathy while positing charity as a means to earn redemption. Some at ELM responsively fundraise large sums, most willing to give at least "a pound a day" for a defined period, sacrificing small earthly pleasures as they lay their paths to paradise. If generosity and even poverty prove salvation, what greater act can illuminate one's path? This of course evokes a comparison to early Calvinists, who found hard work and resulting wealth revealed one's deserved place in heaven.[19] Here my interlocutors search for what Bloch terms "*Vorscheine* (pre-illuminations/glimpses)" of a hoped-for better world to come.[20] Eyes and hearts cast temporally outwards towards the future and (in solidarity with a prophet) past, my ELM interlocutors project themselves ever further into messianic time.

The Rewards of Suffering

Over our epicurean everyday of brewed black tea and curry in her kitchen, Amaya answers one of theology's most difficult questions: why people suffer if there is a God, that is theodicy. She believes that this question is simply "a test that leads to greater rewards in heaven." It is not, according to Amaya, in the least contradictory that God exists alongside of earthly travails. Suffering may serve as a blessing leading to paradise and/or as a test of faith; or it may signal the misgivings of the Muslim community, brought on through misguidance or lack of piety. Following one of our learning circles, Nala, a middle-aged convert, says she feels sorry for people caught in the Syrian conflict but that she also finds, "It must be coming from somewhere. They are lacking in what they are doing spiritually, or we are lacking somewhere in the *umma* . . . Syria is a test. That's why they keep killing each other."

When Cohen writes of messianism, he argues that "the value of human life lies not in happiness but rather in suffering."[21] Cohen articulates this value at once through Jewish theology and Jewish history, "a continuous chain" of suffering.[22] The idealization of poverty and suffering among my interlocutors at ELM similarly emerges at the nexus of theological teachings and lived circumstances, present and past. "It's not an easy thing to be a walking Qur'an," asserts a teacher, Samiya, at a women's learning circle in winter 2014. During Ramadan in summer 2016, Imam K. articulates the rewards attained in the hereafter for suffering in this life.

> The hardship is a sign of strength, physical strength, mental strength, spiritual strength. If you give up easily than you are not somebody expected to do something very good in your life . . . We know that the longer day brings very high reward. There is a hadith from Sahabi [companion of the Prophet Muhammad] Abu Musa . . . they are on the board of the ship, when it is the darkness of the night after midnight they hear some kind of noise, OK . . . Someone is making an announcement to them. They don't see them but they hear it . . .

"O people of the ship, people of the boat, listen, I am giving you good news. Allah has decided something very important . . ." Then Abu Musa said, "If you are giving us any good news, give us, don't delay. What is it?" . . . Indeed, Allah *Subhanahu wa-ta'ala* had decided, he made compulsory on him that whoever facing thirst in longer day by fasting during summer, in hot days, Allah *Subhanahu wa-ta'ala* provide him drink in the day of judgment when everybody will be having thirst.

In such sermons, as well as workshops and women's meetings in the mosque, we are advised by leadership to seek meaning in our travails, many of them embodied hardships, whether long summer Ramadan days of fasting, washing our feet with cold water in winter, staying up late for extra prayers, or a life with little economic stability. "The one who knows it best is the one who choked on it," says speaker Nouman Ali Khan, founder of Bayyinah Institute, an American institution that uses media and technology for Islamic education. Here the interdependence of ways of knowing and ways of being in the process of "corporeal remolding" again comes to the fore.[23]

Only recently able to walk after a year confined to bed by a mysterious illness, Melia describes this as a blessing. "Maybe Allah wanted me to become ill so that I could change the way that my life was going. Now I leave the house to spend time with friends, go regularly to the mosque." As a quote attributed to medieval Islamic jurist and theologian Ibn Qayyim al-Jawziyya that is shared in a women's WhatsApp group reads, "The soul will never become pious and purified except through undergoing afflictions. It is the same as gold that can never be pure except after removing all the base metals in it." In a weekend workshop with women soon after in spring 2014, Shaykh P. reiterates this sentiment:

> Even if we think we've done well, we should constantly say to ourselves, "I haven't done enough" . . . We are hard on ourselves and think the worst of ourselves. This is a good thing, to always check the self. One of the purest was Yusuf [protagonist of an often-cited Qur'anic narrative], who resisted so many tests that were put in his way. He was pure even though the wife of the minister tried to seduce him. But he does not say "I'm so innocent, so pure." No, he says, "The soul is capable of, commands evil, but in my case it is Allah *Subhanahu wa-ta'ala* who saved me."

To protect both the self and the collective, one thus seeks purity, stripped of debris by the granules of hardship for the sake of God, with purity achieved through the will of God. In this respect, the community to a great extent re-flects a Weberian sect. Weber writes, "Everything which arose later from sects is linked in the decisive points to the demand for purity, the *ecclesia pura*—a community consisting only of those members whose mode of conduct and life style do not carry public signs of heavenly disfavor, but proclaim the glory of God."[24]

My interlocutors at ELM respond to the socioeconomic injustices that have deep and lasting implications on their lives in East London. Rather than tacit acceptance of a subordinate societal position, they transform their perspectives such that ethical strivings and lived experience reflect one another. This community, temporally distinct from the immediacy of the city, animates a messianic timeline in which Muslims focus both on those less fortunate than themselves, giving beyond their means, and on the hereafter, where they will be rewarded for living virtuously in the world. In this form of Benjaminian "counter-earth"—a term he likens to an earth cast under the light of moon rather than the light of sun—or rather counter-time, their inhabitance of met-ropolitan Europe is unexpected and unorthodox.[25] Yet understanding how justice-seeking in the present—which is again "shot through with chips of Messianic time"—relates to the alignment of the social and the moral helps to make sense of human-material relations in and beyond the mosque.[26] On the surface, what appears at first as paradox emerges from the nexus of socioeco-nomic schism in the British capital and Islamic epistemological resources—producing that realm of dreams deferred.

Hasan: "The turmoil is strong"

Hasan, a youth worker in Tower Hamlets, meets me at a small café by the train station abutting Victoria Park. Over tea and biscuits, he speaks of his threshold position, as a Muslim man working for the Tower Hamlets government. His phone buzzes with messages from his wife, photographs of their new baby girl flashing on the screen throughout our meeting. He moves somehow fluidly from describing his immense love for his daughter to the troubled waters that Muslim youth in the district, the city, and the country wade within.

Born in Tower Hamlets to parents who migrated from the Sylhet region of Bangladesh, Hasan is intimately familiar with the borough's rough edges. To explain the present, he often turns to his personal past and the continuity of marginality experienced by Muslims. "Gang life, I *lived* this," Hasan explains. "Most [local Muslim youth] grow up on these estates. When we went to school we had to go in groups to be safe, from Shadwell to Stepney Green. It was only a ten-, fifteen-minute walk. If we were late, we weren't going to school, it wasn't safe. We had to pass through five estates." From such harrowing micro-experiences to a tenuous positionality within broader society—"we *are* the Other," he asserts with emphasis—Hasan sees how the cultural degradation of Muslims can turn individuals inwards, away from society. He gives a telling example of an acquaintance whose act of ritual cleansing for prayer [*wudu'*] was designated as "dirty," seen to upend the "order" of his workplace. "Some workplaces, they have feet washing basins for *wudu'*. Others don't. There is a man who washes his feet in a sink at work before prayer and everyone says 'you're disgusting.' He replies, 'I wash my feet five times a day, they are cleaner than your face.'"

The ultimate task, Hasan says, is full inclusion—inclusion in the London metropolis, and the British nation-state, not only present but past. "We say it's your country, but after Brexit hate crime is up five times. Jo Blog says to you, 'It's not yours, get out.' Young people respond with a slap." To ameliorate experiences of cultural subordination requires a celebration of Muslim contributions to British society, he explains, an unearthing of buried pasts: from the "service of Asians" in WWI and WWII to those who helped rebuild the country after WWII. Then they can say, " 'Actually I do belong here.' Young people can respond then with a literature-based slap."

Looking down, Hasan smiles at the photographs of his child that appear intermittently on his screen. Looking up, he returns to our conversation about a harsh reality, on the surface glossed over by gentrification in establishments like the one where we now sit, delicate porcelain teacups balanced in our hands. "You have an expectation of being a victim of hate . . . the turmoil is strong," he says, shaking his head. His own turmoil results not only from assumptions in mainstream society but also from Muslim groups and institutions that look at him with a similar sense of suspicion because he works for the government. He was recently expelled from the Islamic Forum of Europe (IFE), straddling an impossible line between Muslim youth and the Tower Hamlets government. Hasan looks down at the photograph and up again, at the sky outside threatening rain.

THE INTIMACY OF TERROR: A MULTICULTURAL HAUNTING

While internally preaching a hard boundary between the halal and the haram, the East London Mosque also engages as an institution with the surrounding metropolis—from the participation of its leadership on local social councils to Open Mosque Days, press engagement, and hosting high-profile visitors,

including Prince Charles and current prime minister Boris Johnson. As with
Şehitlik's Bahira Project, this mosque's representation within local networks
and alliances, such as the Tower Hamlets Community Cohesion Contingency
Planning and Tension Monitoring Group (CCCPTMG),[27] illuminates how
Muslim individuals and institutions become implicated in state security projects. They too seek enactive (through self-advocacy) and protective (buffering
communities from interventions) possibilities in coercive sociopolitical contexts. Here the East London Mosque's dealings with securitization reveal a
schism between the narratives of hope emerging from Islam and the narratives
of threat that color Muslim life in London.

Forcibly entrenched within a dominant security paradigm, terror plays an
active role in the lives of all ELM community members, as it does in all Muslim
communities in Europe. It constrains what they can make; it constrains how
they can dwell. They are called to not only continuously condemn terrorist
attacks, but also to somehow prove their loyalty to the targeted states, cities,
and individuals. They proclaim, time and again, that this is not Islam, that
"terror has no religion," and that the Qur'an clearly states, "if anyone kills a
person . . . it is as if he kills all mankind." This Qur'anic verse is uttered so
often that it becomes a sort of mantra, the go-to quotation given to journalists when Muslim leaders are summoned to denounce the violence of others.
Securitization, however, including the surveillance of mosques and neighborhoods, affects not only public images, but also intimate lives. It exposes deep
disappointments in the liberal state and its underlying values, including the
ephemerality of multiculturalism, the intolerance embedded in the notion of
"tolerance," the inequality inherent to equality discourses, and the limits of
freedom. While we cook in her kitchen, Kasia describes freedom as an agentive
act of detachment—freedom from her family's cultural mores, freedom from
her husband through a hoped-for separation, freedom from the state as locus
of identity. On one occasion, however, I use the word "freedom" in the context
of the metropolis to describe the sentiment I feel when I wander its streets, and
Kasia shakes her head. "Freedom for who?," she asks, an unanswerable question that reverberates now, as I narrate the terror that shakes my interlocutors
awake from their dreams.

Operation Trojan Horse

The London Metropolitan Police, formed in the early twentieth century, was
the first police force in England. While policing in London, as the UK more
broadly, unduly focuses on immigrant and postmigrant populations, police

have historically belonged to the urban working class, many themselves hailing from immigrant backgrounds.[28] Mark, a white British middle-class man who has worked in the Tower Hamlets police force for three decades, articulates the layered in-betweenness of London for Muslims under the gaze of a security state. He is, in many ways, more reflective on the complexities of state-Muslim relations than the police officers I interview in Berlin, his surveilling role somehow softened by a combination of compassion and hope for plurality. Mark helps to guide me through both the history and present sociopolitical fragmentation of Tower Hamlets, London, and the British state. In so doing, he often turns towards the multicultural project, terming multiculturalism "a blobby sort of thing."

> If we're looking for certainty or discernable edges, we all now agree that multiculturalism is a success, you'll never get that. Here in Britain you can wear anything you want. You can wear a veil—well not at the bank or giving witness, but the rest of the time, I don't care. Who cares whether a man loves a man or loves a woman? I think if you're looking for certainty, you won't see it. Multiculturalism is something with rough edges that requires people to be decent to each other and vigilant against corrosive forces.

Mark's description of multiculturalism centers on a normative rather than political project, one based in mutual respect and the "right to indifference" described by Mayanthi Fernando.[29] Still, he recognizes that the rhetoric of multiculturalism has increasingly been employed in reference to an enduring period of pathology by the conservative political wing, in which "Muslimness" alludes the integrative capacity of states. The danger of this multicultural haunting is its reference to a mythic time, an eroded, ephemeral moment of the recent past. If we approach it as such, as a "spongy referent" perpetually disintegrating without ever taking form, multiculturalism loses its innocuous exterior.[30]

Even in his own hope-filled vision of multiculturalism, the terror specter remains, as Mark speaks of the need to be "vigilant against corrosive forces," signaling extremism in its many forms; he not only discusses the Muslim community, but also—more so—far right-wing movements. As a leader in the local police precinct and the wider borough community, Mark is concerned with maintaining equilibrium in a place that has become grounds for conflict between those celebrating diversity and those striving for homogeneity, like the so-called Christian patrols and so-called Muslim patrols mentioned earlier. Tower Hamlets' denizens, he assures with a smile, "we get on all right."

Mark straddles the line between hard and soft power, collaboration and surveillance. The ultimate position of liminality in the policing of Muslim communities, however, is inhabited by Muslim state employees, whether police officers, like those I interview in Berlin, or other civil servants, including youth workers like Hasan. Let me return, for a moment, to the café near Victoria Park, where Hasan evokes the problematic notion of the "model Muslim" who has not cast off his religious identity, but rather explicitly chosen to work for the state.[31] Aware of his own in-betweenness, Hasan pushes back against this conceptualization. He describes himself not as partner in policing, but rather a buffer, the last defense before a spiral of securitization takes hold. "Once the police get involved, it's too late," he explains, noting the weakening of already "weak ties" when police enter into intimate spheres including schools and homes. Mark Granovetter argues that weak ties undergirded by trust, like those between acquaintances, create social cohesion.[32] Consequently, undermining trust, an inevitable outcome of securitization and surveillance, erodes these weak ties, here deepening the social and emotional distance of Muslim populaces from the British state.

Like Hasan, the East London Mosque appears as an ambiguous, liminal space in the borough's policing. The distinct community infrastructure of institutions like ELM becomes somehow both partially blamed for radicalization—as disconnected or so-called "parallel" communities—and implicated as a collaborator in the state security project. Within a context corrosive of trust, it appears paradoxical that the UK, as Europe more broadly, depends on the very communities it fears to impede the radicalization of Muslim youth. Hasan, for instance, describes the mentorship that an ELM imam provides to youth seen at risk for radicalization. "I don't have a beard," he explains, they are "not going to trust me." Here Hasan notes his own limitations, with the ascendency of embodied markers not only in the mainstream abstraction of Muslims, the breaking apart of bodies, but also signaling authenticity in Muslim communities.

Hasan soon turns our conversation to a crisis that took place in the borough in January 2015, when three schoolgirls from the Bethnal Green Academy traveled to Syria, joining ISIS. This moment shocked the local Muslim community, parents shaken by the sense that global forces could penetrate their only safe spaces in the city, their homes in "away."[33] The dwellings they had made—their "fashioned shells"—were breached by an immaterial, virtual network.[34] Hasan describes the fear expressed by parents in the months after the girls left Tower Hamlets, asking him to help protect their children from global forces beyond their control. At the same time, on a local level, ELM was targeted by the media as a space potentially fomenting extremist views; an uncle of one of the schoolgirls told a British newspaper that his niece had been radicalized at ELM by the Muslimat, the women's wing of the Young Muslim Organisation.[35] This moment, its layering of local and global political contentions, fomenting both suspicion and fear, contributed to what Mark terms a "turning point for the [Tower Hamlets Muslim] community" in 2016. Since then, Mark explains, Muslims in Tower Hamlets have experienced a notable upsurge in contact with security forces, facilitated by the expanded mandate of the Prevent strategy.[36] He reflects, "Recent events have made people warier, raids on the *madrasas* . . . being under watch, Prevent programming in school, makes people feel the community is really under the thumb. More kids than ever are having contact with police officers."

I cannot help but repeat, in my mind and also on this page, Hasan's words that "once the police get involved, it's too late," signaling the deep structural problems at the heart of the security apparatus and the insecurity that so often takes hold. In making sense of the schoolgirls' motivations to flee outwards from the city, Hasan describes a grappling for alternative realities in the face of deep marginality, one made accessible by technology; online forums provide an opportunity for both inward and outward flight—an attempt to escape—from difficult lived experiences. Sarah Glynn writes of the rise of Islamism in the East End via its direct relationship to marginalization:

> It is not hard to understand how Islamism can be seen as a potent antidote to alienation, socio-economic disadvantage and lack of opportunity, and how it has been effectively counter-posed as an alternative to hedonistic capitalist materialism and (more specifically) to Tower Hamlets' drug and gang culture.[37]

It is not, however, only the lack of socioeconomic opportunity that grates and separates, but also the emotional distancing that makes full belonging as Muslims in the mainstream impossible. In Zygmunt Bauman's words, the stranger (here the Muslim) "poison[s] the comfort of order with suspicion of chaos."[38] "Muslims are suspect," Hasan says with a sigh, as he looks through the café window to the skies threatening rain. He explains how some youth in the borough respond to this suspicion, which fractures and fragments their sense of groundedness—the "double absence" that results from feeling that they belong neither to where their families migrated from nor to the UK.[39] Hasan here juxtaposes the glamor of possibility that attracts with disappointment that repels, potential agency and authority portrayed in virtual worlds with lived experiences of vulnerability and subordination.

The attraction to sensational materials, such as ISIS videos targeting young women by promising romance in the desert to dedicated jihadi brides, must be contextualized within the deprivation and violence of Tower Hamlets. Hasan describes this attraction as a response to being neither imagined, nor able to imagine oneself, as part of the society at hand. Animated by potentially devastating hope, this leads to the imagining of new communities in and across virtual space. "We live here multiple lives," Hasan asserts.

> Now you live three lives: home/friends/online . . . a glimpse of glamorized call of duty through social media, which is the biggest gateway . . . ISIS has glamor, for example outsourcing film, it was almost like a trailer to the gladiator, with costumes, lighting, music. It creates a very emotive experience.

Such virtual other-lives thus provide *affective* opportunities for Muslim youth who feel doubly dislocated from the cultural mindsets of their parents and a mainstream that casts them as uncivil. Hasan points to the grave failure of the British state to address the roots of this problem, where opportunities to build emotional bonds with the city and state are continuously undercut by securitization and surveillance.

As he describes the local schoolgirls' disappearance in terms of the impossible promises to soothe lived disappointments, Hasan speaks of an earlier societal scandal geographically further afield—one that has reverberated in Muslim communities across the country: "Operation Trojan Horse." In 2014, Operation Trojan Horse rose as the epitome of "muscular liberalism," which has come to characterize the British security state.[40] An anonymous letter sent to the Birmingham City Council in 2013 outlined the "infiltration of Islamist ideology" through an agenda to replace non-Muslim teachers with those espousing Islamism in the city's schools, leading to twenty-one school investigations.

While no such agenda was found in schools, the subsequent report criticized five of them for their faith-based visions. And it cast not only the schools but the entire city of Birmingham, one of the most diverse in the UK, in light of a neoliberal security agenda—sacrificing the security of Muslim families and educators in its justification of government investigation. The language of the report, and reporting on it by the media, further deepened the perceived linkages between Islam and extremism, reinforcing stereotypes about the covert danger of Muslim communities in the UK.[41] This incident at the same time echoed the tenor of earlier European state investigations into Jews, from the French Dreyfus Affair to the German *Judenzählung*, with factual findings overshadowed by suspicion and unfounded accusations of disloyalty invoked.

Operation Trojan Horse has since come to represent the deep and enduring intimacy—the unfortunate familiarity—of terror in Muslims' lives.

There is widespread recognition in the Tower Hamlets borough, including at the East London Mosque, that this far-reaching *discourse* of radicalization, extremism, and terrorism has become synonymous with Muslim bodies and institutions. In one of our learning circles in winter 2014, our teacher Biva describes a companion of the Prophet Muhammad who publicly recited the Qur'an facing not only social outcry but violence as a "terrorist of the time." "When he went in front of the Kaaba it's a bit like us now, going in front of the Parliament holding a sign for Palestine or Syria and being labeled as terrorists. People are labeled as terrorists for their religion. He was the terrorist of the time." By appropriating this terminology through the Islamic tradition, but turning it on its head, Biva seeks to disarm the potency of the terror discourse. And yet by employing this terminology as a common and recognizable discursive form, she also speaks to the intimacy of terror in Muslims' lives.

The most public and debated of government security schema that has deepened this intimacy of terror in Muslims' lives is the UK's Prevent strategy, as described earlier.[42] During our conversation, Hasan gives an example of Prevent in action within the local community, citing "a student [who] didn't want to go to assembly. He knew he needed a better excuse than that and said that 'music is against my faith.' This was seen as extremist." This mislabeling of extremism, creating a spiral of interventions, thereby deepening alienation, is far more common than actual involvement in extremist groups or acts. Here discursive labeling in security terms again allows for illiberal sanctioning by the liberal state, disregarding individual autonomy and freedom in the name of an ambiguous "greater good," eroding the very values that it claims to protect. Like Hasan, police captain Mark is aware that something dark bubbles underneath the surface in London and the UK more broadly, as in Europe as a whole. "Beneath this patina of reasonableness is something much more unreasonable: hatred of Muslims and the idea that all Muslims are extremists."

This unreasonable yet powerful idea reverberates on a macro level in the overarching security strategy of the British state, but also on a more micro level in the violent reprisals so often experienced by Muslims for crimes they did not commit. On June 3, 2017, in an attack claimed by ISIS, three men drove a vehicle into pedestrians on London Bridge and thereafter stabbed Borough Market shoppers, killing seven and injuring dozens of people.[43] At a press conference in response to this attack, Sufia Alam, a representative of the Maryam Centre, reflects on the subsequent danger faced by members of the ELM community:

We have seen in the past how such incidences have led to an increase in reprisals—arson on mosques, abuse and attacks on individuals, especially our sisters in hijab and niqab. Already we are getting information of such reprisals. We are in touch with the police for more presence from them. We urge you to be extra vigilant. Don't travel unnecessarily or alone especially in the night. Sisters, please take extra note.

Here we see how the terror discourse, institutionalized but not contained in a far-reaching state security agenda, strips Muslims of their agency through both authorized and unauthorized violence against bodies of flesh and bodies, like ELM, of stone.

This terror discourse and the repercussions it has on the everyday lives of Muslims in the metropolis cannot be easily disarmed. In fact, it has been deepened under the current Conservative Party government, justified by the supposed failures of multiculturalism, with Muslim communities blamed for separation from a mainstream that fails to fully include them. In her June 4, 2017, speech following the London Bridge attack, Prime Minister Teresa May asserts:

> While we have made significant progress in recent years, there is, to be frank, far too much tolerance of extremism in our country. So, we need to become far more robust in identifying it and stamping it out across the public sector and across society. That will require some difficult and often embarrassing conversations, but the whole of our country needs to come together to take on this extremism, and we need to live our lives not in series of separated, segregated communities, but as one truly United Kingdom.[44]

Let us pause here at a single word: *tolerance*. No, not only a word, a seemingly innocuous but dangerous term key to the Muslim experience in the East End and far beyond. While May here alludes to a negative link between tolerance and extremism, the discourse of tolerance in politics and the media, portrayed as a European value, has largely been one of aspiration.[45] As Wendy Brown explains, tolerance is at once a "discourse of power and a practice of governmentality" achieved through a practice of toleration, a making do with that which makes the dominant group in society uncomfortable.[46] Neither individual nor group receives tolerance; its target is the essentialized subject of covert aversion. Tolerance, often attached to rhetoric about Muslims in Europe, is a bitter civilizing discourse disguised by a saccharine rhetorical wrapper of the enlightened, liberal sensitivity—a contranym, perfectly synonymous with its own antonym: intolerance.[47] For Muslims in today's Europe, "tolerance conferred . . . shores up the normative standing of the tolerant and the liminal standing of the tolerated—a standing somewhere between civilization and barbarism."[48] To invoke tolerance reveals the perpetuity of policing the stranger dwelling in the threshold of the European metropolis—"somewhere between civilization and barbarism"—and thereby the unrelenting hierarchy inherent to an undercaste status.

Hanan: "I like to ask questions"

I am skimming suras about Yusuf, while listening to the soft, somehow audible recitation of a young woman across the room, when a woman approaches me and introduces herself as Hanan. Hanan smiles, curling her small feet under her legs, telling me she is twenty-four and employed in the local Tower Hamlets government. Like Hasan, Hanan crosses the boundaries between the Muslim community and the state, contending through a complex lived reality with the rhetorical vision of separateness preached at the East London Mosque. She stands out, although not for lack of modest attire, with leggings, and a semi-transparent long black skirt, a striped shirt and maroon sweater, a taupe-colored animal print scarf covering her hair. "I like to ask questions," Hanan says with sincerity.

We discuss my research project, the time I have spent at ELM. Hanan then proceeds to talk about Islam, intertwined with snippets from her life. Her vision contrasts with that preached by ELM leaders, who encourage adherents to discipline themselves in the minutiae of everyday habits. "What is important is being good, becoming pure in our souls . . . It's important to get the big things right and then the little things will fall into place. To have a good heart." She used to attend this mosque with her mother, but would "rebel" in small ways, such as chewing gum during prayers. Hanan became pious after the death of her father, when she was eighteen, taking her religious practice more seriously in the wake of loss. She describes her turn toward piety as a softening—"I was hard before he died, then I became soft. I was a typical London girl"—and a way to remain connected with her father, who taught her to read the Qur'an as a child, the sound of each Arabic letter still reminding her of his voice. His loss sent her full force into the arms of all that lingered from what they had shared.

Rather than tightening her topographical boundaries, like many of my interlocutors, to focus on the neighborhood surrounding ELM, Hanan regularly travels outside of the country: most recently to Turkey and Mexico. This has helped to open her eyes to the world. Her mother forbids it and yet she does it anyway. "I'm not going to do haram," she assures me. "If I were, I could do it here. I could do it anywhere."

Hanan sees "a lot of questions" as challenging her acceptance in the community. She tries to find the answers, but this makes others, from her family to the older "aunties" at ELM, uncomfortable.

> My friend at work also told me that it's idol worship, worshiping the footprint of Muhammad. So, I went to my brother and asked him, "Yes, it kind of is, why do we do that?" And he told me, "No, you cannot question that, it's haram. You just do it. It's that way." I like to question things, to think about them. That's why we have intellect. It says so in the Qur'an.

At the End of a Dead-End Street: On Brexit

I begin my morning in a local coffee shop by Victoria Park, where long faces meet long faces, the public sphere suddenly alive with chatter over the Brexit vote. It is June 24, 2016, a turning point, or perhaps a punctuated ending to debates on the UK's role in the European project: a remarkable day in British history. Just a week earlier, the murder of a member of Parliament, Jo Cox, by a far-right extremist, Thomas Mair, shook the nation. Yelling "This is for Britain. Britain will always come first," Mair stabbed and then shot Cox, representative of Batley and Spen, in Birstall outside of Leeds. In the buildup to the Brexit vote, Mair had identified Cox as a staunch supporter of the Remain Campaign and of immigration.[49]

Set against a physically beautiful and politically shaky backdrop, I participate in a moment of privileged disenchantment within the gentrifying pocket of Victoria Park Village, where men and women sit at the idyllic Pavilion Café, watching the queen's fishing swans dip their necks below the surface of a man-made pond. An American woman in the café speaks to me, as her pug jumps up and down between us; she feels uncertain about remaining in the UK, having moved abroad in response to the election of George H. W. Bush. A young Danish woman laments that she has not transferred her sterling into Danish kroner, pushing her blond ponytail to the side as she speaks with great animation. Along with the energy of uncertainty, a sadness lingers in the air, in these conversations of fear brought to fruition.

Shaded by the arc of old willow trees, we are all here caught off guard by our illiteracy in many other pockets of the city, such as the East London Mosque, where no one mentions Brexit in our conversations later that same afternoon. This political climate arguably affects the mosque constituents far more than these coffee shop goers two miles away, with rising incidents of verbal and physical attacks against identifiable Muslims in both the lead-up to and aftermath of the vote, as documented by TellMAMA (a project recording and measuring anti-Muslim violence). The Brexit vote is, however, not a shock moment for Muslims in London, but rather a continuation along a trajectory of partial inclusion, the inevitable end of a dead-end street. From the colonies to the postcolonial metropole, Brexit comes as no surprise to my interlocutors who encounter the impossibility of full belonging time and again in their everyday lives. While they are deeply affected by politics—from Prevent to Brexit—my interlocutors express a staunch political agnosticism, reflecting the Benjaminian notion that "to politicize an idea was to deprive it of its ethical and spiritual validity . . . sullied by politics, ethical ideas lose their substance."[50] Concerned with, and motivated by, closing distance not to society but to God, they thus turn away from politics, seen to disorient from the messianic north star that will one day lead them home.

I see Kasia the same day, the air between us unsettled by a distinct sense of disappointment. She has been avoiding me, along with the other women in our group who once met to cook and to learn. At the time, eighteen months earlier, all sought to distance themselves from their husbands, rooting more deeply in Islam as a means to forge new paths in their individual lives. Melia perceived a year-long bout of debilitating illness as a sign that she should gain independence through increased religious devotion. Amaya found herself in Qur'anic recitation, first as student, then as teacher, with hope to relocate abroad. Kasia set a separation from her husband in motion—one that has since been halted. "Elisabeth!," Kasia exclaims when she sees me at the Maryam Centre. "Are you a Muslim now?" I shake my head. I ask how things are going and she quickly responds, "Things are different now," turning away. I have heard through others that Melia stays home with her newlywed daughter and grandchild. Amaya, once a vocal leader at the Maryam Centre, is no longer present at all. I wonder if she made it to Mecca.

Following the disappearance—the flight—of the Bethnal Green school girls, *madrasa* raids, and the borough's first Muslim mayor, Mohammad Lutfur Rahman, being found guilty of electoral corruption charges in 2015, the atmosphere in the neighborhood has shifted towards one of deepened mistrust.[51] An insecurity not present during my first time at the mosque in winter 2014 prevails less than two years later, undergirded by deepening sociopolitical divisions and a rising right wing that has gained not only popular support but positions in established political institutions. The neighborhood has, as earlier explored, experienced multiple blows, its children preyed upon by extremists and increasingly under the eye of teachers officially tasked with identifying signs of potential radicalization through the national Prevent strategy.[52] As discontent has surged in the city, and the country, the proliferation of policies targeting Muslims through a security lens has emerged in the wake of those protecting group identities and spaces.[53] The Brexit vote now further destabilizes the metropolis, the nation and beyond, bringing a pluralist European project to its knees.

Kasia does not want to continue speaking to me, yet my toddler approaches her relentlessly, eying a Styrofoam box filled with French fries delicately balanced on her knees. Beside Kasia, a babbling baby: another son. As determinant as political affairs, personal letdown passes through her troubled gaze. She never left her husband with her half-grown children. She began at the beginning again. "I don't come here much anymore," she explains, as she offers my toddler French fries. "You know, I think about it, things changed. There used to be so much life at the mosque, so much was going on here. But now there are so many regulations, we women don't meet anymore." I am filled with questions I do not, cannot ask. What regulations is she referencing—that is, what aftermath am I not only witnessing, but wading within? And where are the wings, the miracles of flies and angels that once united us?

The same day, which is also the day before Eid al-Fitr, the celebration marking the end of Ramadan, I am intercepted by a white, middle-aged man after I tie a headscarf loosely around my hair close to the Maryam Centre. "What is this! What is this! What is this!," he demands, rather than questions, blocking my way in front of the Tesco Express supermarket. I fix my eyes on the ground, transported to the first time I arrived on Whitechapel Road, eighteen months prior, a bloodied butcher running alongside stall upon stall selling gem-colored saris, surrounded by women in headscarves, *jilapi* freshly fried in front of my eyes. The surface of that initial encounter suggested a certain ease to Muslim life in this corner of the city, if economically uncertain—a sense that no one stood out on Whitechapel Road, that the indifference so desired by Fernando's French interlocutors, and also my own in Germany and the UK, might exist in this postcolonial city.[54] That was only the surface, of course, and the depths revealed plurality without cohesion, tension without productive friction: that there are not two sides to each story, nor six—like the seals of Solomon that mark the mosque—but so very many that we will never hear or see. And time, ebbing and flowing, pulling us forwards and backwards at once, has also brought winds of change: to ELM, to Tower Hamlets, to the

London metropolis. Time has moved us into this uncertain moment, where the personal and political collide.

Only upon reflection years later do I recognize the temporal importance of my entrance into the lives of my closest ELM interlocutors: a moment of empowerment, of opening, inviting me into their intimate spaces, detaching from husbands who had disappointed them. It is within Amaya's home that I learn to recite the first verse of the first chapter of the Qur'an. And it is within Kasia's home that I watch the tearful explanations of Jewish women converting to Islam, revealing an understandable hope given my ambivalent positionality, as a pregnant, Jewish American woman married to a Muslim man. The new distance between us is filled with unspoken and unfulfilled hopes, layered betrayals in the concentric circles that move outwards from the home to the mosque surveilled, the unforgiving metropolis to the uncertain world.

That evening, after I meet Hanan for iftar, I ascend the stairs to the Maryam Centre's main area to retrieve my shoes. I have taken the wrong staircase and find myself again in the men's section of ELM. I descend, frustrated at my lack of direction, not wanting to reenter the room where women sit awaiting the *tarawih* prayer, undertaken after the night prayer during Ramadan. I enter the bathroom in hopes I will find someone familiar. With no such luck, I ask a woman I have not seen before, standing at the sink washing her hands, if she knows how to get back to the Maryam Centre. "We are going there in a minute, I am just making *wudu*'," she replies with a smile. She proceeds to hand her young daughter the headscarf draped over her shoulder, subsequently washing her face and arms. She runs a wet hand quickly through her hair. "Are you American?" she asks, recognizing my accent. "We were in America," she explains, and then asks where I am from. "New York," I answer. She replies, "We visited New York . . . People were so lovely, many had never met a Muslim before but they were so nice to us. Our lawyer there did everything for us." "What were you doing there?," I ask. "Oh, it's a long story. My brother was extradited."

I know I cannot hide my shock as she says this nonchalantly, throwing her headscarf back over her hair in a single swoop. She continues without pause, shifting into the familiar terrain of mundane small talk. "We are from south London, we don't usually come here but we thought we would for a change. There's a lovely bazaar behind the mosque too." I am still astonished. "I hope everything is OK for your brother," I say. "*Al-hamdulillah*, he is back home," she replies, and smiles again, this time with a shrug. We exit the bathroom together, my unease palpable as we climb the stairs to the Maryam Centre.

This moment, among many others, teaches me the intimacy of terror, which is at the same time "the terror of bigotry" in the lives of Muslims, coloring the early lives of their children and also their families' possibilities.[55] I don't know anything about her brother or what he was accused of, but I am certain from the straightforwardness with which she shares this information that her experience is part and parcel of mundane life. Terror may live as a sudden, violent, extraordinary act outside of state bounds for most citizens, but at the very same time, for Muslims, the terror of securitization and bigotry lives as a daily threat to destabilize their dwelling in the city at hand.

This moment, this intangible but inevitable place where my research leads, in which I am suddenly lost in a familiar place, is also where my research ends. We ascend the final steps, where I thank the woman and we say goodbye, Walter Benjamin's words echoing in my body and in my mind. "The staircase I climbed would prove to be the stronghold of a ghostly apparition, which at first rendered all my limbs heavy and powerless, and then, when only a few steps separated me from the longed-for threshold, left me transfixed in a spell."[56] It appears out of thin air, this sense, this sight of a minotaur that was always there—one that my interlocutors tried, together and apart, to ignore as they strived for a better tomorrow in the securitized labyrinth of the London metropolis.

I am here transported in mind, if not body, to the streets of Madrid, where before I stood on the words of Spanish literary greats and the ruins of Islamic empire, that city a palimpsest; that city as labyrinth, where I walked through doors, but found so many walls. Now, I am lost in a place whose twists and turns I thought I knew by heart, another urban labyrinth presided over by the very same minotaur—state surveillance in its shifting, elusive form. "Here we are left with hope," interrupted.[57] A stirring of disenchantment in the self. A sense of boundedness in time and place, the invisible but inescapable constraints of an undercaste status that contends with the power to make, and the power to dwell. There is nothing to do but collect my shoes, taking in the walls of shelves, women gazing out of broad glass windows, the sound of water rushing as others make *wudu'*, children skittering across the floor. I recall the *shahada* spoken on the carpeted prayer room below, new babies born into our weekend learning circle—where things began—and the burials of the beloved, family members in mourning—where things end. I slowly descend the stairs, taking in the calligraphy on the wall, pushing open the doors into London's busy night, their weight against my frame a final time.

The air is warm, the stars disguised by city light.

CHAPTER 7

Unsettled Europe:
On the Threshold of Remembrance

The current amazement that the things we are experiencing are "still" possible in
the twentieth century is *not* philosophical. This amazement is not the beginning of
knowledge—unless it is the knowledge that the view of history which gives rise to it is
untenable.

WALTER BENJAMIN[1]

We are now face to face, *Angelus Novus* and I.

It is December 26, 2019, and I am at the Israel Museum, in the hills of
Jerusalem, looking into the eyes of the Paul Klee sketch that inspired Walter
Benjamin's final work, *Theses on the Philosophy of History*. Before his death,
Benjamin resisted moving to Israel, where his closest friend, the philosopher
and historian Gershom Scholem, had secured an academic position for him.
He died by his own hand in Portbou, Spain, as he fled the Nazis. Today, a
memorial to his tragic end that also speaks to the end of this book stands in
Portbou. It is an enclosed staircase leading down to the mouth of the open sea,
made of wood (evoking trees, evoking books) and glass that one may see out of,
but not move beyond. Words from his *Theses* are etched into the glass: "The
construction of history is consecrated to the memory of the nameless."[2]

Nearly eighty years later, thousands of miles, and two seas away, I am immediately taken by the face of *Angelus Novus*, gap-toothed and wide-eyed,
hair that appears to be made out of scrolls, wings open in surrender. Like the
Theses it inspired, passed through the hands of Klee, Benjamin, and Scholem,
the painting continues to occupy a threshold between present and past; it is
a *malakh*, meaning both angel and messenger in Hebrew. Before his demise,
Benjamin gifted *Angelus Novus* to Scholem and the writings it had inspired to
Hannah Arendt, dividing the image and the text between two global metropoles. Arendt carried his writings to New York City when she too fled the
Third Reich. And here in Jerusalem, the angel came to adorn Scholem's living room.[3] An intimate bedfellow of migration and the insider-outsider sta-

tus of Jews in twentieth-century Europe, *Angelus Novus* as muse, Benjamin speaks through his *Theses* to the contemporary challenges faced by Muslims in Europe—challenges of remembrance masked as challenges to modernity. "Doesn't a breath of the air that pervaded earlier days caress us as well?"[4] Looking into the face of *Angelus Novus*, Benjamin writes,

> This is how one pictures the angel of history. His face is turned toward the past. Where we perceive a chain of events, he sees one single catastrophe which keeps piling wreckage upon wreckage and hurls it in front of his feet. The angel would like to stay, awaken the dead, and make whole what has been smashed. But a storm is blowing from Paradise; it has got caught in his wings with such violence that the angel can no longer close them. The storm irresistibly propels him into the future to which his back is turned, while the pile of debris before him grows skyward. This storm is what we call progress.[5]

In her introduction to Benjamin's collection of essays and reflections, *Illuminations*, Arendt evokes a tension at the heart of his vision: first outright rejecting modern, enlightened Europe through a Marxist lens, and later turning towards its critique with a messianic vision rooted in the Jewish tradition.[6] The questions embedded in Benjamin's writings—concerning how to make, and make better, under the constraints of power—are questions asked and attended to by both mosque communities at the heart of this book. And the tragedy of pain repeated, pain *repeating* as I write and as you read, is one, I hope, obviated in this story that ties together the words and the lives of Muslims and Jews in the European metropolis.

In the preface to Benjamin's *One-Way Street*, Greil Marcus likens his collective works to "an invitation to the apprehension of one's own modernity."[7] In this book, I have extended this invitation to apprehend Europe's understanding of modernity, as I have apprehended my own through the threshold space of the mosque in the metropolis. This story is thus one that not only unsettles spatial borders, but also taken-for-granted notions of time. Benjamin calls us to surrender to intertwined time, connections between present, future, past—countering the perception of "progress as a 'fact'" in which Europe monopolizes not just modernity, but along with it memory.[8]

In an iteration of intertwined time, I have asked the reader to time travel with me, to engage the intellectual paradigms of Jewish thinkers, many from nineteenth- and twentieth-century Europe, as a lens to better understand the experiences of Muslims in Europe today. Here I have connected the Jewish intellectual tradition, imbued with a perspective of marginality, so many unrealized dreams, to the lives of Muslims experiencing such marginality through what I term an undercaste status, set against the "impossible dream" of civility.[9] The discourse *on* Muslims in Europe constructs even citizens as both historical and present threats to so-called European values, rooted in notions of "incivility": "language crafted to lock creative people into cages of inferiority and hopelessness."[10] Such cultural marginality permeates—thereby constraining opportunities across—the residential, educational, and economic spheres. For my interlocutors, an undercaste status rises to the surface of their early experiences in school, solidified in residential segregation and barriers to inclusion in the full economic opportunities of the metropolis. Perpetuated through securitization, it further divides and disciplines Muslim bodies, human and architectural alike.

In both London and Berlin, thousands migrated to Europe in a postcolonial/postimperial era, called by governments seeking to rebuild their economies in the wake of WWII. Reverberations of Max Frisch's words ("We called for labor, but people came instead") can be heard and felt to this day, as diverse and dynamic postmigrant populaces make dwellings for themselves in Europe's metropoles.[11] From demand for legal inclusion resulting in revised citizenship regimes in Germany to solidarity movements like that of political blackness in the UK, a politics of recognition[12] reigned in the latter half of the twentieth century.[13] Those once cast in the role of the worker, later the migrant, and the ethnic minority demanded equality and justice in an unequal, unjust social world. And as the framework of naming shifted to one where the concept of Muslimness dominated, this demand further deepened among those born and raised in Europe, seeking equality and justice as Muslims in the cities and states at hand.

The two mosque communities at the heart of this book embody an Arendtian legacy: that marginality, socially constructed but concrete in its effects, should not be equated with powerlessness. Domination does not equal obliteration, as destructive forces can also cultivate an impetus for resistance, resuscitation, and renewal. The concrete body of the mosque, as an interstice in European public life, and the concrete—*not conceptual*—lives of Muslims critique and contest assumptions about coherence and order in modernity. At the Şehitlik and East London mosques, an opportunity arises to collectively shape discourse and practice through Islamic knowledge in order to contend with externally imposed labelling as uncivil. Mosques, as thresholds between the door and the wall of the European metropolis, become frontiers on which Muslims resist the singular imagination of Europe as a place and time through forms of crossing, making, and dwelling infused at once with history and a striving for redemption. "And in the heavens," writes Jorge Luis Borges, "the verbs preserve and create are synonymous."[14] And in this world, creation and preservation fall to prophets and to poets.

Like *Angelus Novus*, the more Europe's Muslims are thrust forward, or sideways, into a social order in which they cannot fully belong, the more they look back—towards Islamic traditions, including a long line of prophets culminating with Muhammad—as a moral, social, and political lifeforce. And while it is impossible to "make whole what has been smashed," Europe's Muslims show that it is in fact possible to revive knowledge that contends with a purist European ideology.[15] Rather than simply lamenting the loss of pasts buried beneath victors' constructed histories, remembrance can be cultivated (to cultivate is the very root of the word "culture"), thereby, in the words of Theodor Adorno, "allow[ing] suffering to speak."[16]

It is not by chance that Mnemosyne, the inventress of language and words, was also the goddess of remembrance. "In the voices we hear, isn't there an echo of now silent ones?," Benjamin asks.[17] The discourse *of* Muslims in Europe—long "a motivated silence"—today "reject[s], alter[s] and expose[s]" that which disfigures Muslim life, in interlinked acts of *phronesis* and *poiesis*.[18] As Muslims increasingly remember and recover their knowledge traditions in and through revivalist movements in the European metropolis, they engage not only in material regulation (of the headscarf, mosque building, etc.), but also in an *unsilencing*: really letting Islam—past, present, and future—speak. Speaking through Islam, my interlocutors' reveal the enduring ambiguity of *European* identity, "not only of the pastness of the past, but of its presence," captured in the misnaming of an ageless angel, both old and eternal, as new.[19]

Looking to the past rather than an imagined future reveals the interstitial fragments where place comes into conversation with time, stressed in various "iterations of tradition."[20] While based largely on the Qur'an and the Sunna, such diverse iterations of Islam lie at the nexus of religious sources and lived experiences, and therefore hermeneutics at the center of each mosque as a lived space. Religiously rooted interpretation focuses on the internalization and expression of Islamic virtues in the making of the Muslim self and Muslim communities in the metropolis, achieved through God-consciousness (*taqwa*), ritual worship (*'ibada*), and right conduct (*adab*) rather than the herein deconstructed European values (e.g. civility, tolerance, equality, freedom) with which Muslims are assumed to clash.

The seeking of these virtues is undergirded by language, Qur'anic speech and the sayings/doings (Sunna) of the Prophet Muhammad. It is not the mere reading but the practice of reciting the Qur'an, often from memory, that allows it to transcend time, its discursive enactment a form of revelation (*tanzil*), wisdom (*hikma*), discernment (*furqan*), and remembrance (*dhikr*). Through recitation, Muslims become links in an unbroken chain beginning with the Prophet Muhammad, called to recite by the Angel Gabriel. In both London and Berlin, this *phronetic* practice of remembrance is deeply embedded in the lives of my interlocutors, offering an opening—in the act of speech—to fuse mundane, everyday life with the divine. For Muslims converting or returning to Islam, recitation is often a first act of deepening devotion, building a bridge between this world and paradise, future and past.

In his groundbreaking book on al-Ghazali, Ebrahim Moosa writes of the *resuscitation* of tradition. Linking poetry to biology, he likens al-Ghazali's work to the botanical concept of palingenesis, rebirth vis-à-vis particular lived environments.[21] As the Jewish thinkers herein engaged, Moosa not only writes about strangers, but is himself a stranger, imbued with ambiguity and liminality. He is intimately familiar with the violence of hierarchical postcolonial/postimperial sociopolitical systems, having grown up during apartheid in South Africa; there and then, he explained to me, he was designated as part of a group deemed "Indians" while living in an area designated for those deemed "coloureds" in a color- and ethnicity-coded racial schema.[22] He has been in exile since violent Islamic extremists bombed his family home in South Africa in 1998. Moosa illuminates the critical capacity endowed to the so-called stranger as maker, who, whether Muslim or Jewish, is forced by circumstance to inhabit a threshold position, and yet, by his/her own imaginative capacity, agentively transforms the threshold from a repressive space, with little air to breathe, into a space for poetic resuscitation.[23] In both mosques, my interlocutors strive, as strangers and makers, to resuscitate Muslim legacies and heritage, histories and memory—"flooded with the light of tradition and ventilated with the air of temporality"—in order to emancipate themselves from present social marginalization.[24]

The Islamic tradition is not, however, isolated, but rather in conversation with other traditions and histories. These traditions and histories unite in today's metropole, in the silenced spaces and the small reminders visible through cracks in façades of novelty and coherence. As I have signaled throughout this book, from the thought of prominent Jewish thinkers to Muslim-Jewish topographic and social intersections in contemporary London and Berlin, echoes of the Jewish past can be heard in the negotiation of an insider-outsider status in the modern European metropolis. Francis Shor describes Benjamin's writings as demonstrating a "working out of a Jewish marginality which is both in the world (historical materialism) and outside of it (Jewish mysticism)."[25] And

Europe has seen this "working out of a Jewish marginality" through forms as divergent as those seen at Şehitlik and ELM in their "working out" of a Muslim marginality that is both in the world and outside of it.

There are echoes of a Jewish past not only in responses to marginality, but also in the body memories of each metropolis. In Tower Hamlets, a center of Bengali culture in East London, amid boiled bagel shops and Jewish symbols, two synagogues have been transformed into mosques. In Berlin, temporally staggered neighbors residing where Jewish residents once lived shine the *Stolpersteine* with cotton cloths. On Münchenerstrasse in the city's former Jewish district, the Löcknitz-Grundschule built where a synagogue once stood, tasks each student with researching a former Jewish resident of the neighborhood. Their names are then inscribed on bricks, stacked as a wall of remembrance, a wall of names on a street where signposts, set amongst the city trees that give us breath, resuscitate a Jewish past.

Not only the presence of certain histories, but also the absences of others matter. Belonging at the level of the metropolis becomes inscribed in myriad ways—both literal and figurative grammars made legible through social and political contexts. At the Grunewald train station memorial in Berlin, for instance, Platform 17, from which Jews were sent to concentration camps, is etched with dates, numbers, and geographies: one reads 19.10.1942/ 963 Juden/ Berlin-Riga. Leonard Barkan suggests that the slash imbues the possibility of "and" into Jewish identity (Jewish *and* Berliner), while also leaving open the possibility of "or" (Jewish *or* Berliner).[26] The intricate cultural grammars of language determine the ways in which we read the world, whether made legible or imbued with aphasia. Returning for a moment to the national sphere, Christian Dietrich likens the German-Jewish hyphen to a point of complex, disputed connection, of difference and overlap, of potentiality and failure.[27] Fatima Besnaci-Lancou, on the other hand, likens the French-Muslim hyphen in the postcolonial context to a bridge.[28]

The experience of Muslims in Europe—with hyphens and slashes, endowed with bridges, failures, and potentialities—cannot be decoupled from its past, near and far, from the medieval conceptualization of caste on the Iberian Peninsula to Jewish marginality, from the colonial projects and guest worker programs that resulted in twentieth-century migrations to European states. Muslims live with the shadows of this European history not only behind but beside them. Yet if we see these shadows, again, as light turned inside out, other histories can contribute to a European project that recognizes plurality not as a challenge, but a second chance.

For instance, the Reconquista was preceded by the Convivencia, an at-times romanticized, but also often overlooked, period of Muslims, Christians, and Jews living together under Umayyad rule, where literal and figurative translations abounded.[29] The Jewish salons of the eighteenth and nineteenth centuries crossed religious, economic, and gender lines.[30] And Islam has inarguably helped to shape "the West," through its scientific and philosophical legacies and through the colonized bodies endowed with Islamic epistemology. Perhaps the ultimate poetic possibility is to unweave our tightly knit histories, and make space for the silenced, the absent, colorful threads that connect us, and to call them by their names. From my grandfather Benjamin and his button store, to Eduard Salinger selling fabrics in West Berlin and Altab Ali in the textile factories of London's East End, so many have sought to make a dwelling in the metropolis, whether in the "new" (New York) or "old" (London, Berlin) world.

As a grandchild of the garment district, my visions of making appear in metaphors of cloth and string. An honest loom: therein lies the potentiality for a new old world. At both Şehitlik and ELM, we see critical un- and reweaving done by those who not only reside, but create in the thresholds of urban life. In the words of anthropologist Franz Boas, "It would seem that mythological worlds have been built up only to be shattered again, and that new worlds were built from the fragments."[31] Which brings us to reconsider the marginal position not only as a point of critical departure, but also itself a vantage point that endows a unique capacity to see deeply into all directions, into the cracks and crevices of the metropolis and modernity alike. In both the Jewish and Islamic traditions, the migrant, the border crosser, the Simmelian stranger situated in the cultural threshold is alone endowed with the capacity to decenter from the margins, to illuminate—as "window mirror"—"re-describing" Europe (the poetic act), by unifying old with new.[32] According to one hadith, the Prophet Muhammad calls for all to "be in this world as if you were a stranger or a traveler along a path," able to see past social guises into the nuance of human life. On this, Moosa reflects, "When asked to identify the characteristics of the exiles, or strangers, the Prophet states: 'They are those who will restore my tradition.'"[33] Similarly, Cohen writes, "Through the laws of the Talmud, the decisive equation is: Stranger = Noahide = pious."[34] Such insider-outsiders, Bauman asserts, "expose the artifice, the fragility, the sham of the most vital of separations . . . This is exactly what the strangers do."[35]

If the city truly is, as Benjamin argued, the epitome of modernity, then it is a site made by strangers, at once experienced and remembered, a place of cyclical rebirths on top of ruins. From London's East End, where the call to prayer can be heard above the urban bustle of Whitechapel Road, to Berlin's east-west border, where a neo-Ottoman structure appears to touch the clouds, Muslims are inarguably not only part, but also poetic makers of the plural metropolis, present, future, past. Like it or not, "the polycultural city is already here; it is among us."[36] And we are not only within, we *are* the polycultural city. Europe must shift both its discourses and sociopolitical practices away from an imagined, homogenous community that strives for an inherently intolerant "tolerance," towards a lived, heterogeneous community, through an unsettling of monopolies on epistemology, history, language, and memory. Only then, when the storm of "what we call progress" relents, can the angel close his wings: tied to the earth, severed from the spirit of caste, he can come to dwell among us beneath the city lights that shroud our heaven's stars.[37]

Afterword: The Memory of Trees

In his memories of growing up in Berlin, Walter Benjamin writes of "always lagging a half-step behind," capturing a child's view of trailing his mother through the city, and yet also describing how we straddle both present and past.[1] So it is with every ethnographic book—a half-step behind, or afterwords in which "the end is simply the beginning of an even longer story."[2]

Since I began my research seven years ago, Europe's metropoles have faced sociopolitical challenges old and new: large-scale migration, a rising right wing, tensions between the global and the local, or rather the global *in* the local, from Whitechapel to Neukölln and far beyond. In 2015, as German chancellor Angela Merkel opened the borders to hundreds of thousands of refugees, sociopolitical tensions rose to the surface and erupted across geographic locales.[3] This moment became a sticking point for already growing right-wing parties throughout Europe, marrying anti-immigrant and anti-Muslim sentiment with Euroskepticism.[4] In the United Kingdom, the UK Independence Party (UKIP) was an active and vocal force in the Brexit Leave Campaign, and secured a significant number of seats in the European Parliament in 2014.[5] In Germany, the AfD entered parliament in 2017 on an anti-immigrant platform, critiquing the project of European integration for overlooking the economic discontents of German citizens left behind by globalization.[6] As noted earlier, in Austria and France, far-right presidential candidates Norbert Hofer and Marine Le Pen came in second in the 2016 and 2017 presidential elections, respectively.[7] And in 2019, the right-wing Spanish Vox party entered parliament.[8] This list goes on.

Whether Europe is now at a moment of political juncture or rocky continuance is a matter of interpretation. Yet it is easy to overlook the place of the longer story in what appears on the surface as a moment of acute conflict and crisis. To my interlocutors in London and Berlin, this moment is not really distinct, but rather embedded in ongoing tensions between ethnonationalism and plurality. They, and now I too (inspired by Benjamin's writings), see not a moment of abrupt change, but instead the echoes of a longue durée reverberating across Europe. That is, this particular sociopolitical moment appears neither sudden nor distinct, but familiar and fitted into a larger historical process that unites decades of cultural, social, political, and economic strife. The undercaste status of Muslims in Europe remains, with Muslims/Islam cast as uncivil. And history here shows its face not as repeating, but blurred, the body memories of each city surfacing with vigor and violence.

The body of the city, made of so many strata, is both archaic and chameleonic: its relentless dynamism countered by its enduring edifices, archways, dead-end streets. Life in the city goes on to the beat of footsteps stepping on ruins, subways cutting through the underground, and a melody where the laughter of children meets church bells, car horns, and, now in Germany at intermittent moments throughout the day, the public *adhan*. This public call to prayer across Germany began at the DITIB mosque in the town of Duisburg-Marxloh as a response to the COVID-19 pandemic. It has, if for a moment, interrupted the removal of Islam from European publics, as a soundscape that acts as comfort or salve, and also awakens the "I" and the "us" as inextricably connected to the stranger. To write the end of this book now, in the middle of this crisis, is to narrate from the depths of the unknown, with life and death in close, discomfiting quarters. And not only the time, but also the place from which I write reminds me of the entwinement of lives and death. Back in Berlin, in the once-Jewish Barn Quarter, I am surrounded by haunting memorials: an empty, fallen chair at Koppenplatz; a sculpture of grieving women caught in embrace on Rosenstrasse; shoeless statues, surrounded by piles of stones—a Jewish tradition that reminds us of eternity—at the gates of a cemetery.

When I think from this temporal and physical perspective of the mosque communities in this book, I cannot help but to revisit the tension faced by my interlocutors—seeking harmony and seeking redemption—in crossing, the making of new beginnings, and dwelling, endings that are of course an entryway to another life ("simply the beginning of an even longer story").[9] At the end of this story, which is the beginning of another, I will briefly return to the threshold of the Şehitlik Mosque in Berlin, which experienced a dramatic sociopolitical overhaul. In 2016, a newly appointed DITIB attaché for religious affairs arrived in Berlin from Turkey. Second-generation mosque leaders describe his influence on Şehitlik in retrospect, detailing his micromanagement of the daily workings of the mosque. In early 2017, with familiar gray skies over Berlin, the leadership of the Şehitlik Mosque suddenly steps down, the doors shut without warning on their harmonizing vision. On social media—these posts quickly removed—Şehitlik's youth group suggests that Ender Çetin has been forced to resign. A virtual reconstruction of the community quickly follows, in language and the photographs that speak a thousand words: German translations removed from the website, pictures of the Turkish flag replacing those of interreligious meetings on Şehitlik's social media.

The change begins but does not end there, traveling from space back to the Muslim body, flesh transformed into battleground. The Muslim body emerges yet again as a fixed site of contention in the body of the metropolis, with a female tour guide fired for failing to wear the headscarf. It is paradoxical that the headscarf debate, turned on its head, is the moment in which Şehitlik's youth realize the unmaking of their project of *sympoiesis*, making together with each other, with other "Others," and with the city of Berlin. Soon after, Wednesday night German lessons on Islam are eliminated. Next, the tours are stopped (although later temporarily reinstated since many have already been booked) and the annual Ramadan celebration with German politicians called off.

One could argue that this shift results from a polarized political atmosphere linking the mosque to the Turkish state, a struggle emerging out of soiled Turkish-German relations, as President Erdoğan increasingly amasses power, imprisoning politicians, academics, civil servants, and journalists, including some with German citizenship; and as Germany reprimands Turkey for supposedly sending imams to spy on mosque constituents, with the goal of identifying Gülen supporters.[10] I would, however, counter that this era was born in Anatolia, with the thousands of migrants who once moved north to reside on uneven ground. The Şehitlik of today was made by the ambiguity and ambivalence of Muslim inclusion, including Germany's longstanding dependence on Turkey to support its Islamic institutions. And this making, with life and death in constant interchange, has displaced Şehitlik both as a protective religious space first forged by Turkish guest workers and their kin at the turn of the twenty-first century and later as a space reflective of the broader city by their children. On my final trip to Berlin in 2017, Mustafa shakes his head. "I don't like what happened there. I don't like the atmosphere now." His college-aged son, Murat, once attended Şehitlik multiple times a week and now echoes his father's words: "I don't even want to go there anymore." They sense loss in a place where birds once sang on window sills as young Berliners recited the Qur'an, where tour guides pointed to the intricate carved-stone arches that symbolize trees. They sense loss in a place that was everything—if not the same thing—to both of them.

Yet loss does not mean that *all* is lost. Both immersive and subversive hope remain—hope, with "its pendant, memory"—in the discourses and the bodies of my interlocutors; in my own body in a city with such erasure, as a presence of Jewish life; and in the body of the mosque.[11] A mosque built at a burial place, rooted in the ground and reaching towards the sky crosses the horizon, connecting the future of paradise to paradise past: from the time of fallen empires to the emptying of thrones. Şehitlik remains a symbolic site of the layered strata of the metropolis, full of mazes and minotaurs, but also angels and openings to the sky. In so many ways, this mosque is a continuation of postwar Berlin's rebuilding, its dream to reconcile: new lives lived adjacent to graves, where the sound of children learning Arabic letters fill the air; where Qur'ans rest on wooden stilts, verse held in reverence above ground; and where sparrows open their wings, crossing the threshold of windows thrown open to change. Even amidst the shifting winds of politics, their external constraints, the stories of my interlocutors here as in London reveal the power of moral agency, the power of making a dwelling in the face of enduring estrangement. These stories intertwine time, and they teach not only the "redemptive power" but also the recollective power of narrative; "perhaps," as Benjamin writes of his childhood reading box, "the mingling of the forgotten with the dust of our vanished dwellings is the secret of its survival."[12] That is, many forgotten faces of modernity intertwine within the body of the mosque in the metropolis, where arches rise in the shape of cypresses and elms, witness to human splendor and ruin: and now also in the pages of this book, once trees, in the enduring afterlife of memory.

ACKNOWLEDGMENTS

"The teacher and student. All bookish cultures are bound to generate them," Amos Oz once wrote. I would like to thank my teachers, present and past, familial, formal, and found within the pages of books. My first teachers were of course my parents, Ellen and Ted Becker, without whom I never would have fashioned myself into a writer. I am so grateful to my parents for nurturing this passion in me, for the walls upon walls of books that insulated our home; and also to my sister, Katrina Becker, for her ceaseless support.

In this endeavor, my mentor Jeffrey Alexander has been invaluable as a teacher and a friend; he not only created a place to ask questions and to indulge in deep intellectual debate, read (and reread) my work, but has also challenged me as a scholar. Philip Gorski lent me his incredibly sharp and critical intellectual eye as a mentor for my scholarship, and I often found myself happily lost in our conversations bridging academia and the "real world." Julia Adams provided not only mentorship, in all of its many layers, but also productive critique, always encapsulated in inspiring conversations. I am indebted to Philip Smith, Yale's secret weapon for learning how to write sociologically, and to Nadine Amalfi, who created a supportive environment for writing and so much more. And I am also grateful to Mabel Berezin, an unwavering mentor since my undergraduate days at Cornell University. Beyond these individuals, the collective opportunities for the presentation and discussion of my writing with the Center for Cultural Sociology, the Comparative-Historical Research Workshop, and the Religion and Politics Colloquium at Yale helped me immensely in writing this book. I would also like to specifically thank the organizers (Zubair Ahmad and Amin El-Yousfi) and participants of "The Ethical and the Everyday" workshop at the Cambridge University Woolf Center for the opportunity to reflect deeply on the ethnographic study of Islam/Muslims in Europe.

I could not have finished this book without the support of Chuck (Charles) Mathewes and Paul Dafydd-Jones, who read and commented on the manuscript extensively during my tenure as a postdoctoral fellow on the Religion & Its Publics project at UVA. Chuck has been an incredible mentor in religious studies, showing me my own blind spots, while—in his larger-than-life way—providing ceaseless laughter and support. Paul has inserted the necessarily skepticism and critical eye into his reading of my work, yet somehow managed to keep it light with his admirable British humor. I am further indebted to the Institute for Advanced Studies in Culture, Tony Lin in particular, which provided me with an intellectual atmosphere to complete the manuscript and an extraordinarily helpful manuscript workshop during my postdoctoral fellowship. From conversations that allowed me to reflect on this project to deep readings of what has become this book, I could not have come to this point without the support of Marion Katz, Kirsten Wesselhoeft, Jeanette Jouili, Armando Salvatore, Nadia Marzouki, Khaled Abu El Fadl, John Bowen, Karen Barkey, Tariq Modood, Johnathan Wyrtzen, Isaac Reed, Vasfiye Toprak, and Fiona Greenland. And of course, I am extremely grateful to Kyle Wagner, my editor at the University of Chicago Press, for having faith in this project since its very beginnings, going above and beyond his duties; for the reviewers, so very generous in giving not only their time but also expertise; and for the editorial work of Dylan Montanari, Michael Koplow, and Amber Herrle on the manuscript.

I have received generous support for my research from the Berkeley Center for Religion, Peace, and World Affairs at Georgetown University; the German Academic Exchange Service (DAAD); the National Science Foundation; the Religious Research Association; the Yale Divinity School; the Yale Program for the Study of Anti-Semitism; and the Yale MacMillan Center. I have also received generous support for the writing of my book from the Center for Islam in the Contemporary World and from the Humility and Conviction in Public Life Project at the University of Connecticut. Without them, these years of research and writing would not have been possible.

I am so very thankful to my many interlocutors, whose willingness to open their lives both amazed and humbled me, who taught me so much about Islam, Europe, and modernity, and who wrote this book with me, as it is their stories that I tell. Together and apart, they cracked open space and time in London and Berlin, providing me with an interstitial opportunity to see so far beyond my own taken-for-granted assumptions about the world in which we live, at once together and apart.

Perhaps it is strange to thank individuals whom I never met beyond the bindings of their books. And yet there is no way to enumerate the intimate intellectual influences of great thinkers, including those with a Jewish positionality, from Georg Simmel to Hermann Cohen, Walter Benjamin to Hannah Arendt, Hans Jonas to Ernst Bloch, Herbert Gans to Zygmunt Bauman and Richard Sennett. I must also thank Ebrahim Moosa, whose theorization of the vitality of threshold positions and strangerhood in Islam continues to inspire me. So much has been lost—and yet, as all of these thinkers teach us from within the bindings of their books, so much hope remains. On hope, I must also thank my dear friend Rachel Wahl, who helped me at once find a place for this book, and for myself, in our unsettled world.

Finally, I cannot thank my husband, Ufuk Topkara, enough; his combination of love and intellect never ceases to amaze me, and he continues to challenge me to open both my heart and my mind. In fact, it is our morning conversations over coffee, in our home lined with books, that became the backbone of this text. And I must thank my children, Sami and Ela, both born during the years in which this book came to fruition—the littlest, but also greatest of my teachers, gifting me the knowledge of what it means to live a truly beautiful life.

NOTES

PREFACE

1. Said, *Culture and Imperialism*, xxx.
2. Bauman, *Modernity and the Holocaust*, 53.
3. Barkan, *Berlin for Jews*, 154.

CHAPTER ONE

1. Henri Lefebvre, *Qu'est-que penser*, 100, quoted and translated in Kofman and Lebas, "Lost in Transposition," 53.
2. Max Frisch's foreword, "Überfremdung," to Alexander Seiler, *Siamo Italiani*, quoted and translated in Mandel, *Cosmopolitan Anxieties*, 51.
3. Ruiz, *Medina Mayrit*.
4. Lowney, *A Vanished World*.
5. Rogozen-Soltar, *Spain Unmoored*.
6. Lowney, *A Vanished World*.
7. Millanes, "The City as Palimpsest."
8. Deupi, *Architectural Temperance*.
9. Milton, *Paradise Lost*.
10. Dante, *The Divine Comedy*.
11. While I invoke the concept of modernity in order to juxtapose today's city with the ancient city, I am cognizant that the hegemonic Orientalist/neo-Orientalist discourse employs "modernity" as a synonym for Western/Eurocentric modernity, rather than the full diversity of modernity in its many forms. Salvatore, *The Sociology of Islam*.
12. Dickinson, "Metropolis."
13. Walter Benjamin was a forebear of the Frankfurt School, a school of thought rooted in critical theory—a neo-Marxist, dialectical approach to studying society. The Frankfurt School in its original incarnation was made up of Jewish thinkers, including Max Horkheimer, Theodor

Adorno, Eric Fromm, and Herbert Marcuse. Jacobs, *The Frankfurt School, Jewish Lives, and Antisemitism.*

14. Benjamin, *Benjamin*, 44 (N16).

15. Gilloch, *Myth and Metropolis*, 1; Benjamin, *Berlin Childhood around 1900*, 42.

16. Schorske, *Thinking with History*, 39, 42.

17. Schorske, *Thinking with History*, 46.

18. Both the labyrinth and palimpsest are metaphors that appear throughout Benjamin's diverse writings on the city. Paetzold, "Walter Benjamin and the Urban Labyrinth"; Millanes, "The City as Palimpsest."

19. Dussel, "Eurocentrism and Modernity," 65.

20. Tester, *The Social Thought of Zygmunt Bauman*, 115; Bauman, *Intimations of Postmodernity*, 178.

21. Dussel, "Europe, Modernity, and Eurocentrism," 474; Benhabib, *The Reluctant Modernism of Hannah Arendt*, 49.

22. I use the word "constituents" to signal those who are part of the mosque; that is, not only do they utilize it, but they make the mosque as a community.

23. Said, *Culture and Imperialism*, 36.

24. Salvatore, *The Sociology of Islam.*

25. Brubaker, *Trans.*

26. J. Alexander, "Civil Sphere, State, and Citizenship."

27. Here, I draw on Renato Rosaldo's theory of "cultural citizenship," specifically her understanding of "cultural citizenship" as an experience at the nexus of belonging and dignity. Rosaldo, "Introduction."

28. Armando Salvatore reinvigorates this Aristotelian term (*phronesis*) in conversation with Alasdair MacIntyre and in contrast to Jürgen Habermas, bringing it to bear on discourses about modernity and its relationship to tradition. Salvatore, *The Public Sphere.*

29. In his book, *Crossing and Dwelling*, Thomas Tweed defines religions as "confluences of organic-cultural flows that intensify joy and confront suffering by drawing on human and suprahuman forces to make homes and cross boundaries": religion constituted both by "being in place" (dwelling) and "moving across space" (crossing). Turning his gaze to the modern urban form, Richard Sennett considers men and women (Homo Faber) makers, exploring the city as a place of both making and dwelling. I center not on the site of religion itself (as Tweed) nor the city in its entirety (as Sennett), but rather on the mosque in the metropolis, as a religion-filled urban threshold space. Tweed, *Crossing and Dwelling*, 54, 80; Sennett, *Building and Dwelling.*

30. Moosa, *Ghazali and the Poetics of Imagination*, 34.

31. Simmel, "The Stranger," 176.

32. Bauman, *Modernity and Ambivalence*, 60–61.

33. Bauman, *Modernity and Ambivalence*, 71, 85; Bauman, *Modernity and the Holocaust*, 39.

34. Bauman, "Modernity and Ambivalence," 145.

35. Sennett, *Building and Dwelling.*

36. Asad, "Muslims and European Identity," 209; Bauman, *Modernity and the Holocaust.*

37. Weil, *The Need for Roots*, 40.

38. Sennett, *Building and Dwelling.*

39. Augustine, *The City of God.*

40. Benjamin, *The Arcades Project*, 1999, 494 (02a, 1).

41. A. Allen, *The End of Progress.*

42. Dussel, "Eurocentrism and Modernity," 65.

43. Arendt, *The Jewish Writings*, 75.

44. El Fadl, *The Great Theft.*

45. I use the term "Bengali" to refer to an ethnic group, one that often shares Bangladeshi origin; in my book this includes those who migrated to London and the UK from the Sylhet region, although some reference the Sylheti people as a distinct ethno-religious group.

46. N. Ahmed, *Family, Citizenship and Islam*, 12; Laraib and Nasir, "The Pakistani Diaspora in UK: Evolution, Integration and Challenges."

47. Castles, "Guestworkers in Europe: A Resurrection?"

48. Yukleyen, "Localizing Islam in Europe"; Rosenow-Williams, *Organizing Muslims and Integrating Islam in Germany*; Pew Research Center, "The Growth of Germany's Muslim Population"; Hackett, "5 Facts about the Muslim Population in Europe."

49. Allievi, *Conflicts over Mosques in Europe.*

50. Lamont, *The Dignity of Working Men*, 4.

51. Mahmood, *Politics of Piety.*

52. Throughout this book, I will reference these two mosque communities, but am cognizant that all mosque communities are very diverse and dynamic. I am thus not aiming to capture the entire life of the mosque, nor the social or political stances of the entire communities, but rather the experiences of making, including dwelling-making, that I witness among my interlocutors in and from the mosques. This limited view into and through the mosque contributes to a broader argument about Europe, and about the opportunities found within the Islamic epistemological tradition to critique and counter cultural subordination. I am thus less interested in the representativeness of the stories herein told than I am in what my interlocutors and their experiences in these mosque communities, as Benjaminan fragments, teach us about notions of "modernity," "progress," and "civility."

53. Benjamin, "The Flaneur's Return," xiv.

54. Oz and Oz-Salzberger, *Jews and Words*, 136.

55. At a workshop at the Cambridge University Woolf Institute in November 2018, Mayanthi Fernando suggested the responsibility of the ethnographer of Islam/Muslim communities to partake in *sympoiesis* as a methodological act. This discussion sparked my interest in thinking through acts of making—together and apart—occurring within Europe's Muslim communities. Soon after, I read Ebraham Moosa's book, *Al-Ghazali and the Poetics of Imagination*, in which he theorizes the threshold position (e.g., that endowed by exile) as an opportunity for al-Ghazali, and arguably also contemporary thinkers, to enact *poiesis*. Moosa, *Ghazali and the Poetics of Imagination.*

56. In *How Judaism Became a Religion*, Leora Batnitzky argues that the premodern status of Jews was one that collapsed culture, religion, and nationality into a singular collectivity. When "religion" became understood as belief or faith, it superimposed a Christian paradigm onto the traditional expression of Jewishness as practice, through law, rather than an assertion of belief. Batnitzky, *How Judaism Became a Religion*; Norton, *On the Muslim Question*, 228.

57. Andijar, "On the European Question."

58. Norton, *On the Muslim Question*; Topolski, "A Genealogy of the 'Judeo-Christian' Signifier"; Topolski, "Good Jew, Bad Jew . . . Good Muslim, Bad Muslim."

59. Benjamin, *The Arcades Project*, 542 (R3, 1).

60. Fassin, "The Endurance of Critique," 22.

61. Murphy and Dingwall, "The Ethics of Ethnography."

62. Some community members at Şehitlik assert that women, most notably Pinar Çetin, married to mosque director Ender Çetin, run the mosque. Pinar is among the loudest voices during Ender Çetin's tenure in this position, demanding gender equality inside of the religious community and representation of Muslim women in local politics outside of it. She herself runs for office in the Berlin House of Representatives in 2016, and while she does not win this race, her bid for office is perceived as a major stride for visibly Muslim women in the city. Pinar both spearheads inward-facing initiatives, asserting that women should be able to pray in the main mosque sanctuary, and takes the lead on outward-facing projects, such as the publicly lauded Open Mosque Day and the controversial Bahira Project, focused on deradicalization.

63. Harding, "Representing Fundamentalism," 373.

64. Benjamin, "The Flaneur's Return," xix.

65. Eiland, "Translator's Foreword," xv.

66. Benjamin, "The Flaneur's Return," xviii.

67. Merleau-Ponty and Smith, *The Merleau-Ponty Aesthetics Reader*, 82.

68. Jonker, "The Mevlana Mosque in Berlin-Kreuzberg"; Bowen, *Why the French Don't Like Headscarves*; Landman and Wessels, "The Visibility of Mosques in Dutch Towns"; DeHanas and Pieri, "Olympic Proportions"; Göle, "The Public Visibility of Islam and European Politics of Resentment."

69. Landler, "In Munich, Provocation in a Symbol of Foreign Faith."

70. "Demonstranten streiten über Moschee-Pläne"; Beardsley, "Across the Atlantic, Another Mosque Splits a City"; DeHanas and Pieri, "Olympic Proportions"; Davidson, *Only Muslim*.

71. Cheng, "Islamophobia, Muslimophobia, or Racism?"

72. Fernando, *The Republic Unsettled*; Hermon-Belot, "French Laïcité and Religious Pluralism."

73. Astor, Burchardt, and Griera, "Polarization and the Limits of Politicization."

74. J. Alexander, *The Civil Sphere*; Salvatore, *The Sociology of Islam*.

75. Howe, *Landscapes of the Secular*, 9.

76. Holston, "The Civility of Inegalitarian Citizenships," 53.

77. Holston, "The Civility of Inegalitarian Citizenships," 51.

78. Beaman, *Citizen Outsider*.

79. A. Roy, *Civility and Empire*, front matter.

80. Bhabha, "Sly Civility," 74; Benjamin, *Illuminations*, 205 (thesis XIV).

81. Bhabha, "Sly Civility"; A. Roy, *Civility and Empire*, 9.

82. Feldman, "Re/Entangling Irish and Nigerian Diasporas," 174.

83. Stoler, "Colonial Aphasia," 121.

84. Sayad, "Immigration and 'State Thought,'" 178.

85. Bhabha, "Sly Civility"; A. Roy, *Civility and Empire*, 9.

86. Shepard, *The Invention of Decolonization*, 231.

87. Benjamin, *Illuminations*, 200 (thesis VIII).

88. Berlant, *The Queen of America Goes to Washington City*, 175.

89. Bowen, *Why the French Don't Like Headscarves*; Bowen et al., "An Institutional Approach to Framing Muslims in Europe."

90. Bhabha, *The Location of Culture*, 2.

91. For example, such research includes the following works: Dwyer and Meyer, "The Institutionalisation of Islam in the Netherlands and in the UK"; Peter and Arigita, "Introduction: Authorizing Islam in Europe"; Peter, "Individualization and Religious Authority in Western European Islam"; Maussen, "Constructing Mosques"; Yukleyen, "Localizing Islam in Europe"; and Kuppinger, "One Mosque and the Negotiation of German Islam."

92. Oxford Reference, "Kulturkampf."

93. Kastoryano, "Religion and Incorporation."

94. Koopmans, "Germany and Its Immigrants"; Rosenow-Williams, *Organizing Muslims and Integrating Islam in Germany*, 165.

95. Charity Commission, "Survey of Mosques in England and Wales"; McClean, "State and Church in the United Kingdom," 657.

96. O. Roy, *Globalized Islam*; Fernando, *The Republic Unsettled*; Jouili, *Pious Practice and Secular Constraints*; Liberatore, *Somali, Muslim, British*; Jacobsen, *Islamic Traditions and Muslim Youth in Norway*.

97. Sennett, "The Public Realm," 270.

98. Arendt, "The Public and the Private Realm," 215.

99. Avishai, " 'Doing Religion' in a Secular World," 413, 409.

100. For Qur'anic citations, this book uses *The Qur'an*, trans. M. A. S. Abdel Haleem.

101. Arendt, *Men in Dark Times*, 18.

102. Salvatore, *The Public Sphere*; Schielke, "The Power of God."

103. Quoted and translated by Szondi, "Introduction," 19–20.

104. This manuscript follows a pattern of triadic discourse: I bring God into the conversation on Muslims and Europe; I bring Jews, Muslims, and Europe into conversation; and I bring the European metropolis into the conversation between Muslims and God. This relational triangulation is an analytical choice that helps to disrupt binaries and question social hierarchies, allowing for new ways of seeing the perpetuation of, and the agentive possibilities of unsettling, inequality.

105. In *On the Muslim Question*, Anne Norton argues that the "Jewish question" was the "axis" of political and ethical questions leading up to, and during the Enlightenment, and that the "Muslim question" has similarly become the "axis" of political and ethical questions, today. Norton, *On the Muslim Question*, 1–5.

106. Bernstein, *Hannah Arendt and the Jewish Question*; Edgar, "Hermann Cohen."

107. Pollock, "Every State Becomes a Theocracy," 7.

108. Şenocak, *Gefährliche Verwandtschaft*, 90, quoted and translated in Cheesman, *Novels of Turkish German Settlement*, 41.

109. Norton, *On the Muslim Question*; Topolski, "A Genealogy of the 'Judeo-Christian' Signifier"; Topolski, "Good Jew, Bad Jew . . . Good Muslim, Bad Muslim."

110. Benhabib, *Exile, Statelessness, and Migration*, xvi.

111. Edgar, "Hermann Cohen."

112. Delaney, *Classical and Contemporary Social Theory*, 90; Sennett, *Building and Dwelling*, 55.

113. Gronow and Pyyhtinen, "Georg Simmel."

114. I use the terms "German Jewish" and "German Jew(s)" here not without recognizing the complexities of German Jewishness, where the emphasis moves between a religious/cultural identifier and a national identifier. Some have argued that German Jewishness was, and is, impossible; and yet most of the Jewish thinkers I employ use the terminology of "German Jew(s)" and "German Jewish" to describe themselves and other Jews in Germany. Dietrich, "Eine Deutsch-Jüdische Symbiose?"

115. Geoghegan, *Ernst Bloch*; Howells, "Ernst Bloch and Utopian Critical Theory."

116. Osborne and Charles, "Walter Benjamin"; Baudelaire, *The Painter of Modern Life and Other Essays*, 9.

117. Wiese, *The Life and Thought of Hans Jonas*.

118. Jonas, *The Imperative of Responsibility*.

119. Minnich, "Thinking with Hannah Arendt," 123; D'entrèves, "Hannah Arendt."

120. Tester, *The Social Thought of Zygmunt Bauman*, 115; Bauman, *Intimations of Postmodernity*, 178; Blackshaw, *Zygmunt Bauman*.

121. Blackshaw, *Zygmunt Bauman*.

122. American Sociological Association, "Herbert J. Gans."

123. Venkatesh and Rosen, "Herbert J. Gans."

124. An "undercaste" suggests, of course, a broader system in which there is an upper or over-caste as well as potentially other caste statuses. While invoking the relationality inherent in an undercaste, I focus on the making and experience of Muslims as an undercaste in the analytical singular (as Weber) rather than the full hierarchical complexity of a caste system. Weber, *From Max Weber*, 188–90, 396–415.

125. Wachtel, "An Interview with Richard Sennett."

126. Sennett, interview and lecture by Richard Sennett.

127. Poma, "Hermann Cohen."

128. Symons, *More Than Life*, 3; Procyshyn, "The Origins of Walter Benjamin's Concept of Philosophical Critique," 657.

129. Scholem, *Walter Benjamin*; Wiese, *The Life and Thought of Hans Jonas*; Benhabib, *Exile, Statelessness, and Migration*.

130. Scholem, *Walter Benjamin*, 133.

131. Leo Baeck Institute, *We Have Wandered Together a Long, Long Way*.

132. Wachtel, "An Interview with Richard Sennett."

133. Benhabib, *Exile, Statelessness, and Migration*. 1.

134. Gillespie and Hill, "On Walter Benjamin's Legacy"; Young-Bruehl, *Hannah Arendt*, 163.

135. Ercolini, "Arendt, Adorno, and Benjamin: Response, Responsibility, and Commitment," 220.

136. Bauman, *Modernity and the Holocaust*, 53.

137. Bird, "Hannah Arendt's Funeral Held."

138. Moosa, *Ghazali and the Poetics of Imagination*, 276.

139. Moosa, *Ghazali and the Poetics of Imagination*, 279.

140. Said, *Orientalism*, 27; Graf, "Das neue Faschismus-Syndrom," 102.

141. Primo Levi, Holocaust survivor and author writes, "Their life is short, but their number is endless; they, the *Muselmanner*, the drowned, form the backbone of the camp, an anonymous mass, continually renewed and always identical, of non-men who march and labour in silence, the divine spark dead within them." That the most degraded on the brink of death in Auschwitz were termed "Muslims" has primarily been explained by their incapacity to stand, kneeling—out of weakness, not in prayer—on the ground in what appeared to be an Islamic form of prostration. The idea of nonidentity, anonymity, a collapsing of many into a singular abstracted form ("always identical") also speaks to an enduring status of strangerness experienced by both Muslims and Jews. Levi, *Survival in Auschwitz*, 90.

142. Cousin and Fine, "A Common Cause," 167.

143. Hafez, "Comparing Anti-Semitism and Islamophobia," 17.

144. Amir-Moazami, "Investigating the Secular Body."

145. Graf, "Das neue Faschismus-Syndrom"; Hafez, "Comparing Anti-Semitism and Islamophobia," 20.

146. Said, *Culture and Imperialism*, 6.

147. Sennett, *Flesh and Stone*, 25.

148. Ewing, *Stolen Honor*, 3.

149. Bauman, *Modernity and the Holocaust*, 51.

150. Gans, "From 'Underclass' to 'Undercaste.' "

151. This can be seen in Frey Francisco de Torrejoncillo's writings, which interchangeably employ the terms "caste," "race," and "nation" to describe Jews, a group he alternatively calls "Hebrews," "Israelites," "New Christians," and "Marranos." Sawyer, *Popularizing Anti-Semitism in Early Modern Spain and Its Empire*, 3.

152. Traverso, *The Jews and Germany*, 43.

153. Arendt, *The Jewish Writings*, xli.

154. Isabel Wilkerson's groundbreaking work *Caste: The Origin of Our Discontents* was released as I completed the final edits on this book. Although I have selectively incorporated some of her ideas into this text, a more engaged dialogue with Wilkerson would—and will be—extremely fruitful at a later point in time. Wilkerson, *Caste*, 28.

155. As cited in Benhabib, *Exile, Statelessness, and Migration*, 4.

156. Oz and Oz-Salzberger, *Jews and Words*, 1.

157. Miles and Cleary, "Britain: Post-colonial Migration Context."

158. Dawson, *Mongrel Nation*, 6.

159. Sayyid, "Introduction: BrAsians: Postcolonial People, Iconic Citizens," 5.

160. DeHanas, *London Youth, Religion, and Politics*, 13, 132–13.

161. Huff, "Rethinking Islam and Fundamentalism," 503; Lacorne, *The Limits of Tolerance*, 108–13.

162. Huntington, "The Clash of Civilizations?"

163. Awan, "I Am a Muslim Not an Extremist"; Vermeulen, "Suspect Communities"; O'Toole et al., "Governing through Prevent?"; Archer, "Welcome to the Umma," 332.

164. P. Thomas, "Prevent and Community Cohesion in Britain."

165. Bonino, "*Prevent*-ing Muslimness in Britain," 387.

166. Kibria, "The 'New Islam' and Bangladeshi Youth in Britain and the US."

167. Vertovec, "Multiculturalism, Culturalism and Public Incorporation"; Modood, *Multiculturalism*, 2.

168. Asthana, "Why Did Multiculturalism Become a Dirty Word?"; Hutcheon, "Is There a Dark Side to Multiculturalism?," 19.

169. Johnston, "Adopt Our Values or Stay Away, Says Blair."

170. Lentin and Titley, *The Crises of Multiculturalism*, 1, 160.

171. Lentin and Titley, *The Crises of Multiculturalism*.

172. Meer, "The Politics of Voluntary and Involuntary Identities."

173. Anderson-Nathe and Gharabaghi, "Trending Rightward."

174. Trumpener, *Germany and the Ottoman Empire, 1914–1918*.

175. Deringil, *Turkish Foreign Policy during the Second World War*.

176. Paxton and Hessler, *Europe in the Twentieth Century*.

177. Chin, *The Guestworker Question in Postwar Germany*, 49; Koopmans, "Germany and Its Immigrants."

178. Cheesman, *Novels of Turkish German Settlement*, 52.

179. Fennell, *Language, Literature, and the Negotiation of Identity*, 32; Rosenow-Williams, *Organizing Muslims and Integrating Islam in Germany*, 106.

180. Constant and Tien, "Germany's Immigration Policy and Labor Shortages," 7.

181. Ewing, *Stolen Honor*; Mandel, *Cosmopolitan Anxieties*; Witte, "Responses to Stigmatisation and Boundary Making."

182. Tibi, *Europa ohne Identität*, 154.

183. Mouritsen et al., "Leitkultur Debates as Civic Integration in North-Western Europe"; Ewing, *Stolen Honor*, 201–2.

184. Amir-Moazami, "Buried Alive," 22.

185. Connolly, "Promoting Tolerance in Germany Could Define Angela Merkel's Leadership."

186. Noack, "Germany Said It Took in More than 1 Million Refugees Last Year. But It Didn't."

187. Peter, "Individualization and Religious Authority in Western European Islam"; Jouili, *Pious Practice and Secular Constraints*, 10.

188. Davidson, *Only Muslim*, 205–20.

189. The Islam Conference was forged in 2006 under the leadership of then–Interior Minister Wolfgang Schäuble to unite representatives from the five dominant Muslim organizations: (1) the Turkish-Islamic Union for Religious Affairs (Türkisch-Islamische Union der Anstalt für Religion, Diyanet İşleri Türk-Islam Birliği, DITIB); (2) the Islamic Council for the Federal Republic of Germany (Islamrat in der Bundesrepublik Deutschland, IRD); (3) the Association of Islamic Cultural Centres (Verband der Islamischen Kulturzentren, VIKZ); (4) the Central Council of Muslims in Germany (Zentralrat der Muslime in Deutschland, ZMD); and (5) the Federation of the Alevi Communities in Germany (Alevitische Gemeinde Deutschland, Almanya Alevi Birlikleri Federasyonu, AABF), as well as ten individuals selected by the German government, in order to create a platform for discussing the role, expression, and representation

of Islam in Germany. Rosenow-Williams, *Organizing Muslims and Integrating Islam in Germany*, 87.

190. Leggewie, Joost, and Rech, *Der Weg zur Moschee*; Frymark, "The Turkish Campaign in Germany"; Ceylan, "From Guest Workers to Muslim Immigrants," 83–86.

191. Barnes, "Brexit: What Happens Now?"

192. Kaufmann, "It's NOT the Economy, Stupid"; Elliott and Stewart, "What Are the (C)HRD Implications of Brexit?"

193. Shepp, "Angela Merkel Won Reelection, But Is She Still the Leader of the Free World?"

194. Said, *Orientalism*, 49.

195. Brown, "Tolerance As/In Civilizational Discourse," 433.

196. Said, *Orientalism*, 49; A. Roy, *Civility and Empire*.

197. Heller, "Remains of the Diaspora," 174.

198. Yilmaz, *How the Workers Became Muslims*; Schiffauer, "Enemies within the Gates," 94.

199. Runnymede Trust, *Islamophobia: A Challenge for Us All*; C. Allen, "Justifying Islamophobia"; Cesari, *Securitization and Religious Divides in Europe*.

200. Bowen et al., "An Institutional Approach to Framing Muslims in Europe," 1–2.

201. Benjamin, *Selected Writings Volume 1*, 15.

202. Bauman, *Modernity and the Holocaust*; Dollard, *Caste and Class in a Southern Town*; Davis, Gardner, and Gardner, *Deep South*; Wilkerson, *Caste*.

203. Martínez, *Genealogical Fictions*, 28.

204. Weber, *From Max Weber*, 188–90, 396–415.

205. Douglas, *Purity and Danger*, 141.

206. Marcus, "Preface," xxiv.

207. Jonas, "Responsibility Today"; Jonas, *The Imperative of Responsibility*.

208. Arendt, *Rahel Varnhagen*.

209. Bauman, "Postmodernity, or Living with Ambivalence," 14.

210. Halal and haram in fact theologically lie on a spectrum—*fard* (obligatory), *mustahabb* (recommended), *mubah* (permissible), *makruh* (reprehensible), and haram (forbidden). Ramadan, *To Be a European Muslim*, 69–72.

211. Miyazaki, *The Method of Hope*; Bloch, *The Principle of Hope*.

212. Benjamin, *Illuminations*, 201 (thesis IX).

CHAPTER TWO

1. Haley, "The Desperate Ottoman," 1; Cohen, *Religion of Reason*, 116.

2. Foremost scholars of caste in India also employ the concept beyond the geographical boundaries of South Asia. For instance, Surinder Jodhka understands caste as both an empirical category and analytical "category of 'status' and 'power'" undergirded by a "framework of prejudice and discrimination as a sociological process which enables and sustains [its] reproduction." Jodhka, *Caste in Contemporary India*, 229.

3. M. Alexander, *The New Jim Crow*.

4. Gans, "From 'Underclass' to 'Undercaste,'" 151.

5. Norton, *On the Muslim Question*, 228.

6. Saunders, *Social Class and Stratification*, 20.

7. Bougle, *Essays on the Caste System*; Runciman, "Towards a Theory of Social Stratification"; Dumont, *Homo Hierarchicus*; Weber, *From Max Weber*, 188–90, 396–415.

8. Weber, *From Max Weber*, 188–90, 396–415.

9. Bleich, "What Is Islamophobia and How Much Is There?" 1582.

10. Wilkerson, *Caste*, 17.

11. Beaman, "But Madame, We Are French Also," 50.

12. Meer and Modood, "Refutations of Racism in the 'Muslim Question'"; Meer, "Racialization and Religion."

13. C. Allen, "From Race to Religion," 49.

14. Brah, Hickman and Mac an Ghaill, "Thinking Identities: Ethnicity, Racism and Culture," 4.

15. Amin, "The Remainders of Race," 8; Meer, "Racialization and Religion," 388; Miles, *Racism*, 75.

16. As Wilkerson writes, "Caste and race are neither synonymous nor mutually exclusive. They can and do coexist in the same culture and serve to reinforce each other. Race, in the United States, is the visible agent of the unseen force of caste. Caste is the bones, race the skin. Race is what we can see, the physical traits that have been given arbitrary meaning and become shorthand for who a person is. Caste is the powerful infrastructure that holds each group in its place. Its very invisibility is what gives it power and longevity." In the European context, I argue that it is not only race, but a collapsing of religion, culture, ethnicity, and race in the classification of Muslims and Jews that is "the skin" on "the bones," "the visible agent of the unseen force" of caste. Wilkerson, "America's Enduring Caste System."

17. Balibar, "Is There a 'Neo-Racism'?," 23, 24.

18. Fassin, "Nommer, interpréter: Le sens commun de la question raciale"; Meer, *Key Concepts in Race and Ethnicity*, 10; Rana, "The Story of Islamophobia," 148; Topolski, "The Race-Religion Constellation," 58.

19. Meer and Modood, "Refutations of Racism in the 'Muslim Question'"; Meer, "Racialization and Religion"; Garner and Selod, "The Racialization of Muslims"; Dagli, "Muslims Are Not a Race."

20. Modood, "Political Blackness and British Asians."

21. Modood, "Muslims and the Politics of Difference."

22. See, for instance, Meer, "The Politics of Voluntary and Involuntary Identities."

23. Geulen, "Warum ist es so schwer, von Rassismus zu sprechen?"

24. Dagli, "Muslims Are Not a Race."

25. Nirenberg, *Neighboring Faiths*.

26. Norton, *On the Muslim Question*.

27. Esra Özyürek understands racism against Muslims in Europe as interconnected with ideas of individual choice inherent to both neoliberalism and secularization, with the Muslim castigated for not choosing to abandon his/her individual identity as such. This language of "choice" is also imperative to my theorization of a Muslim undercaste. When an individual does choose to abandon Muslim identity, like one of the police officers I interviewed in Berlin, he/she is often seen as a "good" or "civil" Muslim. Yet disavowal of Muslim identity promises *conditional*, and

thus arguably impossible, hope for escaping the undercaste status. That is, discrimination against those socially coded as Muslim continues; religion is a key, but not exclusive marker, of how one is relegated to the category of the (uncivil) Muslim. This shifts across and through the collapsing of religion, culture, ethnicity, and race. In a study of Muslims who changed their names to gain greater social inclusion (access to employment, housing etc.) in Sweden, for instance, Shahram Khosravi found stigma alleviated only in "the initial phase of social interaction" (e.g., receiving a job interview). Similarly, Guillaume Pierné found that job applicants in the Paris area were refused both on account of identifiers of having a North African background and/or signaling Islam. Khosravi, "White Masks/Muslim Names"; Pierné, "Hiring Discrimination Based on National Origin and Religious Closeness"; Özyürek, *Being German, Becoming Muslim*.

28. Meer, "Semantics, Scales and Solidarities in the Study of Antisemitism and Islamophobia."

29. Benhabib, *The Reluctant Modernism of Hannah Arendt*, 37; Arendt, *Men in Dark Times*, 18.

30. Benhabib, *The Reluctant Modernism of Hannah Arendt*, 37; Arendt, *Men in Dark Times*, 18.

31. Norton, *On the Muslim Question*, 228

32. Dagli, "Muslims Are Not a Race."

33. Asad, *Formations of the Secular*, 16.

34. Jodhka, "Ascriptive Hierarchies," 1.

35. Wilkerson, *Caste*, 30.

36. Benjamin, *Berlin Childhood around 1900*, 129.

37. Ravid, "From Yellow to Red."

38. Kouwer, *Colors and Their Character*, 113.

39. Shachar, *The Judensau*.

40. Luther, *Vom Schem Hamphoras, und vom Geschlecht Christi*, quoted and translated in Harvey, *Luther and the Jews*, 103.

41. While lesser known than the Jewish ghetto, in the seventeenth century the Venetian authorities created a separate *fundaco* (from the Arabic word, *funduq*, meaning "hotel") in which they housed all Muslims—Ottoman Turks, Albanians, and Bosnians—the doors to the exterior locked from the outside at night. Ravid, "Venice and Its Minorities."

42. Sennett, *Flesh and Stone*, 215, 217.

43. Sennett, *Flesh and Stone*.

44. The idea of second-class citizenship is better captured by "undercaste citizenship," which suggests partial inclusion and subordination not necessarily based on economic status, but rather reflective of perceptions of cultural difference, and resulting social closure and hierarchy.

45. Fredrickson, *Racism*, 18–26.

46. Arendt, *The Jewish Writings*, 74–75, xli.

47. "The word comes in the 17th century from Tamil, '(hereditary) drummer,' from *parai* 'a drum' (pariahs not being allowed to join in with a religious procession)." Knowles, "Pariah"; Arendt, "The Jew as Pariah," 275.

48. Weber, *Ancient Judaism*, 3; Wilson, *Bernard-Lazare*, 144.

49. Momigliano, "A Note on Max Weber's Definition of Judaism as a Pariah-Religion."

50. Higginbotham, *Ghosts of Jim Crow*, 36, 78.

51. Wilkerson, "Americas's Enduring Caste System."

52. Fox, "Intimations of Citizenship."

53. Chalmers, *Hooded Americanism*; Christian, "Class and Caste"; M. Alexander, *The New Jim Crow*, 30.

54. Dollard, *Caste and Class in a Southern Town*.

55. Davis, Gardner, and Gardner, *Deep South*.

56. Wood, *Lynching and Spectacle*, 48.

57. Bouie, "Christian Soldiers."

58. M. Alexander, *The New Jim Crow*, 20.

59. M. Alexander, *The New Jim Crow*, 190.

60. A. Allen, *The End of Progress*, 16.

61. Bauman, *Modernity and the Holocaust*.

62. Bauman, *Modernity and the Holocaust*, 39; Bauman, *Modernity and Ambivalance*, 72.

63. Bauman, *Modernity and the Holocaust*, 45.

64. Bauman, *Modernity and the Holocaust*, 39, 45.

65. Bauman, *Modernity and Ambivalence*, 2.

66. Bauman, *Modernity and Ambivalence*, 4.

67. Berreman, "Caste in India and the United States," 122.

68. Badger, "How the Rise of American-Style Segregation Is Feeding Division in Europe."

69. Wike, Stokes, and Simmons, "Europeans Fear Wave of Refugees Will Mean More Terrorism, Fewer Jobs."

70. Poushter, "European Opinions of the Refugee Crisis in 5 Charts."

71. Awan, "I Am a Muslim Not an Extremist," 1173.

72. Cue, "For France, Girls in Head Scarves Threaten Secular Ideals."

73. Malkiel, "Hispano-Arabic Marrano and Its Hispano-Latin Homophone," 184; Eaude, *Catalonia*, 44; Martínez, *Genealogical Fictions*, 222.

74. Martínez, *Genealogical Fictions*, 75, 83.

75. Dussel, "Eurocentrism and Modernity," 66.

76. Zapata-Barrero and Zapata-Barrero, "The Muslim Community and Spanish Tradition"; Navarro and Santos, *El Islam en las aulas*.

77. In the British colonial apparatus in Egypt, Leila Ahmed contends, unveiling became a signal of progress, an unshackling from "backwardness" under the colonial gaze. Here white men were represented as potential saviors, rather than oppressors of Muslim women—with degradation blamed on Muslim men instead of colonial projects and the human bodies that upheld them. L. Ahmed, *A Quiet Revolution*, 19–45.

78. Fanon, *A Dying Colonialism*, 63.

79. Fanon, *A Dying Colonialism*.

80. Padamsee, *Representations of Indian Muslims in British Colonial Discourse*, 78.

81. Douglas, *Purity and Danger*. See also Ewing, *Stolen Honor*.

82. Cheesman, *Novels of Turkish German Settlement*, 48; Haley, "The Desperate Ottoman," 1.

83. Ewing, *Stolen Honor*, 34; Wyatt, "The Sociocultural Context of African American and White American Women's Rape."

84. Trumpener, *Germany and the Ottoman Empire, 1914–1918*, 43.

85. Said, *Orientalism.*

86. Baczynska and Ledwith, "How Europe Builds Fences to Keep People Out."

87. "Marine Le Pen: Muslims in France 'like Nazi Occupation.'"

88. Harris, "Two Mosques, Two Different Reactions in Germany."

89. McGraw and Warner, "The Danish Cartoon Crisis of 2005 and 2006."

90. Cooper, "Controversial Dutch MP's Visa Bid Stalls"; Bayraklı and Hafez, *European Islamophobia Report 2015*, 385.

91. Amnesty International, "Choice and Prejudice," 385.

92. Amnesty International, "Choice and Prejudice," 84.

93. Van Bohemen and Kemmers, "Secular Intolerance in a Post-Christian Society."

94. Yurdakul, "Jews, Muslims and the Ritual Male Circumcision Debate," 77; Amir-Moazami, "Investigating the Secular Body."

95. Özyürek, *Being German, Becoming Muslim*, 12; Özyürek, "The Politics of Cultural Unification, Secularism, and the Place of Islam in the New Europe."

96. Davis, "Lifting the Veil"; Pipes, *The Rushdie Affair*, 56–62.

97. Wike, Stokes, and Simmons, "Europeans Fear Wave of Refugees Will Mean More Terrorism, Fewer Jobs."

98. Gallup, "Islamophobia: Understanding Anti-Muslim Sentiment in the West."

99. Özyürek, "Creating Parallel Communities of Perpetrators."

100. York, "Post-Brexit Racism Documented on Social Media"; Yeung, "EU Referendum"; TellMAMA, "Press."

101. Smale, "Austria Rejects Far-Right Presidential Candidate."

102. Stanley-Becker, "Marine Le Pen Falls Short in Far-Right Bid for the Presidency of France."

103. Fraser, "France's Much Vaunted Secularism Is Not the Neutral Space It Claims to Be."

104. Huggler, "Germany's Far-Right AfD Party 'Has More Public Support than Ever'."

105. "Survey Finds One in Three Germans Supports PEGIDA 'Anti-Islamicization' Marches."

106. Brown, *Regulating Aversion*, 37.

107. In Britain, for instance, 16 percent of all prisoners are Muslims, increasing from 8 percent in 2002, a far greater increase than any other group. Sturge, "Briefing Paper CBP-04334: UK Prison Population Statistics."

108. Latour, *We Have Never Been Modern*, 99.

109. Arendt, "The Jew as Pariah," 121.

110. Stowasser, "The Turks in Germany: From Sojourners to Citizens," 70.

111. Woods, "England in 1966: Racism and Ignorance in the Midlands."

112. Dremeaux, "The Way People Look at Us Has Changed."

113. Laurence, *The Emancipation of Europe's Muslims*, 11.

114. Koenig, Maliepaard, and Güveli, "Religion and New Immigrants' Labor Market Entry in Western Europe."

115. Adida, Laitin, and Valfort, "Identifying Barriers to Muslim Integration in France," 22388.

116. Valfort, *Religious Discrimination in Access to Employment: A Reality*, 14.

117. Kaas and Manger, "Ethnic Discrimination in Germany's Labour Market," 3.

118. Open Society Foundations, "Muslims in Europe," 111.

119. Haug, Stichs, and Mussig, "Muslim Life in Germany."

120. Peucker and Akbarzadeh, *Muslim Active Citizenship in the West*, 44.

121. Amnesty International, *Choice and Prejudice*, 33.

122. Brems, "Belgium: Discrimination against Muslims in Belgium," 88.

123. Women Equalities Committee, "Employment Opportunities for Muslims in the UK," 15.

124. Equalities Review Commission, *Fairness and Freedom*, 35.

125. S. Ali, *British Muslims in Numbers*, 18.

126. Luciak, "Documenting Discrimination and Integration in 15 Member States of the European Union," 19–20.

127. Bonefeld and Dickhäuser, "(Biased) Grading of Students' Performance."

128. Amnesty International, *Choice and Prejudice*, 70–71.

129. Hamel, "Muslim Diaspora in Western Europe," 297–98; Rubin, "French School Deems Teenager's Skirt an Illegal Display of Religion."

130. Gieryn, "A Space for Place in Sociology," 474.

131. Martin, "Germany's Guestworkers."

132. Nilsson, *Open Source Jihad*, 4; Slooter, *The Making of the Banlieue*.

133. Stewart, "A Global View of Horizontal Inequalities," 7.

134. S. Ali, "British Muslims in Numbers," 19.

135. Brubaker, "Categories of Analysis and Categories of Practice," 5.

136. Douglas, *Purity and Danger*, 141.

137. Benhabib, *The Reluctant Modernism of Hannah Arendt*, 10.

138. Marcus, "Preface," xxiv.

139. Marcus, "Preface," xiv.

140. Benjamin, *Berlin Childhood around 1900*, 54.

141. Ware, *The Walking Qur'an*, 37.

142. Peek, "Becoming Muslim"; Avishai, "'Doing Religion' in a Secular World," 412.

143. Benjamin, *The Arcades Project*, 221 (14, 5).

144. Here Dussel is interpreting and translating Aristotle's *Nichomachean Ethics*. Dussel, *The Underside of Modernity*, 141.

145. Sherif, *Ghazali's Theory of Virtue*, 32.

146. Widlock and Fassin, "Virtue," 195.

147. Germann, "Al-Farabi's Philosophy of Society and Religion."

148. Salvatore, *The Sociology of Islam*, 110.

149. Bloch, *The Principle of Hope*, vol. 1, vi.

150. Fadil, "Managing Affects and Sensibilities," 439.

151. Mahmood, *Politics of Piety*.

152. Jouili, *Pious Practice and Secular Constraints*.

153. Fernando, "Reconfiguring Freedom."

154. Gidley, "Diasporic Memory and the Call to Identity," 662.

155. Moosa, *Ghazali and the Poetics of Imagination*, 39.

156. Demetz, "Introduction," ix.

157. Jacobs, *The Frankfurt School, Jewish Lives, and Antisemitism*, 14.

158. Walter Benjamin writes in "fragments" of the city as both aesthetic and critical form, resisting the rise of totalitarianism that led to his death. In his preface to Benjamin's text, *One-Way Street*, Greil Marcus explains of Benjamin's historical context, "The moment was all towards what was not yet called totalitarianism, and the embrace of the fragment, its investigation, its interrogation, the affirmation of the fragment's truth and beauty" (Marcus, "Preface," xvii).

159. Lefebvre, *Writings on Cities*, 53.

160. Lefebvre, *Writings on Cities*, 53.

161. Ivic, *Paul Ricoeur's Idea of Reference*, 8.

CHAPTER THREE

1. Eiland, "Translator's Foreword," xiii, xiv.

2. Arendt, *The Origins of Totalitarianism*; Cohen, "The Concept of God after Auschwitz."

3. Baudelaire, *The Painter of Modern Life and Other Essays*, 9; Benjamin, "The Flaneur's Return," xiii.

4. Sayad, *La double absence*.

5. Benjamin, *Berlin Childhood around 1900*, 89.

6. Sonnevend, *Stories without Borders*.

7. Soederberg, "Governing Stigmatised Space," 479.

8. Clack, "Neukölln: Your Guide to Berlin's Hippest 'Hood."

9. Juhnke, "The Allure of Diversity, Creativity and Space" (I thank the author for permission to cite this); Novy, "The Selling (Out) of Berlin and the De- and Re-politicization of Urban Tourism in Europe's 'Capital of Cool'"; Hubbard, "Hipsters on Our High Streets."

10. For instance, see Langer, *Ein Jude in Neukölln*, as an example of such a conversation.

11. I pieced together the history of the mosque from tours, conversations with mosque leadership, and the mosque website, which previously had a section on its history.

12. Bulliet, "The Shaikh Al-Islām and the Evolution of Islamic Society"; Gözaydın, "Diyanet and Politics."

13. Gözaydın, "Diyanet and Politics"; Öztürk, "Turkey's Diyanet under AKP Rule."

14. T. Smith, "Between Allah and Atatürk"; Gözaydın, "Diyanet and Politics."

15. Chaker, "The Life of Abu Mansur Al-Maturidi and the Socio-political and Theological Context of Central Asia in the Tenth Century"; Kam, "Das Böse als ein Gottesbeweis."

16. Kamali, *The Middle Path of Moderation in Islam*.

17. According to the anecdotal accounts of my interlocutors, Şehitlik serves Kurdish Muslims in the city, albeit less than other mosques like the Merkez Mosque in Berlin, which is located in a neighborhood with a large Kurdish population. Yet it is also important to note that the Kurdish independence movement in Turkey, historically causing deep conflict with the Turkish state, has moved through migration to other geographical contexts, like Germany. Ostergaard-Nielsen, *Transnational Politics*, 47–48, 61.

18. Barkey, "Islam and Toleration."

19. Responsibility is a trope that emerges in German society vis-à-vis the Holocaust; Germany, through both education and memorialization, seeks to foster collective responsibility for

this past. The Şehitlik Mosque, on the other hand, focuses on responsibility within, and to, present society. These differing time scales matter, especially as Muslims have been unjustly accused of lacking interest in, or appropriate empathy for, those who suffered or perished during the Holocaust. Özyürek, "Rethinking Empathy," 456, 463.

20. Asad, "The Idea of an Anthropology of Islam," 20.

21. Wilkerson, "America's Enduring Caste System."

22. Jung, "Stille Gebete zu Allah."

23. Mamdani, "Good Muslim, Bad Muslim."

24. Cohen, *Religion of Reason*.

25. Foucault, "Was ist Aufklärung?"

26. Ware, *The Walking Qur'an*, 8.

27. Firestone, *Journeys in Holy Lands*, 63–71.

28. Cohen, *Religion of Reason*, 454.

29. There is an interesting parallel between the experience of nostalgia among Turkish Berliners and so-called *Ostalgie*, a nostalgia for East Germany that has colored the experiences, rememberings, and current discontents of some who lived in the German Democratic Republic (Deutsche Demokratische Republik, DDR). Berdahl, " '(N)Ostalgie' for the Present."

30. Moosa, *Ghazali and the Poetics of Imagination*, 275–76.

31. Heller, "Remains of the Diaspora," 170.

32. Appadurai and Breckenridge, "On Moving Targets," i.

33. Batuman, "Architectural Mimicry and the Politics of Mosque Building," 325.

34. Appadurai and Breckenridge, "On Moving Targets," i.

35. Benjamin, *Berlin Childhood around 1900*, 42, 62.

36. Pamuk, *Istanbul*, 104.

37. The comparative silence on economic status and deprivation throughout my research at the Şehitlik Mosque is one that many can literally afford to have—if not objectively well-off, those in Berlin are certainly more financially secure, at least partially due to a robust welfare state, than my interlocutors at the East London Mosque. While this may affect class, it does not affect the undercaste position of my interlocutors in Berlin. As Wilkerson writes of the caste system in the US: "Through the years, wealth and class may have insulated some people born into the subordinate caste in America but not protected them from humiliating attemtps to put them in their place or remind them of their caste position." Wilkerson, *Caste*, 106.

38. Benjamin, *Reflections*, 335.

39. Topolski, "A Genealogy of the 'Judeo-Christian' Signifier."

40. Bauman, *Modernity and Ambivalence*, 72.

41. Arendt, "The Jew as Pariah," 110.

42. Fanon, *A Dying Colonialism*, 35–64.

43. Scott, *The Politics of the Veil*, 81.

44. Rubin, "French School Deems Teenager's Skirt an Illegal Display of Religion."

45. Dearden, "Burkini Ban: Why Is France Arresting Muslim Women for Wearing Full-Body Swimwear and Why Are People So Angry?"

46. Korteweg and Yurdakul, *The Headscarf Debates*.

47. Jones and Braun, "Secularism and State Neutrality"; Elver, *The Headscarf Controversy*.

48. Uhlmann, "Der ewige Streit um das Kopftuch."

49. Taylor, "Teachers' Religious Headscarves in German Constitutional Law," 93.

50. J. Alexander, *The Civil Sphere*, 423, 466.

51. "Germany's Top Court Rules Muslim Schoolgirls Must Join Swimming Lessons."

52. Ewing, *Stolen Honor*, 190–98.

53. Fadil, "Not-/Unveiling as An Ethical Practice."

54. Foucault, *Discipline and Punish*, 25.

55. Ewing, *Stolen Honor*, 180.

56. Morrison, "Nobel Lecture."

57. Said, *Orientalism*; Hall, "The West and the Rest."

58. Simmel, "The Stranger," 176.

59. Hafez, "Comparing Anti-Semitism and Islamophobia," 25.

60. Bauman, *Modernity and Ambivalence*, 72.

61. M. Alexander, *The New Jim Crow*, 248.

62. Topolski, "Good Jew, Bad Jew . . . Good Muslim, Bad Muslim."

63. Arendt, "The Jew as Pariah," 121.

64. Benhabib, *The Reluctant Modernism of Hannah Arendt*, 190.

65. Gimaret, "Taklīf."

66. Jonas, "Responsibility Today," 89.

67. Gimaret, "Taklīf"; Hallaq, *Sharī'a*, 1.

68. Jouili, *Pious Practice and Secular Constraints*, 43.

69. Mardin, *Religion and Social Change in Modern Turkey*; Gingeras, *Mustafa Kemal Atatürk*.

70. Hendrick, *Gülen*, 62–69.

71. Mahmood, "Feminist Theory, Embodiment, and the Docile Agent," 215.

72. Bourdieu, *The Logic of Practice*, 53.

73. Winchester, "Embodying the Faith."

74. Ware, *The Walking Qur'an*, 8.

75. Moosa, *Ghazali and the Poetics of Imagination*, 210; Jouili, *Pious Practice and Secular Constraints*.

76. Jouili, *Pious Practice and Secular Constraints*, 91–92.

77. Salvatore, *The Sociology of Islam*, 13.

78. Winchester, "Embodying the Faith."

79. *Iman* is understood as "faith (in God), *maṣdar* of the 4th form of the root ʾ*mn*. The root has the connotations of 'being secure, trusting in, turning to'; whence: 'good faith, sincerity' (*amana*), then 'fidelity, loyalty' (*amāna*), and thus the idea of 'protection granted' (*amān*)." Gardet, "Īmān." "Faith," although not a perfect translation, is thus the best approximation of *iman* in the English language and is used as such throughout this text.

80. Sayad, *La double absence*.

81. Jouili, *Pious Practice and Secular Constraints*, 54, 56.

82. Bourdieu, *The Logic of Practice*, 58; Nava, *Visceral Cosmopolitanism*, 14; Friedman, "What Is the Habitus Clivé?"

83. Winchester, "Embodying the Faith."

84. Ware, *The Walking Qur'an*, 7.

85. Benhabib, *The Reluctant Modernism of Hannah Arendt*, 12.

86. Cohen, *Religion of Reason*, 1–4, 249–51.

87. Reconciliation is another symbolically potent social concept in the German context, as society seeks to reconcile with its past, specifically the violence of the Holocaust. It is, at the same time, a potent religious concept within all of the Abrahamic traditions: in Judaism relating directly to peace, as stated here by Hermann Cohen; in Christianity to atonement; and in Islam to seeking balance and justice. Cohen, *Religion of Reason*, 446–62; Brümmer, "Atonement and Reconciliation," 436; Moosa, "Reconciliation in Islamic Thought and Practice."

88. Cohen, *Religion of Reason*, 456.

89. Cohen, *Religion of Reason*, 446.

90. Benjamin, *Berlin Childhood around 1900*, 95.

91. Ware, *The Walking Qur'an*, 49.

92. While the tour is employed to foster feeling among contemporary German citizens for the victims of the Holocaust, a particular form of empathy is forged among Muslims in Germany—seeing their own experiences of marginality as different and yet reminiscent of this past. Özyürek argues that empathy is cultivated through seeing the self in "the Other," as the intersubjective perspective is one of bodily experience, and thus emotive relations or attachments to this past are not uniform but deeply personal. She traces how appropriate forms of feeling are stressed in a society/state project that seeks to shape the ways in which contemporary citizens relate to the past, finding that Muslims are deemed "outside of the moral fold" when they express empathy, emerging from their lived experiences, rather than responsibility for the past. Being deemed "outside of the moral fold" contributes to and fortifies Muslims' labeling as uncivil. Özyürek, "Rethinking Empathy," 471.

93. Opotow, "Absence and Presence," 53.

94. Stoler, "Colonial Aphasia."

95. Schmid, "Hermann Cohen's Theory of Virtue," 255.

96. Uekotter, *The Greenest Nation?*

97. The six-pointed star, which is also called the "seal of Solomon," is portrayed in mosques throughout the world. This hexagram historically appeared in both Jewish and Muslim architecture as a symbol of protection. Israel Ministry of Foreign Affairs, "King Solomon-s Seal."

98. Shepard, *The Invention of Decolonization*, 231.

99. Enjelvin and Korac-Kakabadse, "France and the Memories of 'Others,'" 155.

100. Avishai, "'Doing Religion' in a Secular World," 409.

101. O. Roy, *Globalized Islam*, 195; Jacobsen, *Islamic Traditions and Muslim Youth in Norway*, 284.

102. Fernando, "State Sovereignty and the Politics of Indifference," 265.

103. Benjamin, *The Arcades Project*, 221 (14, 5).

CHAPTER FOUR

1. Sennett, "The Open City," 101–2.

2. Glucroft, "A Desperate Need for a Third Way."

3. Said, *Culture and Imperialism*, xiii.

4. Benjamin, *Berlin Childhood around 1900*, 37.

5. Rogowski, " 'To Be Continued': History in Wim Wenders's *Wings of Desire* and Thomas Brasch's 'Domino'"; Bordo, "The Homer of Potsdamer Platz."

6. Barkan, *Berlin for Jews*, 13, 98.

7. Bezirksamt Tempelhof-Schöneberg, "Zeugnisse jüdischen Lebens in Schöneberg"; Barkan, *Berlin for Jews*, 177.

8. Arendt, *The Jewish Writings*, 88.

9. Arendt, *Rahel Varnhagen*; Benhabib, *The Reluctant Modernism of Hannah Arendt*, xii.

10. Overlapping with my own period of research in this mosque, local artist Kirsten Kötter paints and sketches everyday life. In her online project diary she writes: "How do they deal with the children in the mosque? The adults do not correct the children. They may play during prayers. Like I am able to paint during prayers." Many of her works are displayed in a temporary exhibition in the mosque on June 22, 2014, and an exhibition hosted by Salaam-Schalom on June 28, 2015, among others (Kötter, "Şehitlik Mosque Project").

11. Benhabib, *The Reluctant Modernism of Hannah Arendt*, 92.

12. Benhabib, *The Reluctant Modernism of Hannah Arendt*, 14.

13. Savelsberg and King, "Institutionalizing Collective Memories of Hate."

14. The Israel-Palestine conflict is by no means overcome and continues to color Jewish-Muslim relations in Berlin. During the 2014 outbreak of war in Gaza, rallies take to the streets of Germany's capital. Mosques project their horror at the attacks on Palestine. Synagogues condemn the violence against Jewish Israelis. Coverage of men wearing Palestinian flags, screaming "Jew, Jew, cowardly pig—come out and fight on your own!" on the central Berlin shopping avenue of Kurfurstendamm proliferate in the news. Comparisons between the Holocaust and the practices (ghettos, subordination) of Israeli leadership in relation to the Palestinian populace are loudly invoked at pro-Palestine protests throughout the city. The overarching sentiment, a Şehitlik youth leader explains: "*Everyone* must choose a side." Rosenberg, "Berlin Protestors Chant: 'Jew, Jew, Cowardly Pig, Come On Out and Fight.' "

15. Shooman, "Zur Debatte über das Verhältnis von Antisemitismus, Rassismus und Islamfeindlichkeit."

16. Wenders, *Wings of Desire*; Bordo, "The Homer of Potsdamer Platz."

17. Wenders, *Wings of Desire*.

18. Langer, "Muslime sind die neuen Juden"; Yurdakul, "We Don't Want to Be the Jews of Tomorrow."

19. Marotta, "Zygmunt Bauman: Order, Strangerhood and Freedom," 46.

20. Chambers, "German Jewish College Shuns Skullcaps after Attack on Rabbi."

21. Sennett, *The Conscience of the Eye*, 123.

22. Bauman, "Postmodernity or Living with Ambivalence," 14.

23. Cohen, *Religion of Reason*, 114; Kaplan, "Suffering and Joy in the Thought of Hermann Cohen."

24. Bauman, *Postmodern Ethics*, 77.

25. Cohen, *Religion of Reason*, 114.

26. Benjamin, *The Arcades Project*, 221 (14, 5)

27. Meet2respect, "Startseite."

28. Arendt, *The Human Condition*, 8.

29. Bauman, "Modernity and Ambivalence," 143.

30. Sartore, "Armin Langer: A Jew in Neukölln."

31. Langer, "Muslime sind die neuen Juden."

32. Said, *Culture and Imperialism*, xxx.

33. Bennhold, "German Parliament Deems B.D.S. Movement Anti-Semitic."

34. Y. Brenner, "In Berlin, Jews and Muslims Fight for Each Other."

35. In his theory of the civil sphere, Jeffrey Alexander argues that only through an expanded sphere of solidarity, a sphere that not only is filled with what is vacant from the state, but also one that can to some extent shape or control the state (through "civil mediation"), can a truly plural society flourish. J. Alexander, *The Civil Sphere*, 412.

36. Sennett, *Building and Dwelling*, 300; Sennett, "The Open City," 102.

37. Arendt, *Rahel Varnhagen*.

38. Bleich, "State Responses to 'Muslim' Violence."

39. Mescher, "Policing and Muslim Communities in Germany," 105.

40. Spencer, "State Power and Local Interests in Prussian Cities."

41. Lozowick, *Hitler's Bureaucrats*, 13–14.

42. Glaeser, *Divided in Unity*.

43. Della Porta, "Protest, Protesters, and Protest Policing."

44. "Polizeigewerkschaft bestätigt Sympathien für AfD."

45. Studio Libeskind, "Academy of the Jewish Museum Berlin in the Eric F. Ross Building."

46. Jüdisches Museum Berlin, *Snip It: Stances on Ritual Circumcision*; Jüdisches Museum Berlin, *Cherchez la femme*; Jüdisches Museum Berlin, *Welcome to Jerusalem*.

47. Eddy and Kershner, "Jerusalem Criticizes Berlin's Jewish Museum for 'Anti-Israel Activity.'"

48. In a scathing article, "The Jewish Museum in Berlin Needs a Cultural Revolution," Alan Posener of *Die Welt* criticized Shooman for bringing BDS supporters (Farid Hafez in particular) to the Academy, soon after echoed by journalist Thomas Thiel. Shooman, half-Palestinian, has since faced both personal and political critique, accused of downplaying Muslim anti-Semitism and denying the "exceptionality" of anti-Semitism by equating it with Islamophobia in her programming. Posener, "Das Jüdische Museum in Berlin braucht eine kulturelle Revolution"; Thiel, "Der Kurswechsel wird zum Kraftakt."

49. Eddy, "What and Whom Are Jewish Museums For?"

50. Yurdakul, "Jews, Muslims and the Ritual Male Circumcision Debate."

51. Yurdakul, "Jews, Muslims and the Ritual Male Circumcision Debate"; Amir-Moazami, "Investigating the Secular Body"; Eddy, "German Lawmakers Vote to Protect Right to Circumcision."

52. Benjamin, *The Arcades Project*, 494 (O2a, 1).

53. Benjamin, *The Arcades Project*, 494 (O2a, 1).

54. Amir-Moazami, "Investigating the Secular Body."

55. Holston, "The Civility of Inegalitarian Citizenships," 53.

56. Sennett, *Flesh and Stone*, 376.

57. Arendt, *The Human Condition*; Bauman, *Postmodern Ethics*, 77.

58. Topolski, "A Genealogy of the 'Judeo-Christian' Signifier."

59. Sarrazin, *Deutschland schafft sich ab.*

60. J. Alexander, *Remembering the Holocaust.*

61. Sarrazin, *Feindliche Übernahme.*

62. Schuetze, "Amid Rising Anti-Semitism, German Official Advises Jews against Wearing Skullcaps in Public."

63. Bittner, "What's behind Germany's New Anti-Semitism?"

64. Silverstein, *Postcolonial France*, 64.

65. "Jewish Council Says Anti-Semitism in Germany Is Increasing."

66. Bergmann et al., "Bericht des unabhängigen Expertenkreises Antisemitismus."

67. Pew Research Center, "Unfavorable Views of Jews and Muslims on the Increase in Europe."

68. Sennett, *Building and Dwelling*, 265.

69. Benjamin, *The Arcades Project*, 542 (R3, 1).

70. Benjamin, *The Arcades Project*, 542 (R3, 1).

71. See Liberatore, *Somali, Muslim, British*, on how Somali Muslims in the UK create boundaries between culture and religion as a means to empower their religious identities.

72. Kocan and Oncu, "Citizen Alevi in Turkey"; Sökefeld, *Struggling for Recognition.*

73. Abdullah, "760 German Citizens Have Joined ISIS, 200 Returned Home."

74. Bleich, "State Responses to 'Muslim' Violence."

75. Rosenow-Williams, *Organizing Muslims and Integrating Islam in Germany*, 124–25.

76. Vermeulen, "Suspect Communities—Targeting Violent Extremism at the Local Level."

77. *Integration fördern, Radikalisierung erkennen.*

78. *Integration fördern, Radikalisierung erkennen.*

79. Bonefeld and Dickhäuser, "(Biased) Grading of Students' Performance."

80. Fereidooni, "Diskriminierungs- und Rassismuserfahrungen von Referendar*innen und Lehrer*innen, mit Migrationshintergrund."

81. "Berlin Court Rules in Favor of Hijab-Wearing Teacher."

82. "Berlin Teacher Headscarf Ban Is Illegal."

83. Mahlmann, "Religious Symbolism and the Resilience of Liberal Constitutionalism"; Brady, "German School in Wuppertal Bans Muslim Children from 'Provocative' Prayer."

84. Arendt, "The Jew as Pariah."

85. Mamdani, "Good Muslim, Bad Muslim"; Becker, "Good Mosque, Bad Mosque: Boundaries to Belonging in Contemporary Germany."

86. Bhabha, "Sly Civility"; A. Roy, *Civility and Empire*, 9.

87. Topolski, "Good Jew, Bad Jew . . . Good Muslim, Bad Muslim."

88. Ewing, *Stolen Honor*, 51.

89. Arendt, "The Jew as Pariah," 121.

90. Benjamin, *Illuminations*, 200 (thesis VIII).

91. Begley, *Why the Dreyfus Affair Matters*, 121; Cahm, *The Dreyfus Affair in French Society and Politics*, 10, 84; Judaken, "Édouard Drumont," 191.

92. Jussem-Wilson, "Bernard Lazare's Jewish Journey," 168.

93. Jussem-Wilson, "Bernard Lazare's Jewish Journey"; Wilson, *Bernard-Lazare.*

94. M. Brenner, "1916: The German Army Orders a Census of Jewish Soldiers, and Jews Defend German Culture"; Brownell and Drace-Brownell, *The First Nazi*; Geheran, "Judenzählung (Jewish Census)."

95. Rogowski, "To Be Continued," 559.

96. Sennett, *Building and Dwelling*, 9.

CHAPTER FIVE

1. Hamnett, "Gentrification and the Middle-Class Remaking of Inner London, 1961–2001"; Watt, "It's Not for Us."

2. H. Thomas, *The Norman Conquest*, 100–101.

3. Roth, *A History of the Marranos*, 99–105.

4. Englander, "Booth's Jews."

5. Englander, "Booth's Jews," 566.

6. Frost, "Green Curry."

7. DeHanas, *London Youth, Religion, and Politics*, 13.

8. Mavrommatis, "The New 'Creative' Brick Lane."

9. Alexander, Chatterji, and Jalais, *The Bengal Diaspora*, 210; East London Mosque, "History."

10. Tower Hamlets Council, *Borough Profile: Population*, 9.

11. Options UK, *Understanding East London's Somali Communities*, 15; Liberatore, *Somali, Muslim, British*, 88.

12. Until its secession in 1971, Bangladesh was East Pakistan, and thus its migrants were designated as Pakistani by the British government. Maxwell, *Ethnic Minority Migrants in Britain and France*.

13. Miles and Cleary, "Britain: Post-Colonial Migration Context."

14. Gardner, "Narrating Location," 67.

15. Gardner, "Desh-Bidesh."

16. Oakes and Price, *The Cultural Geography Reader*, 308.

17. Werbner, "Theorising Complex Diasporas."

18. Bowen, *On British Islam*, 40.

19. Salvatore, *The Sociology of Islam*, 10.

20. Gardner, "Desh-Bidesh"; Gardner, "Narrating Location"; Alexander, Chatterji, and Jalais, *The Bengal Diaspora*.

21. Bowen, *On British Islam*, 38.

22. Bowen, *On British Islam*, 41; Pedziwiatr, "Islam and Empowerment," 40.

23. Hamid, "British Muslim Young People"; Hamid, "Mapping Youth Work with Muslims in Britain."

24. Husain, "Maulana Sayyid Abul A'la Maududi"; Nasr, *Mawdudi and the Making of Islamic Revivalism*, 64; Bowen, *On British Islam*.

25. Bowen, *On British Islam*, 40.

26. Metcalf, "Traditionalist Islamic Activism"; El Fadl, *The Great Theft*.

27. Qadeer, *Pakistan: Social and Cultural Transformations in a Muslim Nation*, 60; Hasan, "Rising Extremism in Bangladesh."

28. Zeitlyn, "The Making of a Moral British Bangladeshi."

29. El Fadl, *The Great Theft*, 47.

30. East London Mosque Trust LTD, "Opening Ceremony of East London Mosque, Whitechapel Road, London E1."

31. DeHanas, *London Youth, Religion, and Politics*.

32. DeHanas, *London Youth, Religion, and Politics*, 54.

33. In contrast to Giulia Liberatore's Somali interlocutors in London, my Bengali and convert interlocutors at ELM explicitly intertwine experiences of lived marginality, from poverty to gender inequality, with religious revivalism. As in Liberatore's work, however, religion here emerges as far more than identity, as religious knowledge gives life to "new forms of aspiration" and thereby facilitates the transformation of subjectivities. Liberatore, *Somali, Muslim, British*, 16.

34. DeHanas, *London Youth, Religion, and Politics*, 20.

35. Sennett, Building and Dwelling, 120.

36. Sennett, Building and Dwelling, 124.

37. Holston, "The Civility of Inegalitarian Citizenships," 53.

38. Fernando, *The Republic Unsettled*, 27.

39. Bhabha, "Sly Civility"; A. Roy, *Civility and Empire*, 9.

40. Discussions on equality often pose its false juxtaposition to "difference," a discursive framing indicative of power relations (undergirding lasting inequality), as illuminated in the work of Joan Scott on feminist theory. Scott, "Deconstructing Equality-Versus-Difference."

41. Walzer, *Spheres of Justice*, xii.

42. A. Roy, *Civility and Empire*, 9.

43. Bloch, *The Utopian Function of Art and Literature*, 3; Liberatore, *Somali, Muslim, British*, 16.

44. Benjamin, *Illuminations*, 208 (thesis XVIII).

45. Cohen, *Religion of Reason*.

46. Benjamin, *Illuminations*.

47. Demetz, "Introduction," xxiv.

48. On oppressive language, see Morrison, "Nobel Lecture."

49. Yusuf, *Purification of the Heart*.

50. This is a nontraditional translation of this verse. According to the Qur'anic translation of M. A. S. Abdel Haleem, it is "tell believing men to lower their eyes and guard their private parts" (Q 24:30).

51. Benjamin, *Illuminations*, 209 (thesis XVIII).

52. Kamali, *The Middle Path of Moderation in Islam*.

53. The idea of the middle path is often signaled in the public-facing activities of Muslim institutions, in order to demonstrate compatibility with European societies; ELM thus stands out in the broader field of Islamic institutions in its notable avoidance of such terminology.

54. Yusuf, *Purification of the Heart*, 32.

55. Bowen, *On British Islam*, 28; Sa'ari, "An Analytical Study of Rise and Development of Sufism," 21.

56. Sennett, *Flesh and Stone*, 244.

57. A. Roy, *Civility and Empire*, 9.

58. Bensaid, "Utopia and Messianism"; Benjamin, *Illuminations*, 205 (thesis XIV).

59. Miyazaki, *The Method of Hope*, 13–24.

60. Bloch, *Literary Essays*, 341.

61. Miyazaki, *The Method of Hope*, 5; Bloch, *Literary Essays*, 341.

62. Sharp, "Why Spinoza Today?"; Bensaid, "Utopia and Messianism."

63. Giroux, "When Hope Is Subversive," 38.

64. Levitas, "Educated Hope."

65. Winchester, "Embodying the Faith."

66. Eiland, "Translator's Foreword," xiv.

67. Sayad, *La double absence*.

68. Ricoeur, *Freud and Philosophy*, 45.

69. Jeffries, *Grand Hotel Abyss*, 20.

70. Ware, *The Walking Qur'an*, 8.

71. Mahmood, "Religious Reason and Secular Affect," 846–47.

72. Ricoeur, *Oneself as Another*, 17.

73. Cohen, *Religion of Reason*.

74. Salvatore, *The Public Sphere*, 38.

75. Yusuf, *Purification of the Heart*, 154.

76. Salvatore, *The Public Sphere*.

77. Bloch, *Literary Essays*, 341.

78. Arendt, *The Human Condition*, 247.

79. Benjamin, *Reflections*, 330.

80. DeHanas, *London Youth, Religion, and Politics*.

81. Liberatore, *Somali, Muslim, British*, 109.

82. Rogozen-Soltar, "Managing Muslim Visibility," 612; Özyürek, *Being German, Becoming Muslim*, 24–50.

83. Özyürek, *Being German, Becoming Muslim*, 52.

84. Laing, *The Lonely City*, 8.

85. Marotta, "Zygmunt Bauman: Order, Strangerhood and Freedom," 43.

86. Sayad, *La double absence*.

87. Helvacioglu, "Melancholy and Hüzün in Orhan Pamuk's Istanbul."

88. Pamuk, *Istanbul*, 104.

89. Pamuk, *Istanbul*, 104.

90. Özyürek, *Being German, Becoming Muslim*, 3.

91. Özyürek, *Being German, Becoming Muslim*; Moosavi, "The Imagining of Muslim Converts in Britain by Themselves and Others."

92. Galonnier, "When 'White Devils' Join the Deen."

93. Arendt, *The Human Condition*, 8.

94. Arendt, *The Human Condition*, 247.

CHAPTER SIX

1. Kus, "Neoliberalism, Institutional Change and the Welfare State."

2. Tower Hamlets Council, *Deprivation in Tower Hamlets*, 2–3, 7; Tower Hamlets Council, *Borough Profile: Poverty*.

3. Ball, "The Semi-Detached Metropolis: Hanif Kureishi's London"; M. Ali, *Brick Lane*; Ray, *V. S. Naipaul*; Z. Smith, *NW*.

4. DeHanas, *London Youth, Religion, and Politics*.

5. Ball, "The Semi-Detached Metropolis: Hanif Kureishi's London," 8, 19.

6. Awn, "The Ethical Concerns of Classical Sufism."

7. Winter, "Introduction," xxv.

8. Reetz, "The Deoband Universe."

9. Khadduri, *The Islamic Conception of Justice*; Rosen, *The Justice of Islam*.

10. Safi, "What Is Progressive Islam?," 49; Izutsu, *Ethico-religious Concepts in the Qur'an*; Safi, *Progressive Muslims*.

11. Smirnov, "Understanding Justice in an Islamic Context," 346.

12. Khadduri, *The Islamic Conception of Justice*, 10.

13. Ayoub, "The Islamic Concept of Justice."

14. Hallaq, *Sharī'a*, 1.

15. Esack, "Three Islamic Strands in the South African Struggle for Justice"; Hoffman and Jamal, "Religion in the Arab Spring."

16. As Hermann Cohen explains in *Religion of Reason*, in Judaism, "the Hebrew word for justice [righteousness] is the same word for piety in general," 429.

17. Cohen, *Religion of Reason*, 259, 264.

18. Barylo, "Neo-Liberal Not-for-Profits," 394.

19. Weber, *The Protestant Ethic and the Spirit of Capitalism*, 78, 105–9.

20. Thompson, "What Is Concrete about Ernst Bloch's 'Concrete Utopia'?," 33.

21. Cohen, *Religion of Reason*, 263.

22. Cohen, *Religion of Reason*, 267.

23. Ware, *The Walking Qur'an*, 7.

24. Toennies et al., "Max Weber on Church, Sect, and Mysticism," 142.

25. Benjamin, *Berlin Childhood around 1900*, 161.

26. Benjamin, *Illuminations*, 208 (thesis XVIII).

27. Founded in 2008, this group unites leadership from local religious organizations, LGBTQ organizations, youth groups, and police—among others—in order to monitor and attend to tensions in Tower Hamlets, and has done so in numerous instances. These include responses to the "non-gay zone" stickers accompanied by Qur'anic verse in public places; an English Defense League protest on the border of the borough; and the so-called "Muslim patrols" on Whitechapel, who aimed to prohibit "un-Islamic" symbols and activities (e.g., short skirts, drinking) near the East London Mosque. Kershen, *London the Promised Land Revisited*, 69.

28. Emsley, *The English Police*, 159, 191–93.

29. Fernando, "State Sovereignty and the Politics of Indifference," 265.

30. Lentin and Titley, *The Crises of Multiculturalism*, 20–21.

31. Arendt, "The Jew as Pariah."

32. Granovetter, "The Strength of Weak Ties."

33. Gardner, "Desh-Bidesh."

34. Benjamin, *The Arcades Project*, 221 (14, 5).

35. Wahid, "Britain's Jihadi Bride Groomer."

36. Bonino, "*Prevent*-ing Muslimness in Britain."

37. Glynn, *Class, Ethnicity and Religion in the Bengali East End*, 49.

38. Bauman, *Modernity and Ambivalence*, 56.

39. Sayad, *La double absence*.

40. Sian, "Spies, Surveillance and Stakeouts," 183.

41. Poole, "Constructing 'British Values' within a Radicalisation Narrative."

42. Awan, "I Am a Muslim Not an Extremist."

43. "London Terror Attack: What We Know So Far."

44. Samuelson, "London Bridge Attack."

45. For instance, former Council of Europe commissioner for human rights Thomas Hammarberg notes that "tolerance" is a strived-for value of an open society. Open Society Foundations, "What Is Islamophobia?"

46. Brown, *Regulating Aversion*, 8.

47. A discourse of Muslim intolerance also exposes hierarchies of inclusion in European states. Mayanthi Fernando skillfully deconstructs the naturalization of Muslim intolerance in relation to LGBTQ issues in France. The rejection of homosexuality in practice within some Muslim circles is not unique to this religious group, but rather part of a larger religiotraditional discourse about sexuality, marriage, and reproduction, one quite dominant in the Catholic Church. Yet when Muslims posit homosexuality as unethical, it can lead to their exclusion—in the case of prominent French imams, to the revocation of citizenship and deportation. Fernando contrasts the Muslim position cloaked in a discourse of intolerance (a discourse that also extends to the "new anti-Semitism" earlier described), cast outside of the bounds of the nation-state and European modernity, with the same position on homosexuality held, and publicly expressed, by Catholic politicians, deemed peripheral, but never uncivil. Fernando, *The Republic Unsettled*, 244–52.

48. Brown, "Tolerance As/In Civilizational Discourse," 432–33.

49. Cobain, Parveen, and Taylor, "The Slow-Burning Hatred That Led Thomas Mair to Murder Jo Cox"; "MP Jo Cox 'Murdered for Political Cause.'"

50. Rabinbach, *In the Shadow of Catastrophe*, 42.

51. "Tower Hamlets Election Fraud Mayor Lutfur Rahman Removed from Office."

52. Awan, "I Am a Muslim Not an Extremist."

53. Fekete, "Anti-Muslim Racism and the European Security State."

54. Fernando, "State Sovereignty and the Politics of Indifference."

55. El Fadl, *The Search for Beauty in Islam*, 12.

56. Benjamin, *Berlin Childhood around 1900*, 88.

57. Demetz, "Introduction," xxiv.

CHAPTER SEVEN

1. Benjamin, *Illuminations*, 200 (thesis VIII).

2. Atlas Obscura, "Walter Benjamin Memorial."

3. Gillespie and Hill, "On Walter Benjamin's Legacy"; Laqueur, *Reflections of a Veteran Pessimist*, 96.

4. Benjamin, *Selected Writings Volume 4: 1938–1940*, 390.

5. Benjamin, *Illuminations*, 201 (thesis IX).

6. Arendt, "Introduction."

7. Marcus, "Preface," xxv.

8. A. Allen, *The End of Progress*, 16.

9. A. Roy, *Civility and Empire*, 9.

10. Morrison, "Nobel Lecture."

11. Max Frisch's foreword ("Überfremdung") to Alexander Seiler, *Siamo Italiani*, quoted and translated in Mandel, *Cosmopolitan Anxieties*, 51.

12. The "politics of recognition" is premised on the idea of the liberal state and liberal democratic gaze as dominant, reinforcing the power imbalance between states and particular ethnic/religious/racial groups. For more on the limits of the politics of recognition, see Fernando, "State Sovereignty and the Politics of Indifference."

13. Modood, "Political Blackness and British Asians"; Rosenow-Williams, *Organizing Muslims and Integrating Islam in Germany*.

14. As cited in, and translated by, Fuentes, *This I Believe*, 269.

15. Benjamin, *Illuminations*, 201 (thesis IX).

16. Adorno, *Lectures on Negative Dialectics*, 99; Craig, *A New Universal Etymological, Technological, and Pronouncing Dictionary of the English Language, Embracing All the Terms Used in Science, Literature and Art*.

17. Benjamin, *Selected Writings Volume 4*, 390.

18. Allen, *The End of Progress*, 1; Morrison, "Nobel Lecture."

19. Eliot, "Tradition and the Individual Talent," 37.

20. Moosa, *Ghazali and the Poetics of Imagination*, 54.

21. Moosa, *Ghazali and the Poetics of Imagination*, 278.

22. Seekings and Nattrass, *Class, Race, and Inequality in South Africa*.

23. Moosa, *Ghazali and the Poetics of Imagination*, 278.

24. Moosa, *Ghazali and the Poetics of Imagination*, 278.

25. Shor, "Walter Benjamin as Guide," 38.

26. Barkan, *Berlin for Jews*, 179.

27. Dietrich, "Eine Deutsch-Jüdische Symbiose?" 43.

28. Enjelvin and Korac-Kakabadse, "France and the Memories of 'Others.'"

29. Hirschkind, "The Contemporary Afterlife of Moorish Spain."

30. Benhabib, *The Reluctant Modernism of Hannah Arendt*, 16.

31. Boas, "Introduction," 18.

32. Ivic, *Paul Ricoeur's Idea of Reference*, 8; Benjamin, *The Arcades Project*, 542 (R3, 1).

33. Moosa, *Ghazali and the Poetics of Imagination*, 277; Ṣaḥīḥ Al-Bukhārī 6053, 4: 118, translated and cited in Moosa, *Ghazali and the Poetics of Imagination*, 277.

34. Cohen, *Religion of Reason*, 123.

35. Bauman, *Modernity and Ambivalence*, 56.

36. Fuentes, *This I Believe*, 300.

37. Benjamin, *Illuminations*, 201 (thesis IX).

AFTERWORD

1. Benjamin, *Berlin Childhood around 1900*, 159.

2. Benjamin, *Berlin Childhood around 1900*, 164; Z. Smith, *White Teeth*, 440–41.

3. Noack, "Germany Said It Took in More than 1 Million Refugees Last Year."

4. Brack and Startin, "Introduction."

5. Halikiopoulou and Vasilopoulou, "Support for the Far Right in the 2014 European Parliament Elections."

6. Art, "The AfD and the End of Containment in Germany?"

7. Smale, "Austria Rejects Far-Right Presidential Candidate"; Bastow, "The Front National under Marine Le Pen."

8. Turnbull-Dugarte, "Explaining the End of Spanish Exceptionalism and Electoral Support for Vox," 1.

9. Z. Smith, *White Teeth*, 440–41.

10. Abbas and Zalta, "'You Cannot Talk about Academic Freedom in Such an Oppressive Environment'"; Esen and Gumuscu, "Rising Competitive Authoritarianism in Turkey"; Hockenos, "Erdoğan's International Network of Muslim Cleric Spies."

11. Bloch, *Literary Essays*, 341; Giroux, "When Hope Is Subversive."

12. Benjamin, *Berlin Childhood around 1900*, 140.

BIBLIOGRAPHY

Abbas, Tahir, Anja Zalta. "'You Cannot Talk about Academic Freedom in Such an Oppressive Environment': Perceptions of the *We Will Not Be a Party to This Crime!* Petition Signatories." *Turkish Studies* 18, no. 4 (2017): 624–43.

Abdullah, Ammar. "760 German Citizens Have Joined ISIS, 200 Returned Home." *Reuters*, November 22, 2015. https://www.rt.com/news/323039-germany-isis-fighters-threat/.

Adida, Claire, David Laitin, and Marie-Anne Valfort. "Identifying Barriers to Muslim Integration in France." *Proceedings of the National Academy of Sciences* 107, no. 52 (2010): 22384–90.

Adorno, Theodor. *Lectures on Negative Dialectics: Fragments of a Lecture Course 1965/1966.* Cambridge: Polity Press, 2008.

Ahmed, Leila. *A Quiet Revolution: The Veil's Resurgence from the Middle East to America.* New Haven: Yale University Press, 2011.

Ahmed, Nilufar. *Family, Citizenship and Islam: The Changing Experiences of Migrant Women Ageing in London.* Abingdon: Routledge, 2016.

Alexander, Claire, Joya Chatterji, and Annu Jalais. *The Bengal Diaspora: Rethinking Muslim Migration.* Abingdon: Routledge, 2016.

Alexander, Jeffrey. *The Civil Sphere.* Oxford: Oxford University Press, 2006.

———. "Civil Sphere, State, and Citizenship: Replying to Turner and the Fear of Enclavement." *Citizenship Studies* 12, no. 2 (2008): 185–94.

———. *Remembering the Holocaust: A Debate.* Oxford: Oxford University Press, 2009.

Alexander, Michelle. *The New Jim Crow: Mass Incarceration in the Age of Colorblindness.* New York: The New Press, 2012.

Ali, Monica. *Brick Lane.* New York: Simon and Schuster, 2008.

Ali, Sundas. *British Muslims in Numbers.* London: Muslim Council of Britain, 2015. http://www.mcb.org.uk/wp-content/uploads/2015/02/MCBCensusReport_2015.pdf.

Allen, Amy. *The End of Progress: Decolonizing the Normative Foundations of Critical Theory.* New York: Columbia University Press, 2016.

Allen, Christopher. "From Race to Religion: The New Face of Discrimination." In *Muslim Britain: Communities Under Pressure*, edited by Abbas Tariq, 49–65. London: Zed Books, 2005.

———. *Islamophobia*. Surrey: Ashgate, 2010.

———. "Justifying Islamophobia: A Post-9/11 Consideration of the European Union and British Contexts." *American Journal of Islamic Social Sciences* 21, no. 3 (2004): 1–25.

Allievi, Stefano. *Conflicts over Mosques in Europe: Policy Issues and Trends—NEF Initiative on Religion and Democracy in Europe*. London: Alliance Publishing Trust, 2009.

American Sociological Association. "Herbert J. Gans." Accessed March 23, 2020. https://www.asanet.org/herbert-j-gans.

Amin, Ash. "The Remainders of Race." *Theory, Culture & Society* 27, no. 1 (2010): 1–23.

Amir-Moazami, Shirin. "Buried Alive: Multiculturalism in Germany." *ISIM* 16 (2005): 22–23.

———. "Investigating the Secular Body: The Politics of the Male Circumcision Debate in Germany." *ReOrient* 1, no. 2 (2016): 147–70.

Amnesty International. *Choice and Prejudice: Discrimination against Muslims in Europe*. London: Amnesty International, 2012. https://www.amnesty.org/en/documents/EUR01/001/2012/en/.

Anderson, Benedict. *Imagined Communities: Reflections on the Origin and Spread of Nationalism*. London: Verso, 2016.

Anderson-Nathe, Ben, and Kiaras Gharabaghi. "Trending Rightward: Nationalism, Xenophobia, and the 2016 Politics of Fear." *Child & Youth Services* 38, no. 1 (2017): 1–3.

Andijar, Gil. "On the European Question." *Belgrade Journal of Media and Communications* 2, no. 3 (37–50): 2013.

Appadurai, Arjun, and Carol Breckenridge. "On Moving Targets." *Public Culture* 2 (1989): i–iv.

Archer, Toby. "Welcome to the Umma: The British State and Its Muslim Citizens since 9/11." *Cooperation and Conflict* 44, no. 3 (2009): 329–47.

Arendt, Hannah. *The Human Condition*. Chicago: University of Chicago Press, 2013.

———. "Introduction." In *Illuminations*, by Walter Benjamin, edited by Hannah Arendt. Boston: Mariner Books, 2019.

———. "The Jew as Pariah: A Hidden Tradition." *Jewish Social Studies* 6, no. 2 (1944): 99–122.

———. *The Jewish Writings*. New York: Shocken Books, 2007.

———. *Men in Dark Times*. Boston: Houghton Mifflin Harcourt, 1968.

———. *The Origins of Totalitarianism*. Boston: Houghton Mifflin Harcourt, 1973.

———. "The Public and the Private Realm." In *The Portable Hannah Arendt*, by Hannah Arendt, 182–230, edited by Peter Baehr. New York: Penguin, 2003.

———. *Rahel Varnhagen: The Life of a Jewess*. Translated by Richard Winston and Clare Winston. Baltimore: John Hopkins University Press, 1997.

Aristotle. *Nicomachean Ethics*. Translated and edited by Roger Crisp. Cambridge: Cambridge University Press, 2004.

Art, David. "The AfD and the End of Containment in Germany?" *German Politics & Society* 36, no. 2 (2018): 76–86.

Asad, Talal. *Formations of the Secular: Christianity, Islam, Modernity*. Stanford: Stanford University Press, 2003.

———. "The Idea of an Anthropology of Islam." *Qui Parle* 17, no. 2 (2009): 1–30.

———. "Muslims and European Identity: Can Europe Represent Islam?" In *The Idea of Europe*, edited by Anthony Pagden, 209–27. Cambridge: Cambridge University Press, 2002.

Asthana, Anushka. "Why Did Multiculturalism Become a Dirty Word? It Made Me Who I Am." *Guardian*, December 18, 2010. https://www.theguardian.com/commentisfree/2010/dec/19/anushka-asthana-multiculturalism-good.

Astor, Avi, Marian Burchardt, and Mar Griera. "Polarization and the Limits of Politicization: Cordoba Mosque-Cathedral and the Politics of Cultural Heritage." *Qualitative Sociology* 42, no. 3 (2019): 337–60.

Atlas Obscura. "Walter Benjamin Memorial." Accessed June 7, 2020. http://www.atlasobscura.com/places/walter-benjamin-memorial.

Augustine. *The City of God*. Irvine: Xist Publishing, 2015.

Avishai, Orit. " 'Doing Religion' in a Secular World: Women in Conservative Religions and the Question of Agency." *Gender & Society* 22, no. 4 (2008): 409–33.

Awan, Imran. " 'I Am a Muslim Not an Extremist': How the Prevent Strategy Has Constructed a 'Suspect' Community." *Politics & Policy* 40, no. 6 (2012): 1158–85.

Awn, Peter. "The Ethical Concerns of Classical Sufism." *Journal of Religious Ethics* 11, no. 2 (1983): 240–63.

Ayoub, Mahmoud. "The Islamic Concept of Justice." In *Islamic Identity and the Struggle for Justice*, edited by Nimat Barazangi, M. Raquibuz Zaman, and Omar Afzal, 19–26. Gainesville: University of Florida Press, 1996.

Baczynska, Gabriela, and Sara Ledwith. "How Europe Builds Fences to Keep People Out." *Huffington Post*, April 4, 2016. https://www.huffpost.com/entry/europe-refugee-fences_n_57026a49e4b083f5c6081121.

Badger, Emily. "How the Rise of American-Style Segregation Is Feeding Division in Europe." *Washington Post*, December 2, 2015. https://www.washingtonpost.com/news/wonk/wp/2015/12/02/how-the-rise-of-american-style-segregation-is-feeding-division-in-europe/?utm_term=.891a1fa3dbd2.

Balibar, Étienne. "Is There a 'Neo-racism'?" In *Race, Nation, Class: Ambiguous Identities*, edited by Étienne Balibar and Immanuel Wallerstein, 17–28. London: Verso, 1991.

Ball, John. "The Semi-detached Metropolis: Hanif Kureishi's London." *Ariel: A Review of International English Literature* 27, no. 4 (1996): 7–27.

Banac, Ivo. *The National Question in Yugoslavia: Origins, History, Politics*. Ithaca: Cornell University Press, 1988.

Barkan, Leonard. *Berlin for Jews: A Twenty-First-Century Companion*. Chicago: University of Chicago Press, 2016.

Barkey, Karen. "Islam and Toleration: Studying the Ottoman Imperial Model." *International Journal of Politics, Culture, and Society* 19, no. 1–2 (2007): 5–19.

Barnes, Peter. "Brexit: What Happens Now?" *BBC News*, February 5, 2020. https://www.bbc.com/news/uk-politics-46393399.

Barylo, William. "Neo-liberal Not-for-Profits: The Embracing of Corporate Culture by European Muslim Charities." *Journal of Muslim Minority Affairs* 36, no. 3 (2016): 383–98.

Bastow, Steve. "The Front National under Marine Le Pen : A Mainstream Political Party?" *French Politics* 16, no. 1 (2018): 19–37.

Batnitzky, Leora. *How Judaism Became a Religion*. Princeton: Princeton University Press, 2011.

Batuman, Bülent. "Architectural Mimicry and the Politics of Mosque Building: Negotiating Islam and Nation in Turkey." *Journal of Architecture* 21, no. 3 (2016): 321–47.

Baudelaire, Charles. *The Painter of Modern Life and Other Essays*. Translated by Jonathan Mayne. London: Phaidon Press, 2001.

Bauman, Zygmunt. *Intimations of Postmodernity*. London: Routledge, 2003.

———. "Modernity and Ambivalence." *Theory, Culture & Society* 7, no. 2–3 (1990): 143–69.

———. *Modernity and Ambivalence*. Cambridge: Polity Press, 1991.

———. *Modernity and the Holocaust*. Ithaca: Cornell University Press, 2001.

———. *Postmodern Ethics*. Malden, MA: Blackwell, 1993.

———. "Postmodernity, or Living with Ambivalence." In *A Postmodern Reader*, edited by Joseph P. Natoli and Linda Hutcheon, 9–24. Albany: SUNY Press, 1993.

Bayraklı, Enes, and Farid Hafez, eds. *European Islamophobia Report 2015*. Istanbul: SETA Foundation for Politics, Economic and Social Research, 2016. https://setav.org/en/assets/uploads/2016/05/eir_2015.pdf.

Beaman, Jean. "But Madame, We Are French Also." *Contexts* 11, no. 3 (2012): 46–51.

———. *Citizen Outsider: Children of North African Immigrants in France*. Berkeley: University of California Press, 2017.

Beardsley, Eleanor. "Across the Atlantic, Another Mosque Splits a City." *NPR*, October 9, 2010. https://www.npr.org/templates/story/story.php?storyId=130440036.

Becker, Elisabeth. "Good Mosque, Bad Mosque: Boundaries to Belonging in Contemporary Germany." *Journal of the American Academy of Religion* 4, no. 30 (2017): 1050–88.

Begley, Louis. *Why the Dreyfus Affair Matters*. New Haven: Yale University Press, 2009.

Benhabib, Seyla. *Exile, Statelessness, and Migration: Playing Chess with History from Hannah Arendt to Isaiah Berlin*. Princeton: Princeton University Press, 2018.

———. *The Reluctant Modernism of Hannah Arendt*. Lanham, MD: Rowman & Littlefield Publishers, 2000.

Benjamin, Walter. *The Arcades Project*. Translated by Howard Eiland and Kevin McLaughlin. Cambridge, MA: Belknap Press of Harvard University Press, 1999.

———. *Benjamin: Philosophy, Aesthetics, History*. Edited by Gary Smith. Chicago: University of Chicago Press, 1989.

———. *Berlin Childhood around 1900*. Cambridge, MA: Belknap Press, 2006.

———. "The Flaneur's Return." Preface to *Walking in Berlin: A Flaneur in the Capital*, by Franz Hessel, xiii–xix. Cambridge, MA: MIT Press, 2017.

———. *Illuminations: Essays and Reflections*. Edited by Hannah Arendt. Boston: Mariner Books, 2019.

———. *One-Way Street*. Cambridge, MA: Harvard University Press, 2016.

———. *Reflections: Essays, Aphorisms, Autobiographical Writings*. Boston: Houghton Mifflin Harcourt, 2019.

———. *Selected Writings*, vol. 1: *1913–1926*. Edited by Marcus Bullock and Michael Jennings. Cambridge, MA: Harvard University Press, 1996.

———. *Selected Writings*, vol. 4: *1938–1940*. Edited by Howard Eiland and Michael Jennings. Cambridge, MA: Harvard University Press, 2003.

Bennhold, Katrin. "German Parliament Deems B.D.S. Movement Anti-Semitic." *New York Times*, May 17, 2019. https://www.nytimes.com/2019/05/17/world/europe/germany-bds -anti-semitic.html.

Bensaid, Daniel. "Utopia and Messianism: Bloch, Benjamin, and the Sense of the Virtual." *Historical Materialism* 24, no. 4 (2016): 36–50.

Berdahl, Daphne. " '(N)Ostalgie' for the present: memory, longing and East German things." *Ethnos* 64, no. 2 (1999): 192–211.

Bergmann, Werner, Marina Chernivsky, Aycan Demirel, Elke Gryglewski, Beate Küpper, Andreas Nachama, and Armin Pfahl-Traughber. "Bericht des unabhängigen Expertenk-reises Antisemitismus." Deutscher Bundestag, April 7, 2017. https://dip21.bundestag.de /dip21/btd/18/119/1811970.pdf.

Berlant, Lauren. *The Queen of America Goes to Washington City: Essays on Sex and Citizen-ship*. Durham: Duke University Press, 1997.

"Berlin Court Rules in Favor of Hijab-Wearing Teacher." *Deutsche Welle*, February 9, 2017. https://www.dw.com/en/berlin-court-rules-in-favor-of-hijab-wearing-teacher/a-37477936.

"Berlin Teacher Headscarf Ban Is Illegal, Rules Top Court." *Deutsche Welle*, August 27, 2020. https://www.dw.com/en/berlin-teacher-headscarf-ban-is-illegal-rules-top-court /a-54722770.

Bernstein, Richard. *Hannah Arendt and the Jewish Question*. Cambridge, MA: MIT Press, 1996.

Berreman, Gerald. "Caste in India and the United States." *American Journal of Sociology* 66, no. 2 (1960): 120–27.

Besnaci-Lancou, Fatima, Benoit Falaize, and Gilles Manceron. *Les Harkis: histoire, mémoire et transmission*. Paris: Editions de l'Atelier, 2010.

Bezirksamt Tempelhof-Schöneberg. "Zeugnisse jüdischen Lebens in Schöneberg," August 12, 2016. https://www.berlin.de/ba-tempelhof-schoeneberg/ueber-den-bezirk/spaziergaenge /2015/artikel.357860.php.

Bhabha, Homi. *The Location of Culture*. Abingdon: Routledge, 1994.

———. "Sly Civility." *The MIT Press* 34 (1985): 71–80.

Bird, David. "Hannah Arendt's Funeral Held; Many Moving Tributes Paid." *New York Times*, December 9, 1975. https://www.nytimes.com/1975/12/09/archives/hannah-arendts-funeral -held-many-moving-tributes-paid.html.

Bittner, Jochen. "What's behind Germany's New Anti-Semitism?" *New York Times*, Septem-ber 16, 2014. https://www.nytimes.com/2014/09/17/opinion/jochen-bittner-whats-behind -germanys-new-anti-semitism.html.

Blackshaw, Tony. *Zygmunt Bauman*. Abingdon: Routledge, 2005.

Bleich, Erik. "State Responses to 'Muslim' Violence: A Comparison of Six West European Countries." *Journal of Ethnic and Migration Studies* 35, no. 3 (2009): 361–79.

———. "What Is Islamophobia and How Much Is There? Theorizing and Measuring an Emerging Comparative Concept." *American Behavioral Scientist* 55, no. 12 (December 2011): 1581–1600.

Bloch, Ernst. *Literary Essays*. Translated by Andrew Joron. Stanford: Stanford University Press, 1998.

———. *The Principle of Hope*. Translated by Neville Plaice, Stephen Plaice, and Paul Knight. Cambridge, MA: MIT Press, 1995.

———. *The Utopian Function of Art and Literature: Selected Essays*. Translated by Jack Zipes and Frank Mecklenburg. Cambridge, MA: MIT Press, 1988.

Boas, Frank. "Introduction." In *Traditions of the Thompson River Indians of British Columbia*, by James Alexander Teit, 1–18. Boston: Houghton, Mifflin and Company, 1898.

Bodemann, Y. Michal. *Jews, Germans, Memory: Reconstructions of Jewish Life in Germany*. Ann Arbor: University of Michigan Press, 1996.

Bonefeld, Meike, and Oliver Dickhäuser. "(Biased) Grading of Students' Performance: Students' Names, Performance Level, and Implicit Attitudes." *Frontiers in Psychology* 9, no. 481 (2018): 1–13.

Bonino, Stefano. "*Prevent*-ing Muslimness in Britain: The Normalisation of Exceptional Measures to Combat Terrorism." *Journal of Muslim Minority Affairs* 33, no. 3 (2013): 385–400.

Bordo, Jonathan. "The Homer of Potsdamer Platz: Walter Benjamin in Wim Wenders' Sky over Berlin/Wings of Desire: A Critical Topography." *Images* 2, no. 1 (2008): 86–109.

Bougle, Celestin. *Essays on the Caste System*. Cambridge: Cambridge University Press, 1971.

Bouie, Jamelle. "Christian Soldiers." *Slate Magazine*, February 10, 2015.

Bourdieu, Pierre. *The Logic of Practice*. Stanford: Stanford University Press, 1990.

Bowen, John. *On British Islam: Religion, Law, and Everyday Practice in Shari'a Councils*. Princeton: Princeton University Press, 2016.

———. *Why the French Don't Like Headscarves: Islam, the State, and Public Space*. Princeton: Princeton University Press, 2006.

Bowen, John, Christophe Bertoosi, Jan Duyvendak, and Mona Krook. "An Institutional Approach to Framing Muslims in Europe." In *European States and Their Muslim Citizens*, edited by John Bowen, Christophe Bertossi, Jan Willem Duyvendak and Mona Lena Krook, 1–28. Cambridge: Cambridge University Press, 2013.

Brack, Nathalie, and Nicholas Startin. "Introduction: Euroscepticism, from the Margins to the Mainstream." *International Political Science Review* 36, no. 3 (2015): 239–49.

Brady, Kate. "German School in Wuppertal Bans Muslim Children from 'Provocative' Prayer." *Deutsche Welle*, March 2, 2017. https://www.dw.com/en/german-school-in-wuppertal-bans-muslim-children-from-provocative-prayer/a-37780162.

Brah, Avital, Mary Hickman, and Máirtín Mac an Ghaill. "Thinking Identities: Ethnicity, Racism and Culture." In *Thinking Identities: Ethnicity, Racism and Culture*, edited by Avital Brah, Mary Hickman, and Máirtín Mac an Ghaill, 1–24. London: MacMillan Press, 1999.

Brems, Eva. "Belgium: Discrimination against Muslims in Belgium." In *State, Religion and Muslims: Between Discrimination and Protection at the Legislative, Executive and Judicial Levels*, edited by Melek Saral and Şerif Onur Bahçecik, 65–108. Leiden: Brill, 2020.

Brenner, Michael. "1916: The German Army Orders a Census of Jewish Soldiers, and Jews Defend German Culture." In *Yale Companion to Jewish Writing and Thought in German*

Culture, 1096–1996, edited by Jack Zipes and Sander Gilman, 348–54. New Haven: Yale University Press, 1997.

Brenner, Yermi. "In Berlin, Jews and Muslims Fight for Each Other." *Forward*, December 1, 2014. https://forward.com/opinion/world/210127/in-berlin-jews-and-muslims-fight-for -each-other/.

Brown, Wendy. *Regulating Aversion: Tolerance in the Age of Identity and Empire*. Princeton: Princeton University Press, 2009.

———. "Tolerance As/In Civilizational Discourse." *Nomos* 48 (2008): 406–41.

Brownell, Will, and Denise Drace-Brownell. *The First Nazi: Erich Ludendorff, the Man Who Made Hitler Possible*. Berkeley: Counterpoint, 2016.

Brubaker, Rogers. "Categories of Analysis and Categories of Practice: A Note on the Study of Muslims in European Countries of Immigration." *Ethnic and Racial Studies* 36, no. 1 (2013): 1–8.

———. *Trans: Gender and Race in an Age of Unsettled Identities*. Princeton: Princeton University Press, 2016.

Brümmer, Vincent. "Atonement and Reconciliation." *Religious Studies* 28, no. 4 (1992): 435–52.

Bugeja, Norbert. *Postcolonial Memoir in the Middle East: Rethinking the Liminal in Mashriqi Writing*. New York: Routledge, 2012.

Bulliet, Richard W. "The Shaikh Al-Islām and the Evolution of Islamic Society." *Studia Islamica*, no. 35 (1972): 53–67.

Cahm, Eric. *The Dreyfus Affair in French Society and Politics*. Abingdon: Routledge, 2014.

Castles, Stephen. "Guestworkers in Europe: A Resurrection?" *International Migration Review* 40 (2006): 741–66.

Cesari, Jocelyne. *Securitization and Religious Divides in Europe: Muslims in Western Europe after 9/11—Why the Term Islamophobia Is More a Predicament than an Explanation*. Paris: Challenge, 2006. http://www.antoniocasella.eu/nume/Cesari_2006.pdf.

Ceylan, Rauf. "From Guest Workers to Muslim Immigrants: The History of Muslims and Their Organizations in Germany." In *Muslim Community Organizations in the West: History, Developments and Future Perspectives*, edited by Mario Peucker and Rauf Ceylan, 75–92. Wiesbaden: Springer Fachmedien, 2017.

Chaker, Aref. "The Life of Abu Mansur Al-Maturidi and the Socio-political and Theological Context of Central Asia in the Tenth Century." *Australian Journal of Islamic Studies* 1, no. 1 (2016): 38–64.

Chalmers, David. *Hooded Americanism: The History of the Ku Klux Klan*. Durham: Duke University Press, 1987.

Chambers, Madeline. "German Jewish College Shuns Skullcaps after Attack on Rabbi." *Reuters*, August 30, 2012. https://www.reuters.com/article/us-germany-rabbi-idUSBRE87 T0UZ20120830.

Charity Commission. "Survey of Mosques in England and Wales." https://assets.publishing .service.gov.uk/government/uploads/system/uploads/attachment_data/file/315594/p _brief_mosques.pdf, n.d.

Cheesman, Tom. *Novels of Turkish German Settlement: Cosmopolite Fictions.* Rochester: Camden House, 2007.

Cheng, Jennifer. "Islamophobia, Muslimophobia, or Racism? Parliamentary Discourses on Islam and Muslims in Debates on the Minaret Ban in Switzerland." *Discourse and Society* 26 no. 5 (2015): 562–86.

Chin, Rita. *The Guestworker Question in Postwar Germany.* Cambridge: Cambridge University Press, 2007.

Christian, Mark. "Class and Caste." In *The Encyclopedia of Black Studies*, edited by Molefi Asante and Ama Mazama, 186–87. Thousand Oaks: SAGE, 2005.

Clack, David. "Neukölln: Your Guide to Berlin's Hippest 'Hood." *Time Out*, October 9, 2015.

Cobain, Ian, Nazia Parveen, and Matthew Taylor. "The Slow-Burning Hatred That Led Thomas Mair to Murder Jo Cox." *Guardian*, November 23, 2016. https://www.theguardian .com/uk-news/2016/nov/23/thomas-mair-slow-burning-hatred-led-to-jo-cox-murder.

Cohen, Hermann. "The Concept of God after Auschwitz: A Jewish Voice." *Journal of Religion* 67, no. 1 (1987): 1–13.

———. *Religion of Reason: Out of the Sources of Judaism.* New York: Frederick Ungar Publishing, 1972.

Connolly, Kate. "Promoting Tolerance in Germany Could Define Angela Merkel's Leadership." *The Guardian.* January 16, 2015. https://www.theguardian.com/world/2015/jan/16 /promoting-tolerance-germany-could-define-angela-merkel-leadership.

Constant, Amelie, and Bienvenue Tien. "Germany's Immigration Policy and Labor Shortages." IZA Research Report, 2011. http://legacy.iza.org/en/webcontent/publications /reports/report_pdfs/iza_report_41.pdf.

Cooper, Hayden. "Controversial Dutch MP's Visa Bid Stalls." *ABC*, September 18, 2012. https://www.abc.net.au/news/2012-09-18/geert-wilders-applies-for-australian-visa/4268532.

Cousin, Glynis, and Robert Fine. "A Common Cause." *European Societies* 14, no. 2 (2012): 166–85.

Craig, John. *A New Universal Etymological, Technological, and Pronouncing Dictionary of the English Language, Embracing All the Terms Used in Science, Literature and Art.* London: George Routledge & Company, 1858.

Cue, Eduardo. "For France, Girls in Head Scarves Threaten Secular Ideals." *Christian Science Monitor*, October 5, 1994. https://www.csmonitor.com/1994/1005/05012.html.

Dagli, Caner. "Muslims Are Not a Race." *Renovatio*, February 6, 2020. https://renovatio .zaytuna.edu/article/muslims-are-not-a-race.

Dante Alighieri. *The Divine Comedy.* Translated by John Ciardi. New York: Berkley, 2003.

Davidson, Naomi. *Only Muslim: Embodying Islam in Twentieth-Century France.* Ithaca: Cornell University Press, 2012.

Davis, Allison, Burleigh Bradford Gardner, and Mary Gardner. *Deep South: A Social Anthropological Study of Caste and Class.* Columbia: University of South Carolina Press, 2009.

Davis, Britton. "Lifting the Veil: France's New Crusade." *Comparative Law Review* 34, no. 1 (2011): 117–45.

Dawson, Ashley. *Mongrel Nation: Diasporic Culture and the Making of Postcolonial Britain.* Ann Arbor: University of Michigan Press, 2007.

Dearden, Lizzie. "Burkini Ban: Why Is France Arresting Muslim Women for Wearing Full-Body Swimwear and Why Are People So Angry?" *Independent*, August 24, 2016. http://www.independent.co.uk/news/world/europe/burkini-ban-why-is-france-arresting-muslim-women-for-wearing-full-body-swimwear-and-why-are-people-a7207971.html.

DeHanas, Daniel Nilsson. *London Youth, Religion, and Politics: Engagement and Activism from Brixton to Brick Lane*. Oxford: Oxford University Press, 2016.

DeHanas, Daniel, and Zacharias Pieri. "Olympic Proportions: The Expanding Scalar Politics of the London 'Olympics Mega-mosque' Controversy." *Sociology* 45, no. 5 (2011): 798–814.

Delaney, Tim. *Classical and Contemporary Social Theory: Investigation and Application*. Abingdon: Routledge, 2016.

Della Porta, Donatella. "Protest, Protesters, and Protest Policing: Public Discourses in Italy and Germany from the 1960s to the 1980s." In *How Social Movements Matter*, edited by Marco Giugni, Doug McAdam, and Charles Tilly, 66–96. Minneapolis: University of Minnesota Press, 1999.

Demetz, Peter. "Introduction." In *Reflections: Essays, Aphorisms, Autobiographical Writings*, by Walter Benjamin, vii–xlv. Boston: Houghton Mifflin Harcourt, 1978.

"Demonstranten streiten über Moschee-Pläne." *Welt*, June 16, 2007. http://www.welt.de/politik/article951708/.

D'entrèves, Maurizio Passerin. "Hannah Arendt." In *The Stanford Encyclopedia of Philosophy*, edited by Edward Zalta. Stanford: Stanford University Press, July 27, 2006. https://plato.stanford.edu/archives/spr2019/entries/arendt/.

Deringil, Selim. *Turkish Foreign Policy during the Second World War: An "Active" Neutrality*. Cambridge: Cambridge University Press, 1989.

Deupi, Victor. *Architectural Temperance: Spain and Rome, 1700–1759*. Abingdon: Routledge, 2014.

Dickinson, James. "Metropolis." In *The Blackwell Encyclopedia of Sociology*, edited by George Ritzer, 289–93. Malden, MA: Blackwell Publishing, 2007.

Dietrich, Christian. "Eine Deutsch-Jüdische Symbiose? Das Zionistische Interesse für Fichte und Sombart, Moritz Goldsteins Überlegungen zur Deutsch-Jüdischen Kultur und die Schwierigkeiten mit mem Bindestrich." In *Das Kulturerbe Deutschsprachiger Juden: Eine Spurensuche in den Ursprungs-, Transit- und Emigrationsländern*, edited by Elke-Vera Kotowski, 43–55. Berlin: De Gruyter, 2014.

Dollard, John. *Caste and Class in a Southern Town*. New Haven: Yale University Press, 1937.

Douglas, Mary. *Purity and Danger: An Analysis of Concepts of Pollution and Taboo*. Abingdon: Routledge, 2002.

Dremeaux, Lillie. " 'The Way People Look at Us Has Changed': Muslim Women on Life in Europe." *New York Times*, September 2, 2016. https://www.nytimes.com/2016/09/03/world/europe/burkini-ban-muslim-women.html.

Dumont, Louis. *Homo Hierarchicus: The Caste System and Its Implications*. Chicago: University of Chicago Press, 1980.

Dussel, Enrique. "Eurocentrism and Modernity." *Boundary* 2 20, no. 3 (1993): 65–76.

———. "Europe, Modernity, and Eurocentrism." *Nepantla: Views from South* 1, no. 3 (2000): 465–78.

———. *The Underside of Modernity: Apel, Ricoeur, Rorty, Taylor, and the Philosophy of Liberation*. Atlantic Highlands: Humanities Press International, 1996.

Dwyer, Claire, and Astrid Meyer. "The Institutionalisation of Islam in The Netherlands and in the UK: The Case of Islamic Schools." *Journal of Ethnic and Migration Studies* 21, no. 1 (1995): 37–54.

East London Mosque, "History." 2016. https://www.eastlondonmosque.org.uk/history.

East London Mosque Trust Ltd. "Opening Ceremony of East London Mosque, Whitechapel Road, London E1," 1985. In the mosque's archives.

Eaude, Michael. *Catalonia: A Cultural History*. Oxford: Oxford University Press, 2008.

Eddy, Melissa. "German Lawmakers Vote to Protect Right to Circumcision." *New York Times*, December 12, 2012. https://www.nytimes.com/2012/12/13/world/europe/german-lawmakers-vote-to-protect-right-to-circumcision.html.

———. "What and Whom Are Jewish Museums For?" *New York Times*, July 9, 2019. https://www.nytimes.com/2019/07/09/arts/design/jewish-museums-germany-berlin-europe.html.

Eddy, Melissa, and Isabel Kershner. "Jerusalem Criticizes Berlin's Jewish Museum for 'Anti-Israel Activity.'" *New York Times*, December 23, 2018. https://www.nytimes.com/2018/12/23/arts/design/berlin-jewish-museum-israel-bds-welcome-to-jerusalem.html.

Edgar, Scott. "Hermann Cohen." In *The Stanford Encyclopedia of Philosophy*, edited by Edward Zalta. Stanford: Stanford University Press, 2020. https://plato.stanford.edu/archives/spr2020/entries/cohen/.

Eiland, Howard. "Translator's Foreword." In *Berlin Childhood around 1900*, vii–xvi. Cambridge, MA: Harvard University Press, 2006.

El Fadl, Khaled Abou. *The Great Theft: Wrestling Islam from the Extremists*. New York: Harper One, 2007.

———. *The Search for Beauty in Islam: A Conference of the Books*. Lanham, MD: Rowman & Littlefield Publishers, 2005.

Eliot, T. S. "Tradition and the Individual Talent." *Perspecta* 19 (1982): 36–42.

Ellermann, Antje. "When Can Liberal States Avoid Unwanted Immigration? Self-Limited Sovereignty and Guest Worker Recruitment in Switzerland and Germany." *World Politics* 65, no. 3 (2013): 491–538.

Elliott, Carole, and Jim Stewart. "What Are the (C)HRD Implications of Brexit? A Personal Reflection?" *Human Resource Development International* 20, no. 1 (2017): 1–8.

Elver, Hilal. *The Headscarf Controversy: Secularism and Freedom of Religion*. Oxford: Oxford University Press, 2012.

Emsley, Clive. *The English Police: A Political and Social History*. Harlow, Essex: Longman, 1996.

Englander, David. "Booth's Jews: The Presentation of Jews and Judaism in 'Life and Labour of the People in London.'" *Victorian Studies* 32, no. 4 (1989): 551–71.

Enjelvin, Géraldine, and Nada Korac-Kakabadse. "France and the Memories of 'Others': The Case of the Harkis." *History and Memory* 24, no. 1 (2012): 152–77.

Equalities Review Commission. *Fairness and Freedom: The Final Report of the Equalities Review*. Norwich: The Crown, 2007. https://webarchive.nationalarchives.gov.uk/20100806180051/http://archive.cabinetoffice.gov.uk/equalitiesreview/upload/assets/www.theequalitiesreview.org.uk/equality_review.pdf

Ercolini, Gina. "Arendt, Adorno, and Benjamin: Response, Responsibility, and Commitment." In *Communication Ethics: Between Cosmopolitanism and Provinciality*, edited by Kathleen Glenister Roberts and Ronald Arnett, 215–40. New York: Peter Lang, 2008.

Esack, Farid. "Three Islamic Strands in the South African Struggle for Justice." *Third World Quarterly* 10, no. 2 (1988): 472–98.

Esen, Berk, and Sebnem Gumuscu. "Rising Competitive Authoritarianism in Turkey." *Third World Quarterly* 37, no. 9 (2016): 1581–1606.

Ewing, Katherine Pratt. *Stolen Honor: Stigmatizing Muslim Men in Berlin*. Stanford: Stanford University Press, 2008.

Fadil, Nadia. "Managing Affects and Sensibilities: The Case of Not-Handshaking and Not-Fasting." *Social Anthropology* 17, no. 4 (2009): 439–54.

———. "Not-/Unveiling as an Ethical Practice." *Feminist Review* 98, no. 1 (2011): 83–109.

Fanon, Frantz. *A Dying Colonialism*. New York: Grove/Atlantic, Inc., 1994.

Fassin, Didier. "The Endurance of Critique." *Anthropological Theory* 17, no. 1 (2017): 4–29.

———. "Nommer, interpréter: Le sens commun de la question raciale." In *De la question sociale à la question raciale*, edited by Eric Fassin and Didier Fassin, 19–36. Paris: La Découverte, 2006.

Fekete, Liz. "Anti-Muslim Racism and the European Security State." *Race & Class* 46, no. 1 (2004): 3–29.

Feldman, Alice. "Re/Entangling Irish and Nigerian Diasporas: Colonial Amnesias, Decolonial Aesthetics and Archive-Assemblage Praxis." *Cultural Dynamics* 30, no. 3 (2018): 173–98.

Fennell, Barbara. *Language, Literature, and the Negotiation of Identity: Foreign Worker German in the Federal Republic of Germany*. Chapel Hill: University of North Carolina Press, 1997.

Fereidooni, Karim. "Diskriminierungs- und Rassismuserfahrungen von Referendar*innen und Lehrer*innen 'mit Migrationshintergrund' im Deutschen Schulwesen: Eine quantitative und qualitative Studie zu subjektiv bedeutsamen Ungleichheitspraxen im Berufskontext." Dissertation, University of Heidelberg, 2015.

Fernando, Mayanthi. "Reconfiguring Freedom: Muslim Piety and the Limits of Secular Law and Public Discourse in France." *American Ethnologist* 37, no. 1 (2010): 19–35.

———. *The Republic Unsettled: Muslim French and the Contradictions of Secularism*. Durham: Duke University Press, 2014.

———. "State Sovereignty and the Politics of Indifference." *Public Culture* 31, no. 2 (2019): 261–73.

Firestone, Reuven. *Journeys in Holy Lands: The Evolution of the Abraham-Ishmael Legends in Islamic Exegesis*. Albany: State University of New York Press, 1990.

Foucault, Michel. *Discipline and Punish: The Birth of the Prison*. New York: Vintage, 1995.

———. "Was ist Aufklärung?" In *Ethos der Moderne: Foucaults Kritik der Aufklärung*, edited by Eva Erdmann, Rainer Forst, and Axel Honneth, 35–54. Frankfurt: Campus Verlag, 1990.

Fox, James W., Jr. "Intimations of Citizenship: Repressions and Expressions of Equal Citizenship in the Era of Jim Crow." *Howard Law Journal* 50 (2007): 113–201.

Fraser, Giles. "France's Much Vaunted Secularism Is Not the Neutral Space It Claims to Be." *Guardian*, January 16, 2015. https://www.theguardian.com/commentisfree/belief/2015/jan/16/france-much-vaunted-secularism-not-neutral-space-claims-to-be.

Fredrickson, George. *Racism: A Short History*. Princeton: Princeton University Press, 2002.

Friedman, Sam. "What Is the Habitus Clivé?" *Sociological Review* (blog), December 3, 2018. https://www.thesociologicalreview.com/what-is-the-habitus-clive/.

Frisch, Max. "Überfremdung." In *Siamo Italiani: Gespräche mit italienischen Arbeitern in der Schweiz*, by Alexander Seiler. Zürich: EVZ Verlag, 1965.

Frost, Nicola. "Green Curry: Politics and Place-Making on Brick Lane." *Food, Culture & Society* 14, no. 2 (2011): 225–42.

Frymark, Kamil. "The Turkish Campaign in Germany: Rising Tensions between Berlin and Ankara." *OSW*, March 23, 2017. https://www.osw.waw.pl/en/publikacje/osw-commentary /2017-03-23/turkish-campaign-germany-rising-tensions-between-berlin-and.

Fuentes, Carlos. *This I Believe: An A to Z of a Life*. Translated by Kristina Cordero. New York: Random House, 2006.

Gallup. "Islamophobia: Understanding Anti-Muslim Sentiment in the West," 2012. http:// www.gallup.com/poll/157082/islamophobia-understanding-anti-muslim-sentimentwest .aspx#2.

Galonnier, Juliette. "When 'White Devils' Join the Deen: White American Converts to Islam and the Experience of Non-normative Whiteness." Paris: OSC, Sciences Po/CNRS, 2015. https://core.ac.uk/reader/35309258.

Gans, Herbert. "From 'Underclass' to 'Undercaste': Some Observations about the Future of the Post-industrial Economy and Its Major Victims." In *Urban Poverty and the Underclass: A Reader*, edited by Enzo Mingione, 141–52. Cambridge, MA: Blackwell, 1996.

Gardet, Louis, "Īmān." In *Encyclopaedia of Islam*, 2nd ed., edited by Peri Bearman, Thierry Bianquis, Clifford Edmond Bosworth, Emeri Johannes van Donzel, and Wolfhart Heinrichs, 2012. http://dx.doi.org/10.1163/1573-3912_islam_COM_0370.

Gardner, Katy. "Desh-Bidesh: Sylheti Images of Home and Away." *Man* 28, no. 1 (1993): 1–15.

———. "Narrating Location: Space, Age and Gender among Bengali Elders in East London." *Oral History* 27, no. 1 (1999): 65–74.

Garner, Steve, and Saher Selod. "The Racialization of Muslims: Empirical Studies of Islamophobia." *Critical Sociology* 41, no. 1 (2015): 9–19.

Geheran, Michael. "Judenzählung (Jewish Census)." In *International Encyclopedia of the First World War (WW1)*, July 9, 2015. https://encyclopedia.1914-1918-online.net/article /judenzahlung_jewish_census.

Geoghegan, Vincent. *Ernst Bloch*. London: Routledge, 2008.

Germann, Nadja. "Al-Farabi's Philosophy of Society and Religion." *Stanford Encyclopedia of Philosophy*, June 15, 2016. https://plato.stanford.edu/entries/al-farabi-soc-rel/.

"Germany's Top Court Rules Muslim Schoolgirls Must Join Swimming Lessons." *Reuters*, December 8, 2016. https://www.reuters.com/article/uk-germany-islam-idUSKBN13X1XW.

Geulen, Christian. "Warum ist es so schwer, von Rassismus zu sprechen?" *Bundeszentrale für politische Bildung*, December 8, 2015. https://www.bpb.de/politik/extremismus /rechtsextremismus/213691/warum-ist-es-so-schwer-von-rassismus-zu-sprechen.

Gidley, Ben. "Diasporic Memory and the Call to Identity: Yiddish Migrants in Early Twentieth Century East London." *Journal of Intercultural Studies* 34, no. 6 (2013): 650–64.

Gieryn, Thomas. "A Space for Place in Sociology." *Annual Review of Sociology* 26 (2000): 463–96.

Gillespie, Susan, and Samantha Rose Hill. "On Walter Benjamin's Legacy: A Correspondence between Hannah Arendt and Theodor Adorno." *Los Angeles Review of Books*, February 9, 2020. https://lareviewofbooks.org/article/on-walter-benjamins-legacy-a-correspondence-between-hannah-arendt-and-theodor-adorno/.

Gilloch, Graeme. *Myth and Metropolis: Walter Benjamin and the City.* Cambridge: Polity Press, 2002.

Gimaret, Daniel. "Taklīf." In *Encyclopaedia of Islam*, 2nd ed., edited by Peri Bearman, Thierry Bianquis, Clifford Edmond Bosworth, Emeri Johannes van Donzel, Wolfhart Heinrichs, 2012. http://dx.doi.org/10.1163/1573-3912_islam_SIM_7344.

Gingeras, Ryan. *Mustafa Kemal Atatürk: Heir to the Empire.* Oxford: Oxford University Press, 2016.

Giroux, Henry. "When Hope Is Subversive." *Tikkun* 19, no. 6 (2004): 38–41.

Glaeser, Andreas. *Divided in Unity: Identity, Germany, and the Berlin Police.* Chicago: University of Chicago Press, 2001.

Glucroft, William. "A Desperate Need for a Third Way." *Qantara*, February 2, 2015. https://en.qantara.de/content/the-anti-semitism-debate-a-desperate-need-for-a-third-way.

Glynn, Sarah. *Class, Ethnicity and Religion in the Bengali East End.* Manchester: Manchester University Press, 2017.

Göle, Nilüfer. "The Public Visibility of Islam and European Politics of Resentment: The Minarets-Mosques Debate." *Philosophy and Social Criticism* 37, no. 4 (2011): 383–92.

Gözaydın, Istar. "Diyanet and Politics." *Muslim World* 98, no. 2–3 (2008): 216–27.

Graf, Wilfried. "Das neue Faschismus-Syndrom: Die gemeinsame Tiefenkultur von Antisemitismus und Islamophobie." *Psychotherapie Forum* 14, no. 2 (2006): 102–7.

Granovetter, Mark. "The Strength of Weak Ties." *American Journal of Sociology* 78, no. 6 (1973): 1360–80.

Gronow, Jukka, and Olli Pyyhtinen. "Georg Simmel." *Oxford Bibliographies.* Accessed March 23, 2020. https://www.oxfordbibliographies.com/view/document/obo-9780199756384/obo-9780199756384-0180.xml.

Hackett, Conrad. "5 Facts about the Muslim Population in Europe." Pew Research Center, November 29, 2017. https://www.pewresearch.org/fact-tank/2017/11/29/5-facts-about-the-muslim-population-in-europe/.

Hafez, Farid. "Comparing Anti-Semitism and Islamophobia: The State of the Field." *Islamophobia Journal* 3, no. 2 (2016): 16–34.

Haley, Charles. "The Desperate Ottoman: Enver Paşa and the German Empire—I." *Middle Eastern Studies* 30, no. 1 (1994): 1–51.

Halikiopoulou, Daphne, and Sofia Vasilopoulou. "Support for the Far Right in the 2014 European Parliament Elections: A Comparative Perspective." *Political Quarterly* 85, no. 3 (2014): 285–88.

Hall, Stuart. "The West and the Rest: Discourse and Power." In *Race and Racialization: Essential Readings*, edited by Tania Das Gupta, Carl James, Chris Anderson, Grace-Edward Galbuzi, and Roger Maaka, 56–64. Toronto: Canadian Scholars Press, 2007.

Hallaq, Wael. *Sharīʿa: Theory, Practice, Transformations.* Cambridge: Cambridge University Press, 2009.

Hamel, Chouki El. "Muslim Diaspora in Western Europe: The Islamic Headscarf (Hijab), the Media and Muslims' Integration in France." *Citizenship Studies* 6, no. 3 (2002): 293–308.

Hamid, Sadek. "British Muslim Young People: Facts, Features and Religious Trends." *Religion, State and Society* 39, no. 2–3 (2011): 247–61.

———. "Mapping Youth Work with Muslims in Britain." In *Youth Work and Islam: A Leap of Faith for Young People,* edited by Brian Belton and Sadek Hamid, 83–97. Rotterdam: Sense Publishers, 2011.

Hamnett, Chris. "Gentrification and the Middle-Class Remaking of Inner London, 1961–2001." *Urban Studies* 40, no. 12 (2003): 2401–26.

Harding, Susan. "Representing Fundamentalism: The Problem of the Repugnant Cultural Other." *Social Research* 58, no. 2 (1991): 373–93.

Harris, Emily. "Two Mosques, Two Different Reactions in Germany." *NPR,* October 11, 2007. https://www.npr.org/templates/story/story.php?storyId=15043704.

Harvey, Richard. *Luther and the Jews: Putting Right the Lies.* Eugene: Wipf and Stock Publishers, 2017.

Hasan, Rakibull. "Rising Extremism in Bangladesh: A Voyage towards Uncertainty." *Journal of South Asian Studies* 3, no. 2 (2015): 143–53.

Haug, Sonja, Stephanie Mussig, and Anja Stichs. *Muslim Life in Germany: A Study Conducted on Behalf of the German Conference on Islam.* Federal Office for Migration and Refugees, 2006. http://www.npdata.be/Data/Godsdienst/Duitsland/fb6-muslimisches-leben-englisch.pdf.

Heller, Michael. "Remains of the Diaspora: A Personal Meditation." In *Radical Poetics and Secular Jewish Culture,* edited by Stephen Miller, Daniel Morris, and Charles Bernstein, 170–83. Tuscaloosa: University of Alabama Press, 2010.

Helvacioglu, Banu. "Melancholy and Hüzün in Orhan Pamuk's Istanbul." *Mosaic: A Journal for the Interdisciplinary Study of Literature* 46, no. 2 (2013): 163–78.

Hendrick, Joshua. *Gülen: The Ambiguous Politics of Market Islam in Turkey and the World.* New York: NYU Press, 2013.

Hermon-Belot, Rita. "French Laïcité and Religious Pluralism." Paper presented at the Yale Religion & Politics Colloquium, New Haven, February 14, 2017.

Higginbotham, Michael. *Ghosts of Jim Crow: Ending Racism in Post-racial America.* New York: NYU Press, 2013.

Hirschkind, Charles. "The Contemporary Afterlife of Moorish Spain." In *Islam and Public Controversy in Europe,* edited by Nilüfer Göle, 227–40. Surrey: Ashgate Publishing, 2014.

Hockenos, Paul. "Erdoğan's International Network of Muslim Cleric Spies." *Foreign Policy,* March 27, 2017.

Hoffman, Michael, and Amaney Jamal. "Religion in the Arab Spring: Between Two Competing Narratives." *Journal of Politics* 76, no. 3 (2014): 593–606.

Holston, James. "The Civility of Inegalitarian Citizenships." In *The Fundamentalist City?: Religiosity and the Remaking of Urban Space,* edited by Nezar AlSayyad and Mejgan Massoumi, 51–71. Abingdon: Taylor and Francis, 2010.

Howe, Nicolas. *Landscapes of the Secular: Law, Religion, and American Sacred Space*. Chicago: University of Chicago Press, 2016.

Howells, Richard. "Ernst Bloch and Utopian Critical Theory." In *A Critical Theory of Creativity: Utopia, Aesthetics, Atheism and Design*, edited by Richard Howells, 29–43. London: Palgrave Macmillan, 2015.

Hubbard, Phil. "Hipsters on Our High Streets: Consuming the Gentrification Frontier." *Sociological Research Online* 21, no. 3 (2016): 106–11.

Huff, Toby. "Rethinking Islam and Fundamentalism." *Sociological Forum* 10, no. 3 (1995): 501–18.

Huggler, Justin. "Germany's Far-Right AfD Party 'Has More Public Support than Ever.'" *Telegraph*, May 5, 2016. https://www.telegraph.co.uk/news/2016/05/05/germanys-far-right-afd-party-has-more-public-support-than-ever/.

Huntington, Samuel. "The Clash of Civilizations?" *Foreign Affairs* 72, no. 3 (1993): 22–49.

Husain, Zohair. "Maulana Sayyid Abul A'la Maududi: An Appraisal of His Thought and Political Influence." *South Asia: Journal of South Asian Studies* 9, no. 1 (1986): 61–81.

Hutcheon, Pat. "Is There a Dark Side to Multiculturalism?" *Humanist Perspectives* 201 (2017): 18–21.

Integration fördern, Radikalisierung erkennen. European Foundation for Democracy, 2017. http://europeandemocracy.eu/wp-content/uploads/2017/04/Handreichung-fuer-Lehrkraefte.pdf.

Israel Ministry of Foreign Affairs. "King Solomon-s Seal." 1999. https://mfa.gov.il/mfa/mfa-archive/1999/pages/king%20solomon-s%20seal.aspx.

Ivic, Sanja. *Paul Ricoeur's Idea of Reference: The Truth as Non-reference*. Leiden: Brill, 2018.

Izutsu, Toshihiko. *Ethico-religious Concepts in the Qur'an*. Montreal: McGill-Queen's University Press, 2002.

Jacobs, Jack. *The Frankfurt School, Jewish Lives, and Antisemitism*. Cambridge: Cambridge University Press, 2015.

Jacobsen, Christine. *Islamic Traditions and Muslim Youth in Norway*. Leiden: Brill, 2017.

Jeffries, Stuart. *Grand Hotel Abyss*. London: Verso, 2017.

"Jewish Council Says Anti-Semitism in Germany Is Increasing." *Deutsche Welle*, July 23, 2017. https://www.dw.com/en/jewish-council-says-anti-semitism-in-germany-is-increasing/a-39805727.

Jodhka, Surinder. "Ascriptive Hierarchies: Caste and Its Reproduction in Contemporary India." *Current Sociology* 64, no. 2 (2016): 1–16.

———. *Caste in Contemporary India*. New Delhi: Routledge, 2015.

Johnston, Philip. "Adopt Our Values or Stay Away, Says Blair." *Telegraph*, December 9, 2006. https://www.telegraph.co.uk/news/uknews/1536408/Adopt-our-values-or-stay-away-says-Blair.html.

Jonas, Hans. *The Imperative of Responsibility: In Search of an Ethics of the Technological Age*. Chicago: University of Chicago Press, 1984.

———. "Responsibility Today: The Ethics of an Endangered Future." *Social Research* 43, no. 1 (1976): 77–97.

Jones, Nicky, and Kerstin Braun. "Secularism and State Neutrality: The Headscarf in French and German Public Schools." *Australian Journal of Human Rights* 23, no. 1 (2017): 61–89.

Jonker, Gerdien. "The Mevlana Mosque in Berlin-Kreuzberg: An Unsolved Conflict." *Journal of Ethnic and Migration Studies* 31, no. 6 (2005): 1067–81.

Jouili, Jeanette. *Pious Practice and Secular Constraints: Women in the Islamic Revival in Europe*. Stanford: Stanford University Press, 2015.

Judaken, Jonathan. "Édouard Drumont." In *Antisemitism: A Historical Encyclopedia of Prejudice and Persecution*, vol. 1, edited by Richard Levy, 191–92. Santa Barbara: ABC-CLIO, 2005.

Jüdisches Museum Berlin. *Cherchez la femme*. https://www.jmberlin.de/en/exhibition-cherchez -la-femme.

———. *Snip It: Stances on Ritual Circumcision*. https://www.jmberlin.de/en/exhibition-snip-it.

———. *Welcome to Jerusalem*. https://www.jmberlin.de/en/exhibition-welcome-to-jerusalem.

Juhnke, Sebastian. "The Allure of Diversity, Creativity and Space: Gentrification and Multi-culture in London and Berlin." RC21 Conference, University of Urbino Carlo Bo: Italy, August 27–29, 2015.

Jung, Elmar. "Stille Gebete zu Allah." *Süddeutsche Zeitung*, May 17, 2010. https://www.sued deutsche.de/politik/islam-besuch-in-einer-moschee-stille-gebete-zu-allah-1.368039.

Jussem-Wilson, Nelly. "Bernard Lazare's Jewish Journey: From Being an Israelite to Being a Jew." *Jewish Social Studies* 26, no. 3 (1964): 146–68.

Kaas, Leo, and Christian Manger. "Ethnic Discrimination in Germany's Labour Market: A Field Experiment." *German Economic Review* 13, no. 1 (2012): 1–20.

Kam, Hureyre. "Das Böse als ein Gottesbeweis: Die Theodizee al-Māturīdīs im Lichte seiner Epistemologie, Kosmologie und Ontologie." Dissertation, University of Frankfurt, 2018.

Kamali, Mohammad Hashim. *The Middle Path of Moderation in Islam: The Qur'anic Principle of Wasatiyyah*. Oxford: Oxford University Press, 2019.

Kaplan, Lawrence. "Suffering and Joy in the Thought of Hermann Cohen." *Modern Judaism* 21, no. 1 (2001): 15–22.

Kastoryano, Riva. "Religion and Incorporation: Islam in France and Germany." *International Migration Review* 38, no. 3 (2004): 1234–55.

Kaufmann, Eric. "It's NOT the Economy, Stupid: Brexit as a Story of Personal Values." *LSE*, July 7, 2016. https://blogs.lse.ac.uk/politicsandpolicy/personal-values-brexit-vote/.

Kershen, Anne. *London the Promised Land Revisited: The Changing Face of the London Migrant Landscape in the Early 21st Century*. Abingdon: Routledge, 2015.

Khadduri, Majid. *The Islamic Conception of Justice*. Baltimore: Johns Hopkins University Press, 1984.

Khosravi, Shahram. "White Masks/Muslim Names: Immigrants and Name-Changing in Sweden." *Race & Class* 53, no. 3 (2012): 65–80.

Kibria, Nazli. "The 'New Islam' and Bangladeshi Youth in Britain and the US." *Ethnic and Racial Studies* 31, no. 2 (2008): 243–66.

Knowles, Elizabeth. "Pariah." In *The Oxford Dictionary of Phrase and Fable*. 2nd ed. Edited by Elizabeth Knowles. Oxford: Oxford University Press, 2005 (on-line ed. 2006). https:// www.oxfordreference.com/view/10.1093/acref/9780198609810.001.0001/acref-978019 8609810-e-5230?rskey=B0mr94&result=5220.

Kocan, Gurcan, and Ahmet Oncu. "Citizen Alevi in Turkey: Beyond Confirmation and Denial." *Journal of Historical Sociology* 17, no. 4 (2004): 464–89.

Koenig, Matthias, Mieke Maliepaard, and Ayse Güveli. "Religion and New Immigrants' Labor Market Entry in Western Europe." *Ethnicities* 16, no. 2 (2016): 213–35.

Kofman, Eleonore, and Elizabeth Lebas. "Lost in Transposition: Time, Space and the City." In Henri Lefebvre, *Writings on Cities*, edited by Eleonore Kofman and Elizabeth Lebas, 3–60. Cambridge, MA: Wiley-Blackwell, 1996.

Koopmans, Ruud. "Germany and Its Immigrants: An Ambivalent Relationship." *Journal of Ethnic and Migration Studies* 25, no. 4 (1999): 627–47.

Korteweg, Anna, and Gökçe Yurdakul. *The Headscarf Debates: Conflicts of National Belonging*. Stanford: Stanford University Press, 2014.

Kötter, Kirsten. "Şehitlik Mosque Project," n.d. http://www.kunstgespraech.de/sehitlik.html.

Kouwer, Benjamin. *Colors and Their Character: A Psychological Study*. Dordrecht: Springer, 1949.

Kuppinger, Petra. "One Mosque and the Negotiation of German Islam." *Culture and Religion* 15, no. 3 (2014): 313–33.

Kus, Basak. "Neoliberalism, Institutional Change and the Welfare State: The Case of Britain and France." *International Journal of Comparative Sociology* 47, no. 6 (2008): 488–525.

Lacorne, Denis. *The Limits of Tolerance: Enlightenment Values and Religious Fanaticism*. Translated by C. Jon Delogu and Robin Emlein. New York: Columbia University Press, 2007.

Laing, Olivia. *The Lonely City*. New York: Picador, 2016.

Lamont, Michèle. *The Dignity of Working Men: Morality and the Boundaries of Race, Class, and Immigration*. Cambridge, MA: Harvard University Press, 2009.

Landler, Mark. "In Munich, Provocation in a Symbol of Foreign Faith." *New York Times*, December 8, 2006. https://www.nytimes.com/2006/12/08/world/europe/08mosque.html.

Landman, Nico, and Wendy Wessels. "The Visibility of Mosques in Dutch Towns." *Journal of Ethnic and Migration Studies* 31, no. 8 (2006): 1125–40.

Langer, Ármin. *Ein Jude in Neukölln: Mein Weg zum Miteinander der Religionen*. Berlin: Aufbau Verlag, 2016.

———. "Muslime sind die neuen Juden." *Der Tagesspiegel*, September 9, 2014. https://www.tagesspiegel.de/politik/rassismus-und-antisemitismus-in-deutschland-muslime-sind-die-neuen-juden/10669820.html.

Laqueur, Walter. *Reflections of a Veteran Pessimist: Contemplating Modern Europe, Russia, and Jewish History*. Abingdon: Routledge, 2017.

Laraib, Niyaz, and Sidla Nasir. *The Pakistani Diaspora in UK: Evolution, Integration and Challenges*. CIMRAD Working Paper, no. 01–18 (2018). http://www.gids.org.pk/wp-content/uploads/2019/10/CIMRAD_WP-01_18.pdf.

Latour, Bruno. *We Have Never Been Modern*. Translated by Catherine Porter. Cambridge, MA: Harvard University Press, 1993.

Laurence, Jonathan. *The Emancipation of Europe's Muslims*. Princeton: Princeton University Press, 2012.

Lefebvre, Henri. *Qu'est-que penser*. Paris: Publisud, 1985.

———. *Writings on Cities*. Edited by Eleonore Kofman and Elizabeth Lebas. Cambridge, MA: Wiley-Blackwell, 1996.

Leggewie, Claus, Angela Joost, and Stefan Rech. *Der Weg zur Moschee: Eine Handreichung für die Praxis.* Bad Homburg: Herbert-Quandt-Stiftung, 2009. http://www.gbv.de/dms /ilmenau/toc/35061296X.PDF.

Lentin, Alana, and Gavan Titley. *The Crises of Multiculturalism: Racism in a Neoliberal Age.* London: Zed Books, 2011.

Leo Baeck Institute. *"We Have Wandered Together a Long, Long Way": The Hans and Eleonore Jonas Collection.* Accessed March 7, 2020. https://www.lbi.org/news/we-have -wandered-together-a-long-long-way-the-hans-and-eleonore-jonas-collection/.

Levi, Primo. *Survival in Auschwitz.* New York: Simon and Schuster, 1996.

Levitas, Ruth. "Educated Hope: Ernst Bloch on Abstract and Concrete Utopia." *Utopian Studies* 1, no. 2 (1990): 13–26.

Liberatore, Giulia. *Somali, Muslim, British: Striving in Securitized Britain.* London: Blooms- bury Publishing, 2017.

"London Terror Attack: What We Know So Far." *Guardian,* June 5, 2017. https://www.the guardian.com/uk-news/2017/jun/04/london-attacks-what-we-know-so-far-london-bridge -borough-market-vauxhall.

Lowney, Chris. *A Vanished World: Muslims, Christians, and Jews in Medieval Spain.* Oxford: Oxford University Press, 2006.

Lozowick, Yaacov. *Hitler's Bureaucrats: The Nazi Security Police and the Banality of Evil.* London: Continuum, 2005.

Luciak, Mikael. "Documenting Discrimination and Integration in 15 Member States of the European Union." Luxembourg: Office for Official Publications of the European Com- munities, 2004.

Luther, Martin. *Vom Schem Hamphoras, und vom Geschlecht Christi: Matthei am i. Capitel.* Wittemberg: Rhaw, 1543.

Mahlmann, Matthias. "Religious Symbolism and the Resilience of Liberal Constitutionalism: On the Federal German Constitutional Court's Second Head Scarf Decision." *German Law Journal* 16, no. 4 (2015): 887–900.

Mahmood, Saba. "Feminist Theory, Embodiment, and the Docile Agent: Some Reflections on the Egyptian Islamic Revival." *Cultural Anthropology* 16, no. 2 (2001): 202–36.

———. *Politics of Piety: The Islamic Revival and the Feminist Subject.* Princeton: Princeton University Press, 2008.

———. "Religious Reason and Secular Affect: An Incommensurable Divide?" *Critical Inquiry* 35, no. 4 (2009): 836–62.

Malkiel, Yakov. "Hispano-Arabic Marrano and Its Hispano-Latin Homophone." *Journal of the American Oriental Society* 68, no. 4 (1948): 175–84.

Mamdani, Mahmood. "Good Muslim, Bad Muslim: A Political Perspective on Culture and Terrorism." *American Anthropologist* 104, no. 3 (2002): 766–75.

Mandel, Ruth. *Cosmopolitan Anxieties.* Durham: Duke University Press, 2008.

Marcus, Greil. "Preface." In *One-Way Street,* by Walter Benjamin, ix–xxv. Cambridge, MA: Harvard University Press, 2016.

Mardin, Serif. *Religion and Social Change in Modern Turkey: The Case of Bediuzzaman Said Nursi.* Albany: SUNY Press, 1989.

"Marine Le Pen: Muslims in France 'like Nazi Occupation.'" *Telegraph*, December 12, 2010. https://www.telegraph.co.uk/news/worldnews/europe/france/8197895/Marine-Le-Pen-Muslims-in-France-like-Nazi-occupation.html.

Marotta, Vince. "Zygmunt Bauman: Order, Strangerhood and Freedom." *Thesis Eleven* 71, no. 1 (2002): 36–54.

Martin, Philip. "Germany's Guestworkers." *Challenge* 24, no. 3 (1981): 34–42.

Martínez, María Elena. *Genealogical Fictions: Limpieza de Sangre, Religion, and Gender in Colonial Mexico*. Stanford: Stanford University Press, 2008.

Maussen, Marcel. "Constructing Mosques: The Governance of Islam in France and the Netherlands." Ph.D. thesis, Amsterdam Institute for Social Science Research, 2009. https://dare.uva.nl/search?identifier=23a73a23-c3f0-4b47-ab62-9e06b5e608f5.

Mavrommatis, George. "The New 'Creative' Brick Lane: A Narrative Study of Local Multicultural Encounters." *Ethnicities* 6, no. 4 (2006): 498–517.

Maxwell, Rahsaan. *Ethnic Minority Migrants in Britain and France: Integration Trade-Offs*. Cambridge: Cambridge University Press, 2012.

McClean, David. "State and Church in the United Kingdom." In *State and Church in the European Union*, edited by Gerhard Robbers, 657–76. Baden-Baden: Nomos Verlag, 2019.

McGraw, Peter, and Joel Warner. "The Danish Cartoon Crisis of 2005 and 2006: Ten Things You Didn't Know about the Original Muhammad Controversy." *Huffington Post*, September 25, 2012. https://www.huffpost.com/entry/muhammad-cartoons_b_1907545.

Meer, Nasar. *Key Concepts in Race and Ethnicity*. London: Sage, 2014.

———. "The Politics of Voluntary and Involuntary Identities: Are Muslims in Britain an Ethnic, Racial or Religious Minority?" *Patterns of Prejudice* 42, no. 1 (2008): 61–81.

———. "Racialization and Religion: Race, Culture and Difference in the Study of Antisemitism and Islamophobia." *Ethnic and Racial Studies* 36, no. 3 (2013): 385–98.

———. *Racialization and Religion: Race, Culture and Difference in the Study of Antisemitism and Islamophobia*. Abingdon: Routledge, 2015.

———. "Semantics, Scales and Solidarities in the Study of Antisemitism and Islamophobia." *Ethnic and Racial Studies* 36, no. 3 (2013): 500–515.

Meer, Nasar, and Tariq Modood. "Refutations of Racism in the 'Muslim Question.'" *Patterns of Prejudice* 43, no. 3–4 (2009): 335–54.

Meet2respect. "Startseite." *Meet2respect*. Accessed April 26, 2020. https://meet2respect.de/.

Merleau-Ponty, Maurice. *The Merleau-Ponty Aesthetics Reader: Philosophy and Painting*. Translated and edited by Michael Smith. Evanston: Northwestern University Press, 1993.

Mescher, Heidi. "Policing and Muslim Communities in Germany." In *Social Cohesion, Securitization and Counter-terrorism*, edited by Charles Husband, 100–135. Helsinki: Helsinki Collegium for Advanced Study, 2012.

Metcalf, Barbara. "'Traditionalist' Islamic Activism: Deoband, Tablighis, and Talibs." *Isim Paper* (2002): 1–24.

Miles, Robert. 1989. *Racism*. London: Routledge.

Miles, Robert, and Paula Cleary. "Britain: Post-colonial Migration Context." In *Europe, a New Immigration Continent: Policies and Politics in Comparative Perspective*, edited by Dietrich Thranhardt. Münster: Lit Verlag, 1996.

Millanes, José Muñoz. "The City as Palimpsest." *CiberLetras* 3 (2000). http://www.lehman.cuny.edu/ciberletras/v03/Munoz.html.

Milton, John. *Paradise Lost*. Edited by John Leonard. London: Penguin Classics, 2003.

Minnich, Elizabeth. "Thinking with Hannah Arendt: An Introduction." *International Journal of Philosophical Studies* 10, no. 2 (2002): 123–30.

Miyazaki, Hirokazu. *The Method of Hope: Anthropology, Philosophy, and Fijian Knowledge*. Stanford: Stanford University Press, 2004.

Modood, Tariq. *Multiculturalism: A Civic Idea*. Cambridge: Polity Press, 2007.

———. "Muslims and the Politics of Difference." *Political Quarterly* 74, no. s1 (2003): 110–15.

———. "Political Blackness and British Asians." *Sociology* 28, no. 4 (1994): 859–76.

Momigliano, Arnaldo. "A Note on Max Weber's Definition of Judaism as a Pariah-Religion." *History and Theory* 19, no. 3 (1980): 313–18.

Moosa, Ebrahim. *Ghazali and the Poetics of Imagination*. Chapel Hill: University of North Carolina Press, 2006.

———. "Reconciliation in Islamic Thought and Practice." Presented at the Religion and Reconciliation in Global Perspective, Butler University Desmond Tutu Center for Peace, Reconciliation, and Global Justice, January 27, 2015.

Moosavi, Leon. "The Imagining of Muslim Converts in Britain by Themselves and Others." In *Debating Islam: Negotiating Religion, Europe, and the Self*, edited by Samuel Behloul, Susanne Leuenberger, and Andreas Tunger-Zanetti, 181–202. Bielefeld: Transcript Verlag, 2013.

Morrison, Toni. "Nobel Lecture." *Nobel Prize*, December 7, 1993. https://www.nobelprize.org/prizes/literature/1993/morrison/lecture/.

Mouritsen, Per, Daniel Faas, Nasar Meer, and Nynke de Witte. "Leitkultur Debates as Civic Integration in North-Western Europe: The Nationalism of 'Values' and 'Good Citizenship.'" *Ethnicities* 19, no. 4 (2019): 632–53.

"MP Jo Cox 'Murdered for Political Cause.'" *BBC News*, November 14, 2016. https://www.bbc.com/news/uk-37978582.

Murphy, Elizabeth, and Robert Dingwall. "The Ethics of Ethnography." In *Handbook of Ethnography*, edited by Paul Atkinson, Amanda Coffey, Sara Delamont, John Lofland, and Lyn Lofland, 339–51. London: SAGE Publications, 2002.

Nasr, Seyyed Vali Reza. *Mawdudi and the Making of Islamic Revivalism*. Oxford: Oxford University Press, 1996.

Nava, Mica. *Visceral Cosmopolitanism: Gender, Culture and the Normalisation of Difference*. New York: Berg, 2007.

Navarro, Josep Maria, and Máximo de Santos. *El Islam en las aulas*. Barcelona: Icaria, 1997.

Nilsson, Per-Erik. *Open Source Jihad: Problematizing the Academic Discourse on Islamic Terrorism in Contemporary Europe*. Cambridge: Cambridge University Press, 2018.

Nirenberg, David. *Neighboring Faiths: Christianity, Islam, and Judaism in the Middle Ages and Today*. Chicago: University of Chicago Press, 2016.

Noack, Rick. "Germany Said It Took in More than 1 Million Refugees Last Year. But It Didn't." *Washington Post*, September 30, 2016. https://www.washingtonpost.com/news/worldviews/wp/2016/09/30/germany-said-it-took-in-more-than-1-million-refugees-last-year-but-it-didnt/.

Norton, Anne. *On the Muslim Question*. Princeton: Princeton University Press, 2013.

Novy, Johannes. "The Selling (Out) of Berlin and the De- and Re-politicization of Urban Tourism in Europe's 'Capital of Cool.'" In *Protest and Resistance in the Tourist City*, edited by Claire Colomb and Johannes Novy, 52–72. Abingdon: Routledge, 2016.

Oakes, Timothy, and Patricia Price, eds. *The Cultural Geography Reader*. Abingdon: Routledge, 2008.

Open Society Foundations. "Muslims in Europe: A Report on 11 EU Cities." *Open Society Foundations*, December 2009. https://www.opensocietyfoundations.org/publications /muslims-europe-report-11-eu-cities.

———. "What Is Islamophobia?" *Open Society Foundations*, April 2015. https://www.open societyfoundations.org/explainers/islamophobia-europe.

Opotow, Susan. "Absence and Presence: Interpreting Moral Exclusion in the Jewish Museum Berlin." In *Justice and Conflicts: Theoretical and Empirical Contributions*, edited by Elisabeth Kals and Jürgen Maes, 53–74. Dordrecht: Springer, 2011.

Options UK. *Understanding East London's Somali Communities*. August 2010. http://karin -ha.org.uk/wp-content/uploads/2013/01/Understanding-East-Londons-Somali-Commu nities.pdf.

Osborne, Peter, and Matthew Charles. "Walter Benjamin." In *The Stanford Encyclopedia of Philosophy Archive*, edited by Edward N. Zalta. https://plato.stanford.edu/archives/win 2019/entries/benjamin/.

Ostergaard-Nielsen, Eva. *Transnational Politics: The Case of Turks and Kurds in Germany*. London: Routledge, 2003.

O'Toole, Therese, Nasar Meer, Daniel Nilsson DeHanas, Stephen Jones, and Tariq Modood. "Governing through Prevent? Regulation and Contested Practice in State–Muslim Engagement." *Sociology* 50, no. 1 (2016): 160–77.

Oxford Reference. "Kulturkampf." Accessed June 5, 2020. https://www.oxfordreference.com /view/10.1093/oi/authority.20110810105233755.

Oz, Amos, and Fania Oz-Salzberger. *Jews and Words*. New Haven: Yale University Press, 2012.

Öztürk, Ahmet Erdi. "Turkey's Diyanet under AKP Rule: From Protector to Imposer of State Ideology?" *Southeast European and Black Sea Studies* 16, no. 4 (2016): 619–35.

Özyürek, Esra. *Being German, Becoming Muslim: Race, Religion, and Conversion in the New Europe*. Princeton: Princeton University Press, 2014.

———. "Creating Parallel Communities of Perpetrators: Muslim-Only Holocaust Education and Anti-Semitism Prevention Programs in Germany." Center for Jewish Studies, University of Illinois, March 2013.

———. "The Politics of Cultural Unification, Secularism, and the Place of Islam in the New Europe." *American Ethnologist* 32, no. 4 (2005): 509–12.

———. "Rethinking Empathy: Emotions Triggered by the Holocaust among the Muslim-Minority in Germany." *Anthropological Theory* 18, no. 4 (2018): 456–77.

Padamsee, Alex. *Representations of Indian Muslims in British Colonial Discourse*. New York: Springer, 2005.

Paetzold, Heinz. "Walter Benjamin and the Urban Labyrinth." *Filozofski Vestnik* 22, no. 2 (2001): 111–26.

Pamuk, Orhan. *Istanbul: Memories and the City*. New York: Alfred A. Knopf, 2004.

Paxton, Robert, and Julie Hessler. *Europe in the Twentieth Century*. Boston: Cengage Learning, 2011.

Pedziwiatr, Konrad. "Islam and Empowerment of the New Religious Brokers in Europe." In *Dangerous Others, Insecure Societies: Fear and Social Division*, edited by Michaelis Lianos, 39–50. Abingdon: Routledge, 2013.

Peek, Lori. "Becoming Muslim: The Development of a Religious Identity." *Sociology of Religion* 66, no. 3 (2005): 215–42.

Peter, Frank. "Individualization and Religious Authority in Western European Islam." *Islam and Christian-Muslim Relations* 17, no. 1 (2006): 105–18.

Peter, Frank, and Elena Arigita. "Introduction: Authorizing Islam in Europe." *Muslim World* 96, no. 4 (2006): 537–42.

Peucker, Mario, and Shahram Akbarzadeh. *Muslim Active Citizenship in the West*. Abingdon: Routledge, 2014.

Pew Research Center. "The Growth of Germany's Muslim Population." November 29, 2017. https://www.pewforum.org/essay/the-growth-of-germanys-muslim-population/.

———. "Unfavorable Views of Jews and Muslims on the Increase in Europe." September 17, 2008. https://www.pewresearch.org/global/2008/09/17/unfavorable-views-of-jews-and-muslims-on-the-increase-in-europe/.

Pierné, Guillaume. "Hiring Discrimination Based on National Origin and Religious Closeness: Results from a Field Experiment in the Paris Area." *IZA Journal of Labor Economics* 2, no. 1 (2013): 2–4.

Pipes, Daniel. *The Rushdie Affair: The Novel, the Ayatollah and the West*. Abingdon: Routledge, 2017.

"Polizeigewerkschaft bestätigt Sympathien für AfD." *Frankfurter Allgemeine Zeitung*, June 24, 2019. https://www.faz.net/1.6251074.

Pollock, Benjamin. "Every State Becomes a Theocracy: Hermann Cohen on the Israelites under Divine Rule." *Jewish Studies Quarterly* 25, no. 2 (2018): 1–19.

Poma, Andrew. "Hermann Cohen: Judaism and Critical Idealism," In *The Cambridge Companion to Modern Jewish Philosophy*, edited by Michael Morgan and Peter Gordon, 80–101. Cambridge: Cambridge University Press, 2007.

Poole, Elizabeth. "Constructing 'British Values' within a Radicalisation Narrative." *Journalism Studies* 19, no. 3 (2018): 376–91.

Posener, Alan. "Das Jüdische Museum in Berlin braucht eine kulturelle Revolution." *Die Welt*, June 6, 2019. https://www.welt.de/kultur/article195347713/Das-Juedische-Museum-in-Berlin-braucht-eine-kulturelle-Revolution.html.

Poushter, Jacob. "European Opinions of the Refugee Crisis in 5 Charts." *Pew Research Center* (blog), September 16, 2016. http://www.pewresearch.org/fact-tank/2016/09/16/european-opinions-of-the-refugee-crisis-in-5-charts/.

Procyshyn, Alexei. "The Origins of Walter Benjamin's Concept of Philosophical Critique." *Metaphilosophy* 44, no. 5 (2013): 655–81.

Qadeer, Mohammad. *Pakistan: Social and Cultural Transformations in a Muslim Nation*. Abingdon: Routledge, 2006.

The Qur'an. Translated by M. A. S. Abdel Haleem. Oxford: Oxford University Press, 2010.

Rabinbach, Anson. *In the Shadow of Catastrophe: German Intellectuals between Apocalypse and Enlightenment.* Berkeley: University of California Press, 1997.

Ramadan, Tariq. *To Be a European Muslim: A Study of Islamic Sources in the European Context.* Leicester: Islamic Foundation, 1999.

Rana, Junaid. "The Story of Islamophobia." *Souls* 9, no. 2 (2007): 148–61.

Ravid, Benjamin. "From Yellow to Red: On the Distinguishing Head-Covering of the Jews of Venice." *Jewish History* 6, no. 1/2 (1992): 179–210.

———. "Venice and Its Minorities." Centro Primo Levi, February 14, 2017. https://primolevi center.org/printed-matter/venice-and-its-minorities/.

Ray, Mohit Kumar. *V. S. Naipaul: Critical Essays.* New Delhi: Atlantic Publishers, 2002.

Reetz, Dietrich. "The Deoband Universe: What Makes a Transcultural and Transnational Educational Movement of Islam?" *Comparative Studies of South Asia, Africa and the Middle East* 27, no. 1 (2007): 139–59.

Ricoeur, Paul. *Freud and Philosophy: An Essay on Interpretation.* Translated by Denis Savage. New Haven: Yale University Press, 1977.

———. *Oneself as Another.* Chicago: University of Chicago Press, 1994.

Rogowski, Christian. "'To Be Continued': History in Wim Wenders's *Wings of Desire* and Thomas Brasch's 'Domino.'" *German Studies Review* 15, no. 3 (1992): 547–63.

Rogozen-Soltar, Mikaela. "Managing Muslim Visibility: Conversion, Immigration, and Spanish Imaginaries of Islam." *American Anthropologist* 114, no. 4 (2012): 611–23.

———. *Spain Unmoored: Migration, Conversion, and the Politics of Islam.* Bloomington: Indiana University Press, 2017.

Rosaldo, Renato. "Introduction." In *Cultural Citizenship in Island Southeast Asia: Nation and Belonging in the Hinterlands,* edited by Renato Rosaldo, 1–15. Berkeley: University of California Press, 2003.

Rosen, Lawrence. *The Justice of Islam: Comparative Perspectives on Islamic Law and Society.* Oxford: Oxford University Press, 2000.

Rosenberg, Yair. "Berlin Protestors Chant: 'Jew, Jew, Cowardly Pig, Come On Out and Fight.'" *Tablet,* July 22, 2014. https://www.tabletmag.com/sections/news/articles/berlin-protesters -chant-jew-jew-cowardly-pig-come-on-out-and-fight.

Rosenow-Williams, Kerstin. *Organizing Muslims and Integrating Islam in Germany: New Developments in the 21st Century.* Leiden: Brill, 2012.

Roth, Cecil. *A History of the Marranos.* Philadelphia: Jewish Publication Society of America, 1932.

Roy, Anindyo. *Civility and Empire: Literature and Culture in British India, 1822–1922.* Abingdon: Routledge, 2005.

Roy, Olivier. *Globalized Islam: The Search for a New Ummah.* New York: Columbia University Press, 2004.

Rubin, Alissa. "French School Deems Teenager's Skirt an Illegal Display of Religion." *New York Times,* April 29, 2015. https://www.nytimes.com/2015/04/30/world/europe/french -school-teenagers-skirt-illegal-display-religion.html.

Ruiz, Ana. *Medina Mayrit: The Origins of Madrid.* New York: Algora Publishing, 2012.

Runciman, Walter. "Towards a Theory of Social Stratification." In *The Social Analysis of Class Structure*, edited by Frank Parkin, 55–81. London: Tavistock Publications, 1974.

Runnymede Trust. *Islamophobia: A Challenge for Us All*. London: Runnymede Trust, 1997. https://www.runnymedetrust.org/companies/17/74/Islamophobia-A-Challenge-for-Us -All.html.

Sa'ari, Che Zarrina. "An Analytical Study of Rise and Development of Sufism," *Jurnal Usuluddin* 10 (1999): 21–42.

Safi, Omid. *Progressive Muslims: On Justice, Gender, and Pluralism*. Oxford: Oneworld Publications, 2003.

———. "What Is Progressive Islam?" *ISIM Newsletter* 13, no. 1 (2003): 48–49.

Said, Edward. *Culture and Imperialism*. New York: Knopf, 2012.

———. *Orientalism*. New York: Vintage, 1979.

Salvatore, Armando. *The Public Sphere: Liberal Modernity, Catholicism, Islam*. New York: Springer, 2007.

———. *The Sociology of Islam: Knowledge, Power and Civility*. Malden: Wiley, 2016.

Samuelson, Kate. "London Bridge Attack: Transcript of Theresa May's Speech." *Time*, June 4, 2017. https://time.com/4804640/london-attack-theresa-may-speech-transcript -full/.

Sarrazin, Thilo. *Deutschland schafft sich ab*. Munich: Deutsche Verlags-Anstalt, 2010.

———. *Feindliche Übernahme: Wie der Islam den Fortschritt behindert und die Gesellschaft bedroht*. Munich: Finanzbuch Verlag, 2018.

Sartore, Vernonica. "Armin Langer: A Jew in Neukölln." *Mozaika*, 2017. http://mozaika.es /magazine/en/armin-langer-a-jew-in-neukolln/.

Saunders, Peter. *Social Class and Stratification*. London: Routledge, 2006.

Savelsberg, Joachim, and Ryan King. "Institutionalizing Collective Memories of Hate: Law and Law Enforcement in Germany and the United States." *American Journal of Sociology* 111, no. 2 (2005): 579–616.

Sawyer, Francois. *Popularizing Anti-Semitism in Early Modern Spain and Its Empire: Francisco de Torrejoncillo and the Centinela Contra Judíos (1674)*. Leiden: Brill, 2014.

Sayad, Abdelmalek. "Immigration and 'State Thought.'" In *Selected Studies in International Migration and Immigrant Incorporation*, edited by Marco Martiniello and Jan Rath, 165–80. Amsterdam: Amsterdam University Press, 2010.

———. *La Double Absence: Des Illusions de l'émigré aux Souffrances de l'immigré*. Paris: Le Seuil, 2016.

Sayyid, S. "Introduction: BrAsians: Postcolonial People, Iconic Citizens." In *Postcolonial People: South Asians in Britain*, edited by Nasreen Ali, S. Sayyid, and V. S. Kalra, 1–10. London: C. Hurst & Co., 2006.

Schielke, Samuli. "The Power of God: Four Proposals for an Anthropological Engagement." Programmatic Texts, no. 13. *Leibniz-Zentrum Moderner Orient*, 2019, 1–20. https://d-nb .info/1175974781/34.

Schiffauer, Werner. "Enemies within the Gates: The Debate about the Citizenship of Muslims in Germany." In *Multiculturalism, Muslims and Citizenship: A European Approach*, edited by Tariq Modood, Anna Triandafyllidou, and Ricard Zapata-Barrero, 94–116. Abingdon: Routledge, 2006.

Schmid, Peter. "Hermann Cohen's Theory of Virtue." In *Hermann Cohen's Critical Idealism*, edited by Reinier Munk, 231–57. Dordrecht: Springer, 2006.

Scholem, Gershom. *Walter Benjamin: The Story of a Friendship*. New York: New York Review of Books, 2003.

Schorske, Carl. *Thinking with History: Explorations in the Passage to Modernism*. Princeton: Princeton University Press, 1998.

Schuetze, Christopher. "Amid Rising Anti-Semitism, German Official Advises Jews Against Wearing Skullcaps in Public." *New York Times*, May 26, 2019. https://www.nytimes.com /2019/05/26/world/europe/germany-skullcaps-antisemitism.html.

Scott, Joan Wallach. "Deconstructing Equality-versus-Difference: Or, the Uses of Post-structuralist Theory for Feminism." *Feminist Studies* 14, no. 1 (1988): 33–50.

———. *The Politics of the Veil*. Princeton: Princeton University Press, 2007.

Seekings, Jeremy, and Nicoli Nattrass. *Class, Race, and Inequality in South Africa*. New Haven: Yale University Press, 2005.

Sennett, Richard. *Building and Dwelling: Ethics for the City*. New York: Farrar, Straus and Giroux, 2018.

———. *The Conscience of the Eye: The Design and Social Life of Cities*. New York: W. W. Norton & Company, 1990.

———. *Flesh and Stone: The Body and the City in Western Civilization*. New York: W. W. Norton & Company, 1994.

———. *Interview and Lecture by Richard Sennett*. Video file, 2010. https://www.repository .cam.ac.uk/handle/1810/224458.

———. "The Open City." In *The Post-Urban World: Emergent Transformation of Cities and Regions in the Innovative Global Economy*, edited by Tigran Haas and Hans Westlund, 97–106. Abingdon: Routledge.

———. "The Public Realm." In *The Blackwell City Reader*, edited by Gary Bridge and Sophie Watson, 261–72. Malden, MA: Wiley-Blackwell, 2010.

Şenocak, Zafer. *Gefährliche Verwandtschaft*. München: Babel, 1998.

Shachar, Isaiah. *The Judensau: A Medieval Anti-Jewish Motif and Its History*. London: Warburg Institute, 1974.

Sharp, Hasana. "Why Spinoza Today? Or, 'A Strategy of Anti-Fear.'" *Rethinking Marxism* 17, no. 4 (2005): 591–608.

Shepard, Todd. *The Invention of Decolonization: The Algerian War and the Remaking of France*. Ithaca: Cornell University Press, 2006.

Shepp, Jonah. "Angela Merkel Won Reelection, But Is She Still the Leader of the Free World?" *New York Magazine*, September 25, 2017. https://nymag.com/intelligencer/2017/09/is-angela -merkel-still-the-leader-of-the-free-world.html.

Sherif, Mohamed. *Ghazali's Theory of Virtue*. Albany: SUNY Press, 1975.

Shooman, Yasemin. "Zur Debatte über das Verhältnis von Antisemitismus, Rassismus und Islamfeindlichkeit." In *Antisemitismus und andere Feindseligkeiten: Interaktionen von*

Ressentiments, edited by Katharina Rauschenberger and Werner Konitzer, 125–56. Frankfurt: Campus Verlag, 2015.

Shor, Francis. "Walter Benjamin as Guide: Images in the Modern City." *Jewish Social Studies* 44, no. 1 (1982): 37–46.

Sian, Katy Pal. "Spies, Surveillance and Stakeouts: Monitoring Muslim Moves in British State Schools." *Race Ethnicity and Education* 18, no. 2 (2015): 183–201.

Silverstein, Paul. *Postcolonial France*. London: Pluto Press, 2018.

Simmel, Georg. "The Stranger." Translated by Ramona Mosse. *Baffler*, no. 30 (2016): 176–79.

Simonsen, Kristina, and Bart Bonikowski. "Is Civic Nationalism Necessarily Inclusive? Conceptions of Nationhood and Anti-Muslim Attitudes in Europe." *European Journal of Political Research* 59, no. 1 (2020): 114–36.

Skeat, Walter William. *A Concise Etymological Dictionary of the English Language*. New York: Harper, 1898.

Slooter, Luuk. *The Making of the Banlieue: An Ethnography of Space, Identity and Violence*. Cham: Springer, 2019.

Smale, Alison. "Austria Rejects Far-Right Presidential Candidate Norbert Hofer." *New York Times*, December 4, 2016. https://www.nytimes.com/2016/12/04/world/europe/norbert-hofer-austria-election.html.

Smirnov, Andrey. "Understanding Justice in an Islamic Context: Some Points of Contrast with Western Theories." *Philosophy East and West* 46, no. 3 (1996): 337–50.

Smith, Thomas. "Between Allah and Atatürk: Liberal Islam in Turkey." *International Journal of Human Rights* 9, no. 3 (2005): 307–25.

Smith, Zadie. *NW*. New York: Penguin, 2000.

———. *White Teeth*. New York: Vintage International, 2000.

Soederberg, Susanne. "Governing Stigmatised Space: The Case of the 'Slums' of Berlin-Neukölln." *New Political Economy* 22, no. 5 (2016): 478–95.

Sökefeld, Martin. *Struggling for Recognition: The Alevi Movement in Germany and in Transnational Space*. New York: Berghahn Books, 2008.

Sonnevend, Julia. *Stories without Borders: The Berlin Wall and the Making of a Global Iconic Event*. Oxford: Oxford University Press, 2016.

Soysal, Yasemin. *Limits of Citizenship: Migrants and Postnational Membership in Europe*. Chicago: University of Chicago, 1994.

Spencer, Elaine Glovka. "State Power and Local Interests in Prussian Cities: Police in the Düsseldorf District, 1848–1914." *Central European History* 19, no. 3 (1986): 293–313.

Stanley-Becker, Isaac. "Marine Le Pen Falls Short in Far-Right Bid for the Presidency of France." *Washington Post*, May 7, 2017. https://www.washingtonpost.com/world/europe/marine-le-pen-congratulates-emmanuel-macron-on-his-victory-in-french-presidential-race/2017/05/07/afe9064e-3021-11e7-a335-fa0ae1940305_story.html.

Stevenson, Angus, and Maurice Waite, eds. *Concise Oxford English Dictionary*. Oxford: Oxford University Press, 2011.

Stewart, Frances. "A Global View of Horizontal Inequalities: Inequalities Experienced by Muslims Worldwide." SSRN Scholarly Paper. Rochester: Social Science Research Network, 2009. https://papers.ssrn.com/sol3/papers.cfm?abstract_id=1433779.

Stoler, Ann Laura. "Colonial Aphasia: Race and Disabled Histories in France." *Public Culture* 23, no. 1 (2011): 121–56.

Stowasser, Barbara. "The Turks in Germany: From Sojourners to Citizens." In *Muslims in the West: From Sojourners to Citizens*, edited by Yvonne Haddad, 52–71. Oxford: Oxford University Press, 2002.

Studio Libeskind. "Academy of the Jewish Museum Berlin in the Eric F. Ross Building." Accessed May 22, 2020. https://libeskind.com/work/academy-of-the-jewish-museum-berlin -in-the-eric-f-ross-building/.

Sturge, Georgina. "Briefing Paper CBP-04334: UK Prison Population Statistics." House of Commons Library, 2020. https://commonslibrary.parliament.uk/research-briefings/sn04334/.

"Survey Finds One in Three Germans Supports PEGIDA 'Anti-Islamicization' Marches." *Deutsche Welle*, January 1, 2015. https://www.dw.com/en/survey-finds-one-in-three-germans -supports-pegida-anti-islamization-marches/a-18166667.

Symons, Stephane. *More Than Life: George Simmel and Walter Benjamin on Art*. Evanston, IL: Northwestern University Press, 2017.

Szondi, Peter. "Introduction." In *Berlin Childhood around 1900*, by Walter Benjamin, 1–36. Cambridge, MA: Harvard University Press, 2006.

Taylor, Greg. "Teachers' Religious Headscarves in German Constitutional Law." *Oxford Journal of Law and Religion* 6, no. 1 (2017): 93–111.

TellMAMA. "Press," 2016. https://tellmamauk.org/press-section/.

Tester, Keith. *The Social Thought of Zygmunt Bauman*. London: Palgrave Macmillan, 2004.

Thiel, Thomas. "Der Kurswechsel wird zum Kraftakt." *Frankfurter Allgemeine Zeitung*, December 17, 2019. https://www.faz.net/aktuell/feuilleton/debatten/zur-lage-des-juedischen -museums-berlin-16538869.html.

Thomas, Hugh. *The Norman Conquest: England after William the Conqueror*. Lanham, MD: Rowman & Littlefield, 2008.

Thomas, Paul. "Prevent and Community Cohesion in Britain: The Worst of All Possible Worlds?" In *Counter Radicalisation: Critical Perspectives*, edited by Christopher Baker-Beall, Charlotte Heath-Kelly, and Lee Jarvis, 36–53. Abingdon: Routledge, 2014.

Thompson, Peter. "What Is Concrete about Ernst Bloch's 'Concrete Utopia'?" In *Utopia: Social Theory and Future*, edited by Michael Jacobsen and Keith Tester, 33–46. Abingdon: Routledge, 2012.

Tibi, Bassam. *Europa ohne Identität: Die Krise der multikulturellen Gesellschaft*. Munich: Bertelsmann Verlag, 1998.

Toennies, Ferdinand, Georg Simmel, Ernst Troeltsch, and Max Weber. "Max Weber on Church, Sect, and Mysticism." *Sociological Analysis* 34, no. 2 (1973): 140–49.

Topolski, Anya. "A Genealogy of the 'Judeo-Christian' Signifier: A Tale of Europe's Identity Crisis." In *Is There a Judeo-Christian Tradition? A European Perspective*, edited by Emmanuel Nathan and Anya Topolski, 267–83. Berlin: De Gruyter, 2016.

———. "Good Jew, Bad Jew . . . Good Muslim, Bad Muslim: 'Managing' Europe's Others." *Ethnic and Racial Studies* 41, no. 12 (2018): 2179–96.

———. "The Race-Religion Constellation: A European Contribution to the Critical Philosophy of Race." *Critical Philosophy of Race* 6, no. 1 (2018): 58–81.

Tower Hamlets Council. *Borough Profile: Population*. London, 2018. https://www.towerham
lets.gov.uk/Documents/Borough_statistics/Research-briefings/Population_2_BP2018.pdf.
———. *Borough Profile: Poverty*. London, 2018. https://www.towerhamlets.gov.uk/Documents
/Borough_statistics/Research-briefings/BP2018_3_Poverty.pdf.
———. *Deprivation in Tower Hamlets: Analysis of the 2015 Indices of Deprivation Data*. Lon-
don, 2015. https://www.towerhamlets.gov.uk/Documents/Borough_statistics/Income
_poverty_and_welfare/Indices_of_Deprivation_Low_resolution.pdf.
"Tower Hamlets Election Fraud Mayor Lutfur Rahman Removed from Office." *BBC News*,
April 23, 2015. https://www.bbc.com/news/uk-england-london-32428648.
Traverso, Enzo. *The Jews and Germany: From the "Judeo-German Symbiosis" to the Memory
of Auschwitz*. Lincoln: University of Nebraska Press, 1995.
Trumpener, Ulrich. *Germany and the Ottoman Empire, 1914–1918*. Princeton: Princeton Uni-
versity Press, 1968.
Turnbull-Dugarte, Stuart. "Explaining the End of Spanish Exceptionalism and Electoral Sup-
port for Vox." *Research & Politics* 6, no. 2 (2019): 1–8.
Tweed, Thomas. *Crossing and Dwelling: A Theory of Religion*. Cambridge, MA: Harvard
University Press, 2009.
Uekotter, Frank. *The Greenest Nation? A New History of German Environmentalism*. Cam-
bridge, MA: MIT Press, 2014.
Uhlmann, Stefan. "Der ewige Streit um das Kopftuch." *Der Tagesspiegel*, October 31, 2006.
https://www.tagesspiegel.de/politik/laendersache-der-ewige-streit-um-das-kopftuch
/769128.html.
Valfort, Marie-Anne. *Religious Discrimination in Access to Employment: A Reality*. Paris:
Institut Montaigne, 2015. https://www.institutmontaigne.org/ressources/pdfs/publications
/discriminations-en.pdf#:~:text=RELIGIOUS%20DISCRIMINATION%20IN%20
ACCESS%20TO%20EMPLOYMENT%3A%20A%20REALITY,and%20ethnic%20
identities.%20For%20more%20than%20a%20decade%2C.
Van Bohemen, Samira, and Roy Kemmers. "Secular Intolerance in a Post-Christian Society:
The Case of Islam in the Netherlands." In *Paradoxes of Individualization: Social Control
and Social Conflict in Contemporary Modernity*, edited by Dick Houtman, Stef Aupers,
and William de Koster, 141–55. Surrey: Ashgate, 2011.
Venkatesh, Sudhir, and Eva Rosen. "Herbert J. Gans: An Introduction." *City & Community* 6,
no. 1 (2007): 1–5.
Vermeulen, Floris. "Suspect Communities—Targeting Violent Extremism at the Local Level:
Policies of Engagement in Amsterdam, Berlin, and London." *Terrorism and Political Vio-
lence* 26, no. 2 (2014): 286–306.
Vertovec, Steven. "Multiculturalism, Culturalism and Public Incorporation." *Ethnic and Ra-
cial Studies* 19, no. 1 (1996): 49–69.
Wachtel, Eleanor. "An Interview with Richard Sennett." *Brick*, November 25, 2013. https://
brickmag.com/an-interview-with-richard-sennett/.
Wahid, Omar. "Britain's Jihadi Bride Groomer: Schoolgirl Radicalised in London Mosque
Recruited Her Three Classmates to Join ISIS in Syria." *Daily Mail*, August 1, 2015.

https://www.dailymail.co.uk/news/article-3182561/Britain-s-jihadi-bride-groomer-School
girl-radicalised-London-mosque-recruited-three-classmates-join-ISIS-Syria.html.

Walzer, Michael. *Spheres of Justice: A Defense of Pluralism and Equality*. New York: Basic Books, 2008.

Ware, Rudolph. *The Walking Qur'an*. Chapel Hill: University of North Carolina Press, 2014.

Watt, Paul. " 'It's Not for Us': Regeneration, the 2012 Olympics and the Gentrification of East London." *City* 17, no. 1 (2013): 99–118.

Weber, Max. *Ancient Judaism*. New York: Simon and Schuster, 2010.

———. *From Max Weber: Essays in Sociology*. Oxford: Oxford University Press, 1946.

———. *The Protestant Ethic and the Spirit of Capitalism: And Other Writings*. Translated by Peter Baehr. New York: Penguin Classics, 2002.

Weil, Simone. *The Need for Roots: Prelude to a Declaration of Duties towards Mankind*. London: Routledge, 2003.

Wenders, Wim, dir. *Wings of Desire*. 1987.

Werbner, Pnina. "Theorising Complex Diasporas: Purity and Hybridity in the South Asian Public Sphere in Britain." *Journal of Ethnic and Migration Studies* 30, no. 5 (2004): 895–911.

Widlock, Thomas, and Didier Fassin. "Virtue." In *A Companion to Moral Anthropology*, edited by Didier Fassin, 186–203. Sussex: John Wiley & Sons, 2012.

Wiese, Christian. *The Life and Thought of Hans Jonas: Jewish Dimensions*. Lebanon: Brandeis, 2010.

Wike, Richard, Bruce Stokes, and Katie Simmons. "Europeans Fear Wave of Refugees Will Mean More Terrorism, Fewer Jobs." *Pew Research Center*, July 11, 2016. https://www.pewresearch.org/global/2016/07/11/europeans-fear-wave-of-refugees-will-mean-more-terrorism-fewer-jobs/.

Wilkerson, Isabel. "America's Enduring Caste System." *New York Times*, July 1, 2020. https://www.nytimes.com/2020/07/01/magazine/isabel-wilkerson-caste.html.

———. *Caste: The Origins of Our Discontents*. New York: Random House, 2020.

Wilson, Nelly. *Bernard-Lazare: Antisemitism and the Problem of Jewish Identity in Late Nineteenth-Century France*. Cambridge: Cambridge University Press, 1978.

Winchester, Daniel. "Embodying the Faith: Religious Practice and the Making of a Muslim Moral Habitus." *Social Forces* 86, no. 4 (2008): 1753–80.

Winter, Timothy. "Introduction." In *Al-Ghazali on Disciplining the Soul and on Breaking the Two Desires: Books XXII and XXIII of the Revival of the Religious Sciences*, by Abu Hamid Muhammad al-Ghazali, xxv–xxiii. Cambridge: Islamic Texts Society, 2016.

Witte, Nils. "Responses to Stigmatisation and Boundary Making: Destigmatisation Strategies of Turks in Germany." *Journal of Ethnic and Migration Studies* 44, no. 9 (2018): 1425–43.

Women Equalities Committee. "Employment Opportunities for Muslims in the UK." House of Commons, 2015. https://publications.parliament.uk/pa/cm201617/cmselect/cmwomeq/89/8902.htm.

Wood, Amy Louise. *Lynching and Spectacle: Witnessing Racial Violence in America, 1890–1940*. Chapel Hill: University of North Carolina Press, 2011.

Woods, Rebecca. "England in 1966: Racism and Ignorance in the Midlands." *BBC News*, June 1, 2016. https://www.bbc.com/news/uk-england-birmingham-36388761.

Wyatt, Gail. "The Sociocultural Context of African American and White American Women's Rape." *Journal of Social Issues* 48, no. 1 (1992): 77–91.

Yeung, Peter. "EU Referendum: Reports of Hate Crime Increase 57% Following Brexit Vote." *Independent*, June 27, 2016. https://www.independent.co.uk/news/uk/home-news/brexit -hate-crime-racism-reports-eu-referendum-latest-a7106116.html.

Yilmaz, Ferruh. *How the Workers Became Muslims: Immigration, Culture and Hegemonic Transformation in Europe*. Ann Arbor: University of Michigan Press, 2016.

York, Chris. "Post-Brexit Racism Documented on Social Media." *Huffington Post*, July 2, 2016. https://www.huffingtonpost.co.uk/entry/post-brexit-racism_uk_5777be69e4b073366f0f 1d06?guccounter=1&guce_referrer=aHR0cHM6Ly9zZWFyY2guewFob28uY29tLw &guce_referrer_sig=AQAAAMEzpWAnxLvIt3XXILJAWHjcktw1Z4HGu9DM39Ddj30 atx2N8ebIzP7700jxdRRI-pS9Wfk32jxXyAMfcBOmiKt52xfC9lX4nusvpGg55P7CYm9 ToCxS-ZFKbCYlRyw4H8gIj16CtqnkvzZh6oD1V8Lk-kl-6X9COAOlx8l5GEMo.

Young-Bruehl, Elisabeth. *Hannah Arendt: For Love of the World*. New Haven: Yale University Press, 1982.

Yukleyen, Ahmet. "Localizing Islam in Europe: Religious Activism among Turkish Islamic Organizations in the Netherlands." *Journal of Muslim Minority Affairs* 29, no. 3 (2009): 291–309.

Yurdakul, Gökçe. "Jews, Muslims and the Ritual Male Circumcision Debate: Religious Diversity and Social Inclusion in Germany." *Social Inclusion* 4, no. 2 (2016): 77–86.

———. " 'We Don't Want to Be the Jews of Tomorrow': Jews and Turks in Germany after 9/11." *German Politics & Society* 24, no. 2 (2006): 44–67.

Yusuf, Hamza. *Purification of the Heart*. Mountain View: Sandala, 1998.

Zapata-Barrero, Ricard. "The Muslim Community and Spanish Tradition: Maurophobia as a Fact, and Impartiality as a Desideratum." In *Multiculturalism, Muslims and Citizenship: A European Approach*, edited by Tariq Modood, Anna Triandafyllidou, and Ricard Zapata-Barrero, 143–61. Abingdon: Routledge, 2006.

Zeitlyn, Benjamin. "The Making of a Moral British Bangladeshi." *Journal of Moral Education* 43, no. 2 (2014): 198–212.

INDEX

Neukölln, 35, 61–62, 107, 111–14, 116, 125–26, 206

neutrality, 29, 78–79, 113

New Synagogue, 109

Nigeria, 14, 115

Nilsson, Per-Erik, 54

9/11 attacks, 126

niqab, 50, 134, 145, 152, 173, 191

no-go zones, 54, 124

Norton, Anne, 19, 43

Nursi, Said, 87

Oakes, Timothy, 140

occupational subjugation, 51–52

Old Testament, 66, 107

Open Mosque Day, 92, 106, 169, 184, 218n62

Operation Trojan Horse, 189–90

Ottoman Empire: caste, 48–49; East London Mosque, 161; Napoleon, 48; remembrance, 205; Şehitlik Mosque, 34, 62, 64–65, 71, 87, 106, 117; tradition, 62, 64–65; World War I, 29, 49, 64

Özyürek, Esra, 165, 224n27, 232n92

Pakistan, 8–9, 32, 53, 140, 142–43, 169, 236n12

Palestine, 110, 114, 116, 121, 190, 233n14

Pamuk, Orhan, 72, 167

paradise, 3, 164, 199; earning, 155–57, 180–81; future, 36, 147, 149, 176, 202, 209; lost, 5; marginality and, 143; past, 8, 36, 202, 209; prayer and, 90

pariahs, 21, 25, 45, 83, 131–32, 225n47

parvenu, 21, 78, 83, 126, 129–33

Patriotic Europeans Against the Islamicization of the West (PEGIDA), 51, 124

peace: Christians, 94; Cohen, 68, 94, 98, 232n87; harmonization, 94; Jews, 112, 232n87; modernity, 48; Muhammad, 89, 95, 101; Muslims, 2, 89, 95, 97–98, 101, 163–64; religious symbols, 79, 128; Salaam-Schalom Initiative, 35, 106–7, 111–17, 233n10

persecution, 19, 24–25, 30, 126

philanthropy. *See* charity

phronetic space, 6, 56, 151, 160–61, 168, 201–2

Pierné, Guillaume, 224n27

piety: caste, 55–57; concept of, 18; context, 36; dignifying, 28; East London Mosque, 12, 55, 142, 154, 156, 159, 162–66, 173–77, 180–81, 192; modernity, 34, 142; professionalization of giving, 177–81; reverts, 162–66; rewards of suffering, 181–84; Şehitlik Mosque, 12, 55, 64, 66, 73, 80, 87–92, 101–2, 108, 128; tours, 96–98; women, 9, 17, 36, 57, 87–88, 148, 173–74, 182

pogroms, 136

poiesis: as Aristotelian making, 6, 34–35, 54, 57–59, 88, 150, 159–60, 163, 173, 201, 217n55; *autopoiesis*, 6, 36, 171–72; method of hope, 159–60; Moosa on, 6, 58–59, 217n55; strangers, 6, 34, 59, 163; *sympoiesis*, 6, 10, 35, 70, 106–7, 113, 171, 208, 217n55

Poland, 22, 47, 154, 160

police: caste, 224n27; East London Mosque, 134, 165, 185–91, 239n27; European metropoles, 27–28, 32, 35; identity, 224n27; London Metropolitan Police, 185–92; Operation Trojan Horse, 189–90; radicalization, 126, 131, 188; Şehitlik Mosque, 66, 78, 82, 94, 96–97, 117–18, 122, 125–31; surveillance, 35, 117–18, 122, 126, 130–31, 186–87; Tower Hamlets, 27, 134, 186, 188, 239n27; Turks, 32, 35, 95, 125

Pollock, Benjamin, 19

Portugal, 136

Posener, Alan, 234n48

postcolonialism, 4, 15, 26–29, 32, 36, 51, 53, 78, 142, 172, 194–95, 200–203

poverty: ascetics, 156, 174, 176; caste, 45; East London Mosque, 172, 174–84, 237n33; Engels on, 5; European metropoles, 5, 22, 27; *fundaco*, 225n41; gentrification, 61–62, 136, 172, 174, 184; ghettos, 44–45, 157, 225n42, 233n14; inequality, 22, 172, 237n33; marginality, 27, 237n33; Marx, 5; Muhammad, 174–75; positioning of poor, 175–76; pride in, 174–76; professionalization of giving,